1. *The A to Z of Buddhism* by Charles S. Prebish, 2001. *Out of Print. See No. 124.*
2. *The A to Z of Catholicism* by William J. Collinge, 2001.
3. *The A to Z of Hinduism* by Bruce M. Sullivan, 2001.
4. *The A to Z of Islam* by Ludwig W. Adamec, 2002. *Out of Print. See No. 123.*
5. *The A to Z of Slavery and Abolition* by Martin A. Klein, 2002.
6. *Terrorism: Assassins to Zealots* by Sean Kendall Anderson and Stephen Sloan, 2003.
7. *The A to Z of the Korean War* by Paul M. Edwards, 2005.
8. *The A to Z of the Cold War* by Joseph Smith and Simon Davis, 2005.
9. *The A to Z of the Vietnam War* by Edwin E. Moise, 2005.
10. *The A to Z of Science Fiction Literature* by Brian Stableford, 2005.
11. *The A to Z of the Holocaust* by Jack R. Fischel, 2005.
12. *The A to Z of Washington, D.C.* by Robert Benedetto, Jane Donovan, and Kathleen DuVall, 2005.
13. *The A to Z of Taoism* by Julian F. Pas, 2006.
14. *The A to Z of the Renaissance* by Charles G. Nauert, 2006.
15. *The A to Z of Shinto* by Stuart D. B. Picken, 2006.
16. *The A to Z of Byzantium* by John H. Rosser, 2006.
17. *The A to Z of the Civil War* by Terry L. Jones, 2006.
18. *The A to Z of the Friends (Quakers)* by Margery Post Abbott, Mary Ellen Chijioke, Pink Dandelion, and John William Oliver Jr., 2006.
19. *The A to Z of Feminism* by Janet K. Boles and Diane Long Hoeveler, 2006.
20. *The A to Z of New Religious Movements* by George D. Chryssides, 2006.
21. *The A to Z of Multinational Peacekeeping* by Terry M. Mays, 2006.
22. *The A to Z of Lutheranism* by Günther Gassmann with Duane H. Larson and Mark W. Oldenburg, 2007.
23. *The A to Z of the French Revolution* by Paul R. Hanson, 2007.
24. *The A to Z of the Persian Gulf War 1990–1991* by Clayton R. Newell, 2007.
25. *The A to Z of Revolutionary America* by Terry M. Mays, 2007.
26. *The A to Z of the Olympic Movement* by Bill Mallon with Ian Buchanan, 2007.
27. *The A to Z of the Discovery and Exploration of Australia* by Alan Day, 2009.
28. *The A to Z of the United Nations* by Jacques Fomerand, 2009.
29. *The A to Z of the "Dirty Wars"* by David Kohut, Olga Vilella, and Beatrice Julian, 2009.
30. *The A to Z of the Vikings* by Katherine Holman, 2009.
31. *The A to Z from the Great War to the Great Depression* by Neil A. Wynn, 2009.
32. *The A to Z of the Crusades* by Corliss K. Slack, 2009.
33. *The A to Z of New Age Movements* by Michael York, 2009.
34. *The A to Z of Unitarian Universalism* by Mark W. Harris, 2009.
35. *The A to Z of the Kurds* by Michael M. Gunter, 2009.
36. *The A to Z of Utopianism* by James M. Morris and Andrea L. Kross, 2009.
37. *The A to Z of the Civil War and Reconstruction* by William L. Richter, 2009.
38. *The A to Z of Jainism* by Kristi L. Wiley, 2009.
39. *The A to Z of the Inuit* by Pamela K. Stern, 2009.
40. *The A to Z of Early North America* by Cameron B. Wesson, 2009.

120. *The A to Z of Middle Eastern Intelligence* by Ephraim Kahana and Muhammad Suwaed, 2009.
121. *The A to Z of the Baptists* William H. Brackney, 2009.
122. *The A to Z of Homosexuality* by Brent L. Pickett, 2009.
123. *The A to Z of Islam, Second Edition* by Ludwig W. Adamec, 2009.
124. *The A to Z of Buddhism* by Carl Olson, 2009.
125. *The A to Z of United States–Russian/Soviet Relations* by Norman E. Saul, 2010.
126. *The A to Z of United States–Africa Relations* by Robert Anthony Waters Jr., 2010.
127. *The A to Z of United States–China Relations* by Robert Sutter, 2010.
128. *The A to Z of U.S. Diplomacy since the Cold War* by Tom Lansford, 2010.
129. *The A to Z of United States–Japan Relations* by John Van Sant, Peter Mauch, and Yoneyuki Sugita, 2010.
130. *The A to Z of United States–Latin American Relations* by Joseph Smith, 2010.
131. *The A to Z of United States–Middle East Relations* by Peter L. Hahn, 2010.
132. *The A to Z of United States–Southeast Asia Relations* by Donald E. Weatherbee, 2010.
133. *The A to Z of U.S. Diplomacy from the Civil War to World War I* by Kenneth J. Blume, 2010.
134. *The A to Z of International Law* by Boleslaw A. Boczek, 2010.
135. *The A to Z of the Gypsies (Romanies)* by Donald Kenrick, 2010.
136. *The A to Z of the Tamils* by Vijaya Ramaswamy, 2010.
137. *The A to Z of Women in Sub-Saharan Africa* by Kathleen Sheldon, 2010.
138. *The A to Z of Ancient and Medieval Nubia* by Richard A. Lobban Jr., 2010.
139. *The A to Z of Ancient Israel* by Niels Peter Lemche, 2010.
140. *The A to Z of Ancient Mesoamerica* by Joel W. Palka, 2010.
141. *The A to Z of Ancient Southeast Asia* by John N. Miksic, 2010.
142. *The A to Z of the Hittites* by Charles Burney, 2010.
143. *The A to Z of Medieval Russia* by Lawrence N. Langer, 2010.
144. *The A to Z of the Napoleonic Era* by George F. Nafziger, 2010.
145. *The A to Z of Ancient Egypt* by Morris L. Bierbrier, 2010.
146. *The A to Z of Ancient India* by Kumkum Roy, 2010.
147. *The A to Z of Ancient South America* by Martin Giesso, 2010.
148. *The A to Z of Medieval China* by Victor Cunrui Xiong, 2010.
149. *The A to Z of Medieval India* by Iqtidar Alam Khan, 2010.
150. *The A to Z of Mesopotamia* by Gwendolyn Leick, 2010.
151. *The A to Z of the Mongol World Empire* by Paul D. Buell, 2010.
152. *The A to Z of the Ottoman Empire* by Selcuk Aksin Somel, 2010.
153. *The A to Z of Pre-Colonial Africa* by Robert O. Collins, 2010.
154. *The A to Z of Aesthetics* by Dabney Townsend, 2010.
155. *The A to Z of Descartes and Cartesian Philosophy* by Roger Ariew, Dennis Des Chene, Douglas M. Jesseph, Tad M. Schmaltz, and Theo Verbeek, 2010.
156. *The A to Z of Heidegger's Philosophy* by Alfred Denker, 2010.
157. *The A to Z of Kierkegaard's Philosophy* by Julia Watkin, 2010.
158. *The A to Z of Ancient Greek Philosophy* by Anthony Preus, 2010.
159. *The A to Z of Bertrand Russell's Philosophy* by Rosalind Carey and John Ongley, 2010.
160. *The A to Z of Epistemology* by Ralph Baergen, 2010.
161. *The A to Z of Ethics* by Harry J. Gensler and Earl W. Spurgin, 2010.

162. *The A to Z of Existentialism* by Stephen Michelman, 2010.
163. *The A to Z of Hegelian Philosophy* by John W. Burbidge, 2010.
164. *The A to Z of the Holiness Movement* by William Kostlevy, 2010.
165. *The A to Z of Hume's Philosophy* by Kenneth R. Merrill, 2010.
166. *The A to Z of Husserl's Philosophy* by John J. Drummond, 2010.
167. *The A to Z of Kant and Kantianism* by Helmut Holzhey and Vilem Mudroch, 2010.
168. *The A to Z of Leibniz's Philosophy* by Stuart Brown and N. J. Fox, 2010.
169. *The A to Z of Logic* by Harry J. Gensler, 2010.
170. *The A to Z of Medieval Philosophy and Theology* by Stephen F. Brown and Juan Carlos Flores, 2010.
171. *The A to Z of Nietzscheanism* by Carol Diethe, 2010.
172. *The A to Z of the Non-Aligned Movement and Third World* by Guy Arnold, 2010.
173. *The A to Z of Shamanism* by Graham Harvey and Robert J. Wallis, 2010.
174. *The A to Z of Organized Labor* by James C. Docherty, 2010.
175. *The A to Z of the Orthodox Church* by Michael Prokurat, Michael D. Peterson, and Alexander Golitzin, 2010.
176. *The A to Z of Prophets in Islam and Judaism* by Scott B. Noegel and Brannon M. Wheeler, 2010.
177. *The A to Z of Schopenhauer's Philosophy* by David E. Cartwright, 2010.
178. *The A to Z of Wittgenstein's Philosophy* by Duncan Richter, 2010.
179. *The A to Z of Hong Kong Cinema* by Lisa Odham Stokes, 2010.
180. *The A to Z of Japanese Traditional Theatre* by Samuel L. Leiter, 2010.
181. *The A to Z of Lesbian Literature* by Meredith Miller, 2010.
182. *The A to Z of Chinese Theater* by Tan Ye, 2010.
183. *The A to Z of German Cinema* by Robert C. Reimer and Carol J. Reimer, 2010.
184. *The A to Z of German Theater* by William Grange, 2010.
185. *The A to Z of Irish Cinema* by Roderick Flynn and Patrick Brereton, 2010.
186. *The A to Z of Modern Chinese Literature* by Li-hua Ying, 2010.
187. *The A to Z of Modern Japanese Literature and Theater* by J. Scott Miller, 2010.
188. *The A to Z of Old-Time Radio* by Robert C. Reinehr and Jon D. Swartz, 2010.
189. *The A to Z of Polish Cinema* by Marek Haltof, 2010.
190. *The A to Z of Postwar German Literature* by William Grange, 2010.
191. *The A to Z of Russian and Soviet Cinema* by Peter Rollberg, 2010.
192. *The A to Z of Russian Theater* by Laurence Senelick, 2010.
193. *The A to Z of Sacred Music* by Joseph P. Swain, 2010.
194. *The A to Z of Animation and Cartoons* by Nichola Dobson, 2010.
195. *The A to Z of Afghan Wars, Revolutions, and Insurgencies* by Ludwig W. Adamec, 2010.
196. *The A to Z of Ancient Egyptian Warfare* by Robert G. Morkot, 2010.
197. *The A to Z of the British and Irish Civil Wars 1637–1660* by Martyn Bennett, 2010.
198. *The A to Z of the Chinese Civil War* by Edwin Pak-wah Leung, 2010.
199. *The A to Z of Ancient Greek Warfare* by Iain Spence, 2010.
200. *The A to Z of the Anglo–Boer War* by Fransjohan Pretorius, 2010.
201. *The A to Z of the Crimean War* by Guy Arnold, 2010.
202. *The A to Z of the Zulu Wars* by John Laband, 2010.
203. *The A to Z of the Wars of the French Revolution* by Steven T. Ross, 2010.
204. *The A to Z of the Hong Kong SAR and the Macao SAR* by Ming K. Chan and Shiuhing Lo, 2010.

The A to Z of
Kant and Kantianism

Helmut Holzhey
Vilem Mudroch

The A to Z Guide Series, No. 167

THE SCARECROW PRESS, INC.
Lanham • Toronto • Plymouth, UK
2010

Published by Scarecrow Press, Inc.
A wholly owned subsidiary of
The Rowman & Littlefield Publishing Group, Inc.
4501 Forbes Boulevard, Suite 200, Lanham, Maryland 20706
http://www.scarecrowpress.com

Estover Road, Plymouth PL6 7PY, United Kingdom

British Library Cataloguing in Publication Information Available

Library of Congress Cataloging-in-Publication Data

The hardback version of this book was cataloged by the Library of Congress as
follows:

Holzhey, Helmut, 1937–
 Historical dictionary of Kant and Kantianism / Helmut Holzhey, Vilem
Mudroch.
  p. cm. — (Historical dictionaries of religions, philosophies, and
movements ; no. 60)
 Includes bibliographical references (p.   ).
 1. Kant, Immanuel, 1724–1804—Dictionaries. I. Mudroch, Vilem. II. Title.
III. Series.
  B2751.H65   2005
  193—dc22   2005004107

ISBN 978-0-8108-7594-4 (pbk. : alk. paper)

☉™ The paper used in this publication meets the minimum requirements of
American National Standard for Information Sciences—Permanence of Paper
for Printed Library Materials, ANSI/NISO Z39.48-1992.
Printed in the United States of America

CONTENTS

EDITOR'S FOREWORD

Immanuel Kant is indisputably one of the most significant philosophers of the modern age. This initially came as somewhat of a surprise, since in his younger years he did not write anything of overwhelming consequence, nor was he widely known. But the things he wrote later in his life — the *Critique of Pure Reason*, the *Critique of Practical Reason* and the *Critique of Judgment*, in particular — became famous, first in Germany, then gradually in the rest of Europe and the United States. Some of his concepts, such as thing-in-itself and the categorical imperative, were debated widely, as was his approach to metaphysics, epistemology and ethics. Not only was there a large number of followers before his death, later schools of Neokantianism became established, and even today Kant is part and parcel of any introductory course of philosophy, and Kantianism is widely disseminated among scholars and quite ordinary beings as well (whether they realize it or not). Does it matter that, even in his own time, his works were interpreted differently by his supporters, and strongly criticized by his opponents, for very different reasons, or that Kantians and Neokantians often disagreed sharply with one another? That is hard to say. It depends on whether one expects philosophy to incorporate the ultimate truth once expounded or to grow and adapt. If the latter, then Kant remains impressively significant.

However, since Kant's writings, and the writings of Kantians and Neokantians can be confusing and contradictory, it is important to have a guide to sort things out. This is actually indispensable for those who do not know German, and are receiving any wisdom second hand in different languages in which, aside from such simple things as mistranslations, they have to contend with the fact there may actually be no 'correct' translation. So, the dictionary aspect of this historical dictionary is double, first to convey just what a given Kantian term may mean, in a glossary, but more precisely with a proper explanation in actual entries. Other entries obviously deal with Kant's intellectual development and writings, those of important adherents and followers, and the founders and members of various Kantian schools. The background to this complex web of schools and commentators is laid out more specifically in the introduction. Certainly not to be overlooked is the extensive bibliography offered in the last section, which focuses both on Kant's own writings and then on the manifold writings of others.

This *Historical Dictionary of Kant and Kantianism* was written by Helmut Holzhey and Vilem Mudroch, both of whom received their Ph.D. at the University of Zurich. Dr. Holzhey is professor emeritus at the University of Zurich, where Dr. Mudroch is presently a research associate. Both of them have written extensively on Kant, Kantianism and Neokantianism, with Dr. Holzhey being especially concerned with the work of the Marburg School and also of Hermann Cohen, whose archive he founded. Dr. Mudroch has, among other things, coedited a book on the Scottish Enlightenment and contributed to a German-language encyclopedia of the history of philosophy. They have worked together often in the past and at present are collaborating on books dealing with 18th-century philosophy in France and Germany (including Kant). Their knowledge of the subject is precious, but no less essential is their knowledge of the German language, which makes them particularly helpful with regard to the tasks indicated above. One way or another, this volume is bound to be a useful addition to the still growing edifice of Kantian studies.

Jon Woronoff
Series Editor

CITATIONS AND ABBREVIATIONS

Following widely accepted practice, the first edition of the *Critique of Pure Reason* (1781) will be referred to simply as 'A' followed by the page numbers, while the second edition (1787) will be cited as 'B' and the page numbers. Further abbreviations:

CJ	*Critique of Judgment* (1790) (Title also translated as: *Critique of the Power of Judgment*)
CPrR	*Critique of Practical Reason* (1788)
GMM	*Groundwork of the Metaphysics of Morals* (1785)
MM	*The Metaphysics of Morals* (1797)
P	*Prolegomena to Any Future Metaphysics that will be able to come forward as Science* (1783)

The so-called "*Academy Edition*," that is, *Kants gesammelte Schriften*, edited by the Prussian, subsequently the German Academy of Sciences, will be cited as 'Ak' followed by the volume and the page numbers. These references will be helpful even to readers not using the *Academy Edition*, given that nearly all recent translations into English provide the corresponding volume and page numbers in the margins. However, where possible, the references are based on the internal divisions of the works and will be traceable in any adequate edition.

Many of the translations into English are our own, though we have greatly benefitted from some of the standard English language renderings of Kant's works. For quotations from the *Critique of Pure Reason*, we have relied heavily on the Cambridge Edition of the work (ed. Paul Guyer, Allen W. Wood, Cambridge: Cambridge University Press, 1998), and, to a much lesser extent, on Norman Kemp Smith's older effort (London: Macmillan, 1929). For the *Critique of Practical Reason*, we have used both Lewis White Beck's (Indianapolis: Bobbs-Merrill, 1956) and Mary J. Gregor's (Cambridge: Cambridge University Press, 1996; part of the Cambridge Edition) translations. For the *Critique of Judgment*, we have consulted mainly the Cambridge Edition (ed. Paul Guyer, trans. Paul Guyer, Eric Matthews, 2000); for other works, the volumes of the Cambridge Edition served us wherever they were available.

CHRONOLOGY

1724   **22 April:** Immanuel Kant is born in Königsberg, East Prussia (today Kaliningrad, Russia) as the fourth child of Johann Georg Kant, a harness-maker, and Anna Regina (maiden name Reuter)

1732-1740   attends the Pietist Collegium Fridericianum; becomes acquainted with classical Latin literature; develops a scorn for the official version of Pietism

1738   death of his mother

1740-1746   studies philosophy, mathematics, and science at the University of Königsberg; influenced by his teacher Martin Knutzen (1713-1751); supports himself mainly by teaching private lessons

1746   death of his father; composes his first piece of writing, *Thoughts on the True Estimation of Living Forces* (published in 1749)

1748-1754   domestic tutor in three families in the vicinity of Königsberg, officially still a student or candidate at the University

1753   death of George Berkeley

1755   publishes the *General History and Theory of the Heavens;* **12 June:** granted the degree of Master of Philosophy on the basis of his Latin thesis, *Concise Outline of some Reflections on Fire*; **27 September:** tested on his doctoral dissertation, also in Latin, *A New Elucidation of the First Principles of Metaphysical Cognition;* Kant is permitted to teach at the university and to charge his students a fee; he lectures on a wide range of subjects in philosophy, science, physical geography and theology

1756   **April:** defends his Latin *Habilitationsschrift*, the *Physical Monadology*, which formally entitles him to apply for a teaching chair; however, his attempt to obtain Martin Knutzen's vacant position is unsuccessful

1762-1764   Johann Gottfried Herder attends Kant's lectures; his notes allow important insights into Kant's thought during this period

1763   publication of *The Only Possible Argument in Support of a Demonstration of the Existence of God* and of the *Attempt to Introduce the Concept of Negative Magnitudes into Philosophy.* For his contribution to the competition organized by the Prussian Royal Academy of the Sciences, Kant wins the second prize with his *Inquiry Concerning the Distinctness of the Principles of Natural Theology and Morality* (published in 1764)

1764   publication of the *Observations on the Feeling of the Beautiful and Sublime;* July: Kant declines the chair of poetry at Königsberg

1765   Kant becomes a librarian at the Library of the Castle, thus securing for himself for the first time a steady if modest income

1766   *Dreams of a Spirit-Seer Elucidated by Dreams of Metaphysics*

1769-1770   Kant is offered teaching chairs in Erlangen and Jena, but, after initially accepting at the former university, refuses them both as he has realistic prospects of obtaining a chair in his native city

1770   **31 March:** appointed to a chair of Metaphysics and Logic at the University of Königsberg; **21 August:** Kant publicly defends a Latin dissertation, *On the Form and Principles of the Sensible and the Intelligible World*

1770-1781   The so-called "Silent Years," during which Kant publishes little, but prepares his critical works

1772   quits his job as librarian

1776   death of David Hume; Kant serves as dean (*Dekan*) of the faculty of philosophy during the summer term

1778   death of Jean-Jacques Rousseau; Kant declines an offer of a teaching chair in Halle

1779–1780   Kant serves as dean during the winter term

1780   permanent member of the Academic Senate of the University of Königsberg

1781   **May:** publication of the first edition of the *Critique of Pure Reason*

1782–1783   Kant serves as dean during the winter term

1783   *Prolegomena to any Future Metaphysics;* Kant purchases a house in Königsberg

1785   **April:** *Grounding for the Metaphysics of Morals*

1785–1786   Kant serves as dean during the winter term

1786   serves as president (*Rektor*) of the University during the summer term; **Easter:** *Metaphysical Foundations of Natural Science;* Karl Leonard Reinhold begins publishing his *Briefe über die Kantische Philosophie* (*Letters on Kantian Philosophy*)

1787   second edition of the *Critique of Pure Reason*

1788   again president of the University during summer term; *Critique of Practical Reason*

1789   Karl Leonard Reinhold: *Versuch einer neuen Theorie des menschlichen Vorstellungsvermögens* (*Essay on a New Theory of the Human Power of Representation*)

1790   *Critique of Judgement;* Salomon Maimon: *Versuch über die Transzendentalphilosophie* (*Essay on Transcendental Philosophy*)

1791   Kant serves as dean during the summer term

1793   publication of *Religion within the Boundaries of Mere Reason*

1794   conflict with the Prussian censorship officials; reduces the
            amount of his teaching; Johann Gottlieb Fichte: *Grundlage der
            gesamten Wissenschaftslehre (Foundation of the Entire Doc-
            trine of Science)*

1794-1795   Kant was to serve as dean during the winter term, Christian
            Jacob Kraus takes his place

1795   *On Eternal Peace*

1796   **23 July:** Kant's last lecture; Jakob Sigismund Beck: *Grundriss
            der critischen Philosophie (The Principle of Critical Philoso-
            phy)*

1797   *Metaphysics of Morals*

1798   *Conflict of the Faculties; Anthropology from a Pragmatic Point
            of View;* Kant is to serve as dean during the summer term, but
            Mangelsdorf takes his place

1799   **August:** declaration against Fichte; Johann Gottfried Herder:
            Metacritique

1800   Kant's health begins to decline; his students and disciples start
            publishing his lectures and other manuscripts

1802   Georg Wilhelm Friedrich Hegel: *Glauben und Wissen (Belief
            and Knowledge)*

1803   **October:** Kant's final illness; death of Herder

1804   **12 February:** death of Kant

1807   Jakob Friedrich Fries: *Neue Kritik der Vernunft (New Critique
            of Reason)*

1831   death of Hegel

1832   Friedrich Eduard Beneke: *Kant und die philosophische Aufgabe
            unserer Zeit (Kant and the Philosophical Problem of our Time)*

1855	first complete English translation of the *Critique of Pure Reason* by J. M. D. Meiklejohn; Hermann Helmholtz: *Über das Sehen des Menschen* (*On the Sight of the Human Being*)
1860	Kuno Fischer: *Immanuel Kant. Entwicklungsgeschichte und System der kritischen Philosophie* (*The Development and the System of the Critical Philosophy*)
1865	Otto Liebmann: *Kant und die Epigonen* (*Kant and his Followers*)
1866	Friedrich Albert Lange: *Geschichte des Materialismus* (*History of Materialism*)
1871	Hermann Cohen: *Kants Theorie der Erfahrung* (*Kant's Theory of Experience*)
1876	Alois Riehl: *Der philosophische Kriticismus*
1897	founding of the *Kant Studies*
1905	founding of the *Kant Society*
1917	Bruno Bauch: *Immanuel Kant*
1918	Ernst Cassirer: *Kants Leben und Lehre* (*Kant's Life and Teachings*)
1929	Norman Kemp Smith's translation of the *Critique of Pure Reason;* Martin Heidegger: *Kant und das Problem der Metaphysik* (*Kant and the Problem of Metaphysics*)
1936	H. J. Paton: *Kant's Metaphysic of Experience: A Commentary on the First Half of the* Kritik der reinen Vernunft
1960	First International Kant-Congress held in Bonn

INTRODUCTION

KANT'S LIFE AND THE DEVELOPMENT OF HIS THOUGHT

In his *Anthropology from a Pragmatic Point of View*, Immanuel Kant offered an affectionate description of his native city of Königsberg (Ak 7, p. 120–21). This "large city" had in 1724 a population of some 50,000. Its university, founded in 1544, was in the early 18th century one of the strongholds of Lutheran orthodoxy. The city enjoyed a favorable position as far as maritime commerce was concerned: it served as one of the major centers of exchange at which English manufacturing products, wine, and colonial goods were traded for raw materials from Poland-Lithuania. Aside from its German majority, the city was inhabited by Polish and Lithuanian-speaking minorities as well as by French Huguenots.

Kant was born on 22 April 1724. His father was a harness-maker; the family, though by no means wealthy, did not suffer from want. Kant grew up in an environment, both at home and at school, that was heavily imbued by Pietism. Between 1732 and 1740, he attended the Collegium Fridericianum, where the pupils spent most of their time studying Latin. Here, Kant was influenced by Franz Albert Schultz (1692–1763), the principal of the school, from whom he learned a combination of Pietism and Wolffianism, that is, a curious blend of a spirituality that appealed to the heart and rational philosophy. Later, Kant was to distance himself sharply from the narrow spirit of Pietism (see Ak 7, p. 57). Among the professors at the University of Königsberg, where Kant began his studies in 1740, Martin Knutzen (1713–1751) was especially important for him; he introduced Kant to the writings of Isaac Newton and to the then popular physico-theology.[1]

In his first work, *Thoughts on the True Estimation of Living Forces*, published in 1749, Kant contributed to the *vis viva*–controversy, attempting to find an intermediate position between the Cartesians and the Leibnizians.[2] During this period, Kant earned his living as a domestic tutor in the vicinity of Königsberg. In 1755, he embarked on an academic career, though it was only in 1770 that he obtained the kind of teaching chair that he considered to be suitable for himself. Thereafter, his existence was firmly bound with the university, and he never left his native city again. Kant's life, which even in its early days was relatively unspectacular, eventually became highly regimented and, from a biographical point of view, in many ways uninteresting. Famous during Kant's later years were his highly punctual walks, by which the people of Königsberg were supposedly able to set their clocks. By far the most interesting feature of Kant's life was his personal contacts. In his younger years, most of these occurred at dinner parties held at the residences of the leading citizens of the city. Later, especially after he acquired his own house, Kant daily invited up to seven guests for lunch, freely discussing a large variety of intellectually stimulating topics. As Kant's fame grew, he was also sought out by other prominent persons, from Moses Mendelssohn to Johann Gottlieb Fichte.

Kant's position at the university bore the title "Chair of Metaphysics and Logic"; officially, he retained it until his death, though he stopped lecturing in 1796. In accordance with university rules, upon the assumption of his professorship, Kant was obliged to publicly defend an inaugural dissertation in Latin; with its theory of time and space as the forms of human sensibility, the corresponding piece *De mundi sensibilis atque intelligibilis forma et principiis* contains the first central elements of his mature, critical philosophy.

In the so-called pre-critical period, Kant dealt especially with two problem areas. Initially, he was interested primarily in the basic concepts and methods of physics and astronomy. In his *General History and the Theory of Heavens* of 1755, he propounded, as the first person ever, a theory of the development of our planetary system in accordance with Isaac Newton's principles; Kant generalized the theory into an all encompassing cosmogony and cosmology. Later, he concentrated more strongly on metaphysical topics such as the principles of cognition, proofs of the existence of God, or a metaphysical method in general. At first, his thought was strongly influenced by the philosophy of the Leibniz-Wolff school.[3] However, with his *Inquiry Concerning the Distinctness of the Principles of Natural Theology and Morality* (published in 1764), Kant soon launched a radical critique of metaphysics, a critique that reached its preliminary climax in the *Dreams of a Spirit-Seer Elucidated by Dreams of Metaphysics* (1766). Kant no longer considered the claims of the cognition of a supra-sensible world to be legitimate, and metaphysics seemed to him possible only as a theory of experience, a theory that could be gained only in accordance with the Newtonian method. Metaphysics was thus for the first time conceived by Kant as a discipline in which the limits of human reason were to be delineated (Ak 2, p. 367–68).

For more than 10 years after he composed his inaugural dissertation, Kant remained publicly more or less silent, indeed, he refrained from publishing anything at all. However, in 1781, Kant surprised the scholarly world with his epoch-making philosophical treatise, the *Critique of Pure Reason*.[4] Judging from the first reactions, one would not have surmised that a work that would eventually revolutionize philosophy had just appeared. This realization started to dawn on philosophers only in the 1870s, but it did not become widely accepted until the 20th century. Initially, the work was viewed as outdated, too profound, and, above all, obscure. Kant's contemporaries would not have had any difficulties understanding his incisive critique of metaphysics, but they struggled with the demanding argumentation of the work, and they were unable to grasp the positive contribution that Kant made with his new theory of experience and especially with his transcendental deduction of the categories.[5]

A first, anonymous review of Kant's *Critique* was published in the *Göttingische Anzeigen von gelehrten Sachen* of 1782; the authors of this superficial and yet highly critical piece were Christian Garve (1742–1798) and Johann Georg Heinrich Feder (1740–1821).[6] In order to unmask the nullity of this review, but also to make the contents of his own work more accessible, Kant produced in 1783 with his *Prolegomena to Any Future Metaphysics* a second version of his critique of reason, in which he built his theory on the sole assumption that we really do possess "a pure natural science" (Ak 4, p. 294), i.e., he presupposed the a priori validity of mathematics and Newtonian physics. Kant continued his work on the "metaphysics of nature" (A 845–46/B 873–74) in his *Metaphysical Foundations of Natural Science* of 1786; his goal here was to ground a general doctrine of matter as an a priori science of outer nature and thus to provide the conceptual underpinnings for Newton's mathematical description of nature. Insights gained from both of these books influenced Kant's attempt to revise the *Critique of Pure Reason;* this second edition appeared in 1787. Especially noteworthy is the fact that Kant completely rewrote the section dealing with the transcendental deduction of the categories, a section that had been decried as extraordinarily impenetrable.

Kant achieved a first breakthrough with his critical philosophy with the publication in 1785 of *Groundwork of the Metaphysics of Morals*, which brought to fruition prolonged attempts on his part to establish moral philosophy on new foundations. Aside from this, several articles that Kant published starting in 1784, mostly in the *Berlinische Monatsschrift*, the journal that acted as the mouthpiece of the Berlin Enlightenment, attracted widespread attention. In these, Kant developed the basic notions of his philosophy of history ("Idea for a Universal History with a Cosmopolitan Purpose," "Conjectures on the Beginning of Human History"), critically reviewed Johann Gottfried Herder's *Ideen zur Philosophie der Geschichte der Menschheit* (*Ideas on the Philosophy of the History of Humankind*), and commented on the controversy over Gotthold Ephraim Lessing's alleged Spinozist leanings ("What Does It Mean to Orient Oneself in Thinking?").

Unexpectedly, in 1788 Kant produced a second critique, the *Critique of Practical Reason*, having decided only in 1787 to compose it. He was initially motivated by his wish to defend himself against critics who had attacked him in reviews of the *Groundwork* and in other hostile pieces. However, the main philosophical motivation stemmed from his desire to supplement the destructive critique of speculative reason's metaphysical pretensions with the proof that the metaphysical ideas of freedom, God, and immortality could regain their 'objective' meaning within the realm of the *practical* use of reason (though they then remained strictly confined to such use).

The second critique was followed by a third one already in 1790, bearing the title *Critique of Judgment*. Kant's critical project, which was originally conceived as a propaedeutic to metaphysics (A 841/B 869), gained with this work the markings of a system, as Kant himself later explicitly admitted to Johann Gottlieb Fichte (Ak 12, p. 371). With his third *Critique*, Kant especially hoped to bridge the gap between theoretical and practical reason; this task was to be assumed by the power of judgment as it reflected on the general and as it stood under the "principle of the formal purposiveness of nature." Reflective judgment then functioned according to Kant in two ways: either as it was related to the aesthetic and subjective or as it was related to the logical and objective representation of the formal purposiveness of nature. With his thesis that aesthetic judgments contained a priori elements, Kant revolutionized the theories of taste in the 18th century. His pre-Darwinian theory of organic nature, which is based on the concept of the objective purposiveness of nature, also contributed to a new conception of nature as it appeared, for example, in Friedrich Wilhelm Joseph Schelling's philosophy.

In the 1790s, Kant's thought stood at the center of philosophical discussions in Germany, even though his 'criticism' seemed to be superseded by interpretations, corrections, and new developments of his teachings by others. Kant himself added to his oeuvre in 1793 a book on the philosophy of religion, *Religion within the Boundaries of Mere Reason*, in which he elucidates how a critically instructed reason is to ingest the Christian religion. This work involved Kant in a severe conflict with the Prussian censorship and led to a temporary prohibition to publish on religion. In addition, Kant also composed the long promised *Metaphysics of Morals* that appeared in 1797 in two parts, namely as a *Doctrine of Right* and as a *Doctrine of Virtue*.

On the other hand, a corresponding *Metaphysics of Nature* no longer appeared. Instead, Kant attempted in the so-called *Opus Postumum* in uncounted drafts and notes to work out the conceptual transition from the metaphysical foundations of natural science to the a priori principles of physics, without, however, being able to achieve satisfactory results. With his *Anthropology from a Pragmatic Point of View* of 1798, Kant accorded a glimpse into the highly successful lectures that he had held at the University of Königsberg since 1772, though neither at this point nor later did this book stimulate much interest. When Kant died on 12 February 1804, based on the contemporary philosophical developments, one would not have been totally unjustified in thinking that his work was obsolete. Kant's funeral, however, presaged the bright future for which his philosophy was destined. Though Kant himself wished to be buried immediately after his death without any pomp, his body was displayed for 16 days and his last passage was attended by thousands of people, including all the city and university officials as well as the officers of the local army garrison.

WHAT IS KANTIANISM?

Kant himself has been characterized as a subjective idealist and as an opponent of subjective idealism, as having advocated reason over faith and faith over reason, as having based himself on science and on ordinary experience.[7] This list of contradictory predicates could be extended; it helps to underscore the difficulty that one faces when attempting to produce a definition of Kantianism which would satisfy most philosophers and historians of philosophy. It may be wiser to avoid basing such an attempt on one-sided and polemical so-called continuations of Kant's philosophy, and to seek instead to locate the concept of Kantianism *between* the above-mentioned or other opposing positions. One should thus follow Kant's own practice of considering his "critical philosophy" as an intermediate stance (for example, between dogmatism and skepticism). Specifically, we may inquire into the characteristics that distinguish Kantianism from other philosophical traditions. What conceptions must a philosopher defend, if he or she is to count as a Kantian? This question will in many ways be answered differently today than it would have been answered, for instance, at the end of the 18th century. In spite of these difficulties, finding a common denominator in the thought of those thinkers who in the last two hundred years have claimed to be Kantians is not impossible.

From a purely formal point of view, a Kantian is obviously someone who orients himself or herself by the central theories of Kant's own thought. In theoretical philosophy, this will indisputably include the concept of a transcendental philosophy that investigates the conditions of the possibility of experience; the acceptance of synthetic cognition (judgments) a priori; the distinction between appearance and thing-in-itself; the further distinction between sensibility, understanding, and reason; the delineation of the limits of human cognition in accordance with the thesis that human thought requires some reference to experience in order not to lose itself in fantasies; and, as a consequence of this last point, the demolition of dogmatic metaphysics. In the realm of practical philosophy, the Kantian will insist on the autonomy of reason when the good will is determined, and will therefore reject affective and material determining grounds of the will; in the theory of justice, the law of reason, understood as an application of the categorical imperative to the external relations of humans, will supersede traditional natural law; history will be conceived as a development toward a cosmopolitan state of peace, in which rationally derived laws hold even between different countries. As far as the philosophy of religion is concerned, a Kantian will accord priority to reason over faith, distinguishing, however, between religious or clerical faith, on the one hand, and rationally grounded faith, on the other; the latter will have as its content only God and the immortality of the soul.

However, to 'orient' oneself along the lines of these theories does not mean that a Kantian must accept them as completely as Kant did. Thus, for instance, in the historical course of the reception of Kant, various theses have been developed in regard to the question of the status of transcendental cognition, a question that Kant himself left open. Similarly, especially in the 19th century, the concept of synthetic cognition a priori was subjected to different interpretations: from the point of view of biology, psychology, transcendental logic, or ontology. Concerning the question of the thing-in-itself and, along with it, of Kantian idealism or realism, fine distinctions are being made to this day, distinctions that may also be found in general epistemological debates. As far as the attitude toward metaphysics goes, there have been repeated attempts in the history of Kantianism to revise Kant's verdict by highlighting his *Critique of Practical Reason* and his *Critique of Judgment*.

When it comes to the topics sketched above, Kant's own texts allow different interpretations, so that it is not always clear what is Kantian and what is not. However, there are also doctrines that, on the whole, never became parts of Kantianism, regardless of the issue of different interpretations. Such are, for instance, Kant's theory of time and space, his transcendental deduction of the categories in the *Critique of Pure Reason*, but also his theory of the subjective character of the judgments of taste from the *Critique of Judgment*.

A General Overview of Kant Interpretations

The reception of Kant was influenced, at times very heavily, by nonphilosophical factors. Political, social, and cultural circumstances occasionally dictated not only how Kant was received, but whether he was received at all. Indeed, the whole of Kantianism was a historically contingent phenomenon, given that there was nothing in the initial rejection of Kant that necessarily had to induce certain philosophers to begin defending and further developing his thought. And that the old Kantianism of the 1790s was eventually followed by a Neo-kantianism in the 1870s also had contingent reasons.

The reception of Kant in the English-speaking world did not, by any means, run parallel to the reception in Germany, and this in spite of much personal contact between the philosophers and scholars of the two countries. Kant was generally interpreted in light of the philosophical currents dominant in the respective country at that particular point in time, and these currents diverged a great deal. Perhaps most striking is the difference in reception in the second half of the 19th century. While in Germany idealism was in decline, in England it enjoyed its heyday; while Germany produced Neo-kantianism, in England Hegelian-shaped interpretations of Kant dominated.

Another important factor in accounting for the differences between the receptions had to do with the availability of translations or with the varying ability in the English-speaking world to read German. Translating and discussing Kant in English was at any rate always affected by terminological problems. A number of the English renderings of Kant's key terms already possessed set meanings that often did not reflect Kant's intentions. The different philosophical traditions of the different countries played an important role in this way, too. In Germany, Kant wrote in a largely Leibnizian type of philosophical climate, even if empiristic tendencies had gained an important foothold; in Great Britain and in North America, he was at least initially received in an atmosphere that was dominated by the thought of John Locke, utilitarianism, and the Scottish Common Sense philosophy.

EARLY OPPONENTS AND ADHERENTS

Early Reception in Germany

The philosophical attacks on the *Critique of Pure Reason* came from three directions: Leibniz-Wolffian philosophy, empiricism, and the insights that were developed only in the 1770s into the relation of language and thought. Kantians were motivated by this criticism to present and interpret Kant's works so as to spread the "critical philosophy." Especially important was the book *Erläuterungen über des Herrn Professor Kant Critic der reinen Vernunft* (*Explications of Professor Kant's Critique of Pure Reason*) of 1784 by Johann Schultz (also: Schulze, 1739–1805), professor of mathematics in Königsberg; further the claim by Christian Gottfried Schütz (1747–1832) in the *Allgemeine*

Litteratur-Zeitung, a journal founded by him, that a new era in philosophy had been inaugurated with the *Critique of Pure Reason* (7 April 1785), and his subsequent collaboration with Kant; finally, Karl Leonhard Reinhold's *Briefe über die Kantische Philosophie* (*Letters on Kantian Philosophy*) that first appeared in the journal *Teutscher Merkur* in 1786/87 and that Reinhold then published in an enlarged and amended version as a book in two volumes in 1790/92. Reinhold emphasized the "reformation of philosophy" that Kant had brought about especially by making it clear that the oppositions between materialism and idealism, empiricism and rationalism, as well as atheism and supernaturalism could be overcome.[8] What followed were numerous further writings by authors who admitted fully or partially their adherence to Kantian philosophy. They paraphrased or interpreted Kant's works, and fought against the diminishing horde of Kant's opponents, but they also left their own marks on Kantianism and thus contributed in a greater or lesser degree to the changes taking place in the Kantian edifice. Aside from Reinhold, an important role in the further development of Kant's philosophy was played by Salomon Maimon (1753–1800) and Jakob Sigismund Beck (1761–1840).[9]

Reinhold attempted to provide the foundation of philosophy that he found lacking in Kant in his own "Philosophy of Elements." This foundational project was taken up by Johann Gottlieb Fichte (1762–1814) in his "Doctrine of Science" (1794); with his formulation of the first principle that was based on the basic concept of the self, Fichte departed from Kant's critical epistemology.[10]

Another point of contention concerned the correct understanding of Kant's thing-in-itself. Friedrich Heinrich Jacobi (1743–1819) brought up the question of how objects affect us. The dilemma[11] that he constructed offered a possible recourse to skepticism, on the basis of which Gottlob Ernst Schulze (1761–1833), who, just as Jacobi, appealed to David Hume, attacked the new 'dogmatism' of the critical philosophy.[12] Although Salomon Maimon, who after 1786 intensively examined the *Critique of Pure Reason*, ultimately labeled himself a skeptic in regard to the question of the existence of objectively valid cognition, he constructively developed, under the influence of Baruch Spinoza, Gottfried Wilhelm Leibniz, and Wolff, Kant's theory of judgments and categories.[13] Jakob Sigismund Beck distanced himself in his book *Erläuternder Auszug aus den critischen Schriften Kants* (*An Explicated Anthology of Kant's Critical Writings*), which he claimed to contain instructions for the only possible understanding of the critical philosophy, from Reinhold's, Maimon's, and Fichte's revisions of Kant. However, with his "doctrine of stance," he himself also deviated strongly from Kant's position. In the third volume of his *Erläuternder Auszug*, he thus contended that as a consequence of his critique of Reinhold's theory of the link between representations and objects, the presupposition of a thing-in-itself or the distinction between the thing-in-itself and appearance would have to be abandoned.[14]

Unlike Friedrich Wilhelm Joseph Schelling and Georg Wilhelm Friedrich Hegel, for whom Kant's significance was by and large only historical, Jakob Friedrich Fries (1773–1843) attempted in the first decade of the 19th century to resurrect Kant's philosophical intentions, without, however, giving Kantianism much of a boost.[15]

Early Reception in Great Britain

The only prominent person in Great Britain in the 18th century who had any appreciable amount of direct knowledge of Kant and of the first German Idealists was Samuel Taylor Coleridge. Coleridge read the *Critique of Pure Reason* in German, making copious notes on it and producing comments on Kant's philosophy in a number of his writings. Coleridge was appreciative of some of the key notions of Kant's thought: of the possibility of reconciling cognition and belief; of the distinction between sensibility, understanding, and reason; and of the distinction between appearances and things-in-themselves. However, Coleridge also combined Kant with German Idealism and with Plato, modifying Kant accordingly. Thus, under the influence of Fichte and Schelling, he rejected the notion of an absolutely unknowable thing-in-itself, and under the influence of Platonism, he advocated a distinction of all objects into those of sense and those of the understanding. He found such a distinction in Kant's *Inaugural Dissertation* of 1770, but apparently failed to realize that by the time of the *Critique*, Kant had abandoned this piece of teaching. Coleridge also displayed a tendency to grasp 'appearance' (*Erscheinung*) as equivalent to 'illusion' (*Schein*), an error that was to be taken up by numerous other English-language authors. Coleridge did not, however, exercise any great immediate influence in Great Britain, if only because his philosophical writings were published much later.[16]

Somewhat surprisingly, there was a brief period during the second half of the 1790s when reports on Kant's philosophy appeared in some of the popular British journals[17] and when Kant's thought was summarized and discussed in a number of book publications, most notably by Thomas Beddoes,[18] J. A. O'Keeffe,[19] Friedrich August Nitsch,[20] John Richardson,[21] and Anthony Florian Madinger Willich.[22] Nitsch, a German disciple of Kant residing in London, also offered private courses on Kant's philosophy between 1794 and 1796. In addition, some of the first translations of Kant's writings appeared at this time, most of them by John Richardson.[23]

This reception apparently owed a great deal to the current political climate in Britain, a climate that was marked by open-mindedness and that favored the publication of a number of journals that were at liberty to print pieces dealing with new intellectual phenomena originating on the European continent. Much of this early reception was superficial, in keeping with the nature of the popular journals that were aimed at a broad public rather than at an academic audience. There was an underlying awareness that Kant's philosophy was something radically new, extremely difficult to understand, and that it was becoming dominant in Germany. However, some of the basics of Kantian philosophy did emerge from these publications, even if Kant was often presented from the point of view of Reinhold and even if he was generally not clearly distinguished from Fichte. It was pointed out that Kant was concerned with an examination of the scope and the limits of human cognition and that he wished to achieve this goal by focusing on the faculty of knowledge itself rather than on the things known or on the genesis of cognition. Also noted were Kant's rejection of the relevance of the historical evidence of religion and of the metaphysical demonstrations of God, along with his treatment of religion as subservient to morals.

The last mentioned point annoyed the conservatives who saw Kant as irreligious and politically subversive, as aligned with the Jacobins. It should be noted, however, that on a philosophical level, Kant at this point in time encountered in England a difficult ground, given the dominance of Lockean epistemology and utilitarian ethics. Only some of the ideas expressed in his essay *Perpetual Peace* fit into the British discussion. Toward the end of the 1790s, the political mood in Great Britain turned increasingly conservative, many of the liberal-minded journals ceased appearing, and a hostile polemic was conducted against German philosophy in the reactionary journals such as *The Anti-Jacobin Review*. The first wave of interest in Kant's philosophy faded and did not begin to revive until about 1820.

For the sake of completeness, it should be noted that at the end of the 18th and the beginning of the 19th centuries, Kant had adherents and opponents in other European countries as well. One may mention the Dutch philosophers Paul van Hemert (1756–1825) and Johannes Kinker (1764–1845); the former wrote an introduction to Kantian philosophy, *Beginsels der kantianische wysgeerte* (Amsterdam, 1796), and founded in 1798 a journal that was devoted exclusively to the goal of spreading Kant's thought, *Magazin voor de kritische wysgeerte*. In France, a notable contribution to Kantianism was made by Charles François Dominique de Villers (1767–1815), who first wrote a number of articles dealing with Kant and who subsequently published the book *Philosophie de Kant, ou principes fondamentaux de la philosophie transcendentale* (Metz, Paris, 1801). In Holland, Kant was vehemently opposed by Daniël Wyttenbach (1746–1820), in France by Destutt de Tracy (1754–1836), each of whom composed articles attacking Kant.

NEOKANTIANISM

Around 1870, Neokantianism developed in Germany and soon became the dominant movement in the German philosophical world.[24] Its precursors advocated, just as the full-blown Neokantians were to do later, a renewal of philosophy by returning to Kant. The earliest precursor of Neokantianism was possibly Eduard Beneke (1798–1854), who in his *Kant und die philosophische Aufgabe unserer Zeit* (*Kant and the Philosophical Task of Our Time*) of 1832 attempted to ground philosophy in inner experience, thus both utilizing and 'correcting' Kantian notions. Christian Weiße (1801–1866) expressed in his inaugural speech *In welchem Sinn die deutsche Philosophie jetzt wieder an Kant sich zu orientieren hat* (*In what sense ought German Philosophy to orient itself on Kant*) (1847) the widespread sentiment that the then predominant isolation of German academic philosophy was to be counteracted by returning to Kantian-style critical thought, that is, one that would be skeptical toward metaphysics and that would stress epistemology.

A further contribution to the development of the movement was made by Hermann Helmholz (1821–1894), who in his lecture *Ueber das Sehen des Menschen* (*On Human Vision*) (1855) highly praised Kant's conception of the relation between philosophy and science. Somewhat later, Otto Liebmann's (1840–1912) motto "Back to Kant," formulated in the course of his criticism of idealism in his *Kant und die Epigonen* (1865), provided a highly influential stimulus to the budding movement.[25] More important for the development of the movement as far as the philosophical substance was concerned were the two volumes on Kant by Kuno Fischer (1824–1907) that he published as part of his *Geschichte der neueren Philosophie* (*History of Recent Philosophy*) in 1860. By insisting on pure reason's spontaneous production, Fischer established a unifying link between Kantian and idealistic philosophy, thus influencing the interpretation of Kant by the Southwestern German School of Neokantianism. But above all, the interest in Kant was promoted by Friedrich Albert Lange (1828–1875) who in a chapter of his widely read *Geschichte des Materialismus* (1866, 2nd ed. 1873/1875) presented a picture of Kant that was readily understandable and ideologically convincing to his contemporaries.[26]

There was a general trend in continental Europe in the second half of the 19th century to renew philosophy by taking up Kant. The most important representative of neo-criticism in France was Charles Renouvier (1815–1903).[27] Aside from him, Kantian motives were taken up by Jules

Lachelier (1834-1898) with his connection of Kantian idealism and spiritualistic realism, his student Emile Boutroux (1845-1921) with his criticism of determinism in naturalistic philosophy, and Léon Brunschvicg (1869-1944) with his determination of the relation of philosophy and science; however, all three ultimately remained within an idealistic framework. In Italy, Kantian philosophy and its German renaissance played a notable role during the years of national unification, which was accompanied by a receptivity to European intellectual debates. At first, this occurred in a Hegelian environment at the school of Bertrando Spaventa (1817-1883) in Naples, but in 1869 Felice Tocco (1845-1911), a student of Spaventa, proclaimed that a return to criticism was necessary and beneficial to further the relation between philosophy and science. Francesco Fiorentino (1834-1884), another student of Spaventa, attempted to link Kant to Giambattista Vico (1668-1744), and he made recourse to Kant in order to reconcile idealism and positivism; at the end of the 1870s, Fiorentino accepted an evolutionary interpretation of Kant's a priori. The most extensive work on Kant was produced by Carlo Cantoni (1840-1906). With his *Emanuele Kant* (3 vols., 1879-1884), Cantoni by his own admission sought to renew Italian philosophy in a Kantian fashion. However, he also overstepped the boundaries of criticism by postulating an "absolute real" (*reale assoluto*) on which not only phenomena but also the cognitive activity of the subject were to be based. This point was attacked by Tocco, who defended against Cantoni's ontologist stance a positivistic and scholarly interpretation of Kant, and who thus became the spokesman of Italian Neokantianism in the 1880s.[28]

However, it was only in Germany that a genuine Kantian movement arose, roughly coinciding with the establishment of the second empire in 1871. Here, the movement separated into different directions and became, at least in part, institutionalized in different schools. As a mark of a philosophical new beginning, the new Kantianism distanced itself both from speculative idealism and from so-called petty bourgeois materialism, positions that it deemed ideologically useless. A philosophy in the spirit of Kant, on the other hand, promised to help in intellectually mastering the changes that occurred with the enormous expansion of science and technology. The historical Kant stood for an epistemologically founded philosophy that would satisfy the new ideal of a science free of metaphysics; at the same time, such a philosophy would, better than any other single discipline, fulfill, even in the new environment dominated by science and technology, the old demand for providing orientation when one was faced with basic and overarching questions of knowledge and action.

The founding fathers of Neokantianism were Hermann Cohen (1842-1918), Alois Riehl (1844-1924), and Wilhelm Windelband (1848-

1915). However, the fact that they were all guided by Kantian philosophy does not in any way mean that they defended a common philosophical position. Cohen, the founder of the Marburg School of Kantianism, tended toward a "critical idealism"; Riehl interpreted Kant against the background of British empiricism and aimed at a "critical realism"; Windelband, the founder of the Southwestern German School of Neokantianism, developed a teleologically oriented Kantian philosophy of value.[29]

The Marburg and the Southwestern German Schools of Neokantianism reached their peaks and their greatest dissemination in the period between roughly 1895 and 1912. This is attested to by the publications of the main representatives Hermann Cohen, Paul Natorp (1854–1924), Wilhelm Windelband, and Heinrich Rickert (1863–1936), by the rise of circles of disciples, and by the resonance both from the specialists and from the wider, philosophically interested public. In spite of significant differences between the two schools, they pursued a common goal: to prove and to secure the rationality of culture. To achieve this task, they considered it of paramount importance to present a convincing philosophical foundation of scientific knowledge. To counteract the spreading disappointment with science, namely, the feeling that science could not, as many had expected, found a comprehensive worldview that would provide guidance in life, the Neokantians concentrated on philosophically working out the *reason in science*.

At the beginning of the 20th century, new opponents appeared on the scene who claimed that science had its irrational ground in 'life.' The weakness of the rationalistic endeavor lay in the fact that the goal of a rational, "systematic interpretation of reality" could not be attained. The thinking of this new era stepped into the shadow of existentialist philosophy. In the 1890s, Friedrich Nietzsche's (1844–1900) philosophy started gaining great popularity, even if the academic world was at first almost completely untouched by this phenomenon. And Wilhelm Dilthey's (1833–1911) existentialist grounding of the humanities in lived experience (*Erleben*), whose subject was no longer the rational human being but the "willing, feeling, imagining" one, did become accepted by philosophers at the German universities. The Neokantians rejected existentialism in all its forms, although the justification of this rejection assumed different shapes in the two Neokantian schools. Interestingly, the Neokantian concept of 'value' derived at least some of its appeal from the fact that it addressed ideological needs, and this it could achieve only thanks to its existentialist foundation. However, in spite of the hostility of the existentialists and in spite of the differences in the interpretation of Kant's works on the part of the two schools, the Kantian critique of reason remained, especially as far as its 'negative' side as the demolition of dogmatic ontology and metaphysics was concerned, the basis of a still thriving Neokantianism. At this point in time, the name of the movement was still appropriate.

The question of the exact date of the demise of Neokantianism remains disputed. There is much indication that Kantianism in its original shape was buried with World War I. In Marburg, the transition was especially noticeable. Cohen left the city after his retirement from the university in 1912 and his teaching chair was not passed on to Ernst Cassirer (1874–1945), but to the experimental psychologist Erich Jaensch. Natorp proclaimed after the war that he had an ambiguous relation to his identity as a member of the Marburg School. The most spectacular effect, however, was achieved by Nicolai Harmann (1882–1950), who in his book *Grundzüge einer Metaphysik der Erkenntnis* (*Foundations of a Metaphysics of Knowledge*) of 1921 distanced himself from the epistemology of his teachers, even if he and Heinz Heimsoeth (1886–1975) had become intellectually estranged from their Marburg school already before 1914. Cassirer accomplished the shift from epistemology to the philosophy of culture in a much steadier fashion; the first volume of his *Philosophy of Symbolic Forms* appeared in 1923.[30]

The Southwestern German School suffered as a consequence of the early death of Emil Lask, who was killed in action. The systematic continuation and development of the basic notions of the school in Rickert's writings of the 1920s and 1930s can no longer be counted as part of Neokantianism. Taking Rickert's earlier criticism as his point of departure, Bruno Bauch (1877–1942) initially retained his ties to Kantian philosophy, but largely discarded, after World War I, the themes of the Neokantianism of the prewar era. In light of these facts, there is good historiographical reason to limit Neokantianism in the narrow sense of the term to the period before 1918. Rickert provided justification for this view in a eulogy for Alois Riehl in 1924; with Riehl's passing, Rickert claimed that Neokantianism as a historical phenomenon had come to an end. Rickert suggested reserving the label 'Neokantian' for those philosophers who "attempted on the basis of a renewed and profound study of Kant to induce philosophy to think about itself" and who "led scientific philosophy forwards by returning to Kant." According to Rickert, the achievement of the Neokantians consisted of their having "given shape to the basic concepts of Kant's writings . . . , a shape in which everybody who was capable of thinking philosophically could understand them." Significantly, Rickert did not think that new Neokantians were needed any more, as there would be no additional work for them.[31] Further systematic development of the critical conception came to an end in Germany with Adolf Hitler's ascension to power in 1933. And, after 1945, Neokantianism in Germany was not resurrected.

KANTIANISM IN GREAT BRITAIN AND AMERICA IN THE 19TH CENTURY

Kantianism in Great Britain

The revival of interest in Kant began with a series of articles in the *Encyclopaedia Londinensis* (1810/1829) by Thomas Wirgman, a disciple of Nitsch,[32] as well as with the publication of the translations of the *Logic* and the *Prolegomena* in 1819 by John Richardson[33] and of "Idea" by Thomas de Quincey.[34] This was followed in 1829 by William Hamilton's substantial discussion of Kant's philosophy that included an appropriation of at least some of its elements.[35] That a proponent of the Scottish commonsense philosophy should come to deal with Kant was not altogether accidental, given that certain similarities between Kant's thought and that of Thomas Reid, the founder of the Scottish school, do exist. Both were concerned with providing an answer to David Hume and both contended that cognition depends on certain a priori principles or concepts in the mind. However, these leads were initially barely noted and they were certainly not greatly pursued by Reid's immediate followers such as Thomas Brown or Dugald Stewart. Brown did review Charles Villers's book on Kant, *Philosophie de Kant, ou principes fondamentaux de la philosophie transcendentale*, in the *Edinburgh Review*,[36] but, never having read Kant himself, he failed to present an accurate picture of Kant's thought. And Stewart too produced his discussion of Kant mainly on the basis of second-hand accounts, having himself had direct knowledge only of the pre-critical *Inaugural Dissertation* (1770). He thus interpreted Kant as a Platonist and mistakenly attributed to him the view that things-in-themselves are objects of the understanding, while appearances are objects of the senses.[37]

Hamilton, on the other hand, was the first of the Scots who was able to read Kant in the original and who was also familiar with the German reactions to Kant. He was aware of the similarity to Reid and referred to Kant on a number of occasions. Just as Kant, Hamilton argued that there was no such thing as simple apprehension since every act of apprehension already contains judgment. This was linked to Hamilton's further Kantian sounding claim that thinking involved submitting the object of thought to the conditions of our thinking faculty (Hamilton's famous doctrine of the conditioned). Indeed, important parts of Hamilton's language are Kantian, such as the expressions "thing-in-itself," "subject of thought," and so forth.[38] However, in spite of these obvious similarities, the precise nature of the relation between Kant and Hamilton is disputed among scholars. According to one view, Hamilton was deeply influenced by Kant,[39] according to another, Hamilton's attempted synthesis of Kant and Reid was doomed to failure and did nothing beyond proving the incompatibility of the two systems of thought.[40] This charge is based on the claim that one could not synthesize Reid's realism, which Hamilton had adopted, with Kant's transcendental idealism. The accusation of incompatibility may be answered by pointing to the fact that Hamilton's realism did not commit him to claiming that we arrive at cognition of things-of-themselves and that Kant himself had admitted that an empirical realism may coexist with his transcendental idealism.[41] Following a third line of interpretation, Hamilton was not greatly influenced by Kant beyond borrowing some language, and, in fact, differed from him profoundly. Along with Kant's distinction of the cognitive faculties into understanding and reason, Hamilton rejected Kant's theory of the phenomena and the antinomies, and he criticized Kant for producing skepticism and for thus provoking the rise of the most extreme forms of absolute idealism.[42]

Kant's philosophy was introduced into Oxford by William Hamilton's disciple Henry L. Mansel, who was reader and then professor of moral philosophy and metaphysics at Magdalen College starting in 1855. Mansel referred to Kant extensively in his criticism of both utilitarianism and idealism and in his defense of Hamilton's philosophy of the 'conditioned.' His understanding of Kant resembled that of Hamilton. He explicitly identified the concepts of the absolute, actual, and unconditioned with things-in-themselves and he refused the distinction of understanding and reason as well as the one between cognition and thinking.[43]

In the 1830s, William Whewell, who freely admitted that his epistemology owed fundamental insights to Kant's first *Critique*, made an attempt to introduce Kant into Cambridge. Whewell agreed with Kant that cognition of an empirically given was possible only when a formal connecting element was provided by the mind and he sought to anchor certainty in what he called "Fundamental Ideas," which, just like Kant's categories, function as laws of thought. However, unlike Kant, he claimed that these laws of thought were not in principle limited in number and that they were ultimately derived from the progress of science. Moreover, Whewell argued that their necessity is proven by the fact that they serve as the necessary foundations of an exact science rather than as the necessary condition for the possibility of experience. Owing mainly to this last mentioned point, Whewell's epistemology has been found to hold certain similarities to that of Hermann Cohen.[44] It should also be added that Whewell was not particularly successful in establishing Kant at Cambridge.[45]

The decline of the Scottish School in Great Britain in the second half of the 19th century was accompanied by a rise of idealism, inspired by the German version, especially by Hegel. This development was marked by an improved ability to read German as well as by a greater interest in Kant. Kant was no longer seen as the critic and skeptic, but as the precursor of German Idealism. The interpretations of Kant did not necessarily differ a great deal from those of the Scottish School, but he was now viewed in a more positive light. The British idealists were occasionally called 'Neokantians' or 'new-Kantians,' though these labels are misleading; the British philosophers had little to do with the German Neokantians, nor did they draw their main inspiration from Kant.[46]

British Idealism is said to have commenced with James Hutchison Stirling's book *The Secret of Hegel* of 1865. Stirling later produced a separate work on Kant, *Text-Book to Kant*,[47] in which he reproduced a part of the *Critique of Pure Reason* and in which he claimed to have been genuinely concerned with understanding Kant. However, he placed Kant in the vicinity of Locke, declaring that Kant's "empirical object" corresponds to Locke's 'representation' and that Kant's 'thing-in-itself' corresponds to Locke's "something I know not what"; Stirling managed this interpretation by rendering Kant's *'Erscheinung'* (appearance) with 'perception.' Another influential monograph on Kant coming out of the idealist school was Thomas Hill Green's *Lectures on the Philosophy of Kant* of 1890. Green rejected Kant's thing-in-itself on the grounds that an object is always an object of consciousness and nothing in-itself. Aside from this, he also rejected Kant's distinction between matter and form in experience. Not surprisingly, he considered the B-deduction of the categories to be a relapse into traditional metaphysics, praising the A-deduction and especially its concept of the transcendental object, since Kant did not search there for a cause of objects outside of consciousness.[48]

Influential were Edward Caird's two books on Kant,[49] not least of all because they were far more readable than the previous works on Kant in English. Although Caird acknowledged the influence of Hermann Cohen, Hans Vaihinger, Benno Erdmann, Friedrich Paulsen, and Alois Riehl, his interpretation does not greatly differ from Green's. Caird criticized Kant's distinctions in general; he also rejected Kant's concept of the thing-in-itself and, along with it, the notion that an unknowable being could affect the subject as well as the notion of the givenness of the manifold. Finally, he reproached Kant for claiming that "being as given" was something over and above "being-for-thought."[50]

The disillusionment with idealism in England that set in toward the end of the 19th century was based on a number of criticisms. It was, for instance, felt that the concept of the absolute was more of a burden than a help, also that idealism could not properly account for the specific, the material, the empirical, and, connected with this, that it could not satisfactorily resolve the question of the relationship between philosophy and the sciences. This had consequences for the reception of Kant. For one thing, German Neokantianism was increasingly taken into account, and Kant was now read more for his epistemological views than as a metaphysician. This change was inaugurated in part by some of the younger representatives of idealism such as Andrew Seth or Robert Adamson, but it was continued by a number of philosophers who had no connection with idealism. In fact, the new interpretations of Kant lasted well into the 20th century.

Kantianism in America

During the first half of the 19th century, philosophy in America was heavily dominated by the Scottish School of Common Sense, and Kant was mentioned only sporadically. A noteworthy contribution to the spread of Kantianism during this period was made by James Marsh, president of the University of Vermont, who in his introductory essay to his edition of Coleridge's *Aids to Reflection* (1829) discussed some of the fundamental positions of Kant's philosophy, such as the distinction between understanding and reason or the transcendental doctrine of freedom. Although Marsh by his own admission owed much of his understanding of Kant to Coleridge, he did exercise some influence on his successors at Vermont, allowing Kant to gain a first foothold in the new world.[51] It should also be noted that the movement known as 'Transcendentalism,' which started in the 1830s and whose most famous proponent was Ralph Waldo Emerson, drew from Kant only very selectively. As has often been pointed out, Kant himself would have labeled these thinkers 'Transcendentists' and would have considered them, unflatteringly, as 'enthusiasts.'[52]

Even as the Scottish Common Sense philosophy began to wane, it still played a role in determining how Kant was received. It was, for instance, not uncommon to claim that investigating the laws of thought was part of psychology; alternatively, one may have turned to logic in the hope of illuminating "Kant by an appeal to Aristotle."[53] Just as William Hamilton in Great Britain had attempted to combine Kant and Reid, so there were attempts in America at a "rapprochement between Scottish philosophy and Kantianism."[54] One philosopher to do so was Francis Bowen (1811–1890), who toward the end of his life introduced the *Critique of Pure Reason* as a textbook into Harvard. Other people continued to hold the Scottish School in high regard, even as they encountered Kant's work. They were then often more or less critical of Kant. Thus, for example, Noah Porter, president of Yale University between 1871 and 1887, preferred the Scots from a theological point of view, thinking they were safer. In a similar vein, James McCosh, president of Princeton from 1868 to 1888, opposed in his book *A Criticism of the Critical Philosophy* (1884) some of the central doctrines of Kant. He rejected Kant's limitation of cognition to phenomena, claiming that we could have direct knowledge of things-in-themselves, and he generally criticized Kant's Copernican Revolution from a Common Sense point of view.[55] Generally though, in the last few decades of the 19th century, the theologically-minded philosophers in America began to read Kant's works directly, instead of continuing to rely on the intermediary role played by the Scottish Common Sense philosophers. Kant now replaced Hamilton as the person toward whom to turn for an answer to Hume's skepticism. Owing to the theological motivation, however, the emphasis tended to be more on practical than on theoretical philosophy.[56]

Another element that greatly influenced the reception of Kant in America was the fact that next to Kant, post-Kantian German philosophy was studied and highly regarded as well, so that Kant was often seen through the prism of German Idealism. Some of this development was no doubt owing to the influence of the British 'new-Kantians,' but as there were early direct contacts with German philosophy, one may assume that a good part of this movement was indigenous. Of the relatively early works introducing Kant to America, one may especially mention Frederic H. Hedge's *Prose Writers of Germany* (1847), a translation of parts of Kant's *Critiques* and of his essay on *Perpetual Peace* as well as of a number of writings by post-Kantian German philosophers, and Laurens Perseus Hickok's *Rational Psychology* (1849), in which Kant's theoretical philosophy is discussed at great length. In a number of places in America, Kant and the German Idealists were translated, read, discussed, and integrated into new strands of philosophy. The most famous of such groups were the so-called St. Louis Hegelians. In connection with them, one may mention as something of a curiosity the existence of a Kant Club in St. Louis before and after the Civil War. Though the particulars of its activities are murky, the members apparently did discuss Kant's and Hegel's writings along with contemporary social and political issues. Perhaps more significant for the reception of Kant was *The Journal of Speculative Philosophy* (1867-1893), founded by W. T. Harris, one of the leading members of the St. Louis Hegelians.[57]

The joint interest in Kant and the Idealists was also apparent at the summer meetings of the Concord School of Philosophy starting in 1879. A number of prominent philosophers took up such an interpretation of Kant. John Dewey wrote in 1884 the article "Kant and Philosophic Method," in which he interpreted Kant as a predecessor of Hegel, crediting the latter with completing Kant's system. In his 1888 book on *Leibniz's New Essays Concerning the Human Understanding*, Dewey further strengthened the idealistic reading of Kant by downplaying the role Hume had played in awakening Kant from his dogmatic slumber and by stressing instead the role of Leibniz in determining what Kant was to write after his sleep.[58] Similarly, the "pragmatic idealist" Josiah Royce, who taught courses on Kant and Hegel at Harvard University, placed the absolute into the center of his philosophy and thus relied far more heavily on Hegel than on Kant. George T. Ladd, on the other hand, was more influenced by Hermann Lotze than by Kant. Ladd, who had introduced courses on Kant into Yale University, resembled most other American philosophers at the turn of the 19th into the 20th century in regarding Kant's rigorous distinction between phenomena and things-in-themselves as a vanquished theory. The things-in-themselves were generally treated in an un-Kantian manner as 'reality,' and it was then held that the "knowledge of reality is necessarily implicated in a knowledge of appearance."[59] Such a position was also expounded by John Watson, professor at Queen's University, Kingston, Canada, in his remarkable defense of Kant against empiricist-oriented attacks by Balfour, Sidgwick, and Hutchison Stirling in his *Kant and His English Critics* (1881). In good Hegelian fashion, Watson regarded Kantianism as having moved "above and beyond" empiricism, suggesting also that Fichte had, in his turn, moved beyond Kant's thought.[60] Finally, Kantian ethics also came to be viewed from a post-Kantian perspective, most prominently by Jacob Gould Schurman, president of Cornell University, in his book *The Kantian Ethics of Evolution* (London, 1881).

A special place in the reception of Kant in America is held by Charles Sanders Peirce, one of the founding fathers of pragmatism. The name of the pragmatist movement was apparently derived from Kant, who had used the term to designate means-ends relations entailed in hypothetical imperatives. But while for Kant pragmatic did not enjoy the highest status in his philosophy, for the American pragmatists focusing on the practical consequences of beliefs became central to their thought.[61] Peirce had come to philosophy mainly by reading the *Critique of Pure Reason*. As early as the 1850s, he distinguished, inspired by Kant's three parts of "The Transcendental Dialectic" (psychology, cosmology, and theology), three classes of entities, namely, thoughts, things, and abstractions or, alternatively, mind, matter, and God. Peirce also held from early on the Kantian thesis that all cognition consists of bringing the manifold of sense to unity, and his mature conception of 'object' owed by his own admission much to Kant. Furthermore, it was the reflection on the merits and demerits of the Kantian categories that led him to investigate at great length the sign relation and to formulate his own categories of quality or firstness, relation or secondness, and representation or thirdness.[62]

METAPHYSICAL KANT INTERPRETATIONS OF THE 1920S

Inaugurated by the work of Heinz Heimsoeth, Kant's critical writings were in the 1920s in Germany interpreted in a way that stressed their metaphysical implications. Heimsoeth himself focused his attention on Kant's metaphysical motives especially as they were linked to Leibniz-Wolffian thought, and he pointed to the fact that Kant himself suggested that his critical writings were to serve as a propaedeutic to the project of a practical, dogmatic metaphysics, a project that Kant, however, never completed. Martin Heidegger construed the *Critique of Pure Reason* as a grounding of metaphysics, in which the "inner possibility of ontology" was justified by the "uncovering of the transcendence, that is, of the subjectivity of the human subject."[63] Further ontological interpretations have been pursued out of different concerns by Gottfried Martin and Ottokar Blaha. Interestingly, the two most important books of this school of interpretation have been translated into English: Heidegger's *Kant und das Problem der Metaphysik* (1929) has been rendered as *Kant and the Problem of Metaphysics*[64] and Martin's *Immanuel Kant. Ontologie und Wissenschaftstheorie* (1951) has been translated under the title *Kant's Metaphysics and Theory of Science.*[65] Especially at the outset, these interpretations arose as reactions against the Neokantian epistemological reading of Kant; this is perhaps also the reason why, in spite of the above-mentioned translations, the "metaphysical Kantianism" never made much of an impact in the English-speaking world, since there was no English Neokantianism to react against.

KANTIANISM IN BRITAIN AND AMERICA IN THE 20TH CENTURY

At the beginning of the 20th century, there was a strong reaction against idealist philosophy, including that of Kant. Most often, Kant was simply ignored by the new analytic philosophers, sometimes he was belittled, and occasionally grossly misinterpreted. Notable in this respect is an early attack on Kant by G. E. Moore, who placed Kant in the immediate proximity of George Berkeley, and who claimed that if it were true that we can have no cognition of the thing-in-itself, then we could have no cognition at all.[66] In spite of this, Kant's thought continued to prosper in the English-speaking world, though, more often than not, its influence became selective and diffuse.

After World War I, as a result of the outcry in America against all things German in academia, Hegel was toppled from the high philosophical pedestal on which he had stood before 1914. Still, Kant remained, though he was now streamlined. The interest was now on Kant the "austere transcendental epistemologist" rather than on the "transcendent metaphysician."[67] An important role in the history of this new type of Kantianism was played by C. I. Lewis, whose lectures on Kant during three decades at Harvard exercised a great deal of influence on the way in which the *Critique of Pure Reason* was taught in America. But though Lewis admitted to the influence of Kant on him, he was a Kantian only in a loose sense of the word. He substituted "pragmatic machinery" for Kant's "transcendental machinery" (that is, for the forms of intuition and the categories), and he claimed that these were not universal and necessary, but open to modification and replacement. In addition, Lewis denied the a priori synthetic, claiming that all a priori was analytic.[68]

Kantian ideas may be found in the thought of diverse 20th-century philosophers who are ordinarily not labeled as Kantians. One may mention as one example the early work of Ludwig Wittgenstein; there are Kantian themes in the *Tractatus Logico-Philosophicus*, such as the notion of the inexpressible limits to our experience, or the notion of the metaphysical self that does not belong to the world but marks a limit. One may even view the grammatical rules that play a key role in Wittgenstein's later *Philosophical Investigations* as a pendant to Kant's synthetic a priori principles. Another case of such 'Kantianism' can be seen in Donald Davidson's theory of "anomalous monism." Davidson quotes from Kant's moral writings, and he presents a solution to the problem of free will that bears explicitly acknowledged similarities to Kant's position.[69] A special mention must be made of Peter Strawson, who not only produced a commentary on Kant's theoretical philosophy but who also utilized Kantian concepts in his book *Individuals*.[70] At present, no specific philosophical kind of Kantianism in the English-speaking world seems to exist.

KANT SCHOLARSHIP

In Germany, exegesis of Kant's works began almost immediately, when various authors attempted to explain Kant's thought without striving for any great interpretation or further development; a good example of this approach is the above-mentioned Johann Schultz. However, true Kant scholarship developed only much later. It required, as a prerequisite, an awareness of the fact that Kant's thought was subject to historical development. Although such an awareness may be located already in Kuno Fischer, Hermann Cohen, and Alois Riehl, it was only with Friedrich Paulsen's *Versuch einer Entwicklungslehre der kantischen Erkenntnistheorie* (*Essay on a Doctrine of the Development of Kantian Epistemology*) of 1875 that the historical and philological interest in Kant began to outweigh the topical and philosophical one. This part of the Kant movement became concerned with discovering unknown texts among the manuscripts, with establishing complete bibliographies, with publishing reliable critical editions, and, finally, with producing a complete and definitive edition of Kant's works. With the latter, it was hoped that the then erratic and confusing state of the publication of Kant's works would be remedied. This task was assumed by the Prussian Academy of Sciences in Berlin in 1894. The edition was to include Kant's correspondence, his unpublished manuscripts as well as student notes from Kant's lectures. Though still not quite complete and in some parts already outdated, the Academy Edition continues to this day to serve as the standard textual point of reference for students of Kant.

On the whole, this kind of scholarship was noted for its abstention from attempts at philosophical and topical reconstructions of Kant.[71] Among other accomplishments, the historical approach to Kant resulted in the founding of the journal *Kant Studies* in 1897 by Hans Vaihinger, a journal that in 2005 is appearing in its 96th volume.

In the English-speaking world, the historical and philological approach to Kant, just as the philosophical one, was closely linked to the availability of translations, though of course a number of British philosophers and scholars were able to read Kant's German. Important were especially the translations of the first *Critique* by J. M. D. Meiklejohn (1855) and Max Müller (1881). Perhaps the first piece of serious Kant scholarship in English was Francis Haywood's *An Analysis of Kant's Critick of Pure Reason* of 1844.[72]

In the 20th century, Kant scholarship in the English-speaking world became a prominent force. An early important role in this movement was played by Norman Kemp Smith. For one thing, Kemp Smith realized that a better translation of the *Critique of Pure Reason* was needed. He criticized the translations by Meiklejohn and Müller especially on the grounds that their translators had insufficient knowledge of the critical philosophy. His own translation appeared in 1929 and remained the standard until it began to be superseded by the new translations by Werner S. Pluhar (1996) and Paul Guyer/Allen W. Wood (1997). On the whole, the work of Norman Kemp Smith set new standards for English-language Kant scholarship. Not only was he familiar with the exegetical work being done in Germany, but he himself paid heed to even very minute details of the *Critique of Pure Reason*. The great knowledge of the work that he acquired while translating the book was helpful in producing his *Commentary*.[73] After Smith's effort, it became much more difficult, and certainly much less frequent, to reproduce Kant in a free philosophical style.[74] Smith's interpretation did, to be sure, contain some blatant errors. Thus he claimed that Kant held the manifold to be structured in some fashion even before the human subject would begin to cognize it,[75] he contrasted appearance with reality, and he asserted that the latter was beyond the former.[76] He also criticized the concept of the "transcendental unity of apperception" as a fallback to Kant's pre-critical philosophy and emphasized instead the transcendental syntheses as the true foundation of transcendental philosophy.[77]

A second milestone in English-language Kant scholarship was set by H. J. Paton with his book *Kant's Metaphysic of Experience: A Commentary on the First Half of the "Kritik der reinen Vernunft"* of 1936. With Paton, the idiosyncracies of Kemp Smith's interpretation became a thing of the past, and Kant students had at their disposal a nonpartisan commentary, whose only serious fault was the fact that it did not cover the whole of the first *Critique*. Since Paton, first class scholarly work on Kant in English has been carried out by a number of persons. One may mention especially Lewis White Beck, Karl Ameriks, Henry E. Allison, Paul Guyer, and Allen W. Wood. The last two mentioned have embarked on a project of producing a new edition of Kant's works in English.[78] The translations are mostly new ones; they adhere to the ideal of literalness and information and strive as much as possible to convey to the readers the kind of impression that they would derive from reading the original German texts. It is very likely that this new edition of Kant's works will remain the standard for English-language scholars for a number of decades.

Although the German and English language scholarships have been treated more or less separately, this movement has, in the second half of the 20th century, become to a large extent international. The *Kant Studies* routinely print German, English, and French articles, and these languages are all more or less well represented at the International Kant congresses. The success of this new, international Kantian scholarship is, incidentally, attested to, among other things, by these very events; at the congress in Berlin in 2000, well over a thousand Kant scholars participated.

Characterizing the scholarly work being done on Kant at present is difficult. Perhaps its most prominent feature is the high level of specialization; not only does one concentrate on theoretical or practical philosophy, but even within these areas, one often focuses on only selected parts. In view of the enormous amount of literature being produced by Kant scholars and of the accompanying difficulty to stay abreast of the latest developments, the trend toward ever greater specialization is unlikely to be halted.

NOTES

1. See the entries NEWTON, ISAAC and GOD, PROOFS OF THE EXISTENCE OF.
2. For more on Kant's early writings, see the entry PRE-CRITICAL PHILOSOPHY.
3. See the entries LEIBNIZ, GOTTFRIED WILHELM; WOLFF, CHRISTIAN; PRE-CRITICAL PHILOSOPHY.
4. For more information on Kant's major publications mentioned in the following account, see the corresponding entries.
5. See the corresponding entries EXPERIENCE and TRANSCENDENTAL DEDUCTION.
6. See also the entry BERKELEY, GEORGE.
7. See Alison Laywine, *Kant's Early Metaphysics and the Origins of the Critical Philosophy* (Atascadero, Calif.: Ridgeview, 1993), p. 1.
8. See also the entry REINHOLD, KARL LEONHARD.
9. See the entry MAIMON, SALOMON. Many of the titles pertaining to Kantianism in this early period have been reprinted in the collection *Aetas Kantiana* (Brussels). For bibliographies of early Kantianism, see Karl Rosenkranz, *Geschichte der Kant'schen Philosophie* (Leipzig: Leopold Voss, 1840), new ed. Steffen Dietzsch (Berlin: Akademie Verlag, 1987), pp. 233–414; Erich Adickes, *German Kantian Bibliography*. 2 vols. (Boston: B. Franklin, 1895–1896 [reprinted, Würzburg, Liebing, 1970]).
10. See the entry FICHTE, JOHANN GOTTLIEB.
11. See the entry THING-IN-ITSELF.
12. G. E. Schulze, *Aenesidemus oder über die Fundamente der von dem Herrn Professor Reinhold in Jena gelieferten Elementar-Philosophie. Nebst einer Vertheidigung des Skepticismus gegen die Anmaassungen der Vernunftkritik* (1792), ed. Arthur Liebert (Berlin: Reuther & Reichard, 1911).
13. For an interesting attempt to solve the problem of the thing-in-itself, see the entry MAIMON, SALOMON.
14. Beck, *Einzig-möglicher Standpunct, aus welchem die critische Philosophie beurtheilt werden muss* (Riga, 1796), p. 26.
15. See the entries FRIES, JAKOB FRIEDRICH; HEGEL, GEORG WILHELM FRIEDRICH; SCHELLING, FRIEDRICH WILHELM JOSEPH.
16. On Coleridge, see Gisela Shaw, *Das Problem des Dinges an sich in der englischen Kantinterpretation*. Kant-Studien Ergänzungsheft 97 (Bonn: Bouvier, 1969), pp. 26–31; John Hoaglund, "The Thing in Itself in English Interpretations of Kant." *American Philosophical Quarterly* 10 (1973): 1–14, p. 4. The ground breaking study of the early reception of Kant in Britain is René Wellek, *Immanuel Kant in England 1793–1838* (Princeton, N.J.:

Princeton University Press, 1931). A more recent overview, one which supersedes Wellek in regard to the last decade of the 18th century and on which the following account is largely based, is Giuseppe Micheli, "The Early Reception of Kant's Thought in England 1785–1805." In *Kant and His Influence*. George MacDonald Ross and Tony McWalter, eds. (Bristol: Thommes, 1990), pp. 202–314.

17. Early articles mentioning Kant appeared, for example, in *The English Magazine* (IX, January 1787, pp. 66–67) and in *The Political Magazine* (February 1787, pp. 94–95). Later, a number of pieces dealing with Kant were published in *The Analytical Review*.

18. *Observations on the Nature of Demonstrative Evidence; with an Explanation of Certain Difficulties Occurring in the Elements of Geometry: and Reflections on Language* (London: J. Johnson, 1793), pp. 89–103.

19. *An Essay on the Progress of the Human Understanding* (London: V. Griffiths, 1795).

20. *A General and Introductory View of Professor Kant's Principles concerning Man, the World, and the Deity* (London: J. Downes, 1796).

21. *The Principles of Critical Philosophy, selected from the Works of Emmanuel Kant . . . and Expounded by James Sigismund Beck . . . Translated from the German by an Auditor of the Latter* (London: Escher, 1797).

22. *Elements of the Critical Philosophy* (London: T. N. Longman, 1798).

23. The early translations of Kant's works were: *Project for a Perpetual Peace* (London: Stephen Conchman, 1796); *Essays and Treatises on Moral, Political, and Various Philosophical Subjects*. 2 vols. Trans. John Richardson (London: William Richardson, 1798–1799) (included the *Foundations of the Metaphysics of Morals, Religion within the Boundaries of Mere Reason* as well as many of the philosophically important pre-critical writings and critical period pieces on the philosophy of history and political philosophy); *The Metaphysic of Morals, Divided into Metaphysical Elements of Law and of Ethics*. 2 vols. Trans. John Richardson (London: William Richardson, 1799). The last-mentioned translation appeared only two years after the first German edition. However, neither it nor the second-mentioned translation exercised much influence, owing to the fact that they were actually printed in Altenburg in Saxony and that only a few of the copies reached England.

24. For an overview of the background to the pre-history and the early phase of Neokantianism, see Klaus Christian Köhnke, *The Rise of Neo-Kantianism: German Academic Philosophy between Idealism and Positivism*. Trans. R. J. Hollingdale (Cambridge: Cambridge University Press, 1991).

25. See the entries HELMHOLZ, HERMANN and LIEBMANN, OTTO.

26. See the entry LANGE, FRIEDRICH ALBERT.

27. See the corresponding entry.

28. See Massimo Ferrari, *Retours à Kant. Introduction au néo-kantisme* (Paris: Les Éditions du Cerf, 2001), pp. 37–45.

29. For more details, see the entries COHEN, HERMANN; MARBURG SCHOOL OF NEOKANTIANISM; NEOKANTIANISM; RIEHL, ALOIS; SOUTHWESTERN GERMAN SCHOOL OF NEOKANTIANISM; WINDELBAND, WILHELM.

30. See the entry CASSIRER, ERNST.

31. Heinrich Rickert, "Alois Riehl." *Logos* 13 (1924/1925): 162–85, esp. pp. 164ff.

32. Articles on Kant, Logic, Moral Philosophy, Metaphysic, Philosophy. See Hoaglund, "Thing-in-Itself," pp. 2–3.

33. *Logic. From the German of E. Kant to which Is Annexed a Sketch of His Life and Writings.* Trans. John Richardson (London: Simpkin and Marshall, 1819); *Prolegomena to Every Future Metaphysic which can Appear as a Science.* Trans. John Richardson (London: Simpkin and Marshall, 1819).

34. *London Magazine* X (1824): 385–93. See Micheli, "Early Reception," p. 307. Translation of Kant's "Idee zu einer allgemeinen Geschichte in weltbürgerlicher Absicht" ("Idea for a Universal History with a Cosmopolitan Purpose").

35. "On the Philosophy of the Unconditioned; in Reference to Cousin's Infinito-Absolute." *Edinburgh Review* 1 (1829). For a recent account of the exact nature of Hamilton's reception of Kant, see Manfred Kuehn, "Hamilton's Reading of Kant: A Chapter in the Early Scottish Reception of Kant's Thought." In *Kant and His Influence.* George MacDonald Ross and Tony McWalter, eds. (Bristol: Thommes, 1990), pp. 315–47.

36. *Edinburgh Review* 1 (1803): 253–80.

37. Dugald Stewart, *Dissertation Exhibiting a General View of the Progress of Metaphysical, Ethical, and Political Philosophy, since the Revival of Letters in Europe.* In *Supplement to the Fourth, Fifth, and Sixth Editions of the Encyclopedia Britannica.* Edinburgh, 1824, vol. 1, pp. 1–66, vol. 5, pp. 1–257. See J. H. Muirhead, "How Hegel Came to England," *Mind* 36 (1927): 423–47, pp. 424–25; Shaw, *Das Problem*, pp. 17–20; Kuehn, "Hamilton's Reading," pp. 318–21.

38. See Kuehn, "Hamilton's Reading," p. 327.

39. Wellek, *Kant in England,* pp. 51, 62; Hoaglund, "Thing-in-Itself," p. 3; J. David Hoeveler Jr., *James McCosh and the Scottish Intellectual Tradition: From Glasgow to Princeton* (Princeton: Princeton University Press, 1981), p. 316.

40. This was already argued in the 19th century by Andrew Seth, *Scottish Philosophy: A Comparison of the Scottish and German Answers to Hume.* 2nd ed. 1885 (reprinted, New York: Burtt Franklin, 1971), p. 153. More recently,

the charge has been repeated by Baruch Brody as well as by Ronald E. Beanblossom: Thomas Reid, *Essays on the Active Powers of the Human Mind.* Ed. Baruch Brody (Boston: MIT Press, 1969), p. xxii; Thomas Reid, *Inquiry and Essays.* Eds. Ronald E. Beanblossom and Keith Lehrer (Indianapolis: Hackett, 1983), p. xl.

41. Kuehn, "Hamilton's Reading," p. 332.

42. Shaw, *Das Problem*, pp. 21–22; Richard Olson, *Scottish Philosophy and British Physics, 1750–1880* (Princeton: Princeton University Press, 1975), p. 131; Edward H. Madden, "Sir William Hamilton, Critical Philosophy and the Common Sense Tradition." *Review of Metaphysics* 38 (1985): 839–66, p. 863; Kuehn, "Hamilton's Reading," pp. 332–45. Kuehn suggests with much plausibility that Hamilton was more influenced by Jacobi than by Kant, or, more precisely, by Jacobi's reading of Kant.

43. Henry Longueville Mansel, *A Lecture on the Philosophy of Kant, delivered at Magdalen College, May 20, 1856* (Oxford: John Henry and James Parker, 1856), pp. 24, 28, 31. See Shaw, *Das Problem*, pp. 23–25.

44. Hoaglund, "Thing-in-Itself," p. 8; see also the editor's introduction to: William Whewell, *Theory of Scientific Method*, ed. Robert E. Butts, Indianapolis (Cambridge: Hackett Publishing Company, 1989), pp. 5–16.

45. See Micheli, "Early Reception," pp. 203–4.

46. See N. H. Marshall, "Kant und der Neukantianismus in England." *Kant-Studien* 7 (1902): 385–408.

47. *Text-Book to Kant. The* Critique of Pure Reason: *Aesthetic, Categories, Schematism. Translation, Reproduction, Commentary, Index. With a Biographical Sketch* (Edinburgh: Oliver & Boyd, 1881).

48. Reprinted in William Hamilton, Henry L. Mansel, Andrew Seth, Thomas Hill Green. *Philosophy of the Unconditioned, On the Philosophy of Kant, The Development from Kant to Hegel, and Lectures on the Philosophy of Kant* (London: Routledge/Thoemmes, 1993).

49. *A Critical Account of the Philosophy of Kant, with an Historical Introduction* (Glasgow: MacLehose, 1877); *The Critical Philosophy of Immanuel Kant.* 2 vols. (Glasgow: James Maclehose & Sons, 1889).

50. On the English Idealists' interpretation of Kant, see Shaw, *Das Problem*, pp. 33–43.

51. J. E. Creighton, "The Philosophy of Kant in America." *Kant-Studien* 2 (1899): 237–52, pp. 240–41.

52. See Bruce Kuklick, *A History of Philosophy in America 1720–2000* (Oxford: Clarendon Press, 2001), p. 78.

53. Elizabeth Flower and Murray G. Murphey, *A History of Philosophy in America.* vol. 1 (New York: G. P. Putnam's Sons, 1977), pp. 204–5.

54. Flower and Murphey, *Philosophy in America*, vol. 1, p. 382.

55. See J. E. Creighton, "Kant in America," p. 249.

56. See Creighton, "Kant in America," pp. 238-9; Bruce Kuklick, "Seven Thinkers and How They Grew: Descartes, Spinoza, Leibniz; Locke, Berkeley, Hume; Kant." In *Philosophy in History*. Richard Rorty, J. B. Schneewind, Quentin Skinner, eds. (Cambridge: Cambridge University Press, 1984), pp. 125-39, p. 129.

57. Many of the key primary sources pertaining to the St. Louis Hegelians have been reprinted recently: Michael DeArmey, James A. Good, eds. *St. Louis Hegelians*. 3 vols. (Bristol: Thoemmes, 2001); James A. Good, ed. *The Journal of Speculative Philosophy, 1867-1893*. 22 vols. (Bristol: Thoemmes, 2002); James A. Good, ed. *The Early American Reception of German Idealism*. 5 vols. (Bristol: Thoemmes, 2002). The last mentioned includes Hedge's *Prose Writers* as volume 3 and Hickok's *Rational Psychology* as volume 4. For a discussion of the background of the group, its activities, and the different interpretations of their philosophical leanings, see Flower and Murphey, *Philosophy in America*, pp. 463-514.

58. John Dewey, *The Early Works, Vol. 1, 1882-1888* (London and Amsterdam: Southern Illinois University Press, 1969), pp. 428-35. See Kuklick, "Seven Thinkers," p. 133.

59. J. E. Creighton, "Kantian Literature in America since 1898." *Kant-Studien* 7 (1902): 409-19, pp. 411-12.

60. John Watson, *Kant and His English Critics. A Comparison of Critical and Empirical Philosophy* (New York: MacMillan, 1881), pp. 2, 24.

61. See Kuklick, *A History*, pp. 132-33.

62. See Flower and Murphey, *Philosophy in America*, vol. 2, pp. 571-72, 588; Kuklick, *A History*, p. 134.

63. Heidegger, *Kant und das Problem der Metaphysik* (1929); 4th ed. (Frankfurt am Main: Klostermann, 1973), p. 199.

64. Trans. James S. Churchill (Bloomington: Indiana University Press, 1962).

65. Trans. P. G. Lucas (Westport, Conn.: Greenwood Press, 1974).

66. G. E. Moore, "The Refutation of Idealism," *Mind* N.S. 12 (1903): 433-53, and "Kant's Idealism," *Proceedings of the Aristotelian Society* 4 (1903/1904): 127-40.

67. Kuklick, "Seven Thinkers," pp. 133-34.

68. C. I. Lewis, "Logic and Pragmatism." *Contemporary American Philosophy*. New York: Macmillan, 1930; *Mind and the World Order* (New York: Charles Scribner's Sons, 1929); *An Analysis of Knowledge and Valuation* (La Salle, Ill.: Open Court, 1946). See Lewis White Beck, "Lewis' Kantianism." In Lewis White Beck, *Studies in the Philosophy of Kant* (Indianapolis: Bobbs-Merrill Co., 1965), pp. 108-24; Flower and Murphey,

Philosophy in America, vol. 2, pp. 893, 957; Kuklick, *A History*, pp. 217–19.

69. Donald Davidson, "Mental Events." In *Essays on Actions and Events* (Oxford: Clarendon Press, 1980), pp. 207–25.

70. See the entry STRAWSON, PETER.

71. From the earlier years, especially Benno Erdmann deserves to be mentioned, specifically his comparison of the two editions of the *Critique of Pure Reason* of 1878, his edition of various works of Kant, and, above all, his *Reflexionen Kants zur kritischen Philosophie* (2 vols., 1882–1884). Also notable was Hans Vaihinger's monumental commentary on the *Critique of Pure Reason*, even if in the end it only covered the beginning of Kant's book (*Kommentar zu Kants Kritik der reinen Vernunft*, 2 vols., 1881–1892).

72. London: William Pickering, 1844 (reprinted, Bristol: Thoemmes, 1990).

73. *A Commentary to Kant's "Critique of Pure Reason."* 2nd ed. (London: Macmillan, 1923).

74. See Shaw, *Das Problem*, p. 75.

75. *Commentary*, pp. 84–85.

76. *Commentary*, pp. liii, 326n., 415–16. This view was also responsible for some mistranslations of the *Critique*. Thus, e.g., Kemp Smith typically rendered a phrase such as "die Grenzen der Sinnlichkeit . . . über alles zu erweitern . . . drohen" with "threaten to make the bounds of sensibility coextensive with the real" (B xxv), thus misinterpreting Kant and misleading generations of scholars.

77. *Commentary*, p. 261.

78. *The Cambridge Edition of the Works of Immanuel Kant*, 1992– . For details, see our Bibliography, Primary Sources, English Translations.

THE DICTIONARY

- A -

ABSOLUTE. Kant makes positive use of this term only in a very specific, limited manner. In accordance with the position he had already developed in his **pre-critical** *Inaugural Dissertation*, he rejects in the *Critique of Pure Reason* **Isaac Newton**'s theory of the absolute nature of **time** and **space** (A 35/B 52). However, Kant's main discussion of 'absolute' occurs in the "**Transcendental Dialectic**" in connection with his remarks on the unconditioned. Kant specifies that he is not using absolute in the sense of valid for a thing as it is in itself or internally, but rather valid in all respects in every relation. Absolute is thus opposed to comparative, that is, valid only in some particular respect. In Kant's **transcendental philosophy**, the "absolute totality in the synthesis of conditions" or the "absolutely unconditioned" is held to be the aim of the **transcendental ideas** of **reason** (A 324-26/B 380-82). The attempt of reason to gain **cognition** on the basis of the three classes of transcendental ideas, namely, the absolute unity of the thinking subject, the absolute unity of the series of conditions of appearance, and the absolute unity of the condition of all objects of thought in general (A 334/B 391), is discussed at great length under the headings **paralogisms**, **antinomies**, and **ideal of pure reason**, where it is demonstrated that such an attempt leads to contradictions and logical quandaries. If, however, the quest for the unconditioned and thus for the absolute fails to produce cognition, it nevertheless remains useful in yielding the notion of the **regulative** use of ideas.

Kant's followers **Johann Gottlieb Fichte**, and even more so **Friedrich Wilhelm Joseph Schelling** and **Georg Wilhelm Friedrich Hegel** abandoned all of Kant's restraint and hoisted the absolute into central roles in their own philosophical systems. In spite of occasional criticism of such usage, for example, on the part of **Arthur Schopenhauer**, philosophies of the absolute remained dominant in Germany during much of the early part of the 19th century before being drastically reduced in size by the advent of **Neokantianism**. Around 1850 the term 'absolute' became popular in Great Britain and America, where it assumed a central role in the philosophical debates during much of the second half of the 19th century, before suffering, at the hands of the analytic philosophy, an even more drastic fate than it had previously endured in Germany.

ABSTRACT, CONCRETE. The concepts of 'abstract' and 'abstraction' did not play a central role in Kant's philosophy. They were discussed and defined mostly in his minor writings, though the results of these efforts were then presupposed in the *Critique of Pure Reason*. Already in his **precritical** *Inaugural Dissertation* (§ 6), Kant distinguished two notions of abstraction, of which, however, he was willing to admit only one. What he wished to rule out was 'abstract' in the sense of being attained by **induction**, that is, of deriving, for example, the color red from the perception of a number of red objects. This conception had been famously advocated by **John Locke**. Kant especially objected to the claim that one could rely on such a process of abstraction to arrive at **a priori concepts**. Instead, he was willing to admit abstraction only in the sense of the separating away of certain qualities from an object, that is, of not attending to them and concentrating on the remaining qualities, for example, removing from the experiential concept of a body everything that is empirical in it, color, hardness or softness, and so forth, and being left only with the **space** that was occupied by the body (B 5; Ak 9, pp. 94–95, § 6). It is only in this latter way that we arrive at a priori concepts and judgments, and it is in this sense that we must understand Kant's claim that such a priori elements are *discovered* in experience, but not *derived* from it (by an inductive process) (B 1–2).

Given that concepts represent numerous individuals and that one thus has to leave out numerous individual qualities when thinking concepts, Kant regarded all concepts as abstract. However, he claimed that their *use* could be either abstract or concrete: the former is the case when a less generic term is employed in regard to a more generic one, the latter in the reverse situation (Ak 9, p. 99, § 16).

ACCIDENT. *See* SUBSTANCE.

ACTION (*Handlung*). Aside from briefly dealing with the concept of logical action of the understanding (A 68/B 93), Kant developed in the *Critique of Pure Reason* the foundations of his theory of action in connection with his treatment of the principle of **causality** and with the resolution of the third **antinomy** of causality and freedom. Under action ("activity and force"), Kant understands the "relation of the subject of causality to the effect." He then argues that actions as the "primary ground of all change of appearances" cannot be attributed to a subject that is itself submitted to change, so that such actions prove this subject as a **substance** (A 204–5/B

249–51). In his discussion of a possible "causality through **freedom**," Kant introduces the idea of the "original action" of a cause, which is not the effect of a preceding cause, but which has an intelligible ground that Kant places in the moral **ought**. Such a causality is distinguished from the "actions of natural causes in a temporal sequence" (A 544–48/B 572–76).

In Kant's **practical philosophy**, action does not play a central role, which is instead assumed by the **will** and the subjective **maxim**. When the will is determined by the categorical **imperative**, then the action, which is joined to it a priori, will be good as such; when the will is subjected to a hypothetical imperative, then **inclination** as "a pathological interest in the object of the action" is involved, and the action is good only as a means to an end (GMM, Ak 4, p. 414). Accordingly, Kant distinguishes between, on the one hand, technically practical and pragmatic actions, which follow the hypothetical imperative, and, on the other hand, moral actions. He divides the latter into 'external' ones, which are marked merely by legality, that is, by an agreement with the **moral law**, and into 'inner' ones, whose incentive is moral obligation and which can be deemed to be moral (CrPR, Ak 5, pp. 71–2; MM, Ak 6, p. 219). Finally, in his theory of virtue, Kant distinguishes juridical laws of action from ethical laws of the maxims of actions; these maxims are grounded in the concept of a purpose that is at the same time **duty** (MM, Ak 6, pp. 388–89, 392).

In his *Ethik des reinen Willens*, **Hermann Cohen** criticized Kant for not having elevated the concept of action to the highest rank in his practical philosophy. First, for Cohen, the will finds its culmination in action, which is its concern and its end. Second, his focus on the juridical aspect of action (*Rechtshandlung*) leads him to view action only in its relationship to another person, with corresponding consequences for the constitution of the ethical subject. Third, law has its origin and actual content in actions, meaning that the law defines what ought to count as an action.

ACTUALITY (*Wirklichkeit, Dasein*). Actuality is one of the **categories** of **modality**. In the **table of the categories** it is presented under the concept of 'existence,' together with its opposite 'nonexistence.' The **schema** of the concept of actuality is "existence at a determinate time" (A 145/B 184). Similarly as in the case of the existential 'is,' Kant stresses that the predicate 'actual' (the same goes for the other modal predicates '**possible**' and '**necessary**') does not augment the determination of the **object**, but expresses the relation to the faculty of **cognition**. It is the mark of an 'actual' object (as opposed to one that is merely thought) that its existence is not only posited in thinking, but that there is an object *outside* the understanding that corresponds to the concept of the object *within* the understanding (Ak 5, p. 139). According to the second **postulate of empirical thinking in general**, we cognize as actual "that which is connected with the material conditions of **experience (of sensation)**" (A 218/B 266). That means that when something is claimed to be actual (existing) and is initially given only conceptually as a possibility, it must subsequently be related to sensation or to **perception**. Kant therefore emphasizes that the cognition of the actuality of something requires perception or at least a connection with other perceptions. On the basis of the postulate of actuality, Kant then refutes in the second edition of the *Critique of Pure Reason* material **idealism** by proving the following theorem: "The mere, but empirically determined, consciousness of my own existence proves the existence of objects in space outside of me" (B 275).

In his *Logik der reinen Erkenntnis* (1902) **Hermann Cohen** clearly distinguished between actuality and reality. The problem of actuality was for him that of the single. In this way he approached the question of the contribution of sensation to cognition, a question he finally resolved within the framework of his discussion of the modal "judgment of actuality." Cohen admits a "demand of sensation," but claims that sensation itself cannot redeem this demand and he reduces it to a critical evaluation of all categorical object determinations in regard to their relation to actuality. This critical evaluation can be carried out only in pure thinking, which in correlation to the demand Cohen determines as a thinking of the **origin**. In his discussion of the actuality of God the later Cohen excluded the attribution of this predicate to God, arguing that it was founded in sensibility.

Paul Natorp relates in his *Die logischen Grundlagen der exakten Wissenschaften* (1910) the modal category of actuality to the discovery of facts in the process of scientific research. Since this process is infinite and there are therefore no absolute facts, the cognition of actuality becomes an everlasting **problem** (*Aufgabe*). Natorp conceives the amplification of possibility into actuality in a structural rather than dynamic or genetic fashion, as a temporal-spatial determination of the object, since time and space are for him the conditions of the determination of existence in possible experience.

Initially in proximity to Natorp, **Ernst Cassirer** recast in his *Substanzbegriff und Funktionsbegriff* (1910) the problem of actuality as the problem of truth. He claimed that the rift between the impression of an object and the object itself is taken up into the concept of cognition, since cognition is a transformation through the form of connection of impressions into objects.

The usage of the expression 'actuality' to summarily signify the world of objects, states, and events does not directly stand in a Kantian tradition. But this was the sense in which **Heinrich Rickert** used the expression "objective actuality" in his *Der Gegenstand der Erkenntnis* (3rd ed. 1915). Rickert developed a concept of actuality that stood between the concept of an aggregate of facts and Kant's concept of **nature**. Such an actuality was supposed to contain more form than the sum of all the given, but less than Kant's nature. It was supposed to be a prescientific and yet coherent actuality, for which one was to seek its forms in the shape of "constitutive categories of actuality."

AESTHETICS. This term was employed in Alexander Gottlieb Baumgarten's book *Aesthetica* (1750) as a label for the new philosophical "science of sensible cognition." From the outset, its task was to integrate the **beautiful** and **art** into the system of philosophy by focusing on **sensation** and **feeling**. This usage eventually became widespread, though, as Kant's *Critique of Pure Reason* demonstrates, the old connotation of an epistemological theory of intuition (perception) subsisted alongside the new meaning. Kant understands aesthetics as a "**critique** of **taste**" (Ak 2, p. 311), not as a science, attributing this conception to Henry Home, Lord Kames (Ak 9, p. 15). "There is no science of the beautiful, only a critique," because a **judgment** of taste is incapable of a scientific foundation (CJ, Ak 5, pp. 304–5). The critique of taste is subordinated only to a "subjective **principle** of the faculty of judgment." Such a subjective critique brings under rules "the reciprocal relation of the **understanding** and the **imagination** to each other" in the representation of a beautiful object. This critique can take one of two forms: either that of art, if it shows the reciprocal relation in examples; or that of science, if it develops and justifies this relation as a **transcendental** condition of the experience of the beautiful. It is the latter with which Kant is mainly concerned (p. 286).

Kant's aesthetics was critically appropriated and further developed by Friedrich Schiller (1759–1805) (*Über Anmut und Würde*, 1793; *Über die ästhetische Erziehung des Menschen*, 1795). In post-Kantian German Idealism, however, Kant's conception was superseded by a philosophy of art which renounced the concept of taste and which parted with the aesthetic determination of art. Among the Neokantians, **Hermann Cohen** established aesthetics as the third part of his system of philosophy; by approaching it via art he viewed it as an ingredient of general culture. Jonas Cohn conceived of aesthetics as a critical science of **value**.

AFFECT. Kant's usage of this word as a noun must be strictly distinguished from his employment of the verb 'to affect' (*affizieren*). Kant discussed affects mainly in the **Critique of Judgment** (§ 29) and in his **Anthropology from a Pragmatic Point of View** (§§ 73–79), each time presenting them in a very negative light, namely, as temper outbursts that preclude the use of **reason**. He distinguished affects from passions, which he considered as even more detrimental to human well-being, defining the latter as enduring and brooding, while the former were tempestuous and not deliberate. Both belonged to **sensibility**, which for Kant made a reliance on them unsuitable to any kind of **moral** conduct.

AFFECTION. Kant employs the noun 'affection' (*Affizierung*) with the corresponding verb 'to affect' (*affizieren*) to express a relation that lies somewhat along the lines of **causality**, but that is not causality itself. There are two different, if related uses of affection. 1) As Kant stresses over and over in the **Critique of Pure Reason**, we are affected by things. This provides us with **sensation**, that is, with the **matter** of **intuition**; in this process we are receptive (for example, A 19/B 33). The upshot of this relationship for Kant is that we do not cognize things as they are in themselves, but only as they **appear** to us.

2) Kant also speaks at a number of places of the subject affecting itself. Here, no new matter is given to us, rather the subject posits the **forms** of **sensibility** and of the **understanding** so that its own **cognition** must then be structured in accordance with these forms. In the "**Transcendental Aesthetic**" Kant says that the **mind** is affected by its own activity, namely, by the act of positing the forms of intuition of **time** and **space** (B 67–68), while in the "**Transcendental Deduction**" he speaks of the understanding affecting **inner sense** (B 153–54).

By means of an analogy between these two kinds of affection, by things and by ourselves, Kant explains his claim that the subject cognizes itself only as it appears to itself and not as it is in itself (B 68, B 165): just as we cognize objects in space "only insofar as we are externally affected," so we intuit ourselves "only as we are internally affected by our selves" (B 166).

Kant returns to the notion of self-affection in the so-called *Opus Postumum*. In keeping with his attempt to discover here concepts that mediate between the philosophy of science and physics, he now utilizes 'affection' to express the idea that the subject posits the concepts of the relations of motive **forces** also into his **perception** (rather than just positing the categories into **experience** as in the first *Critique*). These concepts constitute the formal elements of perception in such a way that the material of perception that the subject takes up is determined by this process of self-affection (Ak 22, pp. 390, 405, 502). *See also* AFFECT; DOUBLE AFFECTION.

AFFINITY (*Affinität, Verwandtschaft*). Kant used the two German terms *'Affinität'* and *'Verwandtschaft'* interchangeably, though in a number of different senses that are only weakly interrelated, if at all. In the *Critique of Pure Reason* 'affinity' plays an important role mostly in the first edition version of the "**Transcendental Deduction**." Here it is distinguished into an empirical affinity, which is apparently equated with **association**, and a **transcendental** affinity; Kant declares that the former is a mere consequence of the latter. Transcendental affinity stands for the thoroughgoing connection of all **appearances** according to necessary **laws** (A 113-14).

Kant once claims that the seat of affinity is in the **understanding** (A 766/B 794), another time that affinity is to be encountered only in the **transcendental unity of apperception**, but he also attempts to relate it to the **productive imagination**, namely, by maintaining that affinity is a necessary consequence of the **synthesis** of imagination (A 122-23). The lack of clarity in regard to the exact status of affinity is a possible consequence of the generally unclear relationship of apperception and imagination in the A-deduction. The realization of this shortcoming may have led Kant to drop the word 'affinity' from the B-deduction.

'Affinity' turns up again in the "Appendix to the **Transcendental Dialectic**," where it is used as a (near) synonym for **'continuity.'** Along with two other **regulative ideas**, those of homogeneity and specification, affinity of forms serves for a higher level ordering of the **cognitions** of the understanding.

Kant uses 'affinity' in yet another sense in his *Anthropology from a Pragmatic Point of View* while discussing the "sensible faculty of literary production." While now clearly distinguishing it from association, he defines it as "the union that arises when the manifold is derived from a common ground," and he compares it to the case of two chemical substances that have a tendency to unite in order to produce a third substance. How distant this is from the other two senses of the word becomes manifest when Kant here suggests that the understanding and sensibility stand in a relationship of affinity so as to produce cognition (§ 33C).

AFFIRMATION. *See* NEGATION.

AGGREGATE. Kant reserved this term for any group of entities of any kind that are disparate and that are not connected by any higher link, that is, that are not systematically ordered. The word 'aggregate' was thus first and foremost opposed to 'system'; in this sense Kant explicitly denied that experience was an "aggregate of perceptions," since experience stands under the pure unity of the understanding, a unity that precedes it a priori and that guarantees systematic connection (P, § 26). In addition, Kant also opposed aggregate, as a number of discrete parts or objects, to continuity (A 170/B 212). As synonyms to 'aggregate' Kant used the words 'rhapsody' or 'rhapsodic'; he did so most famously to accuse Aristotle of compiling the categories in a rhapsodic, rather than in a systematic fashion (P, § 39).

AGREEABLE (*Angenehmes*). In his ethics, Kant opposes the agreeable to the morally good; the former affects the will by sensations in a subjective manner, not as a principle of reason (Ak 4, p. 413). In his aesthetics, the opposition becomes one between satisfaction derived from the agreeable combined with interest, on the one hand, and the disinterested satisfaction with the beautiful on the other (Ak 5, pp. 204–5). In this context, the agreeable is described as that which pleases the senses in the representation of an object, that is, as that which delights. Such pleasure is basically private so that in regard to the agreeable it may be granted that each person has his or her own taste. However, agreement as to whether something is agreeable does occur and Kant explains it by recourse to empirical rules of sociability (pp. 212–13). Regardless of how an agreeable representation may vary from an objective point of view, the assessment that something is agreeable is based on an "incentive of the desires," whose influence depends purely quantitatively on the number of stimuli (p. 266). On the other hand, when the feeling of pleasure involves the beautiful, a "certain quality of the object" also plays a role.

ALTERATION (*Veränderung*). An important auxiliary concept in Kant's epistemology, of which, however, no sustained discussion is ever offered. As a general definition one may take the following statement: "Alteration is the combination of contradictorily opposed determinations in the existence of one and the same thing" (B 291). Kant employed the concept 'alteration' already in his pre-critical piece *Nova Dilucidatio* in the course of his critique of Gottfried Wilhelm Leibniz's theory of preestablished harmony, arguing that only when substances genuinely interact can there be any alteration at all (prop. 12).

In the *Critique of Pure Reason* Kant first stresses that alterations are empirically real and that they occur only in real time, and do not, therefore, yield any cognition of things-in-themselves (A 37/B 53–54). Subsequently, Kant does struggle with the concept somewhat. In the "First Analogy" he distinguishes alteration from change (*Wechsel*), claiming that while it is proper to say that **substance** is altered, its states should be said to change. Substance cannot arise and perish, only its determinations, that is, accidents can do so (A 187-88/B 230-31). However, in an addition to the B-version of the "Second Analogy," Kant seems to abandon his previous distinction, since he now states that "all change (succession) of **appearances** is only alteration." He does, nevertheless, retain the gist of his earlier argument, reiterating that substances indeed do not arise or perish (B 232-33).

The concept of alteration plays a prominent part in Kant's debate of **causality** in the "Second Analogy." Crucial here is his claim that "every alteration has a cause" (A 208/B 253) or his later proclamation that alteration is possible only through a cause (B 291). In keeping with the highly formal nature of his discussion, Kant admits that we have no **a priori** notion of "how in general anything can be altered, how it is possible that upon a state in one point of time an opposite one could follow in the next." To explain specific cases of alteration we would need to be acquainted with moving **forces**. However, the **form** of such alteration, "the condition under which alone it, as the arising of another state, can occur (whatever the content, i.e., the state, that is altered might be), consequently, the succession of the states itself can still be considered a priori according to the law of causality and the conditions of time" (A 206-7/B 252). Moreover, we can also stipulate a priori that alteration occurs through a continuous action of causality. Kant speaks here of a "law of **continuity** of all alteration," meaning that there is no smallest part to time or to the appearances in time, but that alteration passes through all the parts (A 209/B 254).

In the second edition of the *Critique* Kant tied alteration to **space**, claiming that we can exhibit alteration only by resorting to **motion**. Inner alteration in the **mind** requires now a similar recourse to space, since the passing of time can be grasped only figuratively by means of a line (B 391-92).

AMPHIBOLY. In his effort to not only eradicate the errors committed by his predecessors but also to explain their origin, Kant pointed out that some of those mistakes were the result of falsely assigning **concepts** to the wrong cognitive power (**sensibility** or the **understanding**), thus creating a "transcendental amphiboly," namely, a "confusion of the pure object of the understanding with the appearance" (A 270/B 326). In the appendix to the **"Transcendental Analytic"** entitled "On the Amphiboly of the Concepts of Reflection through the Confusion of the Empirical Use of the Understanding with the Transcendental," Kant nearly exclusively concerns himself with the misapplication of the so-called concepts of reflection, that is, of special concepts that do not represent **objects**, but only the relations among themselves. As such concepts, he lists the pairs "identity and difference," "agreement and opposition," "inner and outer," and "matter and form." In order to avoid the amphiboly, one must engage in a **transcendental** reflection that determines to which cognitive power a given concept belongs, that is, that assigns it to its "transcendental place"; the complete doctrine of positioning all concepts would be called "transcendental topic."

The section on the "Amphiboly" is largely directed against **Gottfried Wilhelm Leibniz**. In the course of his attempt to account for the differences between his own and Leibniz's philosophy, Kant accuses the latter of lacking a transcendental topic and therefore of 'intellectualizing' the **appearances**. Thus Kant, within his discussion of identity, argues that Leibniz extended the principle of the identity of indiscernibles to appearances, although properly, it only holds for concepts of things in general. Leibniz's conception of **space** and **time** as the orders of relations of objects is for Kant the result of a similar confusion, namely, of an intellectualization of what in reality are the **forms** of sensibility. In passing, Kant also takes a swipe at **John Locke**, whom he accuses of having 'sensitivized' the concepts of the understanding, that is, of having interpreted them as empirical or abstracted concepts of reflection (A 271/B 327).

ANALOGIES OF EXPERIENCE (*Analogien der Erfahrung*). The third class of the synthetic **principles of pure understanding**. Their "general principle" as stated in the first edition version of the *Critique of Pure Reason* reads: "As regards their **existence**, all **appearances** stand a priori under rules of the determination of their relation to each other in one **time**" (A 176); in the second edition this is amended to: "**Experience** is possible only through the representation of a necessary connection of perceptions" (B 218). Kant carefully selected the title "Analogies of Experience" out of a number of similar expressions (Reflection 4675, Ak 17, p. 648; Reflection 4681, Ak 17, pp. 667–68), making it plain that these principles concerned the **relation** of appearances. The principles are therefore not 'constitutive,' as are the **Axioms of Intuition** and the **Anticipations of Perception**, but only 'regulative.' Within them, the **schemata** of the **categories** of relation are applied: persistence (schema of **substance**), succession (schema of **causality**), and simultaneity (schema of **community**). The analogies of experience belong to the group of **dynamical principles**. They ground the lawful connection of appearances in regard to their **being**, and, in addition, they secure the basis for the **unity** of **nature**, by providing, as principles of general metaphysics, the foundation of the Newtonian laws of motion (see *Metaphysical Foundations of Natural Science*, "Mechanics"). As formal principles a priori they also help to determine the transition from **metaphysics to physics** in the *Opus Postumum* (e.g., Ak 22, p. 294).

ANALOGY. According to Kant, thinking in analogies is permissible only when they are not employed as an inference that extends our **cognition**. In philosophy, analogy may be used solely in a **qualitative** sense, that is, one may determine on the basis of three given members only the **relation** to a fourth one, but not this fourth member itself (A 179–80/B 222). Thus, for example, when we compare the reasons for the artificial constructions of animals with those of humans, we may conceive an 'instinct' as an analogue to human **reason**, without, however, knowing what this instinct is. In a similar fashion, we may, based on the comparison of human products with the purposive products of the supreme cause of the world, conceive the latter in analogy to an **understanding**, without, yet again, being able to transfer the properties of the understanding onto the cause of the world (CJ, Ak 5, p. 464; see also A 698/B 726). A **soul**, an intelligible **world**, and a supreme being cannot be cognized as they are in themselves, but may be assumed "at the boundary of all permitted use of reason" by means of an analogy with the sensible world. This yields the concept of these **noumena**, though such a concept is for us insufficiently determined; Kant here speaks of a "symbolic anthropomorphism" (P, Ak 4, pp. 356–58). *See also* ANALOGIES OF EXPERIENCE; SYMBOL.

ANALYSIS (*Analyse, Zergliederung*). Kant essentially employed the term 'analysis' and the corresponding adjective 'analytic' in two different senses. In a rare case he used it to signify the search for the conditions to an assumed fact (**analytic method**), more commonly, however, he used it in the (chemical) sense of taking apart, resolving a complex whole into simpler parts. In this latter sense, 'analysis' turns up already in Kant's **pre-critical** writings, though there it is assigned a far greater scope than it later assumes in his mature thought. In his *Prize Essay* of 1763/1764 Kant claims that while **mathematics** proceeds by synthesizing elements, **philosophy** ought to resort to analysis; attempts at introducing the two methods outside their proper fields lead to error. Analysis is described here specifically as the resolution of a given, confused concept into its different features, which are then compared "among each other together with the concept in various situations"; the final result should be a determinate **thought** (Ak 2, 276–77).

In the *Critique of Pure Reason*, Kant greatly reduces the importance of such analysis. It is now associated with general **logic**, while **synthesis** is associated with **transcendental logic**. Kant stresses that analysis does not yield any new cognition, but involves only a clarification or perhaps an ordering of concepts by processes such as abstraction, generalization, comparison, and so forth; alternatively, it is characterized as the means of bringing different representations under one **concept** (A 78/B 104). In this sense, Kant somewhat loosely describes **transcendental** critique, which is to serve as preparation for **transcendental philosophy**, as an analysis that would only "provide insight into the principles of **a priori** synthesis in their entire scope." The reason why Kant claims here that analysis is involved is that the aim is not an amplification (synthesis) of the **cognitions** a priori, but only their examination and correction (A 12/B 25–26). The fact that synthesis along with transcendental logic now gains for Kant far greater importance than analysis and general logic is consonant with his remark that analysis is always preceded by synthesis, since where nothing is combined, nothing can be dissolved (B 130). In a similar vein, the analytic unity of consciousness is described as being only posterior to the synthetic unity of apperception (B 133n.).

ANALYTIC (*Analytik*).   In each of his three *Critiques*, Kant divided at least one large part of the work into an 'Analytic' and a '**Dialectic**.' In each case the former was concerned with presenting some positive content, while the latter was aimed at debunking fundamental errors (mostly those committed by Kant's predecessors or by the young, **pre-critical**, Kant himself), or at showing how only restricted use could be made of certain concepts, or at pointing out how seemingly irreconcilable positions could sometimes be reconciled (**antinomy**). In the *Critique of Pure Reason*, Kant divided the "**Transcendental Logic**" into a "**Transcendental Analytic**" and a "**Transcendental Dialectic**." The Analytic was supposed to present in two books, the "Analytic of Concepts" and the "Analytic of Principles," "the elements of **pure cognition** of the **understanding** and the **principles** without which no **object** can be thought at all" (A 62/B 87). Within the context of the "Analytic of Concepts," Kant at least partly accounted for his choice of the term 'analytic,' namely, by explaining that it refers to an "analysis of the faculty of understanding itself" rather than to an analysis of the contents of **concepts** (A 55/B 90). In the Dialectic Kant then sought to refute or at least to curtail leading doctrines of traditional **metaphysics**.

   In the *Critique of Practical Reason*, the "Analytic of Pure Practical Reason," because it deals with the **will** rather than with cognition, reverses the order of the first *Critique:* it begins by showing the possibility of practical **principles a priori**, then it proceeds to a discussion of the concepts of the objects of **practical reason**, before arriving at the **sensibility** (in practical philosophy, this is the role of moral sentiment); the "Dialectic of Pure

Practical Reason" deals with the consequences of the quest for the unconditioned (the highest good) for the practical conditioned (inclinations). Finally, in the ***Critique of Judgment***, each of the two major parts has its own analytic and dialectic. In the "Analytic of Aesthetic Judgment," Kant presents his theory of the beautiful and the sublime (under the headings "Analytic of the Beautiful" and "Analytic of the Sublime"), while the corresponding dialectic concerns the critique of taste rather than **taste** itself and is therefore focused solely on a conflict of principles, that is, an **antinomy**. Similarly, in the "Analytic of Teleological Judgment," Kant presents his teachings on **purpose**, while the "Dialectic of Teleological Judgment" again seeks to disentangle a conflict of principles, that is, another antinomy.

ANALYTIC AND SYNTHETIC JUDGMENTS.   Analytic judgments are the subject matter of general **logic**, are subordinate only to the principle of contradiction, and may be erroneous even if they are not contradictory, since it may be the case that they are applied mistakenly or that they apply to no **object** at all. In analytic judgments one remains within the given concept in order to discern something about it, that is, the predicate is (covertly and confusedly) contained in the subject. In an affirmative analytic judgment, we thus ascribe to a concept something that is already included in it, in a negative analytic judgment, we exclude the opposite of the concept. In synthetic judgments, on the other hand, we go beyond the given concept to consider something different from it that stands in a relation to it, a relation other than identity or contradiction. The error of a synthetic judgment cannot be discovered in the judgment itself, one must go beyond it. Kant calls the former type of judgments clarifying or explicative, the latter type ampliative (A 6–8/B 10–11, A 154–55/B 193–94; P, § 2).

This distinction is not totally unprecedented in the history of philosophy, though it was generally not made within the Leibniz-Wolff school. Here the tendency was to claim that all judgments were analytic, though already **Gottfried Wilhelm Leibniz** did distinguish logically necessary judgments from contingent ones. During his **pre-critical** period, Kant initially adhered to this practice with some reservations in the *Nova dilucidatio* (1755), though already in his *Attempt to Introduce Negative Magnitudes into Philosophy* (1763), he presaged the distinction analytic/synthetic by suggesting that next to logical contradiction there is also a real one. He may have been inspired by **David Hume**'s distinction between "relations of ideas" and "matters of fact."

Kant's distinction is reasonably unproblematic and has generally gained acceptance as long as one only combines analytic with **a priori** and synthetic with a posteriori. However, Kant's classification of judgments becomes revolutionary (and problematic), when he asserts the existence of **synthetic a priori** judgments. It is along with these that the distinction between general and **transcendental logic** comes into play; it is the latter that provides the main foundation of Kant's **transcendental philosophy**.

ANALYTIC METHOD (*Analytische Lehrart*). In the *Prolegomena* (§§ 4–5) Kant distinguishes the analytic method from the synthetic one. In the former, for which Kant also suggests the label "regressive method," one commences by assuming certain **facts** as if they were given, such as the fact of the existence of a **pure mathematics** and of a pure **science**, or, more precisely, of the existence of **a priori** propositions in mathematics and science, and proceeds (regresses) to investigate the conditions under which alone such facts are possible. Kant asserts that this is the procedure used in the *Prolegomena* themselves, whereas for the *Critique of Pure Reason* he claims to be resorting to the synthetic method, also termed 'progressive,' in which one assumes no facts at all, but commences with the powers or **faculties** of the human **mind**, proving the facts as one moves along. In accordance with Kant's intention to present his theoretical philosophy in the *Prolegomena* in a much more accessible manner than in the *Critique*, the analytic method is rated as the simpler one, as better suited for beginners, while the synthetic method is admitted to be clearly more demanding both on the philosopher employing it and on the reader attempting to follow it.

ANTHROPOLOGY FROM A PRAGMATIC POINT OF VIEW. Starting with the winter semester of 1772–1773, Kant regularly held popular, well attended lectures on anthropology. The work of 1798 is loosely based on these lectures, though it is newly composed; there is hardly any overlap between its formulations and those of the student lecture notes that have been preserved (and recently published in Ak 25).

Anthropology as an area of study had been present in German philosophy at least since Otto Casmann's *Psychologia Anthropologica* of 1594. Originally, anthropology was understood as an empirical investigation of man as a being composed of body and soul; in this form, it was dealt with by Kant's more immediate predecessors Alexander Gottlieb Baumgarten and **Christian Wolff** under the heading "*Psychologia empirica.*" In the 18th century, the field of 'anthropology' roughly corresponded to the contemporary British "science of man." As this latter project was conceived by, for example, **David Hume**, the basic idea was to found philosophy on it. However, in his critical writings, Kant rejected such an approach as illconceived or at least as insufficient, since it failed to deal with the question of the legitimacy of **cognition**. His own anthropology was then not meant to provide any foundations for philosophy, rather, it was intended as a supplement to philosophy; it did not belong to his **critical philosophy** in the strict sense of the word, containing an appreciable amount of empirical material. The term 'pragmatic' was fashionable in the 1770s, though Kant seems to have been the first one to have combined it with 'anthropology.' In his other writings, Kant used 'pragmatic' usually in opposition to moral, in which case it referred to teachings on prudence; however, in his work of 1798, this distinction did not apply, as Kant here included morals. As one of its main characterizations, Kant stressed that his "pragmatic anthropology" dealt with psychological and cultural aspects of **humans**, and he clearly distinguished it from physiological anthropology.

In large parts of the work, Kant proceeded by first briefly (and often not very accurately) summarizing his critical position in regard to a given topic, then by switching, more or less abruptly, to offering his own observations and pieces of wisdom or even direct advice (mostly addressed to young persons) on how to get along in the world, how to act prudently, how to deal with other human beings. Kant's perspective throughout the work is that of an enlightened, cosmopolitan wise man. If the work has any overriding, general goal, then it is to develop themes from Kant's philosophy of **history**. Kant assumes a providential **nature**, a conception that could have been inspired by deist or Stoic thought. Within such a nature, cognitive errors, painful feelings, and moral evil could all be interpreted by Kant as incentives for the advancement of a better future.

The work has no strict **architectonic** of the kind that may be found in Kant's three *Critiques*. It is divided into two major parts, called "Anthropological Didactic" and "Anthropological Characteristics." The former is subdivided into three books, along the lines of the division in the *Critique of Judgment* of the **faculties** or powers of the mind (*Gemütsvermögen*): faculty of cognition, **feeling** of **pleasure** and pain, faculty of **desire**. These books are structured only loosely. For reasons that are not immediately apparent, Book 1 begins with consciousness (§§ 1–6), proceeds to **sensibility** (§§ 7–39), and ends with the higher faculties of cognition (§§ 40–59). It is in this last section that Kant deals, among other issues, with mental frailty and infirmity (§§ 45–53). Book 2 focuses on pleasure from an empirical point of view, but also takes up **taste**, Book 3 deals with **affects**, passions, health, and, at the end, with the **highest** moral and physical **good**. The second part is concerned with the character of the individual person, gender, nation, race, and species. Especially the last mentioned section is devoted to themes of the philosophy of history. Here, Kant specifies that the progress of humankind chiefly consists of turning beings that possess the capability of reason (*animal rationabile*) into rational beings (*animal rationale*). The work enjoyed no great immediate success, and, at least until recently, did not inspire much scholarly endeavor.

ANTICIPATIONS OF PERCEPTION (*Antizipationen der Wahrnehmung*). Along with the "**Axioms of Intuition**" one of the two **mathematical principles** of the **pure understanding**. In general, these principles establish the formal **a priori** conditions under which **appearances** are displayed in sensible **intuition**. The "Anticipations" are derived from the **category** of **quality**, and, as such, they determine that a **perception** possesses **reality, negation, or limitation**. The principle of the "Anticipations" as stated in the second edition version of the *Critique of Pure Reason* is: "In all appearances the real, which is an object of the sensation, has intensive **magnitude**, i.e., a **degree**" (B 207). Given that **sensation** is not an objective **representation** and, therefore, has no extensive magnitude, an intensive magnitude or degree of reality is its only quality that we can anticipate a priori. As examples of qualities that allow intensive magnitudes, that is, an infinite number of degrees, Kant offers the color red, warmth, and the moment of gravity (A 169/B 211). The intensity of such qualities can continuously diminish until it equals zero, at which point reality is replaced by negation, meaning that the quality is no longer present. Intensive magnitudes again come into play in the *Metaphysical Foundations of Natural Science*, in the section "Dynamics," which corresponds to the category of quality. The original forces of **attraction** and repulsion, by means of which Kant explains **matter**, are likewise susceptible to continuous diminution or augmentation.

Hermann Cohen transposed in his *Das Prinzip der Infinitesimal-Methode* (1883) Kant's principle of the "Anticipations" into the "Principle of Intensive Magnitude," with which he then attempted to provide an epistemological foundation of the concept of the differential, and, along with it, an epistemological foundation of reality (§ 18). Cohen went beyond Kant in identifying the attribution of intensive magnitude (degree) with the positing of reality. The result of the application of the category of reality found its mathematical expression in the "infinitesimal method." Cohen conceived of the infinitesimally small not as a real, actual infinitesimally small magnitude, but as a realizing element of productive thought. *See also* CONTINUITY.

ANTINOMY. In his **critical philosophy**, Kant claimed that **reason** was fated to attempt to take up certain questions it could never answer, and that it therefore became entangled in contradictions which could be clarified only by a critique of reason itself. His technical term for such contradictions was antinomies. Forerunners of such problems may be found in his **pre-critical philosophy**. In the *Monadologia Physica* of 1756, he noted that the **metaphysical** doctrine of the monadology was incompatible with geometry, given that the one denied while the other affirmed the infinite **divisibility** of **space**; this was later to become transformed into the second antinomy. In the *Inaugural Dissertation* of 1770, Kant discussed at some length cases in which predicates of **sensibility** were applied to intelligible **objects**, leading invariably to muddles (Section V). It has been suggested, especially on the part of older scholarship, that the realization of the importance of antinomial contradictions provided Kant with the decisive impulse to develop his critical philosophy, but this interpretation has been disputed by more recent scholarship, which tends to emphasize other factors, such as the development of the theory of the subjective nature of time and space as the forms of our sensibility, or the separation of sensibility from the **understanding**, or the development of the **transcendental deduction** of the categories, or yet the concentration on the problem of the limits of human **cognition**.

In the second chapter of the **"Transcendental Dialectic"** of the *Critique of Pure Reason*, Kant treats antinomies in a systematic fashion. He divides them into two groups, mathematical and dynamical, and identifies two antinomies in each group. For each of the four antinomies there is a thesis and an antithesis, and Kant provides seemingly irrefutable proofs for each (though beginning with **Arthur Schopenhauer** the validity of these proofs has repeatedly been questioned). In his resolution of the antinomies he shows that in the case of the mathematical ones, both the thesis and the antithesis are false, but that for the dynamical antinomies, both claims are true if assigned to their proper sphere of validity. According to the thesis of the first antinomy, the world has a beginning in **time** and is enclosed in spatial boundaries, whereas the antithesis denies such limits and claims that the world is infinite. The thesis of the second antinomy asserts that every composite **substance** consists of simple parts, while the antithesis denies the existence of anything simple. Kant considers these four statements to be false because they involve assertions about things beyond the **limits** of our cognition. The third antinomy deals with **freedom**. The thesis argues that aside from a **causality** in accordance with the **laws** of **nature**, there is a causality through freedom, while the antithesis denies the latter part of the claim. According to the thesis of the fourth antinomy, there is an absolutely necessary being belonging to the world either as a part or as its **cause**, while the antithesis denies the existence of any such being. Kant thinks that the antitheses of the dynamical antinomies are true for the **appearances** and that they are subject to human cognition, while the theses are true of the **things-in-themselves** and are not subject to human cognition, but can be thought. Kant identifies a further antinomy in Part I, Book II (Dialectic of Pure Reason) of his *Critique of Practical Reason*, an antinomy that is related to the one of freedom and that is solved in a similar fashion. The two claims, "the desire for **happiness** must be the motive to **maxims** of **virtue**," and "the maxim of virtue must be the efficient **cause** of happiness," are both proved to be impossible, as happiness belongs to the phenomenal world while virtue is part of the noumenal one, which precludes any causal relationship between the two. Nevertheless, the two realms may be thought as connected, even if the nature of this connection cannot be known.

There are two antinomies in the *Critique of Judgment*, one in each of the two major parts. In the "Critique of Aesthetic Judgment," Kant summarizes the essentially English conception of aesthetics in the thesis "aesthetic judgment is not based on concepts," and the basically German theory in the antithesis "aesthetic judgment is based on concepts." He claims that both assertions may be valid, if one takes 'concept' not in its strictly cognitive signification as entailing the cognition of an object, but in its indeterminate sense as having to do with the ground of the subjective **purposiveness** of nature (§§ 56–57). In the "Critique of Teleological Judgment," Kant presents the two seemingly opposed assertions, "all production of material things and their forms must be judged to be possible in accordance with mere mechanical laws" and "some products of material nature cannot be judged to be possible only in accordance with mechanical laws." He shows that the two statements are contradictory only if converted into **constitutive principles** of determinant **judgment**, but that they are compatible as maxims of reflective judgment (§§ 70–71). *See also* CONTINUITY; TRANSCENDENTAL ILLUSION.

APODICTIC. *See* MODALITY; NECESSITY.

APPEARANCE (*Erscheinung*). Appearances are things as far as they are related to our **sensibility**; outside this relation they would be unknowable **things-in-themselves** (B xxvii). Crucial to an understanding of Kant's account is the fact that he contrasts appearances with **illusion** and that he claims that appearances have empirical **reality** (B 69). This is one part of what he means when he says that appearances are objects of possible **experience** (A 239/B 298). The other point is that **cognition** is possible only of appearances, not of things-in-themselves; both bodies and the empirical self are cognized by us only as appearances. An appearance contains both material components, namely, **sensation**, which is **a posteriori** and is the consequence of our being **affected** by things, and formal elements that are **a priori** and that are contributed by the activity of the subject; these formal elements are the **forms of intuition space** and **time** as well as the **categories** (A 20/B 34).

As the word 'phenomenon' means "that which appears," it is not surprising that Kant links appearances to phenomena, sometimes even treating the two terms as synonyms. However, the relation is not completely straightforward, since Kant also tends to equate phenomena with the lawful relations of appearances. This tendency goes back to his **pre-critical** writings. Kant used the term appearance in a philosophically meaningful way for the first time in his *Inaugural Dissertation*, where he introduced the distinction between phenomena and **noumena** (§ 3). Here, he held that phenomena were given by the sensibility, while noumena were contributed by the **understanding**. And though he pointed to ancient philosophy as the source of this distinction, he deviated from some of the standard ways of defining it. Thus he claimed that certain kinds of cognition, namely, **mathematics**, would fall on the side of the phenomena, whereas, for example, for Plato, mathematics remained on the side of the noumena.

In the *Inaugural Dissertation*, Kant at least initially associated phenomena with appearances, describing the former as sensible objects and holding the latter to be things as they are presented by sensibility (§§ 3–4). However, infusing greater precision soon after, he then distinguished the two in the course of his description of the difference between appearance and experience. Appearance was whatever preceded the use of the understanding, while experience was held to be the cognition that arises when the understanding compares different appearances. Here Kant associated phenomena not with appearances, but with experience, calling the objects of experience phenomena, and the laws of experience the laws of phenomena (§ 5). This distinction between appearances and phenomena is at least partially preserved in the first edition of the *Critique of Pure Reason*, where Kant says that "appearances, insofar as they are thought as objects in accordance with the unity of the categories, are called phenomena" (A 248).

Just as the relationship between appearances and things-in-themselves is somewhat murky because of the unclear status of the latter, so the relationship between phenomena and noumena is obfuscated by Kant's complicated use of the term noumenon. In both these cases, however, the problem lies less with appearance or phenomenon than with their counterparts.

APPEARANCE OF APPEARANCE (*Erscheinung von der Erscheinung*). Kant employed this slightly confusing expression in the so-called *Opus Postumum* in the course of his attempt to find concepts that would effect the transition from the philosophy of **natural science** to **physics**. With "**appearance** of appearance" he presumably wished to convey the idea that formal elements would be present not just in **experience**, as in the *Critique of Pure Reason*, but also in what previously would have counted as **perception**. Kant now claimed that the subject posits the **concepts** of the relations of motive **forces** into perception or intuition and that, as a consequence, all appearances stand under these concepts. The simple appearance, also called direct, still presents the **manifold** of sensible data, while the appearance of the appearance, also labeled indirect appearance, represents those elements that we have placed into perception or intuition. When carrying out work in physics, one only advances as far as the appearance of appearance; Kant here remarks that appearance of appearance from the point of view of the physicist is the **thing-in-itself**. However, to the metaphysician who enjoys a wider perspective, appearance of appearance is not the thing-in-itself but refers to the activity of the subject of placing concepts into perception or intuition (Ak 22, pp. 22, 311, 326, 329, 333–34, 340, 401). It should be noted that "appearance of appearance" does not represent as radical a departure from the use of the term 'appearance' in the first *Critique* as may seem at first sight; already in his earlier work Kant allowed that appearances contain both material and formal elements (A 20/B 34).

APPERCEPTION. *See* TRANSCENDENTAL UNITY OF APPERCEPTION.

APPREHENSION. Kant thought that the raw data, the **manifold**, provided by our **sensibility** could not yield **cognition** unless it was acted on by the **understanding**. In the first edition version of the "**Transcendental Deduction**" of the *Critique of Pure Reason*, he described this action in terms of a threefold **synthesis**. In plain language Kant spoke of taking up, going through, and combining the manifold (A 77/B 102–3), in technical terminology this amounted to the distinction between, first, a "synthesis of apprehension in **intuition**," which Kant also called a "synopsis of the manifold **a priori** through sense," second, a "synthesis of **reproduction** in the **imagination**," and third, a "synthesis of **recognition** in the **concept**" (A 95).

Along with the other two syntheses, the **pure** synthesis of apprehension grounds the corresponding empirical synthesis and "constitutes the transcendental ground of the possibility of all cognition in general," both of empirical and of pure cognition (A 102). The synthesis of apprehension is directed at the manifold of intuition, which it "runs through and takes together," thus producing a (preliminary) **unity**. While dealing with the synthesis of apprehension in the A-version, Kant greatly stresses **time**. Thus he mentions as a basic fact that all our representations belong to **inner sense** and are subject to its formal condition, namely, time. And we become aware that the manifold is a manifold only because the mind distinguishes the time in the succession of **impressions** (A 99).

In the B-version of the "Transcendental Deduction" Kant drops the conception of the threefold synthesis and he no longer mentions reproduction and recognition. However, he does retain the synthesis of apprehension, modifying it in a way that reflects some of the alterations that are characteristic of the second edition in general. His formal definition of the synthesis of apprehension as the "composition of the manifold in an empirical intuition, through which **perception**, i.e., empirical consciousness of it becomes possible" (B 160), does not yet greatly depart from the A-version, in spite of the inclusion of 'perception.' However, his subsequent claim that the synthesis of apprehension must occur in accordance with the forms of intuition **space** and time, a claim buttressed by examples pertaining to both of the forms, is remarkable for its inclusion of space. His other ideas, namely, that the empirical synthesis must stand under the intellectual one, and that apprehension must always stand under the categories, echo similar views from the first edition.

Kant makes further use of the term 'apprehension' outside the "Transcendental Deduction," especially in the "**Analogies of Experience**." Reflecting the tension between these two parts of his work, Kant's use of the term differs. In the "Analogies," the stress when talking about apprehension is on the lack of order, rather than on unity. Thus Kant says that apprehension of the manifold is always successive and therefore always changing (A 182/B 225, A 189–95/B 234–40), that it yields data that are underdetermined, that is, that may possibly be merely subjective. He emphasizes that subsequent acts of the understanding are required in order to arrive at the cognition of an **object**; apprehension would have to stand under a **rule** to be the **representation** of an object. However, somewhat confusing the issue is Kant's later claim that the synthesis of the manifold through the imagination yields an undetermined order of the sequence, while in the case of "a synthesis of apprehension (of the manifold of a given appearance), the order in the object is determined," that is, "there is therein an order of the successive synthesis that determines an object, in accordance with which something would necessarily have to precede and . . . the other would necessarily have to follow" (A 201/B 246). One way of reconciling the two seemingly disparate notions of apperception in the "Analogies" is to take the bracketed expression "given appearance" to refer to an (objective) event. *See also* COMPREHENSION.

A PRIORI, A POSTERIORI. Kant derived this term from a wide-ranging tradition stretching back to **Aristotle**. According to an older signification, a piece of **cognition** was labeled 'a priori' when it proceeded from prior causes to their effects, and, conversely, 'a posteriori' when it moved from posterior effects to their causes. However, this meaning was largely abandoned in the 18th century in favor of a new one, already present in **Gottfried Wilhelm Leibniz**, following which 'a priori' and 'a posteriori' refer to the origin of cognition in **reason** or in **experience**, respectively. It is in this sense, in which Kant established these two concepts (B 1–6; P, § 5). The term 'a posteriori' was used by him to indicate that a piece of cognition was drawn from experience, that is, from sensible impressions. A posteriori then referred to both the genesis of cognition in **time** and to the **empirical** founding of cognition. A posteriori cognition is empirical and **contingent**; Kant considered it to be always synthetic and never **pure**, necessary, or universal.

On the other hand, cognition is called by Kant a priori when it is independent of all experience. The term 'a priori' has no temporal connotation; the priority that it expresses is exclusively the logical independence from experience as far as founding is concerned. The characterizing marks of a priori cognition are **necessity** and strict (as opposed to 'comparative') **universality**. A priori judgments could be either **analytic** or **synthetic**. Kant did not regard the former, which he viewed as the subject matter of general **logic**, as especially problematic or important. Similar distinctions as the one between synthetic a posteriori and analytic a priori had indeed been made earlier, for example, by **David Hume**, who distinguished between "matters of fact" and "relations of ideas." Interesting is Kant's highly original theory of the **synthetic a priori**, a class he accused Hume of having missed and that essentially provides the founding stone of his **transcendental logic** and thus of his whole **critical philosophy**. Kant identified a priori **forms** of sensible **intuition** (space and time), a priori **concepts** of the **understanding**, and a priori **judgments**.

Though the a priori is not derived from experience by **abstraction**, the philosopher carrying out the project of the critique of pure reason *discovers* the a priori elements by a process of abstraction in the sense of separating from them or not attending to the empirical; this holds both for the a priori elements of **sensibility**, that is, the pure forms of intuition, and for the a priori elements of the understanding, that is, the **categories** and the **principles of pure understanding** (B 2, A 22/B 36). Such a procedure for investigating the concepts of the understanding had already been suggested by Kant in his **pre-critical** *Inaugural Dissertation*, where he argued that a priori concepts are gained by attention during experience to the action of the understanding (§ 8).

It is the task of the **transcendental philosophy** to examine "our mode of cognition of objects insofar as this is to be possible a priori" (A 11–12/B 25). The a priori elements of sensibility are proven by a transcendental **exposition**; those of the understanding by a **transcendental deduction**.

In post-Kantian German Idealism, the sharp Kantian distinction between a priori and a posteriori was in part reversed, since only two modes of consideration of one and the same absolute knowledge were admitted. Among the **Neokantians**, there was unanimity in objecting to a psychological interpretation of the a priori in the way in which it had been carried out by **Hermann Helmholtz** and **Friedrich Albert Lange**; the latter grasped Kant's concept of the a priori as an indication of the "psycho-physical organization" of the human being. **Hermann Cohen** distinguished in his first book on Kant, *Kants Theorie der Erfahrung* of 1871, three stages of meaning of the Kantian a priori: metaphysical origin, form, and the formal condition of the possibility of experience. Cohen regarded the pre-critical disjunction of innate and acquired to be definitely overcome by the transcendental cognition of the third stage of the a priori.

ARCHITECTONIC. With this term Kant underscores his high regard for systematic order. Formally, he defines architectonic as the "art of systems" and as "the doctrine of what is scientific in our **cognition** in general." Architectonic unity is then what arises as a consequence of an idea "where **reason** provides the ends **a priori** and does not await them empirically" (A 832–33/B 860–61). Kant employs the word on three closely related levels. First, he claims that reason in the sense of the entire higher faculty of cognition is itself architectonic. Second, corresponding to reason's architectonic nature, all our cognition must be ordered systematically and must therefore belong to a **system** (A 474/B 502). Thus, for instance, in the "Introduction" to his *Logic* Kant claims that the architectonic of sciences is a system in accordance with ideas. And third, our way of attaining cognition must proceed in accordance with an architectonic **method**. For all these reasons, the structure of Kant's three *Critiques*, both as single works and jointly, is based on the architectonic of pure reason. Kant opposed architectonic to **aggregate** or rhapsody, that is, to a merely **empirical** and **contingent** compilation of data that is not governed by an overriding a priori idea.

ARGUMENT FROM DESIGN. *See* GOD, PROOFS OF THE EXISTENCE OF.

ARISTOTLE. Although at the end of the *Critique of Pure Reason* Kant listed Aristotle among the empiricists (A 854/B 882), in general, he referred to him as a logician, directing his critique of **empiricism** usually against **John Locke** or, with some reservations, against **David Hume.** Kant's view of Aristotle was closely related to his own assessment of formal **logic.** On the one hand Kant considered logic, together with **mathematics** and **natural science,** to be a rigorous, well-established discipline that could serve as a model for **metaphysics.** On the other hand, however, he claimed that a well-founded metaphysics could be arrived at only by means of his **transcendental philosophy**; and given that the latter was to be based on his **transcendental logic,** Kant tended to consign formal logic to a subservient position. Accordingly, Kant gives Aristotle credit for having founded formal logic (B viii), but he makes it plain that this, in itself, was insufficient. Kant's charge that Aristotle compiled the **categories** in an unsystematic, 'rhapsodic' fashion, owing to the fact that he lacked a guiding principle for this process (A 81/B 107; P, § 39), is closely joined to his conviction that for Aristotle the categories had a largely logical role to play and did not serve as the necessary conditions for the possibility of **experience.** Revealing is Kant's "Remark to the **Amphiboly** of the Concepts of Reflection." Here he acknowledged that Aristotle produced a "logical topic" for assigning concepts to their proper "logical place," but he again considered this to be clearly inferior to his own "transcendental topic," which would allocate **concepts** their "transcendental place," that is, determine their epistemological status as concepts either in **sensibility** or in **pure understanding,** and thus prevent them from encroaching on areas in which they have no legitimate use (A 268/B 324). *See also* DIALECTIC.

ART (*Kunst*). Kant circumscribes the general concept of art by resorting to three distinctions: art differs 1) from **nature** by virtue of the fact that its works are produced "by freedom," namely, on the basis of purposeful reflections of human beings; 2) from science in a similar fashion as practical skills differ from **cognition;** 3) from handicraft, which Kant views as remunerative rather than liberal (Ak 5, pp. 303–4). Of the subdivisions of the concept of art, Kant emphasizes **aesthetic** art. The latter aims immediately at the **feeling** of **pleasure:** as **agreeable** art it aims at the pleasure of the senses, as **beautiful** art at the production of pleasurable representations, because these are, from the point of view of the cognitive faculties of the spectator, **purposeful** ones. Unlike other results of human exertion, a beautiful work of art must seem to be nature, even if we are aware of its artificiality (p. 306). However, this perspective is possible only if the work of art is produced by a **genius**.

Kant bases his tentative division of the fine arts on the different modes of expression used by human beings in communication: word, gesture, sound. To these he assigns the three genera of art, namely speech, pictorial art, and the art of the play of sensations. Of the fine arts, Kant ascribes the highest rank to poetry (pp. 320–30).

In post-Kantian German Idealism, art occupied a high place in the system of philosophy, as the beauty of artistic works was taken to represent the absolute. For **Friedrich Wilhelm Joseph Schelling**, art was "the only true and eternal organon and document of philosophy."

Hermann Cohen emphasized that art was a specific part of culture, grounding it in the aesthetic consciousness that he labeled "pure feeling." This **feeling**, as the "love of nature by humans," forms the basis of the production and reception of art. Among the fine arts, Cohen, just as Kant, assigns poetry to the highest position. Poetry unifies concept and "the feeling for words" (*Wortgefühl*) in the medium of language. For **Ernst Cassirer**, art is also a "symbolic form." This mental function constitutes the world of pictures as an aesthetic world of illusion, in which the mind reveals itself to itself. The **Southwestern German Neokantians**, on the other hand, took as their point of departure more strongly the Kantian determinations, which they then transformed within the conceptual framework of their own philosophy of **value**: pieces of art are for them "conveyors of value."

AS IF (*Als ob*). Kant used this expression frequently and in a number of different if related senses. Thus, for instance, he claims, using the expression in a more or less nontechnical manner, that the synthetic method commences by assuming certain **facts** as if they were given. Kant also employs the expression in a negative way in order to criticize his philosophical opponents for treating **appearances** as if they were **things-in-themselves** or of treating things-in-themselves as if they could produce **cognition**; such errors, arising out of the failure to distinguish between appearances and things-in-themselves, lead either to **transcendental illusion** or to **amphiboly**.

The most important technical use of 'as if' occurs in respect to concepts that cannot be cognized, but that can be thought. Although such concepts do not, strictly speaking, have an **object**, we may benefit from a theoretical, practical, and aesthetic point of view by treating them as if their objects did exist. In Kant's terminology, though these ideas have no **constitutive** use in possible **experience**, they may be employed as regulative principles. Even if we therefore cannot prove the simplicity of the **soul**, or the beginning of the **world** in time, or the existence of **God**, we may nevertheless consider the soul as if it were simple, the world as if it had a beginning in time, and God as if he existed. Similarly, the regulative idea of "**nature in general**" cannot be demonstrated in experience, since it implies an infinite series, but it may be used as a rule for explaining given appearances as if the series were infinite.

Kant utilized the expression in a number of different ways in his **ethics**. Thus, although we cannot cognize that a subject is free, we may yet treat him as if he were truly endowed with **freedom**, that is, we must act according to the **maxims** of freedom as if they were the **laws** of **nature**. Or, the categorical **imperative** commands every rational being to act "as if he were by his maxims at all times a lawgiving member of the universal kingdom of ends" (Ak 4, p. 438).

A further use of 'as if' occurs in Kant's discussion of aesthetics and teleology. With the claim of the **purposiveness** of nature, we view the order of the world "as if it had sprouted from the intention of a highest **reason**" (A 686/B 714; see also CJ, Introduction). And an object of art may be found to be aesthetically pleasing when we regard it as if it were a product of nature (CJ, § 45).

Taking recourse to **Albert Friedrich Lange** and Friedrich Nietzsche, **Hans Vaihinger** resurrected the conception of the 'as if' in his *Philosophie des Als Ob* (1911). However, Vaihinger went well beyond Kant in holding that all ideal representations, even contradictory ones, were fictions that in their respective scientific, practical, ethical, and religious realms could not only prove meaningful, but sometimes even be necessary.

ASSERTORIC. *See* MODALITY.

ASSOCIATION. Attempts to explain the genesis of human and sometimes also animal **cognition** by means of association psychology figured prominently in the 18th century in the work of thinkers such as **David Hume**, David Hartley (1705–1757), or Joseph Priestley (1733–1804). Kant, too, integrated association into his **critical philosophy**, according it a clear if minor role in his **epistemology**. Although in general Kant's *Anthropology from a Pragmatic Point of View* is not very helpful in shedding light on the *Critique of Pure Reason*, in the case of association one may safely resort to the definition offered in the former work to explain its meaning in the latter one. In fact, Kant's definition also agrees reasonably well with that assumed by his predecessors. He describes the law of association as the custom that arises in the mind when the sequence of empirical **representa-**

tions is frequently repeated, so that when in the future the first representation arises, the mind expects or produces the following ones (§ 33B). However, while for instance Hume attempted to explain **causality** and other key philosophical notions by recourse to such a psychological mechanism, Kant claimed that this would yield only empirical cognition, but could not account for the existence of **pure mathematics** and pure **science**. He therefore criticized Hume for his reliance on association (A 765–66/B 793–94), and attempted to find a ground for this empirical process in some **a priori** concept such as that of **affinity** (A 113).

ASTRONOMY. In his early **pre-critical** days, Kant made a major contribution to astronomy by proposing a new theory of the origin of the solar system. In his *Universal Natural History and Theory of the Heavens* of 1755, Kant suggested that the origin of the solar system should be explained not by recourse to **God**, but by assuming that a cloud of more or less uniformly distributed particles of matter would gradually begin to coalesce at a number of points under the joint influence of the forces of **attraction** and repulsion to form the sun and the planets. A similar theory was advanced later, though independently, by Pierre Simon Laplace in his *Exposition du système du monde* of 1796; since the two explanations differed only in details, they were called the Kant-Laplace theory. In the second half of the 20th century, a refined version of it under the title "nebular hypothesis" has reemerged in astrophysics to account for the origin of the solar system.

Later in his writing career, Kant utilized his command of astronomy for philosophical purposes. In the *Critique of Pure Reason*, he famously compared his own revolution in philosophy to the **Copernican revolution** in astronomy (B xvi), and he used the account of the progress in astronomy from Nicolaus Copernicus to Johann Kepler and to **Isaac Newton** to demonstrate the employment of the **ideas of reason** of homogeneity, specification, and **continuity**. Both in the *Metaphysical Foundations of Natural Science* and in the *Opus Postumum*, Kant often returned to astronomy in the course of his investigation of the conceptual foundations of **physics**.

ATOM. Kant never subscribed to a straightforward atomistic explanation of **matter**, though in his **pre-critical** writings he did defend the theory of physical monads. These were, however, not so much particles of matter as points endowed with the forces of **attraction** and repulsion. During the **critical** period, specifically in his *Metaphysical Foundations of Natural Science*, Kant then discussed two possible explanations of matter: a 'dynamical' one based not on monads or any other points, but strictly on the forces of attraction or repulsion; and a 'mechanical' one based on atoms and the void. Although Kant preferred the former to the latter, since he did not wish to accept either absolutely hard atoms or the void, at this point, he treated both theories as mere hypotheses.

Toward the end of his life, however, he came to feel that the mechanical theory was so riddled with problems as to be untenable, and that therefore the dynamical explanation was the only possible one. The seeds of this view are present already in the *Critique of Pure Reason*. It is one of the lessons of Kant's teachings on intensive **magnitudes** in the "**Anticipations of Perception**" that we could have no **experience** of an entire absence of everything real in **appearance**, meaning that a proof of empty **space** or empty **time** could not be drawn from experience (A 172/B 214). From this, Kant concluded that there was no empty space or empty time in the world, since neither is an object of possible experience, and, drawing out the full implications of these thoughts in the *Opus Postumum*, that nothing can be explained by recourse to inner or outer void in matter (Ak 22, p. 192).

ATTRACTION, REPULSION (*Anziehung, Abstossung*).   From early on, Kant accepted **Isaac Newton**'s force of gravity, criticizing those like **Gottfried Wilhelm Leibniz** who had disparagingly called it an "occult quality" because they were unwilling to admit effects on distant bodies. Generally, Kant did not distinguish attraction from gravity, though at one point he did call gravity the effect of general attraction (Ak 4, p. 518). He opposed attraction to the force of repulsion, conceiving both, however, as universal properties of **matter** that acted regardless of the latter's state, be it **motion** or **rest**, and that required no external cause. Although employing the two **forces** mostly to explain matter, in the **pre-critical** writing *Universal Natural History and Theory of the Heavens* of 1755, Kant also used them to account for the origin of the solar system, and indeed, of the whole physical universe.

The most important discussion of attraction and repulsion occurs in the section "Dynamics" of the *Metaphysical Foundations of Natural Science*, where Kant calls the two forces 'original' and 'fundamental' and where he uses them to explain matter, thus avoiding **atomism**. He considered the two forces to be of equal significance, claiming that without attraction matter would scatter to infinity and there would be nothing, while without repulsion matter would coalesce into an infinitesimally small area and there would again be nothing. In the *Metaphysical Foundations*, Kant also attempted to derive Newton's inverse square law in an **a priori** manner. Attraction and repulsion continued to be present in the *Opus Postumum*, though they no longer commanded Kant's undivided attention as he introduced here other forces in order to account for more specific phenomena of **physics** than just matter. *See also* ASTRONOMY; IMPENETRABILITY.

AUTONOMY, HEAUTONOMY, HETERONOMY. Following **Jean-Jacques Rousseau**'s *Social Contract* (1762), Kant understood autonomy as self-legislation. However, he elevated the concept to serve as the supreme ethical principle, with which he specified the only way in which the demand of the categorical **imperative** could be fulfilled, thus repealing Rousseau's confinement of the term to the realm of political philosophy. While Kant in his ***Opus Postumum*** attributed autonomy to **transcendental philosophy**, that is, to self-determining theoretical **reason** (Ak 21, p. 59), he otherwise used the concept primarily as a characterization of **practical reason**, namely, of the **will** that is its own **law** (GMM, Ak 4, p. 440). Kant also employed 'autonomy' to describe institutional self-determination, for example, of a university (Ak 7, p. 17) or of a **state** (*civitas*) (Ak 6, p. 318).

In his ***Critique of Judgment***, Kant ascribes autonomy in the sense of self-legislation also to the **faculty** of reflective **judgment**. However, this involves not an objective autonomy of **nature** or of the **will**, but a merely subjective one, which Kant would rather call 'heautonomy,' because the faculty of judgment gives a law to itself as to a subjective power (Ak 20, p. 225). The universality of the judgment of **taste** is based, as it were, "on an autonomy of the subject judging about the feeling of pleasure in the given representation, i.e., on his own taste" (Ak 5, p. 281); in the same way, a heautonomy of the reflective faculty of judgment exists in regard to the particular laws of nature (p. 389). Friedrich Schiller (1759–1805) took up this concept and stressed that its significance lay in its difference to "mere autonomy," which exercises an external power against the matter that is to be formed.

According to Kant's theory of **ethics**, heteronomy occurs when some object materially determines the faculty of choice (*Willkür*), because the latter is then dependent on a law of nature (Ak 5, p. 33). Such a determination is external regardless of whether pleasurable objects of the senses or of the understanding, that is, sensuous or intellectual pleasures, are involved (pp. 22–24). All material determinations of the **maxims** of our **actions** aim at our own advantage; they are rooted in self-love or in the pursuit of one's own **happiness**, that is, in **empirically** conditioned contents (pp. 25–26).

In post-Kantian times, there was a tendency in Germany to employ the concept of autonomy in a broad and increasingly vague sense. This was again corrected by the **Neokantians**, who rendered the concept more precise and returned it to its central position in philosophy. **Heinrich Rickert** argued in his *Allgemeine Grundlegung der Philosophie* (*General Ground-*

ing of Philosophy) of 1921 that autonomy is not only an ethical concept, but that it also contains a general philosophical principle. And **Hermann Cohen** analyzed in his *Ethik des reinen Willens* (*Ethics of Pure Will*) the moral autonomy of self-consciousness under the four aspects of self-legislation, self-determination, one's own responsibility, and self-preservation. See also *CRITIQUE OF PRACTICAL REASON*.

AXIOMS OF INTUITION (*Axiome der Anschauung*). Along with the "**Anticipations of Perception**" one of the two **mathematical principles** of the **pure understanding**. In general, these principles establish the formal **a priori** conditions under which **appearances** are displayed in sensible **intuition**. The "Axioms" are derived from the **category** of **quantity**, and, as such, they determine that all appearances are intuited as "multitudes of antecedently given parts," or, in Kant's technical terminology, as "extensive **magnitudes**." After defining extensive magnitudes as "that in which the **representation** of the parts makes possible the representation of the whole" (A 162/B 203), and after explaining that representing a line or a period of time is possible only by successively generating the parts, Kant offers a relatively simple argument in favor of extensive magnitudes in appearances. He starts by claiming that the form of intuition in appearances is **space** or **time**; however, since every appearance as intuition can be cognized only through successive **synthesis** of the manifold, every appearance is therefore an extensive magnitude.

Kant makes use of the principle of extensive magnitudes in his philosophy of **mathematics**, by claiming that geometry and its axioms are based on this successive synthesis in the production of shapes. Moreover, the "Axioms" help to explain the applicability of mathematics, as Kant conceives it, to **objects** of **experience**: given that empirical intuition is possible only through pure intuition, geometrical statements about the latter are necessarily valid for the former (A 165/B 206).

- B -

BAUCH, BRUNO (1877–1942). Bauch first made a name for himself with his works on Kant, especially with his comprehensive examination of Kant's philosophy (*Immanuel Kant*, 1917). Following in the footsteps of his predecessors **Hermann Cohen** and **Wilhelm Windelband**, Bauch placed historical research at the disposal of the program of further developing the "system of critical idealism." Unlike **Ernst Cassirer**, who in 1918 attempted to clarify Kant's thought by taking the concept of **freedom** as his point of departure, Bauch sought to establish the conception of a system on the basis of Kant's critique of teleological judgment. Initially, Bauch stood nearer to the **Marburg School of Neokantianism**, but later, he aligned himself with the **Southwestern German School** by investigating the notions of **value** and **actuality**.

BEAUTIFUL, BEAUTY. Kant's notes from 1769 reveal how at this point he oscillated between a subjective concept of beauty and an objective one. He based the experience of beauty both on a subjective principle, "namely the conformity with the laws of intuitive cognition" (Reflection 625, Ak 15, p. 271), and on the natural relation to the inner perfection of a thing (Reflection 628, Ak 15, p. 273). The **pre-critical** piece *Observations on the Feeling of the Beautiful and the Sublime* of 1764 dealt with the beautiful, which as charming and pleasing was distinguished from the sublime, in the psychological manner of Edmund Burke. On the other hand, Kant was prompted by Alexander Gottlieb Baumgarten's metaphysical definition of beauty as "the perfection of sensible **cognition**" to think about the unison in the play of sensible **intuition** and the **understanding** in response to the beautiful.

The analysis of the beautiful in the *Critique of Judgment* proceeds in line with **aesthetic judgment** or judgment of **taste**. Kant determines satisfaction with the beautiful mostly negatively: 1) it is disinterested; 2) it occurs without any concept and yet claims to be valid for everyone; 3) it implies no representation of a purpose; 4) it is not **contingent**, but **necessary** (Ak 4, pp. 203–40). The aesthetic assessment of an object does not repose on the concept of the object, but on the subjective state of mind of the free play between the **imagination** and the understanding, which is responsible for the **unity** of the **concept** (Ak 5, p. 220). There is, in addition, no "objective rule of taste which would determine by concepts what is beautiful" (p. 231). The ascription of universal validity to a judgment of taste is founded on the communicability of the above-mentioned state of mind.

Unlike the **sublime**, the beautiful is concerned merely with the form of the object, a form that limits the object. Kant describes beauty as "the presentation of an indeterminate concept of the understanding." As sublime, on the other hand, one may also experience a formless object, as long as limitlessness is represented in it or by it and this limitlessness is completed by an indeterminate concept of **reason** to totality (p. 244).

Within his discussion of the theory of the fine arts, Kant distinguishes between beauty of **nature** and beauty of **art**. The former involves a "beautiful thing," the latter "a beautiful representation of a thing." While appreciation of natural beauty requires only taste and not a concept of the thing, the beauty of art needs **genius** (p. 311), who makes an intentionally produced piece of art seem to be unintentional, or, in Kant's words, the object "must be regarded as nature" (p. 307). Kant prefers beauty of nature because it is able to awaken an "immediate interest" that makes it possible "at least to suspect a predisposition to a good moral **disposition**" (pp. 300–1). Finally, with the expression "beauty as a symbol of morality" Kant draws an analogy between aesthetic judgment and **practical reason** (pp. 353–54).

Friedrich Schiller (1759–1805) further pursued the idea of the mediation between nature and freedom within the beautiful, an idea that was contained in Kant's concept of reflective judgment. Kant's distinction between beauty in nature and beauty in art was attacked in **Johann Gottfried Herder**'s *Kalligone* (1800), preserved in **Friedrich Wilhelm Joseph Schelling**'s teachings on the genius at the end of his *System des transzendentalen Idealismus* (1800) and demolished by **Georg Wilhelm Friedrich Hegel**'s preference for the beauty of art that was born in the mind. However, Theodor W. Adorno restored Kant's distinction in his posthumously published *Ästhetische Theorie* (1970).

BEING (*Sein, Dasein*).   Where Kant pointedly speaks of 'being,' especially in connection with his critique of the ontological proof of the existence of **God**, he uses the term synonymously with existence. His main point is that being is not a real predicate that could be added to the concept of a thing, but "merely the positing of a thing or of certain determinations in themselves" (A 598/B 626, see already his **pre-critical** piece *The Only Possible Argument in Support of a Demonstration of the Existence of God*, Ak. 2, pp. 72ff.). In distinction to the logical usage of 'is' as a copula, the existential 'is' states that the subject and its predicates are *posited*. Such a positing (*Position*) concerns the **object** in relation to its **concept** (Reflection 6276, Ak. 18, p. 543). *See also* ACTUALITY.

BELIEF (*Glaube, Glauben*).   The German word '*Glaube(n)*' has both a cognitive and a religious connotation. In the process of discussing the traditional distinction between having an opinion, knowing, and believing (A 820–31/B 848–59), Kant defined belief as a 'taking-to-be-true' which, unlike the having of an opinion, is subjectively sufficient, but, unlike knowing, objectively insufficient. As speaking of belief in the theoretical sphere apparently made no sense to Kant, he restricted his usage of the term to the realm of the **practical**. Here he distinguished between the pragmatic belief that is concerned with the means necessary for attaining a certain goal, and the practical belief that is directed at necessary **ends**. Although Kant recognized a "doctrinal belief" in the existence of **God** and in a future life of the human **soul**, he held this to be unstable in view of the speculative difficulties involved. "**Moral** belief" of the same content, on the contrary, is linked to the final end of moral **action** by imperturbable certainty. This practical or moral belief was at the center of Kant's attention in the "Preface" to the second edition of the *Critique of Pure Reason* when he declared that he had to deny (alleged metaphysical) **cognition** "in order to make room for faith" (B xxx). Belief in the supernatural in this moral sense comprises the rational or '**pure**' form of religious faith. In distinction to this, religious belief in the sense of "ecclesiastical faith" is based on decrees that are traced back to divine **revelation**, and is therefore no more than mere "historical faith." Kant was convinced that "ecclesiastical faith" would gradually be superseded by pure "rational belief," thus bringing the "kingdom of God" nearer (Ak 6, pp. 102-7).

BERKELEY, GEORGE (1685-1753). In the 18th century, Berkeley was famous, or rather infamous, for having worked out a philosophy of immaterialism, that is, the conception that only God and ideas exist, but not matter. His accentuation of the role of ideas earned his thought the label 'idealism,' in spite of the fact that strong **empiricist** as well as rationalist components were equally present. Berkeley found few adherents and many detractors and his philosophy was generally regarded as harebrained, so that philosophers would have wished to dissociate themselves from it at all cost. This is precisely what Kant saw himself compelled to do after the first edition of his *Critique of Pure Reason* was subjected to a hostile review written by Christian Garve (1742-1798), rewritten, so as to appear even more unfavorable to Kant, by Johann Georg Heinrich Feder (1740-1821), and published in the *Göttingische Anzeigen von gelehrten Sachen* of 1782. The authors misinterpreted a number of key tenets of the **critical philosophy** and claimed that Kant had essentially presented a regurgitated version of Berkeley's idealism.

Kant reacted both in his *Prolegomena to any Future Metaphysics* and in the second edition of the first *Critique* of 1787, in which a number of the changes and additions (most famously the section entitled "Refutation of Idealism") were specifically geared to combat the reviewers' charge. In his desire to emphatically distance his own **idealism** from that of Berkeley, Kant branded the latter's philosophy a "mystical or visionary idealism" and a "dogmatic idealism," and underlined the fact that he himself upheld the real **existence** of **objects** and regarded only **time** and **space** as ideal. The gist of Kant's attack on Berkeley boiled down to the assertion that his predecessor had failed to realize that space was the **form** of **sensibility** and not a property of **things-in-themselves**; Kant claimed that this 'error' necessarily led to the conclusion that things in space were merely imaginary. Furthermore, Kant pointed to the fact that his own conception of the **principles of pure understanding** guaranteed the coherence of **experience** (B 71, 274; P, § 13, remarks 2 and 3, Appendix). It should be noted that Kant, in his effort to differentiate between his idealism and that of Berkeley, misrepresented the latter's thought. Contrary to Kant's claim, Berkeley had not demoted bodies to mere illusion, clearly distinguishing within the realm of our perceptions between illusion and reality. One may suspect that Kant's alarm at the review of 1782 had caused him to overreact.

BODY (*Körper, Leib*). The English word 'body' is a rendering of two different German terms, one of which mainly refers to body in the sense of **physics** (*Körper*), while the other is used nearly exclusively for the human body (*Leib*). However, in keeping with everyday German usage, Kant often employed '*Körper*' in either sense. Although Kant touched on the subject of body several times in his writings, it was almost always tangential to whatever his main purpose at that point was, and there is no clear cut doctrine of body to be found in Kant's work.

In his **pre-critical** piece *Thoughts on the True Estimation of Living Forces* (1749), Kant commenced with a brief inquiry of what a body is, rejecting the **Aristotelian** view of bodies as entelechies as well as the Cartesian conception that bodies are defined by their extension, and defending the **Leibnizian** notion that bodies are endowed with **forces** even before extension (§ 1). However, his concern in this whole book was primarily with forces, and only secondarily with bodies. In a similar fashion, Kant remarks offhandedly in the *Monadologia Physica* (1756) that bodies are composed of physical monads (prop. 5), though here the emphasis was on the monads rather than on bodies.

In the *Critique of Pure Reason* Kant did not greatly occupy himself with the problem of bodies, which is unsurprising given the level of abstraction reached in this work. Kant of course maintained that we cognize bodies only as **appearances**, not as **things-in-themselves** (B 69). He did employ bodies, however, when requiring an example for the distinction between **analytic and synthetic judgments**, pointing out that the judgment "all bodies are extended" was analytic, since extension was contained in the concept of body, while the judgment "all bodies are heavy" was synthetic (A 7/B 11). Although Kant does not explain this, it becomes reasonably clear if one bears the historical fact in mind that air (a body) was thought to possess no weight until the experiments of Evangelista Torricelli (1608–1647) and others proved the opposite; the judgment "bodies are heavy" can therefore be cognized only empirically and is thus synthetic.

Another peripheral mention of bodies occurs in the section dealing with the **antinomies**, where Kant claims that a body is divisible to **infinity**, without therefore consisting of infinitely many parts (A 525/B 553). The situation is not much different in the *Metaphysical Foundations of Natural Science*, where Kant offers two definitions, namely, that "a body in a physical sense is **matter** between determinate boundaries" (Ak 4, p. 525), while a body in a mechanical sense is a mass of determinate shape (p. 537); at the first place, however, his main concern is with matter, while at the second it is with mass. There is more on the subject of body in the *Opus Postumum*, though even here it is not the main focus of Kant's investigation, which is rather concerned with forces and **ether**. Kant here defined body by recourse to the forces of **attraction** and repulsion (Ak 22, p. 269).

On the subject of the human body, Kant was concerned with three different issues. First, he touched on the mind-body problem. In the pre-critical piece *Dreams of a Spirit-Seer* (1766), Kant realized that this problem was a quagmire and he did more to evade it than to solve it. In the chapter on the **paralogisms** in the *Critique of Pure Reason*, Kant confidently proclaimed that thanks to his restriction of **cognition** to appearances he had solved the problem: what is truly at stake is not the relation between two radically different **substances**, but between our **representations** of different appearances.

Second, it is a biographical fact that questions of health were of great personal concern to Kant throughout his life, and this is reflected in various of his writings, where control over the body is a prominent topic, for example, in *On the Philosophers' Medicine of the Body* of 1786, in the *Conflict of the Faculties*, or in the *Metaphysics of Morals*.

Finally, Kant made some unsystematic attempts to explain certain concepts of theoretical philosophy by recourse to the human body. Thus in his pre-critical piece "Concerning the Ultimate Ground of the Differentiation of Directions in Space" of 1768, he claimed that one's own body was required in order to distinguish directions in **space**, for example, left from right. In addition there are a few scattered attempts undertaken in the *Opus Postumum* to ground the special laws of physics by recourse to the human body. However, Kant did not develop this in any significant manner and it would be a mistake to regard it as a key to his project of the transition from **metaphysics** to physics. Needless to say, the writings of 20th-century authors such as Maurice Merleau-Ponty or Michel Foucault, who greatly concentrated on the human body, go far beyond anything ever envisaged by Kant.

BOUNDARY (*Grenze*). Kant uses this term to clarify the question of the legitimate scope of our **cognition** as well as to point to the realm of ideas lying beyond. In the *Critique of Pure Reason*, he explains that a boundary is provided by a problematic **concept** that is not contradictory and that is connected with cognitions whose objective reality cannot be cognized, and he holds the **noumenon** in its negative use to be such a boundary concept (*Grenzbegriff*). The noumenon, on the one hand, serves to limit the pretension of **sensibility**, that is, it indicates that sensibility cannot be extended to **things-in-themselves**. On the other hand, Kant also maintains that the **understanding** sets boundaries for itself and hence for our sensible **cognition** by calling things-in-themselves noumena, thus admitting that it does not cognize these things under the **categories**, but only thinks them under the title of an unknown something (A 254–56/B 310–12, A 288–89/B 345).

The benefits provided by the conception that certain **ideas** may only be thought without being able to be cognized, are stressed in the *Prolegomena*. Here, Kant distinguishes between limits (*Schranken*), which contain mere negations and which are applicable to **mathematics** and **natural science**, since these disciplines are forever restricted to **appearances** and are never complete, and boundaries, which always indicate something positive, namely, some space that lies on the other side of them (see also A 433/B 461). Boundaries are the concern of **metaphysics**, and, in Kant's perspective, they ultimately give an intimation of the existence of a **moral** realm.

Hermann Cohen also emphasized the difference between boundary and limit, asserting that the concept of the thing-in-itself was a "boundary concept" and thus an infinite **problem**. In general, he developed Kant's teachings on ideas into a philosophy of boundary concepts. **Salomon Maimon**, taking the metaphysical interpretation of the method of limits in calculus as his point of departure, determined already in 1790 things-in-themselves as "differentials of consciousness." Cohen declared in his examination of the principle of the infinitesimal method (*Prinzip der Infinitesimalmethode*, 1883) that the differential was the means of the production of the **reality** of objects, thus hoping to be able to dispose of the annoying problem of the thing-in-itself.

As a consequence of his attempt to situate religious transcendence within the realm of human experience, **Paul Natorp** developed an independent philosophy or logic of boundary, the gist of which was to locate religion on the boundary of experience. This boundary was to be reached from the 'inside,' namely, on the basis of the encounter with the infinity of everything that can be experienced. This boundary is not a limit, it is rather human consciousness which confines itself as it oversteps every limit. *See also* ANTICIPATIONS OF PERCEPTION.

- C -

CALORIC. *See* ETHER.

CANON. Although this term, which in Kant's time literally meant measuring rod, has the potential of explaining much of the intent of the **critique of pure reason**, Kant used it only sparingly and did not greatly bother to clarify it. His main discussion of it occurs in the section entitled "Canon of Pure Reason" in the "Doctrine of Method" of the *Critique of Pure Reason*, where, however, he discusses mainly the difference between theoretical and practical philosophy and only briefly touches on the function of a canon in theoretical philosophy. Nevertheless, Kant does offer here a definition of a canon, claiming that it is "the sum total of the **a priori** principles of the correct use of certain cognitive faculties in general." He mentions general **logic** and the **transcendental analytic** as examples, pointing out that the former provides a canon for the **understanding** and **reason** in general, but only as far as form is concerned, while the latter yields the canon for the **pure understanding**. The main point of the section is expressed first in Kant's contention that there is, properly speaking, no canon for theoretical reason, since such reason has the inevitable tendency to become entangled in contradictions when it aspires to extend **cognition** beyond the bounds of possible **experience**, second, in his admission that there is a canon for reason in its practical use (A 796/B 824; see also A 131/B 170; Ak 9, p. 13). Although Kant in this section discusses a number of key concepts of his **moral** philosophy and thus presages his later works on **ethics**, the term 'canon' does not figure prominently in any of those books. One exception occurs in the *Groundwork of the Metaphysics of Morals* where Kant links 'canon' to the categorical **imperative** by identifying the "canon of moral appraisal of action in general" with our ability "to will that a **maxim** of our action become a universal **law**" (Ak 4, p. 424). *See also* ORGANON.

CASSIRER, ERNST (1874-1945). Having studied under **Hermann Cohen** and **Paul Natorp**, Cassirer became the most prominent representative of the second generation of the **Marburg School** philosophers. He concentrated on the history of philosophy more systematically than his predecessors had done, though he did employ, as his point of departure, Cohen's notion that philosophical problems are inherently shaped by the historical development of philosophical and scientific **thought**. In his major work based on this conception, *Das Erkenntnisproblem in der Philosophie und Wissenschaft der neueren Zeit* (4 vols., 1906, 2nd ed. 1911, 3rd ed. 1922), Cassirer presented a historical analysis of the unfolding of the problem of

cognition in modern philosophy. This project deviated from Kant's notion of the **a priori** in that it regarded all **epistemological concepts** as historically contingent. As a consequence, Cassirer held, in keeping with the **critical idealism** of **Neokantianism**, that ultimate **truth** could never be attained, that it was always given as a **problem** *(aufgegeben)*. In his epistemology Cassirer differed from the tenets held by his teachers by refusing to concentrate solely on **form**; he maintained that form and **content**, the general and the particular, **validity** and **being** could not be treated in separation, but that they were linked in a basal relationship *(Urverhältnis)*. In his further work, devoted to an analysis of the function of concepts, *Substanzbegriff und Funktionsbegriff* (1910), Cassirer demonstrated that the concepts of **mathematics** and science were relational rather than referential, thus rejecting **substance**-based logic. With this, he radicalized a notion that had already been suggested by Cohen. Later, not unlike some of the other Neokantians, he broadened his philosophy to encompass all of **culture**, not just **science**. In his work *Philosophy of Symbolic Forms* (1923–1929, Engl. trans. 1953–1957) he developed the conception that all human cognition and culture depend, in one way or another, on symbolic representation and he attempted to describe the **categories** that determine the symbolizing activity of humans.

Among his many other works Cassirer wrote an intellectual biography of Kant (*Kant's Life and Thought*, 1918, Engl. trans. 1981) as well as a book on the philosophy of the Enlightenment (*The Philosophy of the Enlightenment,* 1932, Engl. trans. 1951); both works are still useful. Having fled Nazi Germany in 1933, Cassirer taught first at Oxford (1933–1935), later at Yale (1941–1944) and Columbia (1944–1945); during his stay in the United States, he composed two of his most famous works, *An Essay on Man* (1944) and *The Myth of the State* (1946).

CATEGORICAL IMPERATIVE. *See* IMPERATIVE, CATEGORICAL AND HYPOTHETICAL.

CATEGORIES. An essential tool for much of Kant's **critical philosophy**, both theoretical and practical. Kant entertained the notion of some such concepts as the categories already during his **pre-critical** years, but he still assumed they would apply to **things-in-themselves** and not just to **appearances** and he did not think of them as constituting the necessary conditions of possible **experience**. Moreover, he did not yet conceive of them as comprising a systematic set of **concepts**. Thus, in § 8 of the *Inaugural Dissertation* of 1770, he mentions, next to the future categories of **possibility, existence, necessity,** and **causality,** also **substance,** but in § 30 he takes up, in a quite different context and in quite a different sense, the notion of the conservation of **matter**, a notion that would later be subsumed precisely under the heading substance.

In the *Critique of Pure Reason*, the categories, also called the **pure concepts** of the **understanding**, serve as the fundamental, **a priori** forms in accordance with which all data is synthesized; this synthesis in turn serves as the basis of experience. Since in this fashion the categories constitute experience, they are valid for all of it, that is, as Kant says, for all possible experience. This is also the reason why Kant can claim that the categories are both a priori and constitute the necessary conditions of the possibility of experience: without their employment there would be no determinate order of our **intuitions**. Furthermore, the categories serve as the necessary conditions of the possibility of the **cognition** of the **objects** of experience, given that such objects are nothing but intuitions determined in accordance with the categories.

Kant claimed that his set of categories was, unlike **Aristotle**'s set, complete, as it was derived systematically, in the so-called **metaphysical deduction**, from the **table of judgments**. Kant also stressed time and again that the categories cannot be fully applied beyond appearances; such an application is possible only in an analogous manner, and the categories cannot then serve as the basis for the acquisition of cognition. Kant was so convinced of the universal validity of the categories that he utilized them in many works during the critical period other than just the two editions of the *Critique of Pure Reason* and its simplified rendition, the *Prolegomena to Any Future Metaphysics*. In the *Critique of Practical Reason*, he offered a table of categories of **freedom**, in the *Critique of Judgment*, he elucidated the **aesthetic** judgments of **taste** in accordance with the categories, only reversing **quantity** and **quality**, in the *Metaphysical Foundations of Science*, he constructed his analysis of the a priori components of the concept of **matter** around the categories and even in the *Opus Postumum*, at the end of his writing career, he attempted to classify the relations of motive forces by resorting to the categories.

The reception has not always been kind to Kant's categories. For a number of philosophers, especially the **empirically** minded ones, no set of categories could be required or justified, for others, Kant's particular set was deemed to be of no value, since his reliance on the logic of the day for deriving them made his effort dated. Especially toward the end of the 19th century, the philosophical interest in working out a universally valid, closed system of categories declined, and was replaced by attempts to produce open systems of categories, which could better accommodate the progress of empirical science. As **Hermann Cohen** based his thought on 'fluid' judgments rather than on 'fixed' concepts, he grounded his transcendental logic of cognition on a system of judgments, which differed considerably from Kant's. Cohen refused to unambiguously relate judgments to categories, so that he could deduce from one type of judgment different categories or claim that a category was represented in different types of judgment.

In his book *Die logischen Grundlagen der exakten Wissenschaften* of 1910, **Paul Natorp** employed the concept of 'category' only in a historical sense when referring to Kant. In his own epistemology, he replaced the term with the concept of "basic logical function" (*logische Grundfunktion*). It was only in his late work, for example, in his *Philosophische Systematik* (published in 1958), that Natorp returned to the categories that he now understood as functions with which "all content of being that can be experienced in regard to its production" was to be grasped. Natorp distinguished the closed system of the basic categories from the open plurality of categorical orders that develop out of it.

In a similar fashion as Natorp, **Wilhelm Windelband** relied on synthesis as his point of departure, making it the basis of his theory of the categories. Windelband was no longer greatly concerned with the question whether the synthesis of data given in intuition is judgment or concept. Without explicit reference to the problem of an open or closed system of categories, Windelband distinguished between categories of objective validity (constitutive categories such as thing and process) and reflective categories such as equality and difference. The theories of the categories developed by **Heinrich Rickert**, Jonas Cohn, and Emil Last loosely followed Windelband, but can no longer be counted as truly Kantian.

The conception of an open system of categories was espoused in the 19th century by a number of thinkers who were inspired by Kant but who did not belong to the circle of the German Neokantians. Already around the middle of the century, William Whewell introduced a pendent to the categories with his "Fundamental Ideas," which function as laws of thought, but which are not necessarily limited in number. By holding that these 'Ideas' serve as the necessary foundations not of the possibility of experience but of an exact science, Whewell anticipated Cohen in at least one important respect.

Charles Sanders Peirce also based his work on the categories on Kant's theory. However, he transformed it thoroughly, by newly determining, on the basis of his analysis of the functions of signs, the relationship between the metaphysical and the transcendental deduction of the categories. In his first attempt of 1867, in the article "New List of Categories," Peirce developed the three fundamental categories quality, relation, and representation. Later, he joined this semiotically conceived triadic division with the trias of the relationally understood fundamental categories: firstness (monadic relation), secondness (dyadic relation), thirdness (mediating relation). To these categories correspond from the point of view of semiotics the three types of signs icons, index, and conventional symbols, and from the point of view of syllogistics abduction or hypothesis, induction, and deduction. Next to these fundamental categories, Peirce also admitted particular categories, each of which is related to a certain phenomenon.

The concept of categories that are neither necessary nor universal has been advocated by various philosophers in the 20th century such as C. I. Lewis, who drew on Kant only selectively. *See also* TABLES OF JUDGMENTS AND CATEGORIES.

CAUSALITY. A key concept in Kant's **epistemology** as well as in his **moral** philosophy, representing a large part of his answer to **David Hume**. Kant confronted the notion of causality already in his **pre-critical** writings. In the *Nova Dilucidatio* of 1755, he discussed the law of succession for the first time, though there he still remained more or less firmly within the framework of the **Leibniz-Wolff** school, claiming that the law is a derived principle based on the law of sufficient (or, as Kant preferred to say at this point: determining) **reason** and trying to demonstrate it by means of a proof that he later came to view as dogmatic (prop. 12). However, already in his *Attempt to Introduce Negative Magnitudes into Philosophy* of 1763 and again in the *Dreams of a Spirit-Seer* of 1766, Kant realized, in a Humean spirit, that we have no simple insight into causal relations: neither can causality be proved by a conceptual analysis based on the principle of identity nor can it be perceived or abstracted from experience (Ak 2, pp. 202–3, 370–71).

However, it was only in the **Critique of Pure Reason** that Kant, by presenting his **transcendental** proof of causality, offered a genuine alternative to Hume's suggestion that our notion of causality is gained by a psychological process on the basis of custom. Kant now claims that causality is part of the conceptual apparatus that makes **experience** possible and that grounds objective, **lawful** successions of **appearances**. Causality is what gives us an **object** of experience in the first place. Without causality there would be no **cognition**. Although Kant claimed that causality played this role in conjunction and on par with the other **categories**, it nevertheless retained in his philosophy much of the primacy that it enjoyed for Hume.

Kant derived the category of causality as the second of the categories of **relation** from hypothetical judgments, namely, from the relation of ground to consequence, that is, implication. His example of implication is the hypothetical proposition "If there is perfect justice, then obstinate evil will be punished" which contains the relations of the propositions "There is perfect justice" and "Obstinate evil is punished." In such judgments it is left undecided whether these propositions in themselves are true (A 73/B 98) and it is only owing to the category of causality that the claim of objective validity can be made. For categories to be applicable to appearances they need to be schematized, that is, temporal elements must be introduced. The **schema** of causality is "the real upon which, whenever it is posited, something else always follows," that is, the schema is "the succession of the manifold insofar as it is subject to a rule" (A 144/B 183). Kant's most extensive discussion of causality occurs in the section dealing with the "**Principles of Pure Understanding**" under the heading "Second Analogy." In the B-version, he claims that the "principle of temporal sequence according to the law of causality" is the proposition that "all alterations occur in accordance with the law of the connection of cause and effect." Kant attempts to prove this assertion by means of an intricate argument, the gist of which amounts to the claim that an objective succession of events can be distinguished from a subjective one only thanks to the presence of a necessary law of succession, namely, the causal law.

In the *Metaphysical Foundations of Natural Science*, corresponding to the "Second Analogy," Kant presents a modified version of **Isaac Newton**'s first law of motion, popularly known as the law of **inertia**, but stated by Kant so as to emphasize the role of causality. Kant begins by stating that "all alteration of **matter** has an external cause" and only adds in brackets the more Newtonian sounding formulation: "Every body remains in its state of rest or motion, in the same direction and with the same velocity, unless it is compelled to leave this state by an external cause" (Ak 4, p. 543).

The "Second Analogy" is perhaps *the* most analyzed passage of all of Kant's writings. His **epistemological** notion of causality has, however, come under fire from several sides. **Empirically** minded philosophers reject the claim that causality is **a priori**, while existentialist thinkers claim that causality is at best a convenient fiction; advances in physics in the 20th century, especially Werner Heisenberg's Principle of Uncertainty, have been claimed to make Kant's theory of causality obsolete, though this has also been disputed, since at a certain level not only everyday experience but also science continues to operate with the classical concept of causality. In addition, numerous authors, for example, Rudolf Carnap, have made various attempts to reformulate the Kantian law of causality.

Next to this epistemological concept of causality of **nature**, Kant introduced the notion of a causality of **freedom**, arguing at some length first in the third **Antinomy**, subsequently in the third Part of the *Groundwork of* *the Metaphysics of Morals*, and finally in the third chapter of the first book of the *Critique of Practical Reason* that the two notions of causality were compatible, provided that the causality of nature was applied to appearances and the causality of freedom to **things-in-themselves**, but then only in regard to morality. However, within Kant's system the conception of a causality of freedom is problematic. Following his teachings in the "Transcendental Analytic," a meaningful employment of the concept of causality is restricted to experience and may never be applied beyond its bounds. In speaking of a causality of freedom, Kant apparently wished to stress that the **will** of the moral subject did have the efficacy to act and in fact to commence causal chains of events outside the causal chain of nature. What he left unresolved was the question of how such different causal chains can be reconciled, that is, how one can maintain the validity of the notion of the uninterrupted natural causal chain, as Kant certainly wanted to do, and yet claim that there can be 'free' actions that can intervene and interrupt it.

CHEMISTRY. Kant was from early on well acquainted with this discipline, staying abreast, toward the end of his writing career, of the revolutionary developments that were then occurring. Although chemistry usually did not figure as the main focus of his interest, Kant used it several times to draw examples from it, and he compared it with other disciplines, mainly in an effort to establish a standard of what ought to count as scientific endeavor.

In the course of his defense of the **principle** of conservation of **absolute reality** in the **world** in the *Nova Dilucidatio* of 1755 (Proposition 10), he resorted to Stephen Hales's (1677–1761) seminal discovery that gases could exist trapped ('fixed') in solids; he thus supported his contention that great concentrations of potentially explosive forces need not serve as evidence against his theory. While discussing real opposition in his *Attempt to Introduce Negative Magnitudes into Philosophy* (1763), he borrowed the then current idea of a special matter that would account for magnetism, electricity, and heat, all phenomena requiring explanations other than merely logical ones (Part 2, Ak 2, p. 187).

While in the 1780s phlogiston-based chemistry still dominated the scene, Kant now became ambivalent in his assessment of this discipline. In the *Critique of Pure Reason*, he considered the chemistry of Georg Ernst Stahl (1659/60–1734) to be an example of an established science and he contrasted it favorably with the unscientific **metaphysics** of his days (B xii-xiii, A 646/B 674, A 653/B 681). However, in the Preface to the *Metaphysical Foundations of Natural Science*, he voiced doubts about the scientific nature of chemistry. Although placing it on a higher rung in the scientific hierarchy than empirical **psychology**, he now denied that it enjoyed the status of a science in the full sense of the word, arguing that chemistry reposed on merely empirical principles, rather than on necessary ones, and that it could not be treated mathematically, since it had no law governing, for example, the movement of particles toward or away from one another. He thus called chemistry a "systematic art" or an "empirical doctrine" rather than a "genuine science," reserving the latter label for **physics**.

The only chemist Kant mentioned in the 1790s, after the advent of the new oxygen-based chemistry, was Antoine Laurent Lavoisier (1743-1794). In the *Opus Postumum*, he relied heavily on Lavoisier's concept of 'caloric' with which he attempted to explain the difference in states of matter (solid, fluid, gas) and which he tried to integrate, under the term 'ether,' into his philosophy by means of a **transcendental deduction**.

Interesting are suggestions that Kant may have borrowed from chemistry not only important terminological elements (for example, **analysis, synthesis**), but also notions that inspired discussions central to the first *Critique* (for example, **limits** of **reason** as parallel to the limits of chemistry as a science).

CHRISTIANITY (*Christentum*). In Kant's philosophy of religion, Christianity was defined as the "**idea** of religion which must generally be based on **reason** and to this extent be natural"; the Bible is then supposed to serve as the vehicle for introducing religion among humans (Ak 7, p. 44). As **pure** religious **belief**, Christianity is neutral in respect to differences in denomination, differences that concern merely the external aspects of "ecclesiastical belief." The universal history of the **church** begins with Christianity, because only Christianity, and not **Judaism**, contains "the germ and the principles of the objective unity of the true and universal religious faith" and thus the foundations of the true church (Ak 6, p. 125). According to Kant, Christianity surpassed Judaism by assuming a "completely new principle." On the basis of the premise that Christianity bears the germ of pure religious faith that develops during the history of the church, Kant also interpreted the central Christian dogmas (Jesus as the son of God, Trinity, and so forth) in terms of their moral worth.

CHURCH (*Kirche*). Under this concept, Kant understood a community of people united under the **laws** of **virtue**, a community that works toward the establishment of the kingdom of **God** on earth by "uniting for a common effect the forces of single individuals, insufficient on their own" (Ak 6, p. 98). Kant called the **idea** of such "a union of all upright human beings" the "invisible church," the realization of this idea under the conditions of human existence the "visible church" (p. 101). The distinguishing marks of a true church were universality (no division into sects), honorableness (no superstition and no enthusiasm), **freedom**, and immutability. The formation of any church is, according to Kant, always based on the 'historical' faith in revelation, a faith which serves as a vehicle for the convergence with **pure religious belief.**

CITIZEN (*Bürger*). *See* STATE (*Staat*).

COGITO. *See* I THINK.

COGNITION (*Erkenntnis*). In Kant's **epistemology**, the word '*Erkenntnis*' plays a central role, while the nearly synonymous '*Wissen*' stands at the periphery. The older English translations of the *Critique of Pure Reason* rendered both of the German words with 'knowledge' and it is only in the recent effort by Paul Guyer and Allen W. Wood that the difference between the two terms is captured by reserving 'knowledge' solely for '*Wissen.*'

Throughout his critical period, Kant displayed great concern with examining and establishing the limits and the legitimacy of cognition. This was, in fact, the main purpose of his project of a **critique of pure reason.** Kant maintained that cognition could be had only of **appearances** and not of **things-in-themselves**, holding this even for the human subject, which he claimed cognizes itself only as it appears to itself and not as it is in itself (B 68, B 165). In general, Kant attempted to demonstrate that cognition does not extend to the traditional objects of **metaphysics** such as **immortality** of the soul, **freedom**, or **God**. Such objects can legitimately only be thought, and they cannot be dealt with by means of **constitutive** principles but only of regulative ones.

But if Kant argues against the dogmatic metaphysicians that human cognition is possible only within the bounds of **experience** and that it would not be possible without sensibility, he also stresses against the **empiricists** that cognition is the result of an activity of the **understanding** and that it must be structured in accordance with the formal elements of cognition, namely, the **forms** of **sensibility** (**space** and **time**) and the forms of the understanding (**categories, pure principles of the understanding**). Cognition for Kant is not the result of a passive reception of data; rather, it is effected by a **synthesis** of the understanding that is performed on the **manifold** given by the sensibility. The relationship between cognition, experience, and the formal elements is summed up by Kant in a famous proclamation at the outset of the "Introduction" to the second edition of the *Cri-*

tique of Pure Reason, where he declares that all our cognition commences with experience in a temporal sense, but that it does not, for that reason, all arise from experience (B 1). With this statement Kant underscores the need for both the material and the formal elements of cognition. Cognition is expressed in **synthetic judgments**; **a priori** ones yield a priori cognition, such as **mathematics** or **pure science**, a posteriori ones yield empirical cognition as it arises from **association** or **induction**. Analytic judgments (and thus also general **logic**) yield no new cognition, they only serve to clarify. Kant turns to determining what knowledge is only toward the end of the first *Critique*. In the process of his discussion of the traditional distinction between having an opinion, knowing, and believing (A 820–31/B 848–59), he defines knowledge as a 'taking-to-be-true' that is, unlike opinion and belief, both subjectively and objectively sufficient.

COHEN, HERMANN (1842–1918).   One of the major figures of **Neokantianism** and the founder, along with **Paul Natorp**, of the **Marburg School**. After an initial phase of attachment to the **psychology** of Johann Friedrich Herbart (1776–1841) and to the cultural anthropology (*Völkerpsychologie*) of Moritz Lazarus and Chaim Steinthal, Cohen entered into the contemporary debates concerning Kant by proclaiming a strict adherence to the "certified writings of Kant," making it clear, however, that he was more interested in a critical reconstruction of the spirit of Kant's philosophy than in a blind acceptance of its letter. Cohen's commentaries on Kant's three *Critiques*, *Kants Theorie der Erfahrung* (1871, 2nd ed. 1885), *Kants Begründung der Ethik* (1877, 2nd ed. 1910), and *Kants Begründung der Ästhetik* (1889), followed Kant more closely than did his *Das Prinzip der Infinitesimalmethode* (1883) or the three further works aimed at establishing his own system of philosophy, *Logik der reinen Erkenntnis* (1902, 2nd ed. 1914), *Ethik des reinen Willens* (1904, 2nd ed. 1907), and *Ästhetik des reinen Gefühls* (1912).

It was especially in the last mentioned four works that Cohen worked out his own version of **critical idealism** for **epistemology** and for **ethics** as well as his own political philosophy with its leading concept of **ethical socialism**. Cohen accomplished this by consistently relying on the idea that what is crucial are not the facts produced by ordinary experience, but the facts that the various sciences represent. In epistemology, these were the facts of **mathematics** and **physics**, in ethics, the fact of the pure science of jurisprudence. The prime concern of Cohen's ethics was to establish the foundations of normative human self-cognition; this would secure the possibility of ethical cognition as well as the notion of the autonomy of the acting person. Such a foundation of ethics was to be idealistic in the sense of refusing to rely on empirical facts of human nature, for example, on instincts or on natural needs; accordingly, it was to be arrived at by the **transcendental method**.

Just as Kant, Cohen also struggled with the problem of linking epistemology and ethics in one system of philosophy, and, following his predecessor, he looked toward **aesthetics** to help to accomplish this task. Aesthetics for Cohen was to be founded on the basis of art as a factual component of general culture. He characterized aesthetic consciousness as "pure feeling," and hoped to distinguish its mode of production of objects from the mode of production of cognition and morality by pointing to the possible relation of aesthetic consciousness to itself rather than to an object. Especially during his last years, Cohen published a number of works dealing with problems of religion (*Der Begriff der Religion im System der Philosophie*, 1915), especially of **Judaism** and its foundation in reason (*Religion of Reason out of the Sources of Judaism*, 1919, Engl. trans. 1972).

COMBINATION (*Verbindung*). See SYNTHESIS.

COMMAND (*Gebot*). In distinction to "rules of skill" or "councils of prudence," commands are for Kant "laws that must be obeyed, that is, must be followed even against **inclination**" (GMM, Ak 4, p. 416). The emphasis here is on obedience, which is owed to the command as an objective principle that coerces the **will** (p. 413). A command therefore stands between the objective moral law and the submission of the will under this law. Kant interprets the biblical command to love God and one's neighbor as a command to "respect the law that commands love." Parallel to this determination in his ethics of the relation of law and command, Kant, in his theory of the three authorities of the **state**, assigns command to the executive authority, which enforces the laws that have been passed by the legislator (MM, Ak 6, p. 313).

COMMUNITY (*Gemeinschaft*). As the third category of **relation**, community (*Gemeinschaft*) is usually defined in terms of interaction (*Wechselwirkung*) or reciprocity (*Wechselseitigkeit*), that is, as the interaction or reciprocal action between agent and patient. The main issue Kant is addressing with this category is that of accounting for the interaction between **objects** in the world.

Historically speaking, he had the choice between the theory of physical influence, that is, real community or interaction between objects; or **Gottfried Wilhelm Leibniz**'s doctrine of windowless substances that do not interact among each other, that is, the theory of the preestablished harmony; or the theory of occasionalism. While Kant consistently rejected all versions of the latter two, he inclined from early on toward an acceptance of the former, even if the path he followed was a winding one. Thus in his **pre-critical** piece *Nova Dilucidatio* (1755), he objected to the theory of physical influence on the grounds that it suggested the independence of substances from God (Prop. 12), and in the *Inaugural Dissertation* (1770), he accepted physical influence only after combining it with the thesis that the substances of the universe are dependent on a single cause (§§ 16–22).

In the *Critique of Pure Reason*, Kant emphasizes that we can have no **cognition** of the dependence of **substances** on a higher cause, and he restricts the concept of interaction of objects to the realm of **experience** (B 292–93, A 771/B 799). The category of community is derived from disjunctive **judgments**; these contain relations of opposition and of community of two or more propositions. Opposition is involved in the sense that the judgments are mutually exclusive, community in the sense that together the judgments exhaust the sphere of cognition in its entirety, meaning that each sphere is a complement of the other. Kant's example of a disjunctive judgment is: "The world exists either through blind chance, or through inner necessity, or through an external cause" (A 73–74/B 99). In his discussion of the **category** of community Kant continues along these lines by stressing that things that are related by interaction exist independently of one another, are not subordinated to each other, but rather coordinated simultaneously and reciprocally. He calls such communities aggregates (B 112–13, A 414/B 441). The **schema** of community, which results when the category is placed under a time determination, is described by Kant as the simultaneity of the determinations of one substance with those of another in accordance with a general rule (A 144/B 183).

The **principle** of community is dealt with in the "Third **Analogy**." It is defined in the first edition as: "All substances, insofar as they are simultaneous, stand in thoroughgoing community (that is, interaction with one another)." In the second edition, in keeping with the general trend, **space** is included: "All substances, insofar as they can be perceived in space as simultaneous, are in thoroughgoing interaction" (A 211/B 256). Here, Kant is primarily concerned with explaining how reciprocal series of **perceptions**, that is, simultaneity can be said to be **objective**. The third analogy is not entirely clear, as Kant here also somewhat cryptically writes that community is dependent on space being filled with **matter** that exercises a reciprocal influence. That this analogy has received far less attention than the incomparably more famous second analogy has, however, very likely, far less to do with any obscurities inherent in its proof than with the historical fact that Kant was here not addressing any philosophical problem that was to prove vital in the following two centuries, as was to be the case with causality.

In the *Metaphysical Foundations of Natural Science*, the third analogy as applied to the motion of matter becomes **Isaac Newton**'s third law of motion, namely, the law of the equality of action and reaction.

In the chapter "**Paralogisms** of Pure Reason" in the *Critique of Pure Reason*, Kant also utilizes the expression 'community' to describe the union of **body** and **soul** as it was conceived by philosophers before him. However, he then rejects the dualistic conception of these two substances and thus also the need to describe their relationship in any other way than in terms of constant **laws** that connect them into one experience; one may therefore dispense with the term 'community' in this context (A 385–86).

Finally, in his practical philosophy, Kant used the word 'community' (*Gemeinschaft*) in the sense of a social or political entity only infrequently, preferring the expressions 'society' (*Gesellschaft*) or 'empire' (*Reich*); however, the last mentioned is occasionally rendered in English as 'community' (or kingdom).

COMPREHENSION (*Zusammenfassung*). Kant used this term in his *Critique of Judgment* (§ 26) to describe one of the two acts by means of which the subject grasps a **magnitude**. The other act, the one which precedes comprehension, is **apprehension** (*Auffassung, apprehensio*). By these two acts, our **intuition** provides the **imagination** with a quantum that can be used as a measure or as a unit for estimating magnitudes by way of **numbers**. It is not by accident that Kant adds to comprehension in brackets the Latin expression *comprehensio aesthetica*. His main concern here is with magnitudes that are sufficiently large to produce in us the idea of the **sublime**. As he explains, increasing the magnitude is no problem as far as apprehension is concerned, since the latter can proceed to infinity, but comprehension at some point reaches a maximum limit, beyond which it cannot go, so that imagination must then, when presented with additional data, give up what it had apprehended in the beginning. One practical consequence of this conception in regard to objects that inspire the idea of the sublime in us may be that there is, for example, a proper distance from which we must view such objects; we cannot grasp all of them, that is, comprehend them, if we are positioned too close.

CONCEPT (*Begriff*). At various places in his writings, Kant offered different if related definitions of what a concept is: "the **unity** of the consciousness of connected **representations**" (Ak 7, p. 113), "the consciousness of the activity of connection of the **manifold** of representations in accordance with a **rule** of the unity" (Ak 7, p. 141), or "a universal representation (*repraesentatio per notas communes*) or a reflected representation (*repraesentatio discursiva*)" (Ak 9, p. 91). Common to these definitions is the view that concepts are the products of the **spontaneity** of the **understanding** and that they unite representations in accordance with a rule.

Kant radically distinguished concepts from **intuitions**, which he regarded as particular representations. However, it was one of the key tenets of his **epistemology** that **cognition** can arise only if both intuitions and concepts are involved. He thus declared that concepts alone are empty, while intuitions alone are blind (A 51/B 75). Kant generally reserved the term 'concept' for products of the understanding, preferring to call the concepts of **reason** 'ideas.'

Within the group of concepts, Kant distinguished empirical and **pure** ones. He was not greatly interested in the former and offered no theory to account for them, mentioning only that they "arise from the senses by a comparison of the objects of experience, and have from the understanding only the form of generality" (Ak 9, p. 92). Instead, Kant focused on the pure concepts, namely, the **categories**. These built the core of his epistemology by providing the structure of cognition, by serving as formal elements by means of which the understanding effects a **synthesis** of the manifold.

In the 1920s, **Bruno Bauch** placed 'concept' into the center of his epistemology, determining it as "the functional law of the constitution of an object." Cassirer and Rickert, on the other hand, dealt with 'concept' within the framework of their respective theories of science.

Ernst Cassirer argued in his *Substance and Function* (1910, Engl. trans. 1923) that mathematical and scientific concepts were relational rather than being concepts of things. While in classical logic a concept is formed by isolating qualitative elements that are common to a set of given objects, in the exact sciences concepts are gained by producing a nomological relation. The relation between the general and the particular is then conceived as a relation between the principle of a series and a member of the series, and no longer as a subsumption in which a specific content loses its particularity.

Heinrich Rickert made an influential examination of scientific and historical "concept formation." He emphasized that science cannot rest content with classifications, but that it must form concepts whose content consists of judgments that express laws of nature. Unlike the scientist who seeks the general, the historian attempts to grasp the individual; he forms his concepts so as to refer the objects to cultural values.

CONCEPTS OF REFLECTION. *See* AMPHIBOLY.

CONCEPTS OF THE UNDERSTANDING. *See* CATEGORIES.

CONFLICT OF THE FACULTIES. In the three treatises of this book, published in 1798, Kant examines the established hierarchy of the university faculties from the point of view of enlightened thought, reevaluating in the process the role of philosophy among the academic disciplines. Kant carries out this project by focusing on the 'lawful' conflict between the 'lower,' that is, philosophical **faculty**, which is committed only to a scholarly interest in **truth**, and the three 'upper' faculties, whose teachings are based on existing writings and are concerned with the shaping of societal life.

In its conflict with the theological faculty, the philosophical one counters the ecclesiastical faith based on a dogmatic Bible interpretation of the theologians with its own conception of pure religious **belief**. The conflict with the faculty of law concerns the question whether humanity is progressing toward a better future. Kant links his affirmative reply to the positive consequences of the French Revolution, which enhanced the tendency to establish a republican **constitution**. For Kant, the great importance of such a constitution lies in the fact "that it cannot be bellicose" (Ak 7, p. 88). The third part of the book, dealing with medicine, consists of Kant's answer to the request of the medical doctor Christoph Wilhelm Hufeland (1762–1836) to pass judgment on his medical "attempt to treat the physical element in the human being morally" (p. 97). Kant's comments on Hufeland's dietetics, defined as "the art of prolonging human life" (p. 99), manifest a concern with mastering morbid feelings; however, he also critically discusses the desire to live a long and healthy life.

CONSCIENCE. Kant formalizes conscience into the "consciousness of an internal court in the human being" (Ak 6, p. 438). On the one hand, it has the task of judging whether the examination of an action's accordance with **duty** has taken place; it does not have the task of judging whether the contents of an **action** are in accordance with duty; this is the responsibility of **practical reason** itself (p. 186). Conscience cannot err while performing this task. On the other hand, Kant determines conscience as practical reason directed at the **subject** and, as such, "holding the human being's duty before him for his acquittal or condemnation in every case that comes under a law" (p. 400). In this function, conscience is the inner judge. Although the examination by conscience is a self-examination, the person who, if we retain the metaphor of the court of law, thus stands accused by his own conscience must represent his judge as another person, be it real or ideal.

The attributes that Kant subsequently ascribes to this person make it apparent that conscience is to be understood as a subjective principle of responsibility before **God** (pp. 438–39).

CONSCIOUSNESS (*Bewusstsein*). *See* PSYCHOLOGY; SOUL; TRANSCENDENTAL UNITY OF APPERCEPTION.

CONSTITUTION (*Verfassung*). *See* STATE (*Staat*).

CONSTITUTIVE AND REGULATIVE PRINCIPLES.   In general, Kant used the word 'constitutive' in his theoretical philosophy to refer to **concepts** or principles that constitute, ground, and determine **experience** and the **objects** of experience, that is, that serve as the necessary conditions for the possibility of experience, and, at the same time, as the necessary conditions for the possibility of the objects of experience. Among such concepts he counted the **forms** of **intuition space** and **time**, the **categories**, and the **principles of the understanding**.

To constitutive he opposed regulative, ascribing this qualifier mostly to **ideas of reason**. As the word 'regulative' suggests, the reference is made to rules that regulate or guide us in our inquiry. Kant thought that such guidance could be provided in realms beyond the **bounds** of experience, where we can expect no **cognition**, but where we can at least **think** certain ideas. In the "**Transcendental Dialectic**," Kant demonstrates that we can have no cognition of a simple soul, the world-whole, or God, so that these ideas can have no constitutive use for our experience. However, he also shows that using these ideas in a regulative manner can be highly useful and indeed indispensable. Thus, the regulative idea of a simple soul leads us to seek a unified **psychology**, the regulative idea of a world-whole serves as "a problem for the **understanding**," inducing us to search for the maximum in the series of conditions, and the regulative idea of **God** leads us "to regard all combination in the world as if it arose from an all-sufficient necessary **cause**" (A 619/B 647).

In addition, Kant specifically discusses the need for ordering the empirical **laws** that the understanding discovers, laws that stand under the merely formal determination of the categories, but that require further grounding and systematizing. He presents the regulative principles that could achieve such a task of guiding our research of nature in the "Appendix to the Transcendental Dialectic," naming here especially the laws of homogeneity, specification, and **continuity** (A 658/B 686). In the *Critique of Judgment*, Kant then introduced another regulative principle, namely, that of a formal **purposiveness** of nature, a principle that can also serve to systematize the empirical laws of nature. Kant put the constitutive/regulative distinction to more specific use in his presentation of the principles of the understanding, applying the distinction here not in respect to experience, but in respect to **appearances**. Kant thus classified the first two principles, the **axioms of intuition** and the **anticipations of perception**, as constitutive, presumably owing to the fact that they permit the application of mathematical **construction** to certain aspects of existence, or, in Kant's own words, that they teach how intuition and the real in perception can be "generated in accordance with rules of a mathematical synthesis" (A 178/B 221). On the other hand, the so-called **dynamical** principles of the understanding, the **analogies of experience** and the **postulates of empirical thinking in general**, are merely regulative, since existence here cannot be constructed, and "these principles can concern only the relation of existence" (A 179/B 222). As Kant explains in regard to **analogy**, it is constitutive only in mathematics, since on the basis of two members of a proportion the third can be constructed, but in philosophy analogy is only regulative, because from given members one can cognize only the relation to a further member, but not this new member itself. However, it is important to note that in regard to experience, all four of the principles of the understanding are constitutive.

CONSTRUCTION. A key notion in Kant's philosophy of **mathematics**, one that serves as the distinguishing mark of mathematics. Unlike **philosophy**, which proceeds by the **cognition** from **concepts**, all of mathematics, not just geometry, but also arithmetic and algebra, is based on the construction of concepts. According to Kant's famous definition, "to construct a concept means to exhibit **a priori** the **intuition** corresponding to it." Kant's main problem was to explain how such a procedure, which is seemingly always singular, could guarantee the certainty and the **universal validity** of mathematics. He admitted that resorting to (non-empirical) intuition means dealing only with an individual object, since only concepts, but not intuitions, are general representations. However, constructing a figure that corresponds to a concept, either through mere imagination, in **pure** intuition, or on paper, in empirical intuition, suffices, because we take "account only of the action of construction of the concept" (A 713-4/B 741-2). That means that the **rules** of construction, being universal, assure mathematics of its universality. These rules, however, are not part of intuition or **sensibility**, but are generated by the **understanding**.

Kant's emphasis on the rules of construction, rather than on images in the mind, serves to set apart his own philosophy of mathematics from that of his more empirically minded predecessors, who debated whether mathematics owed its universality to its manipulation of indeterminate images (**John Locke**) or to its operating on individual images that somehow represent all other, similar images (**George Berkeley, David Hume**).

CONTINGENCY (*Zufälligkeit*). In the *Critique of Pure Reason*, Kant introduces contingency as the negation of **necessity** (A 80/B 106). With 'contingent' in a purely categorical sense, Kant labels entities that do not include **existence** in their **possibility**, that is, entities whose nonexistence may be thought (B 290). From the point of view of propositional logic, 'contingent' is something whose contradiction is possible (A 459/B 487). And this is the case for experience or empirical judgments (B 142). When the use of the **category** of contingence in **cognition**, that is, under the determinations of **time**, is involved, Kant excludes contingency: natural processes must be thought as hypothetically necessary (A 228/B 280). While reflecting on this law of the **understanding** in the course of his discussion of the **idea** of an absolutely necessary being in the fourth **antinomy**, Kant introduces the distinction between empirical and intelligible contingency (A 459–60/B 487–88). He resorts here to the modal category of contingency in considering the whole of experience or of nature. In the *Critique of Judgment*, Kant links the supposition of objective **purposiveness** in nature to the thesis of its contingency (Ak 5, pp. 268–69, 335).

Hermann Cohen takes up the problem of intelligible contingency in his *Ethik des reinen Willens*. When the whole of experience is thought by reason, it becomes apparent that this whole hovers over the abyss of intelligible contingency. In order to cover up this abyss, Cohen introduces, on the one hand, the Kantian conception of the systematic **unity** of particular empirical natural **laws** standing under the idea of **purpose**, identifying this idea with Charles Darwin's principle of selection. On the other hand, he shifts the problem into his ethics, where he attempts to solve it by opposing the intelligible contingency of endlessly conditioned human actions to the **noumenon** of **freedom**.

CONTINUITY. Kant held already in his **pre-critical** period that **space** and **time** are divisible to **infinity** and therefore continuous. In his *Thoughts on the True Estimation of Living Forces* of 1749 he approvingly mentioned the law of continuity (§ 26), in the *Monadologia Physica* of 1756 he maintained that space does not contain simple parts and is thus infinitely divisible (prop. 3), and in the *Inaugural Dissertation* of 1770 he argued that time is a continuous **magnitude**, that is, one that does not consist of simple or smallest parts; between any two intervals of time there is always another time segment, and instants are only boundaries (§ 14).

Although in the *Critique of Pure Reason* Kant did not repeat the continuity thesis at the corresponding place in the "**Transcendental Aesthetic**," mentioning only offhandedly much later in the book that space and time are "*quanta continua*" (A 169/B 211), the continuity of time and space is, nevertheless, assumed throughout his critical period. Based on the continuity of time is the claim that there is continuity in change, that is, that **causality** acts in a continuous manner: a thing passes from one state to another through an infinite number of intervening parts. Kant considered this to be an **a priori law** of the **form** of alteration (A 208-11/B 254-56). Based on the continuity of space is Kant's assertion that extensive magnitudes are continuous ("**Axioms of Intuition**"), whereas his claim that intensive magnitudes are continuous ("**Anticipations of Perception**") (A 170/B 212) is independent of the theory of the continuity of the two forms of **intuition**. Although Kant did make an analogy between time and **appearance**, saying that time, appearance in time, and the real in the appearance are all continuous, that is, do not consist of smallest parts, he did not base his contention that there are infinite **degrees** of **reality** on the properties of time (A 209/B 254). The importance of continuity for magnitudes is plain from the fact that this is their only quality that we can cognize a priori (A 176/B 218).

In the section "Dynamics," which in the *Metaphysical Foundations of Natural Science* corresponds to the "Anticipations of Perception," Kant again resorts to continuity, explaining **matter** out of the action of the (continuous) forces of **attraction** and repulsion rather than on the basis of (discontinuous) **atoms** and the **void**; matter is thus also declared to be divisible to infinity (prop. 4).

However, continuity and divisibility to infinity as well as the assertion of the opposite thesis, namely, that simple parts do exist, can be affirmed or denied only with respect to **experience**; extending such claims beyond the realm of experience leads to contradictions. That is the lesson taught by the "Second **Antinomy**." Dividing an appearance (not in a spatial or temporal sense) into parts is a process that is carried out in experience, and, unless such a division is completed, we cannot determine whether it is finite or infinite; however, completing the division in finite time is not possible, so that humans cannot determine whether appearances have a finite or an infinite number of parts.

Finally, in the "Appendix to the **Transcendental Dialectic**," Kant also assumes the law of continuity (affinity), along with homogeneity and specification, as one of the principles of systematic **unity**. In a language modeled on biological classification, Kant speaks of a continuity of the forms of nature. This means that between any two species there will be no gap, but further species, or, in other words, that no species or subspecies will be proximate, but that there will always be intervening species. In spite of the fact that this law is not merely a logical one, but that there is also a **transcendental** law of continuity, it remains only an **idea**, that is, a **regulative** principle that only *points* toward systematic unity (A 657–68/B 685–96).

In his book *Das Prinzip der Infinitesimalmethode* of 1883, **Hermann Cohen** raised the question as to which **category** and which schema is to be used in constructing a continuum. Cohen applied Kant's teachings on **schematism**, according to which all a priori concepts can be constructed as schemata of time, to the method of infinitesimals, thus linking continuity and the continuum to time and motion. Over and above the grounding of infinitesimal analysis, he expanded this determination of continuity into a *mathesis intensorum*, with which *reality* was to be constructed. In his *Logik der reinen Erkenntnis* (*Logic of Pure Cognition*) of 1902, Cohen, in addition, determined continuity no longer as a category, but as a "law of **thought**" (*Denkgesetz*): the continuous unity of thought in its object-producing motion is identical with the continuity of the produced **object**.

COPERNICAN REVOLUTION (*Kopernikanische Wende*). In the "Preface" to the second edition of the *Critique of Pure Reason*, Kant famously compared his own revolution in philosophy to Nicolaus Copernicus's heliocentric revolution in **astronomy**. Kant pointed out that Copernicus had failed to explain celestial motions with the assumption that the observer was in the center, and that he had achieved better results by placing the observer in a revolving position. Kant claimed that, in a similar way, **metaphysics** would be unable to account for **cognition a priori** as long as we continued regarding **intuition** and **concepts** as having to conform to the constitution of **objects**. Instead, success is possible only by assuming that the object must conform to the constitution of our faculty of intuition and to our a priori concepts (B xvi–xvii).

The exact meaning and appropriateness of the analogy has been widely questioned. It is clear that Copernicus, unlike Kant, did not produce a revolution in methodology, also it is clear that Kant intended to prove his hypothesis himself, again unlike Copernicus, whose theory was confirmed only by the subsequent work of Johann Kepler and **Isaac Newton**. Less clear is whether Kant chose Copernicus because the latter, by demoting the earth from its preeminent position in the center of the universe, effected an exceptionally far-reaching revolution, or simply because both Copernicus and Kant exchanged certain components, be these planets or epistemological entities. It is quite possible, however, that, as a third alternative, Kant had knowledge of Copernicus's work *De Revolutionibus*, in which the role of the observer is emphasized, and that he thus saw the similarity in the fact that both revolutions concentrated on the position of the human subject (B xxii). At any rate, Kant's own analogy and the subsequent coining of the expression "Kant's Copernican Revolution" by the commentators have succeeded in providing a succinct label for Kant's teachings that we can cognize only **appearances** but not **things-in-themselves** and that our cognition is dependent on the **forms** of human **sensibility** and of the **understanding**.

COSMOLOGY. Kant was concerned with questions of cosmology during most of his philosophical career, but his treatment of the subject underwent a radical development. In his **pre-critical** piece *Universal Natural History and Theory of the Heavens* of 1755, Kant attempted to account for the origin of the solar system and indeed of the whole universe by relying solely on physical **laws** inherent to **matter**. In doing so, he was seeking to improve both on **Isaac Newton's physics** as well as on the standard version of the physico-theological argument for the **existence** of **God**. Newton felt that he could not explain the origin and the conservation of the solar system without recourse to divine intervention, while the more popular renderings of the argument from design similarly presupposed God's action in even the most minute cases of seemingly purposeful functioning in natural beings. By claiming that God was responsible only for the laws, but not for individual instances of **purposiveness**, Kant presented a more naturalistic account of the universe. However, the *Universal Natural History* was based on analogical reasoning and was filled with speculation, for example, about the intellectual capabilities of the inhabitants of the other planets of our solar system.

While repeating the gist of his earlier argument in *The Only Possible Ground of Proof for a Demonstration of the Existence of God* of 1763, Kant clearly distanced himself from his earlier speculative position in the *Critique of Pure Reason*. In the "**Transcendental Dialectic**," he subjected rational cosmology along with rational psychology and rational theology, the three subjects of traditional special **metaphysics**, to a critical examination. Cosmological ideas were dealt with in the four "**Antinomies of Pure Reason**," in which Kant showed that it is meaningless to ask whether or not the world has a beginning in time and is enclosed in spatial boundaries, and whether or not every composite substance consists of simple parts. Kant now claims that such issues lie beyond the **limits** of our **cognition**. Under the heading of cosmology, he also maintains that **freedom** and the existence of an absolutely necessary being must be denied for the **appear-**

ances, since these questions, too, fall outside of the scope of human cognition, but may be thought in respect to the **things-in-themselves.**

COSMOPOLITANISM.   Since the middle of the 18th century, this topic had been the subject of a lively discussion in Germany, oddly compensating for the political turmoil in the country. The debate focused on the possible connection between a cosmopolitan attitude and a patriotic one. Kant's contribution consisted of his declaration that the **purpose** of nature in history was the creation of a "cosmopolitan state" or of the "perfect civic union within the human species" (Ak 8, pp. 28–29). As he explained in his *Anthropology from a Pragmatic Point of View*, he regarded it as a **regulative** principle that nature determines **humans** to feel that they are destined to progress toward a "cosmopolitan society" (Ak 7, p. 331). Such a society would ideally take the shape of a "state of nations" or of a "global republic," though, realistically, one may only hope for a "league of nations" (Ak 8, p. 357); with the attainment of the latter, "cosmopolitan right" would be limited to providing legal security to people visiting foreign countries and nations, that is, it would amount to "universal hospitality" (pp. 357–60).

Friedrich Bouterwek argued in a similar vein in his *Fünf kosmopolitische Briefe* (*Five Cosmopolitan Letters*) of 1794. However, soon after, under the influence of romanticism, patriotism gained the upper hand in Germany. **Hermann Cohen**'s criticism of the rampant tendency to decry cosmopolitanism as the neglect of one's fatherland amounted to only a feeble reflection of Kant's old position.

CRITICAL IDEALISM.   Kant himself generally did not refer to his philosophy as critical idealism (for some exceptions see *Prolegomena to Any Future Metaphysics*, § 13, remark 3; Appendix, Ak 4, pp. 293–94, 375), preferring instead the labels formal or **transcendental idealism** or **critical philosophy.** After **Johann Gottlieb Fichte** declared that his own "Doctrine of Science" (*Wissenschaftslehre*) was critical idealism, claiming that the self (*Ich*) in its position was to be considered neither idealistically, merely as a subject, nor dogmatically, merely as an object, a version of critical idealism became the characterizing feature of **Neokantianism.** As it was developed by **Hermann Cohen** in the 1880s, critical idealism differed both from speculative idealism and from Kant's **epistemology.** Cohen censured attempts on the part of the former to construct a **system** of rational **cognition** on the basis of a **principle** or a set of principles, just as he rejected the idea of the self-explication of absolute cognition. Speculative idealism, which Cohen also branded as "fundamentalist **metaphysics,**" went astray, according to him, by claiming to have discovered the "absolute foundations" of **truth**; he himself advocated the more modest notion of the "laying of foundations," foundations that would always be capable of revision. Cohen deviated from Kant by abandoning the dualism of **sensation** and **thought**, that is, by stressing that the giving of the real was to be accomplished by thought rather than by sensation as was held by Kant. This led him to concentrate exclusively on the formal conditions of the **possibility of experience** and to consider **matter** as fully subsumed under **form**. Thought, which Cohen conceived of as essentially foundational, as the "thought of the origin," was to provide the basis of all cognition and was thus to replace the sensibly given to which thought would otherwise have to refer. Although this conception of the "constructive character of thought" brought Cohen dangerously close to the very kind of idealism he had rejected, he nevertheless insisted on the appropriateness of the predicate 'critical,' claiming that the reference to the **fact** of **science** was a sufficient safeguard against fundamentalist metaphysics: epistemological analysis was to be concerned with the type of given that had already been critically appraised within science.

For **Paul Natorp**, "critical idealism" signified, in **Plato**'s sense, the placing of all finite cognition into relation with the "infinity of the idea"; critical idealism, nevertheless, remains 'critical' insofar as philosophical questions are addressed to the work of science and of culture.

CRITICAL PHILOSOPHY. Kant's project of a critical examination of the faculties of human **cognition**; placed by Kant into an intermediary position between, on the one hand, dogmatic **philosophy**, which makes metaphysical assertions without questioning their legitimacy and which he associated mainly with the **Leibniz-Wolff** school, and, on the other hand, the **empiricism** of a **John Locke**, or, alternatively, between dogmatism and the **scepticism** of a **David Hume**. Present-day scholarship also distinguishes Kant's critical philosophy from a **pre-critical** one, which was not necessarily dogmatic or even uncritical, but which was not primarily concerned with an examination of the foundations of human cognition. In that sense Kant's critical philosophy starts with the publication of his *Critique of Pure Reason* in 1781 or perhaps with the preparatory phase during the so-called silent decade of the 1770s; the *Inaugural Dissertations* of 1770 may then be considered as a transitional work. Owing to the fact that Kant's early writings have often been ignored, his whole philosophy is frequently, though inaccurately, characterized as critical. *See also* CRITICISM; CRITIQUE.

CRITICISM (*Kritizismus*). Unlike the English term, the German one cannot be used in the sense of "literary criticism." Kant himself introduced this term in 1790 to characterize his **method** in **metaphysics** as an intermediary between dogmatism and **skepticism** (Ak 8, pp. 226–27), and used it again in 1798 to situate, in questions of religion, his "criticism of **practical reason**" between orthodoxy and mysticism (Ak 7, p. 59). In the 1790s Kant's philosophy was interpreted partly as "**critical philosophy**," partly as 'criticism.' However, **Johann Gottlieb Fichte** claimed that he had developed the 'semi-criticism' of Kant and his followers into a "higher, completed criticism." In **Neokantianism, Alois Riehl** distinguished, in opposition to the then common tendency to equate criticism with Kantianism, between criticism as a method for examining the objective validity of the basic concepts of experience, and Kantianism as a specific instance of this method. Accordingly, Riehl identified, in volume one of his *Der philosophische Kritizismus und seine Bedeutung für die positive Wissenschaft* (1876), positions of criticism (that is, of critical philosophy) before Kant, specifically a "psychological criticism" in John Locke and a 'skeptical' one in David Hume. Leonard Nelson also understood his own critical method as criticism, a method that, based on the example of **Jakob Friedrich Fries**, he conceived as psychological. In a related fashion, Paul **Natorp** labeled as criticism the "**transcendental method**" that was based on the interrelation between philosophy and science. More recently, Karl Popper's critical rationalism has been designated as a "new" or "rational criticism."

CRITIQUE (*Kritik*). In accordance with contemporary usage, Kant employed the term 'critique' during his **pre-critical** period in reflections on **aesthetics** and **logic**, holding, however, only the "critique of **reason**" performed by logic, but not the critique of **taste**, to be theoretically important. Although in 1765–1766 Kant shifted logic to the end of the whole of **philosophy**, he already assigned to it, as "the critique and **canon** of all real learning," the task of considering the origin of the insights and errors of philosophy as well as of sketching the plan of a permanent building of reason (Ak 2, p. 310). A **metaphysics** that has been subjected to such a critique can then only be "the science of the **limits** of human reason" (Ak 2, p. 368). Kant defined such a metaphysics in 1769 explicitly as "a **critique of pure reason** and not a doctrine," thinking at this point that logic was a doctrine (Ak 17, p. 368).

The critique of pure reason was not to be understood as "a critique of books and systems," but rather as "a critique of the **faculty** of reason in general" (A xii). This critique, which Kant conceived on the model of a court of justice (A 751/B 779), was to be carried out by reason itself. 'Critique' is opposed to dogmatism (but not to the dogmatic **method**) and to **skepticism** (but not to the skeptical method); it avoids metaphysical conflicts in order to first determine whether the human cognitive powers are at all capable of dealing with metaphysical problems ("**transcendental** critique," A 12/B 26). This examination produces both a negative and a positive result. The former consists in the destruction of metaphysical **cognition** of **God, freedom,** and **immortality,** the latter in permitting the **practical** use of reason. In distinction to the literary critique of the early 18th century, a critique that operated with fixed rules, Kant did not dogmatically presuppose any standard, obtaining it rather "from the ground-rules of the critique's own constitution" (A 751/B 779).

Within his **system,** Kant assigned to the critique (of pure reason) the status of a "propaedeutic to the system of pure reason"; this contains the "complete **idea** of **transcendental philosophy,**" but not yet such a philosophy itself (A 11ff./B 25ff.), which in its turn should constitute the first part of the metaphysics of nature (A 845/B 873). Kant completed the definitive systematization of his critical philosophy in the *Critique of Judgment:* the expression "critique of pure reason" now acquired a narrower meaning, as the critique of the **understanding,** and a wider one, encompassing the triple conception of the critique of the pure understanding, of pure judgment, and of pure practical reason (Ak 5, pp. 167ff.). With the *Critique of Judgment,* Kant considered his critical task to be accomplished; in his remark on **Johann Gottlieb Fichte**'s "Doctrine of Science" (*Wissenschaftslehre*) in 1799, Kant described his own philosophy as a "system of critique" that rested on a completely secure foundation (Ak 12, p. 371).

Johann Georg Hamann (1784) and **Johann Gottfried Herder** (1799) each composed a *Meta-critique,* in which they attempted to correct and to surpass Kant's critique of reason especially by performing a critique of the usage of language in philosophy. In post-Kantian German Idealism, the concept of critique disappeared from its central position in philosophical reflection. Only **Jakob Friedrich Fries** attempted in his *Neue Kritik der Vernunft* (1807) to revive Kant's critique of reason from an anthropological point of view. In **Neokantianism, Friedrich Albert Lange** again countered metaphysics with a philosophical critique, examining the concepts of the former with the latter's empirical and rational means. **Hermann Cohen,** however, again restricted the function of the critique in his *Logik der reinen Erkenntnis* (2nd ed. 1914), allowing it only to exercise a methodical control of cognition-generating **thought. Wilhelm Windelband** distinguished the critical method from a genetical one, assigning to the former the task of examining the **validity** of principles.

CRITIQUE OF JUDGMENT (Kritik der Urteilskraft). The title has also been rendered into English as *Critique of the Power of Judgment;* it is popularly known also as the "Third Critique." In this work, Kant takes up problems that had remained unresolved in the critiques of theoretical and of practical reason; this involved especially the notion of the systematic unity of his theoretical and practical philosophy, and the teleological approach common both to the "critique of taste" (**aesthetics**) and to the theory of **organisms**. Kant had dealt with aesthetics as well as with problems of a teleological consideration of nature earlier, but up to then separately. While working on the "Critique of Taste" in 1787, he came to the conclusion that **a priori principles** would have to be found also for the feelings of **pleasure** and pain, that is, for the third "faculty of the mind," which he planned to include in the third part of philosophy labeled 'teleology' (Ak 10, pp. 514–15).

In order to establish the critique of taste as part of his **transcendental** philosophy, Kant needed to present an analysis of the logical structure of aesthetic judgment. However, he succeeded in linking aesthetic judgment to teleology (in the consideration of nature) only after he introduced the concept of reflective **judgment** as the origin of the a priori of feeling. Kant now realized that the general, on which the faculty of judgment reflects when it departs from the particular of the manifold empirical laws of nature, stands under the principle of the formal **purposiveness** of nature. This principle is subjective and yet transcendental, as it specifies the conditions under which nature does not proceed chaotically, but is purposively structured in accordance with the faculty of judgment. One may hope to find, as Kant puts it, "in the immeasurable manifold of things in accordance with possible empirical laws, sufficient kinship among them . . . and thus reach an empirical system of nature" (Ak 20, p. 215).

This formal purposiveness of nature that functions as a transcendental principle of the faculty of judgment can be represented either as aesthetic or as logical. A representation is called aesthetic when it follows out of a merely subjective ground and rests "on the immediate pleasure in the form of the object," a pleasure arising out of the reflection on this form. A representation is called logical when it follows out of an objective ground "as a correspondence of its form with the possibility of the thing itself" (Ak 5, p. 192). This distinction provides the basis for the main division of the work into a "Critique of the Aesthetic Faculty of Judgment" and a "Critique of the Teleological Faculty of Judgment."

In the introduction to the third critique, Kant summarizes the results of the above thought process in a systematic form. In the first part of the work, he examines the validity of aesthetic judgments. Such judgments require a special justification because they do not repose on concepts. The "Analytic of the **Beautiful**" is divided in accordance with the four main types of function of judgment (§§ 1–22). Kant then continues with the "Analytic of the **Sublime**" (§§ 23–29) and the "Deduction of Pure Aesthetic Judgments" (§§ 30ff.), before proceeding to discuss the convergence of the interest in the beautiful and of moral interest (§ 42); the concept of art and the difference between the beautiful in nature and in art (§§ 43ff.); the concept of **genius** (§§ 46–50); the different kinds of fine arts (§§ 51–54). The first part closes with a "Dialectic of the Aesthetic Faculty of Judgment" (§§ 55–60).

The second part (§§ 61–91) is again divided into an "Analytic," where Kant deals with organisms, and a "Dialectic of the Teleological Faculty of Judgment," which includes the teachings of the critical limitation of the principle of the objective purposiveness of nature. A "Methodology of the Teleological Faculty of Judgment" follows in an appendix.

CRITIQUE OF PRACTICAL REASON. In the ***Critique of Pure Reason,*** Kant had not foreseen a further '*Critique,*' thinking that with his examination of the possibility of a priori cognition his critical propaedeutic to a **metaphysics** of both nature and morals was complete. However, already in the ***Groundwork of the Metaphysics of Morals,*** when he came to deal with the question of what the foundations of the metaphysics of morals consist of, Kant discussed the project of the "critique of a pure practical reason." Such a critique did not appear to him to be as urgent as the "critique of a pure speculative reason"; in addition, Kant still overburdened it here with the task of carrying out the unification of speculative and **practical reason** (Ak 4, p. 391), an undertaking that he was later to assign to the ***Critique of Judgment.***

Finally appearing in 1788 under the title "Critique of Practical Reason," the work is divided, just as the first *Critique,* into a "Doctrine of Elements" and a (brief) "Doctrine of Method." The "Doctrine of Elements" is subdivided into an '**Analytic**' and a '**Dialectic.**' In the first chapter of the 'Analytic,' Kant distinguishes between moral ('practical') **principles,** which are grounded exclusively in **reason,** and **rules** that presuppose certain objects of the will and, along with these, "material of the faculty of desire." The latter are subjected to the principle of self-love, since they express the conditions of the attainment of subjective **happiness.** Only the moral principles can, thanks to their formal nature, be **universal** and therefore objectively valid: the **will** must be thought as determined independently of empirical conditions merely by practical reason, that is, "by the mere **form** of the **law**" (Ak 5, p. 31). Accordingly, Kant states at the beginning of section 7 the "fundamental law of pure practical reason" in the form of the categorical **imperative**: "Act so that the maxim of your will could always at the same time hold as a principle of a universal legislation" (p. 30). Kant calls the consciousness of this fundamental law a **fact** of reason, recognizing it as "the sole fact of pure reason" (p. 31).

The fundamental moral law is the expression of **autonomy** and therefore of the **freedom** of the will to be able to determine itself independently of every desire. Unlike **cognition** that arises from theoretical (speculative) reason and that requires **intuition** and is thus possible only in the sensible world, Kant founds practical cognition, that is, the determination of the will by practical reason, on freedom; in this way the transition to the intelligible world is achieved. However, attaining insight into the connection between subjection to **nature** and freedom would require an "intellectual intuition," and Kant denies that such an intuition is available to humans (p. 31, see also p. 100).

Kant deals with the object and the **incentive** of pure practical reason in two further chapters. The moral law must determine the will immediately. This is possible only when the law itself acts as an incentive. It accomplishes this task by producing a **feeling** of **respect** for itself. This is the only feeling that Kant admits in his foundation of **ethics**, as it is a feeling that is produced by a nonsensible ground. The moral law therefore functions not only as a formal and, in regard to good and evil, as a material, but also, as far as it is an incentive, as a subjective determining ground of the will (p. 75). Kant comprehends good and evil as objects of practical reason. Only they and not the **agreeable** (well-being) or the disagreeable (ill-being) are the possible products of a free will, that is, of a will that is thoroughly and immediately determined by the law of reason (p. 60) and that as such may be called "absolutely and in every respect good" and that forms "the supreme condition of all good." The concept of the **good** (and **evil**) is derived from moral law, it is not conceived as the latter's foundation (pp. 62–63).

Kant continues to deal with these points in the "Dialectic of Pure Practical Reason," specifically under the heading of the **highest good**. Within this concept, Kant connects **virtue** and happiness. First, however, he notes an **antinomy** in this connection: according to the principles of his ethics, happiness may not be a motive of virtue, and virtue cannot be a cause of happiness (pp. 113–14). He solved this antinomy by claiming that the second clause holds only for people in the sensible world, but not in the noumenal one, to which people as moral subjects belong. It is not impossible that the "morality of the disposition" could have a "necessary connection as cause with happiness as effect in the sensible world," but such a connection could only be brought about by the mediation of an intelligible author of nature (p. 115). As a consequence of his concept of practical reason, Kant developed the **postulate** of immortality, freedom, and the existence of God (p. 132), thus moving beyond the position of the *Groundwork of the Metaphysics of Morals* and toward a practical-dogmatic metaphysics, as has been stressed especially by Heinz Heimsoeth. The postulates have for Kant the status of theoretical propositions that, though unprovable, are inextricably linked to the absolutely valid moral law.

CRITIQUE OF PURE REASON. This book is one of the most important treatises on the theory of **cognition** in the history of Western philosophy. Its chief declared aim is to decide whether **metaphysics** is possible or not and to delineate the limits of human cognition (A xi). Kant accomplishes this task by examining the human cognitive **faculties**, and by ascertaining their true scope and their legitimate and illegitimate employment. That such an examination was a primary target of the book is reflected to some extent already in the provisional title that Kant had originally entertained, namely, "The Limits of Sensibility and Reason," but his intention comes forth even more prominently in the title that he eventually did settle on, a title he considered for the first time in a letter to Marcus Herz on 21 February 1772 (Ak 10, p. 132): for one thing he wishes to provide a **critique**, not a doctrine of **pure reason**, that would presumably amount to merely formal, not to **transcendental logic**; for another, as the word 'pure' indicates, he is not interested in presenting a psychological study, but, taking **reason** in its most encompassing sense, strives to develop a procedure to decide the validity of philosophical claims.

Kant emphasizes at a number of points in the book that he is steering a middle course between, on the one hand, the dogmatic metaphysics represented by the **Leibniz-Wolff** school and, on the other hand, the **skepticism** of **David Hume** and the **empiricism** of a **John Locke**. He wishes to avoid the errors of each of these traditions, while taking note of their respective strong points. Thus he agrees with the empiricists that cognition is limited to the realm of **experience** and he agrees with the dogmatists that moral judgments are possible beyond the limits of **sensibility**. He criticizes the former for concentrating only on the empirical origins of cognition, while reproaching the latter with being preoccupied with the a priori elements of human **thought**. Kant defends the middle ground between the two schools by developing a theory according to which pure **concepts** and **principles** of the **understanding** serve as the necessary conditions of the possibility of experience, while **ideas** of reason may be employed in a **regulative** way.

There is a number of catchphrases in the *Critique* that capture many of its basic intentions, even if they do not, of course, do justice to the great complexity of the work. Thus Kant compares his project of depicting reason as a faculty that does not simply follow **objects**, but that rather prescribes them conditions and **rules**, with some justice to the **Copernican Revolution** (B xvi–xvii). Here he marks his difference to the empiricists and gives an inkling of the role that the concepts of the understanding play in grounding possible experience. Another way of expressing the aim of the book is by asking the question "how are **synthetic judgments** a priori possible" (B 19, 73). Within the scope of this inquiry, Kant demonstrates how such propositions exist in **mathematics** and science and he discusses under what conditions they would be possible in metaphysics. To stress the need to combine sensibility with the understanding and thus to underscore the merits of the middle course between empiricism and dogmatism Kant coined the phrase "thoughts without content are empty, intuitions without concepts are blind" (A 51/B 75). Yet another often-quoted sentence expresses the conception that objects stand under the necessary conditions of the **synthesis** produced by the subject: "the conditions of the possibility of experience in general are at the same time conditions of the possibility of the objects of experience" (A 158/B 197).

Although the book has a reasonably clear and well-thought out structure (**architectonic**), it is not always obvious how all of its parts fit together; in fact, there are even passages that seem to belong to Kant's **precritical philosophy** and that the *Critique* supposedly supersedes. Some of these problems can be explained by recalling how Kant composed the book. He spent a decade working on the different parts in an apparently random order, compiling the whole only shortly before the publication of the first edition in 1781. Hence it is conceivable that drafts of various sections were placed by Kant into the final manuscript without being reread with the necessary caution. In the literature, such an attempt at explaining some of the incongruities of the book is referred to as the patchwork theory. Kant retained the structure in the second edition of 1787, though he did rewrite large parts of the first half of the book. Much, incidentally, has been made of the similarity of the structure of the *Critique* to the structure of logic treatises of his day, for example, to *La Logique ou l'Art de Penser* (1662) by Antoine Arnauld and Pierre Nicole or to the work of Joachim Georg Darjes (1714–1791). However, one should bear in mind that Kant had radically different aims in mind than did his predecessors. Owing to his intention of examining the limitations of human cognition, Kant deviated from the common schema of concept, judgment, conclusion, method in significant ways. For instance, the all important "Transcendental Aesthetic" does not fit into the old scheme at all and the "Transcendental Dialectic" is for Kant not a lesson in syllogistic reasoning but rather a critique of **illusion**.

The *Critique* starts with a "Preface" that Kant completely rewrote for the second edition; the B-version is interesting for its comparison of metaphysics with mathematics and science. In the "Introduction," Kant explains some of his technical terminology (**analytic, synthetic, a priori, a posteriori, pure**) as well as his conception of **transcendental philosophy**. The main body of the book is divided into two major parts, the "Doctrine of Elements" and the "Doctrine of Method." The first of these is, in its turn, divided into two parts, namely, the "Transcendental Aesthetic" and the "Transcendental Logic," and the last named is further divided into the "Transcendental Analytic" and the "Transcendental Dialectic." The Aesthetic, Analytic, and Dialectic deal with the human faculties of, respectively, sensibility, understanding, and reason.

In the relatively brief "**Transcendental Aesthetic**," Kant claims that **space** and **time** are neither relational orders of objects as Leibniz had maintained nor the self-subsisting entities of the **Newton**ians, but rather the **forms** of our sensibility. Here, he also formulates his doctrine of **transcendental idealism**, which forms the basis of much of his subsequent critical thought. In regard to space and time, the doctrine states that we do not cognize **things-in-themselves**, but rather only **appearances** as they stand under the conditions of our sensibility.

In a similar way, the "**Transcendental Analytic**" discusses the forms of our understanding, forms that constitute the necessary conditions for the possibility of experience and its objects. The "Analytic" is divided into two books, the "Analytic of Concepts" and the "Analytic of Principles." The former deals mainly with the **categories**. First Kant derives these concepts in a metaphysical **deduction** from the **table of judgments**, then he attempts to prove their validity for objects of experience in a **transcendental deduction**. The last mentioned section is one of the most difficult parts of the whole book, in part owing to the fact that Kant rewrote it completely for the B-edition without ever explaining his reasons for doing so. The "Analytic of Principles" is divided into three chapters. The first, "**Schematism**," again takes up the problem of the applicability of the categories to sense data, the second, "System of All Principles of the Understanding," shows how the categories apply to the forms of **intuition**, and in the third chapter, "On the Ground of the Distinction of All Objects in General into **Phenomena** and **Noumena**," Kant limits the applicability of the categories to appearances. The Appendix to the "Analytic," titled "On the **Amphiboly** of Concepts of Reflection" contains some of Kant's most concerted criticism of the dogmatists and empiricists.

The "**Transcendental Dialectic**" shows how an application of ideas of reason beyond their legitimate bounds leads to illusion. In the chapter "**Pa-**

ralogisms of Pure Reason," completely rewritten in the B-edition, Kant refutes the notion of a substantial self, while in the chapter "The Ideal of Pure Reason," he demonstrates why all arguments for the **existence of God** fail. In the in-between chapter, "**Antinomy** of Pure Reason," Kant shows the limits of the application of cosmological ideas. However, not content with merely refuting unjustified claims, he here also sketches a program for moral philosophy: while cognition of freedom is impossible, **thinking** it is legitimate. The "Appendix to the Transcendental Dialectic" contains further remarks on the regulative, rather than **constitutive** employment of certain principles of reason.

In the "Doctrine of Method," Kant presents various additions to and reflections on the first part of the book. This part is divided into four chapters. The "Discipline of Pure Reason" contains an important discussion of the difference between mathematical and philosophical method, the "Canon of Pure Reason" further explains Kant's stance on moral philosophy by pointing out that practical reason can justify rational belief about things (immortality of the soul, freedom, and God), about which theoretical reason cannot deliver cognition. The chapters "Architectonic of Pure Reason" and "History of Pure Reason" discuss in yet more detail the philosophical and historical positions of the empiricists and the dogmatists as well as Kant's own middle course between them.

The *Critique* was not an immediate success, owing perhaps to its great complexity and difficulty, but within the course of a decade, it did start attracting widespread attention, eventually becoming the subject of a vast field of scholarly endeavor, and serving as the stimulus for numerous developments in philosophy.

CULTURE. In the second half of the 18th century, an encompassing concept of culture (English and French authors often spoke of 'civilization') emerged within the European Enlightenment, a concept that referred to all of human activity both as a process and as regards its results. However, culture was also investigated as a historical phenomenon. Kant's understanding of culture gained its contours from his critical examination of **Jean-Jacques Rousseau**'s theory of historical development and of **Johann Gottfried Herder**'s philosophy of history. Kant defines culture as "the production of the aptitude of a rational being for any ends in general (thus in his freedom)"; in this sense, culture is the ultimate **purpose** that **nature** pursues with the **human** species (Ak 5, p. 431). Thanks to their "unsociable sociability," human beings left the rawness of their historical beginnings for culture, whose highest end is the perfect civic constitution, in which there is no conflict between the two natural predispositions of humans, namely, between that for the preservation of the human species as of an animal species and that for the attainment of the moral state (Ak 8, pp. 116-17). As steps in this path followed by humankind and by the individual Kant distinguishes: cultivation by art and science; social civilization; and finally, becoming moral (Ak 7, p. 324; Ak 8, p. 26). He established a **duty** to cultivate the powers of one's mind, soul, and body (Ak 6, pp. 387, 444), a duty that must commence in education with **discipline** (Ak 9, pp. 442, 449).

Although the concept of culture played a central role in **Neokantianism**, neither **Hermann Cohen**'s theory of the directions of cultural consciousness nor **Heinrich Rickert**'s theory of the sciences of culture drew on Kant's concept of culture. *See also* HISTORY.

- D -

DEDUCTION. In his **transcendental logic**, Kant did not denote with this term the inference of a conclusion from given premises, but used it in the legalistic sense of justifying a given claim. By including at least one deduction in each of the 'Analytics' of his three *Critiques*, he was legitimizing the claims raised by, respectively, the **concepts of the understanding (categories)**, the **principles** of **practical reason**, and the aesthetic **judgments** of **taste**.

The first deduction in the *Critique of Pure Reason* is the 'metaphysical' one, aimed at demonstrating that the set of **categories**, which Kant would be employing throughout his **critical philosophy**, was complete and unique. Kant accomplishes this task by deriving the table of categories from the **table of judgments**. He is satisfied that the former will possess the required characteristics, since he grasps the latter as the "universal logical functions of thinking," functions that must apply not only to all features of logical thinking but also to all judgments about **objects** (B 159). The most famous of Kant's deductions is the **transcendental deduction**, in which he attempts to prove that the categories constitute the objects of **experience** and are therefore objectively valid.

The deduction in the *Critique of Practical Reason* takes as its point of departure **moral** law, which, as an apodictically certain fact of **reason**, itself stands in no need of a deduction. Moral law then serves as the **principle** of the deduction, a deduction that aims to legitimize **freedom** and, along with it, to permit the possibility of a supra-sensible **nature**. The need for a deduction of the judgment of taste in the *Critique of Judgment* arises out of the fact that such judgments are not objective, but claim, nevertheless, universal validity. Kant's solution consisted in his emphasis on the intersubjective nature of the human faculties from which such judgments originate.

DEFINITION.   Kant already held in his **pre-critical** *Prize Essay* of 1763/1764 that **mathematics** begins with definitions, but that **philosophy** can only hope to arrive at definitions at the end of a long process of philosophical analysis (Consideration 1, § 3). Mathematical definitions are produced arbitrarily in a **synthesis**; the **concepts** contained in these definitions are constructed in accordance with the definitions. The fact that *we* construct the concepts of our definitions guarantees that we have certain **cognition** of them. In philosophy, on the other hand, we begin with concepts that we do not construct ourselves, but that are given to us, and they are indeterminate, abstract and universal, so that no definition of them is possible.

Kant retained the gist of this position in the *Critique of Pure Reason*. Given that a definition would have to exhibit "the exhaustive concept of a thing within its boundaries," Kant admits that neither empirical nor **a priori** concepts can be defined in a strict sense. In regard to the former, one can never be sure which characterizing marks are crucial and which not; in regard to the latter, the exhaustiveness of the analysis of the concept is always uncertain. Kant thus suggests explication for empirical concepts and **exposition** for a priori ones as alternatives to definitions. In addition, he reaffirms the infallible status of mathematical definitions in much the same manner as he had established them in 1763 (A 727–32/B 755–60).

DEGREE (*Grad*).   Kant generally described **magnitudes** that were continuous in terms of their possession of degrees, that is, he claimed that they were capable of diminution by infinitesimally small steps until they would be equal to zero. Such magnitudes, labeled by him intensive, were a necessary property of **sensation** (in fact they were the only such property of sensation), a property that could therefore be anticipated **a priori**. Kant dealt with intensive magnitudes in the *Critique of Pure Reason* under the heading "**Anticipations of Perception**." He had derived these **principles of pure understanding** by way of the **schemata** from the **categories of quality** and he therefore depicted the diminution of a degree, that is, of an intensive magnitude, as the transition between two of these categories, namely, **reality** and **negation**. Not surprisingly, Kant designated degree as the schema of quality. In the *Metaphysical Foundations of Natural Science*, Kant explained **matter** as far as it was subsumed under the category of quality in terms of the original **forces** of **attraction** and repulsion. Since these two forces were intensive magnitudes and thus susceptible of having degrees, matter was also conceived as filling **space** by degrees, that is, continuously. Kant expressed a clear preference for this theory of matter over the only alternative discussed by him, the atomistic hypothesis, which relied on a discontinuous magnitude, namely, absolute impenetrability.

DEMONSTRATION. Kant held that only apodictic **proofs** should be called demonstrations and that these were possible only in **mathematics**. In areas where **experience** had to be consulted, we could only be certain of a given state of things, but we could not exclude the possibility of different states. And in **philosophy**, which proceeds by acroamatic (**discursive**) proofs, we cannot arrive at intuitive certainty. Mathematics owes its special status to the fact that it derives its **cognition** from the **construction** of concepts, that is, "from the **intuition** that can be given **a priori** corresponding to the **concepts**" (A 734/B 762; Ak 9, p. 71).

DESCARTES, RENÉ (1596–1650). Although Kant's conception of the **self** ultimately differed from the one held by Descartes in significant ways, there were obvious points of contact and Kant did discuss at a number of places in his *Critique of Pure Reason* the Cartesian precept *cogito, ergo sum* (I think, therefore I am). Regarding this as no inference, but rather as a tautology, since the 'I think' immediately asserts **existence** (A 355), Kant accused Descartes of committing precisely such an error, namely, inferring existence from the **proposition** 'I think.' Kant pointed out that such an inference would have to be carried out by means of a syllogism, in which the premise "everything that thinks, exists" would have to precede the supposedly initial proposition 'I think.' Moreover, Kant asserted that on the assumption of this premise, all beings possessing the property of **thinking** would be turned into necessary ones (B 422). Kant was apparently unaware of the fact that Descartes himself had rejected such an inferential procedure in his *Reply to Objections* (Second Set, Third Point), citing exactly the same grounds as Kant did in the first part of his criticism.

Related to Kant's discussion of the *cogito* was his understanding of Descartes as a proponent of problematic **idealism**. Kant interpreted the *cogito* as the claim that only the existence of the I was indubitable, and that this left the existence of external objects unproven. He contrasted problematic idealism with the dogmatic version, which he attributed to **George Berkeley**; while disdainful of the latter, he evidently held the former in higher regard, calling it "rational and appropriate for a thorough philosophical manner of thought." In his "Refutation of Idealism," a section added to the second edition of the *Critique of Pure Reason*, Kant nevertheless suggested that problematic idealism could be invalidated, by showing that we have **experience** and not just **imagination** of external things. This proof could be achieved by demonstrating that inner experience was possible only on the presupposition of outer experience. The actual argument then begins with the assumption that the **consciousness** of my existence as determined in **time** presupposes, as all time-determinations do, something persistent. Such a persistent, however, could not be in me, since my own existence in time can be determined only by this persistent something. Kant concluded that the **perception** of this persistent was therefore possible only because of an external thing and not thanks to the mere **representation** of an external thing (B 275). In this proof, incidentally, Kant's picture of Descartes is again out of focus. Descartes claimed to have proved the existence of external objects in his *Sixth Meditation*, and he would have been equally unhappy with the label "problematic idealism," since he viewed his skepticism in regard to the senses as merely methodological, that is to say, provisional.

A further point of disagreement concerned the so-called ontological argument for the existence of **God**, which Kant repeatedly attributed to Descartes in spite of the fact that it had first been proposed by Anselm and was later taken up by a number of other thinkers as well.

The **Marburg School Neokantians** regarded Descartes as a historical predecessor of Kant. **Paul Natorp** presented in 1882 a Kantian-type study of the essential Cartesian themes in his *Descartes' Erkenntnistheorie (Descartes's Epistemology)*; **Hermann Cohen** praised especially Descartes's philosophical contribution to the founding of a "mathematical science"; **Ernst Cassirer** examined in his doctoral dissertation of 1899 Descartes's epistemological foundation of mathematics and science. *See also* GOD, PROOFS OF THE EXISTENCE OF (*Gottesbeweise*).

DESIRE (*Begierde, Begehren*).   The **faculty** of desire is, according to Kant, the power of a being "to be by means of its representations the cause of the reality of the objects of these representations" (Ak 5, p. 9; Ak 6, p. 211); by 'objects' he understands the **ends** of an action. The lower faculty of desire is involved when a material object is desired, which thus becomes the determining ground of the **will**; desire is here connected with the **pleasure** taken in the reality of an object, just as loathing is joined with displeasure. The higher faculty of desire comes into play when the will is determined by merely formal **laws** (Ak 5, pp. 21–22). Kant explicitly rejects the possibility of linking the difference between the lower and the higher faculty of desire with the different origin of pleasurable representations in the **senses** and in the **understanding** (p. 23). He speaks of desire (*Begierde, appetitio*) in cases, in which pleasure precedes the determination of the faculty of desire as its cause (Ak 6, p. 212); the faculty of desire is called will only when it is determined by **reason** (conceptually, that is, by the representation of an end) (Ak 5, p. 5; Ak 6, p. 213). In the *Anthropology from a Pragmatic Point of View*, desire is defined as the "self-determination of the power of a subject by the representation of some future thing as an effect of this representation" (Ak 7, p. 251); in his lectures on anthropology, Kant treated desire as parallel to a motive **force** in the corporeal world. *See also* FEELING; INCLINATION.

DETERMINISM. Kant had assumed from the first that nature and human **action** were determined by causal **laws** from which there was no exception. The device of explaining various phenomena by recourse to divine intervention was still in wide use at that point in time, but it was increasingly coming under attack, and Kant studiously avoided the use of miracles, explaining everything instead in terms of laws of nature. This approach is prominent in the **pre-critical** writing *Universal Natural History and Theory of the Heavens* of 1755, in which Kant tries to account for the origin of the solar system and the whole physical universe by restricting himself only to the **forces** of **attraction** and repulsion; he criticizes **Isaac Newton** for assuming that divine intervention is required in setting up and occasionally correcting the orbits of the planets.

However, Kant was then faced with the task of reconciling determinism with human freedom, a **freedom** he had always assumed to be necessary in order to guarantee a meaningful account of moral responsibility. In a dialogue inserted into the *Nova Dilucidatio* of 1755 (Ak 1, pp. 401–4), Kant combined determinism and freedom by denying the freedom of the will. This position, today known as compatibilism, had, in the 17th and 18th centuries, been defended in various forms by a number of prominent philosophers such as Thomas Hobbes, **John Locke**, **Gottfried Wilhelm Leibniz**, or **David Hume**. Along with these thinkers, Kant ended up stressing the so-called liberty of spontaneity at the cost of the liberty of indifference, that is, advocating the conception that the actor is morally accountable for her action simply because of the fact that she performed it and regardless of the fact that an alternate course of action was impossible.

During his **critical** stage, Kant became dissatisfied with this account, claiming such a liberty to be no better than the "freedom of a turnspit" (Ak 5, p. 97). His own solution, outlined for the first time in the third **antinomy** in the *Critique of Pure Reason*, was based on the conception that determinism was indeed universal at the level of **phenomena**, but that it did not have to be assumed at the level of **noumena**. This would make it possible to **think** freedom, even if **cognition** of it was unavailable. Although this solution is undoubtedly ingenious, it is so riddled with problems as to be untenable. The most common criticism is that Kant was unable to explain how **causality** of **nature** could coexist with the causality of freedom in respect to one and the same human action. However, Kant's solution is interesting, especially in view of the fact that all the alternatives (compatibilism, incompatibilism, and so forth) are also difficult to maintain.

DIALECTIC. In the course of the history of philosophy, the valuation of this term has undergone radical oscillations. While **Plato** referred with 'dialectic' to the theory of knowledge that arises from the discussion of opposing conceptions, and therefore to the highest goal of philosophical endeavor, **Aristotle** opposed it to analytic and determined it in his *Topics* as the method for drawing conclusions from the probable (*endoxa*); as probable Aristotle viewed conceptions or propositions "that appear to be true to most or to the wise."

As part of the resurrection of this Aristotelian distinction in the 18th century, Kant employed it in dividing each of his three *Critiques* into their respective parts. However, when he brands dialectics as the "logic of **illusion**" and when he further denies that it is a "doctrine of probability" (A 293/B 349), he joins the opponents of dialectics as it was developed by Cicero and his followers into a logical and rhetorical art of invention and argumentation. For Kant, the "logical topics of Aristotle" was merely an instrument of "schoolteachers and orators" who only "rationalize or garrulously chatter" about a given topic under "certain titles of thought." Kant replaced the Aristotelian topics with his own "**transcendental** topic," which has the task of judging the proper place (**sensibility** or the **understanding**) of the basic **concepts** of philosophical reflection such as identity and difference (A 268–69/B 324–25).

Kant uses the term 'dialectic' in two senses: on the one hand, it refers to the tendency of **reason** to draw false conclusions and to become entangled in contradictions (logic of illusion), on the other hand, understood as a transcendental **discipline**, it designates the procedure of uncovering such false conclusions and contradictions (**critique** of dialectical illusion) (A 293ff./B 349ff.). Kant regarded dialectical illusion as an unavoidable consequence of the quest of human reason to illegitimately extend its proper sphere of influence and to therefore go astray. As he explains, a dialectic is present both in theoretical and practical use of **pure** reason, because reason "demands the **absolute totality** of conditions for a given conditioned thing, and this can be reached only in **things-in-themselves**"; the illusion arises from the mistaken application of the **idea** of the totality of conditions to **appearances** as if they were things-in-themselves (CPrR, Part 1, Bk. 2, Ch.

1). Given the generally negative connotation of the term 'dialectic,' it is not surprising that Kant presented in his three *Critiques* much of his positive teachings in the respective **analytics**.

While **Georg Wilhelm Friedrich Hegel** presented his whole philosophy in the form of a speculative dialectic and a refined version of the concept assumed a central position in Marxist social theory, the **Neokantians** initially showed no interest in dialectic. It was only in **Paul Natorp**'s book *Platos Ideenlehre* of 1903 that the concept of dialectic in **Plato**'s positive sense was reintroduced. This inspired Nicolai Hartmann to attempt to develop the systematic connections of the principles of philosophy by making recourse to the dialectical method. After World War I, the concept of dialectic was utilized not only by the Neo-Hegelians, but also by the younger Neokantians: Jonas Cohn presented with his *Theorie der Dialektik* of 1923 a "theory of the forms of philosophy," in which he understood dialectic as a purely theoretical procedure; Siegfried Marck systematically worked out in his *Die Dialektik in der Philosophie der Gegenwart* (*Dialectic in Present Day Philosophy*) of 1929/1931 a standard of "critical dialectic," defining as dialectic "every conception of thought as a process that moves forward by means of proposition and anti-proposition." Richard Kroner, who explicitly espoused Hegel, determined dialectic in his *Von Kant bis Hegel* of 1921/1924 as a "rationally produced irrationality." *See also* TRANSCENDENTAL DIALECTIC.

DIGNITY (*Würde*). Under dignity, Kant understood an intrinsic and unconditional worth, one that can be attributed only to morality or to a rational being that determines itself to morality (Ak 4, pp. 435–36). This being, which as an **end** in itself belongs to the **kingdom of ends**, is above all price, since everything that has a price, such as skill, diligence, or wit, can be replaced by something else that is equivalent to it; however, morality cannot be replaced by anything. The ground of this dignity of the rational nature of humans lies in their **autonomy**, that is, in the self-determination of the **will** of a rational being through **moral law**, by means of which the being posits itself as an end and avoids being used as a means by the will of another being.

In his *Ethik des reinen Willens*, **Hermann Cohen** claimed that it was the "great question of modern politics" whether the "market value of labor" was compatible with the dignity of the person. Although he employed Kant's concept of dignity for his ethical reform of society, Cohen also distanced himself from the concept: on the one hand, in his criticism of capital punishment, where he found it better to make recourse to self-preservation than to dignity, and on the other hand, in his theory of virtue, where he preferred the more sober expression 'honor' to 'dignity.'

DIMENSIONS OF SPACE. In his **pre-critical** writing *Thoughts on the True Estimation of Living Forces* of 1749, Kant expressed the revolutionary idea of the possibility of Non-Euclidian spaces. By linking the properties of **space** to the properties of **forces** and by regarding the tridimensionality of space as a consequence of **Isaac Newton**'s inverse square law, which he regarded as arbitrary, Kant realized that other types of space must be possible. Thus, for instance, an inverse cube law would dictate a space endowed with different properties and different dimensions. Kant contended that along with the different laws of forces, there would be other sciences of possible spaces, claiming that these would comprise the highest geometry that a finite understanding could establish (§ 10). Unfortunately, Kant failed to pursue this possibility, which was not fully exploited by mathematicians until well into the 19th century. In his **critical** period, Kant then held that space was tridimensional, linking this property inextricably to the nature of our **sensibility**. Since Kant's philosophy of **mathematics** was thus intimately interrelated with his theory of the transcendental ideality of space, it has often been argued that the advent of Non-Euclidian geometries undermined not only Kant's theory of geometry, but also his whole teachings on space and sensibility. This charge, however, has been countered in attempts to show that Kant's theories of space and sensibility could be interpreted in such a way that they were not dependent on any specific type of geometry.

DISCIPLINE (*Disziplin, Zucht*). Kant maintained that discipline should be used against **reason**, the **inclinations**, and in education. The most interesting case of using discipline against reason is discussed in the section entitled "Discipline of Pure Reason" in the "Doctrine of Method" of the *Critique of Pure Reason*. Here, Kant deals with the different procedures in mathematics and in philosophy and comments on his transcendental **method** in order to again emphasize the need for an examination of the human cognitive faculties, especially of pure reason. He defines discipline in general as "the compulsion through which the constant propensity to stray from certain rules is limited and finally eradicated" (A 709/B 737). The discipline of reason checks the trespasses of reason and helps to avoid the deceptions that follow from them; reason must impose this discipline on itself, not for discovering truth, but for determining its own boundaries and thus for guarding against error (A 795/B 823). In general, Kant contrasted discipline with **culture**, viewing the former as a mostly negative, restraining tendency, while the latter was marked by a positive effort to cultivate, educate, or teach (A 709/B 737; Ak 9, p. 449). He deviated from this practice somewhat in the *Critique of Judgment*, where he concocted the expression "culture of discipline" (*Kultur der Zucht*) (§ 83). Discipline in the moral sphere means restraining the inclinations, "freeing the **will** from the despotism of desires" (ibid.). Discipline also plays a major role in Kant's piece *On Education;* here it is understood as a taming of the wildness of humans and as a holding back of their animal nature (Ak 9, p. 449). In the *Metaphysics of Morals* Kant, however, also warns against excessive (self-)discipline and claims that it can be meritorious only if it is accompanied by joyousness (Ak 6, pp. 452, 485).

DISCURSIVE. Throughout his **critical philosophy**, Kant consistently distinguished discursive procedure that was based on **concepts** from an intuitive one. He considered the former to fall within the sphere of the **understanding**, while the latter belonged for him to the domain of **sensibility**. Accordingly, Kant separated discursive **cognition** through concepts from intuitive (*intuitiv*) cognition through **intuitions** (*Anschauungen*). In the introduction to his *Logic*, Kant defined discursive cognition as based on the characteristic features of things, that is, as occurring "through representations that elevate to the ground of cognition something that is common to several things." Since the **method** of **philosophy** is based on concepts, it is discursive, in contrast to the method of **mathematics**, which is intuitive (A 734–35/B 762–63). Kant introduces a less general and encompassing distinction in his discussion of the **principles of pure understanding**, where he demarcates the discursive certainty of the so-called **dynamical principles** from the intuitive certainty of the **mathematical principles**. This distinction does not imply any major consequences for Kant's epistemology, given that he himself admits that the certainty is complete in both cases (A 161–62/B 201).

DISJUNCTIVE JUDGMENTS. *See* COMMUNITY.

DISPOSITION (*Gesinnung*). The word '*Gesinnung*' was introduced into German by Gotthold Ephraim Lessing as a rendition of the French term '*sentiment.*' Shortly after, Kant employed the noun as a label for the inner **principle** of the **maxims** of the **will**, holding it distinct from the Latinate '*Disposition,*' by which he understood a merely subjective kind of attitude irrelevant to ethics (Ak 4, p. 435). In his treatment of the problem of **evil** in the first part of his *Religion within the Boundaries of Mere Reason*, Kant develops the notion that disposition as "the first subjective ground of the

adoption of the maxims" can only be a single one, that it concerns the entire use of our **freedom**, and that it pertains to our power of choice by nature (Ak 6, p. 25). This leaves him with the task of explaining how the transition from an evil or merely lawfully acting **person** to a morally good one can be effected "by a revolution in the disposition of the human being" (pp. 47ff.).
Morality consists for Kant in the "morally good disposition," which he equates with **virtue** (Ak 4, p. 435), not in **actions** or their success. This opposition has frequently been criticized in post-Kantian discussions. Max Weber accentuated it by speaking of a bottomless chasm between actions that stand under maxims based purely on an ethics of disposition (*Gesinnungsethik*) and maxims founded purely on an ethics of responsibility (*Verantwortungsethik*), claiming that in politics these two kinds of ethics would have to supplement each other. From a Kantian point of view, it may seem somewhat paradoxical that the German word '*Gesinnungsethik*' has come to signify a morality based on convictions of the heart, and it would therefore be an error to classify Kant under this heading, as, e.g., Weber had done. *See also* DUTY; ETHICS.

DIVISIBILITY (*Teilbarkeit*). *See* CONTINUITY.

DOGMATISM. *See* EMPIRICISM; SKEPTICISM.

DOUBLE AFFECTION. A theory proposed by the Kant-scholar Erich Adickes to account for the multiple relationships holding between the self as it appears to us and as it is in itself as well as between the **appearance** of an object and the **thing-in-itself**. The theory states that the thing-in-itself is not the direct cause of our **intuitions**, but affects only the self-in-itself, while the object of appearance affects the appearing self. One may represent these relations by means of a rectangle, whose upper corners stand for, from left to right, the thing-in-itself and the self-in-itself, while the lower two corners represent, again from left to right, the object of appearance and the appearing self. The vertical lines mark Kant's claim that the thing-in-itself is only the other side of the appearance, while the upper horizontal line expresses some relation that is unknown to us and the lower horizontal line represents **causality**. The textual evidence for such a reading of Kant is slim, not only in the *Critique of Pure Reason*, but also in the *Opus Postumum*, on which Adickes's conjecture is largely based. Not surprisingly, the theory does not enjoy much support among Kant scholars, though it is still occasionally mentioned. *See also* AFFECTION.

DURATION (*Dauer*). In his 'Proof' of the **principle of pure understanding** of **substance**, Kant argues that since **time** in itself cannot be perceived, all temporal relations or time determinations are therefore possible only thanks to "that which persists in a substratum of the empirical representation of time." Given that duration, defined as the magnitude of **existence** in different parts of the temporal series, is such a temporal relation, it too is possible only thanks to something persistent, namely, substance. Kant claims that in a mere sequence without substance, existence "is always disappearing and beginning, and never has the least magnitude" (A 182-3/B 226). In other words, substance is the necessary condition for the possibility of duration.

DUTY. No concept of Kant's **ethics** has received as much attention as the concept of duty. In academic discussions, it has supplied the name to a whole theory of morality, namely, deontological ethics. Kant was, however, by no means the first one to have utilized duty as a basic concept of ethics. In the 18th century, it figured prominently in the moral philosophy of **Christian Wolff** and especially in that of his opponent Christian August Crusius, and knowledge of the ancient tradition that had originated with the Stoics was disseminated in Germany by Christian Garve's translation of Cicero's *De Officiis* (1783). But it was Kant who first elevated duty to the forefront of an ethical theory.

To have a duty means for Kant to submit one's **will** under an **ought** in the form of an unconditionally valid norm, by which one is not already abiding of one's own accord. A part of duty is the constraint by moral **law** that is ordinarily opposed to and certainly not founded in actually existing **incentives**, namely, **inclinations**. As the only subjective motive for abiding by the objective duty imposed by moral law, Kant admits **respect** for the law (Ak 4, p. 400; Ak 5, pp. 73ff.). Moreover, performing one's duty has a moral value only if one acts not merely in conformity with duty when an inclination, for example, pity, is present, but out of duty, without any inclination or even against it. This difference is captured in the *Critique of Practical Reason* by the distinction between legality and morality (Ak 5, p. 81). The moral worth of an **action** out of duty is also independent of the intention of the action; the worth lies exclusively in the **principle** of the will. The principle of such a duty can only be the categorical **imperative**, since duty as a "practical unconditional necessity of action" is thought as relevant to all rational beings (except for God) (Ak 4, p. 425). As a correlative to the categorical imperative, the awareness of duty that Kant ascribes to every human being contains both the knowledge of an obligation and the constraint to fulfill the obligation, a constraint that originates in **pure prac-**

tical reason. Kant distinguishes between the awareness of the human being that he "ought to perform his duty quite unselfishly" and the experience "that no one can become aware with certainty of having performed his duty quite unselfishly" (Ak 8, p. 284). The sublimity and greatness of duty (Ak 5, p. 86) proceeds from the insight gained in the *Critique of Practical Reason* that the moral law is not deducible, but that the awareness of the law imposes itself on us as a "fact of pure practical reason" (p. 31).

From the categorical imperative, there must also be derived the particular "imperatives of duty" (Ak 4, p. 421). Following the tradition of **natural law**, Kant distinguishes between duties toward oneself and duties toward others, which he both further divides into complete and incomplete ones. Complete duties, for example, the proscription of lying and of committing suicide, are characterized by the fact that they must be obeyed unconditionally and that the proscribed and prescribed actions are determined unambiguously. Kant is also in agreement with the natural law tradition in claiming that there can be no conflicts between duties, though he differs by founding this claim on the concept of duty. Although a conflict of obligations is for him inconceivable, he does admit that the "grounds of obligation" may be in conflict, in which case the stronger ground should prevail (Ak 6, p. 224). Kant's distinction between legal and ethical duties has proven to be helpful for formulating rules for deciding cases of conflict (pp. 218-19). The former are characterized as external, and coercible, though he still understands them as moral, namely, as "indirectly ethical" duties (p. 221).

Friedrich Schiller (1759-1805) voiced a common misgiving, when in his *Anmut und Würde* (1793) he complained of the severe nature of Kant's concept of duty. Schiller wished for a conception of human beings that would allow pleasure and duty to be combined: reason should be gladly obeyed, because an inclination to perform duty is a necessary prerequisite on the path to moral perfection.

In **Hermann Cohen**'s *Ethik des reinen Willens*, the concept of duty does not play a central role anymore. Cohen considered the general idea of duty to be contained in the concept of law. Particular duties are treated as virtues, the feeling of duty finds its expression in loyalty.

Wilhelm Windelband recognizes the mere awareness of duty as a universal principle of morality, but he refuses to take up, as Kant did, the concept of generality in the formulation of this principle. Instead, Windelband claims that the content of particular moral rules cannot be derived from the principle, but that it is rather conditioned by experiential circumstances. Nevertheless, he admits that it is possible to develop further duties out of the formal principle of the awareness of duty, if fulfilling the principle is understood as the highest end. These further duties also remain formal, but they, for example, self-control, do form the means for the production of the content of the awareness of duty.

Bruno Bauch characterizes the awareness of duty as nonarbitrariness, attachment, and voluntariness; the last mentioned point replaces the Kantian notion of the constraining nature of duty, a notion that in the post-Kantian philosophy remained highly controversial.

For Leonard Nelson, just as for Kant, the unconditioned precept of an action that amounts to duty originates in self-legislation. Unlike for Kant, however, the principle of duty for Nelson needs to be supplemented by some content. Nelson distinguishes his position in moral philosophy not only from consequentialistic ethics (*Erfolgsethik*), but also from "formalistic ethics," for which moral law can have no further content. For Nelson, this content cannot consist of the precept to aim at just any end, but only of limiting the aim in the process of following positive ends in view of the conflict between one's own and others' interests. All duties ultimately originate from the precept of justice to "act justly." With this very brief version of moral law, Nelson declares justice to be the one and only criterium of all duties, including the so-called duties toward oneself such as self-preservation, honor, and truthfulness. He thus connects the determination of duties and of rights: the content of a duty is the respect for the interests of others; the duty receives its content from the rights of the others.

DYNAMICAL AND MATHEMATICAL CATEGORIES, PRINCIPLES, AND IDEAS. *See* MATHEMATICAL AND DYNAMICAL CATEGORIES, PRINCIPLES, AND IDEAS.

DYNAMICS. *See* *METAPHYSICAL FOUNDATIONS OF NATURAL SCIENCE.*

- E -

EDUCATION. *See* DISCIPLINE.

EGO. *See* PSYCHOLOGY; SOUL; TRANSCENDENTAL UNITY OF APPERCEPTION.

EMPIRICISM. With his **critical philosophy**, Kant claimed that he was steering a middle course between the traditions of rationalism, which he generally referred to as dogmatism, and empiricism, which he often closely associated with **skepticism**. He understood empiricism as an approach that recognizes **sense experience** as the sole source of **cognition** and that seeks to explain only the genesis of cognition, but not its legitimacy, while he viewed dogmatism as the attempt to explain everything merely on the basis of **ideas** without (sufficient) recourse to sensory experience. Kant argued against the two schools throughout his critical works. Typical of his general attitude is his remark in the section on the "**Amphiboly**," where he accused the 'rationalist' **Gottfried Wilhelm Leibniz** of intellectualizing the **appearances** and the 'empiricist' **John Locke** of sensitivizing the **concepts** of the **understanding** (A 271/B 327).

The most concerted effort to deal with the two positions occurs in the "**Antinomies**." Here, Kant presented rationalist tenets in each of the four theses and the empiricist replies in the antitheses. In this connection, Kant discussed at some length the advantages and the disadvantages of each tradition. He praised the empiricist for providing "a maxim for moderating our claims" and for extending our understanding to its maximum through experience, that is, for being useful in the realm of theoretical philosophy. He criticized the empiricist for not being able to deal properly with **moral** ideas, since these extend beyond the bounds of experience, and he also accused the empiricists of often turning dogmatic, thus sharing that vice with the rationalists. He alleged that both parties end up saying more than they are entitled to. The empiricist wrongly denies moral ideas, the rationalist admits those, but attempts to explain natural appearances in terms of ideas rather than by means of physical explanation (A 468–72/B 496–500). Kant's own critical stance seeks to derive the best from both traditions while avoiding their respective errors. Thus, he admits with the empiricists that all cognition commences with experience, but agrees with the rationalists that it must draw on **pure** concepts and **judgments**. In the moral sphere, the empiricists are correct with their denial of cognition, but Kant goes along with the rationalists in not leaving things at that. His compromise consists of the claim that **thinking** rather than cognizing is the only legitimate approach that, moreover, also turns out to be fully sufficient for grounding moral judgments.

Kant assigned many of his philosophical predecessors to one of the two camps. In order to do so, he often simplified their true positions, presenting ideal philosophies rather than true historical ones. In various places in his critical writings, Kant named as empiricists **Aristotle**, Epicure, and Locke for epistemology, **David Hume** and Francis Hutcheson for ethics, and, along with the last two, Edmund Burke and Lord Kames for aesthetics, while situating **Plato**, **René Descartes**, Leibniz, **Christian Wolff**, and Alexander Gottlieb Baumgarten in the rationalist camp. *See also CRITIQUE OF PURE REASON.*

END. *See* PURPOSE (*Zweck*); PURPOSIVENESS (*Zweckmässigkeit*).

ENLIGHTENMENT (*Aufklärung*). Kant expressed his views on enlightenment fairly late, at a point at which the era of Enlightenment in Germany was nearly over. He did so in the journal *Berlinische Monatsschrift* (December 1784) in answer to the question "What is enlightenment?" raised in that journal a year earlier by Johann Friedrich Zöllner. Kant linked his famous definition of enlightenment, namely, "the human being's emergence from his self-incurred tutelage" (especially in matters of religion), to the postulate "have courage to use your own reason" (Ak 8, p. 35). He did not think that it was justified to speak of his own day and age as an "enlightened era," since in such an era all humans would have to be able to abide by the above postulate. Instead, he described his own time as a "period of enlightenment," because it seemed evident that there was a reduction of the hindrances to universal enlightenment (p. 40).

What Kant regarded as essential in this process was the kind of use that humans make of their **freedom**. For him, enlightenment is significantly advanced when, especially in matters of religion, the freedom to publicly use **reason** is secured. In making this demand, Kant was primarily concerned with the freedom of the men of learning to be able to express their thoughts publicly. This freedom was also to be extended to government officials, the clergy, and army officers, though not in their official functions, but in their occasional role as men of learning; if they used reason in their official acts, then this was, in fact, private use of reason that was subject to limitations.

When Kant passed his judgment on the dispute about Spinozism between Friedrich Heinrich Jacobi and Moses Mendelssohn two years later in his further article for the same journal, "What Does It Mean to Orient Oneself in Thinking?" he was already troubled by the possibility that enlightened thinking could have undesirable consequences, namely, atheism and fatalism. He therefore tied thinking for oneself (*Selbstdenken*) to the **postulates** of **practical reason**, which constitute the contents of rational **religion** (pp. 146–47).

ENTHUSIASM (*Schwärmerei*). In his **pre-critical** writing *Observations on the Feeling of the Beautiful and Sublime* of 1764, Kant distinguished, in a similar fashion as the Earl of Shaftesbury, enthusiasm from fanaticism, defining the former as an inflamation of the mind beyond the appropriate measure by "a maxim of patriotic virtue, friendship, or religion," and the latter as a state in which one believes to be "in an immediate and extraordinary community with a higher nature" (Ak 2, p. 251). In the *Critique of*

Judgment, Kant again denied that reason could approve enthusiasm, defining the latter now as "an idea of the good with **affect**." He classified it, nevertheless, as aesthetically sublime, because it strongly and enduringly supports the commitment to morality, for example, to the willingness of the citizens of a state to defend their rights (Ak 5, p. 272; Ak 7, p. 86).

EPISTEMOLOGY (*Erkenntnistheorie, Theorie der Erkenntnis*). The German expressions for epistemology or theory of **cognition** were coined only after Kant's death, probably sometime during the 1820s or 1830s, and did not become established parts of the German academic discourse until Eduard Zeller's article "Bedeutung und Aufgabe der Erkennntnistheorie" (Meaning and Task of Epistemology) of 1862. However, questions of the origin, conditions, presuppositions, extent, boundaries, and principles of cognition had been raised already during antiquity, and, at least according to a very common conception, philosophy underwent a decisive turn toward epistemology during the 17th century, owing especially to the work of **René Descartes, Gottfried Wilhelm Leibniz,** and **John Locke.** So there is no contradiction involved in claiming that Kant contributed with his **transcendental philosophy** in a highly significant fashion to the development of the theory of cognition, even if he himself never used the corresponding expression nor any of its standard, contemporary equivalents such as 'gnoseology.' Kant's *Critique of Pure Reason* is first and foremost an examination of the human cognitive powers. Although he was concerned with placing **metaphysics** on a secure foundation, he attempted to do this by inquiring into the cognitive validity of metaphysical propositions, and he based this inquiry on a concerted effort to establish the conceptual apparatus that would mark the necessary conditions of the possibility of **experience** and thus also of the **objects** of experience. The gist of Kant's contribution to epistemology is perhaps best summarized by his emphasis on the question *quid juris*, that is, on the inquiry into the *legitimacy* of philosophical claims.

In spite of various departures from Kant, the **Neokantians'** theories of knowledge essentially adhered to Kant's philosophy by dealing with transcendental theories of the conditions of the possibility or of the validity of cognition, by leaving questions of the genesis of cognition to empirical psychology, and by rejecting an ontology understood as a basic, underlying discipline. **Hermann Cohen** determined epistemology, which he also labeled "critique of cognition," as a theory of 'pure' thought that produces the foundations of mathematical and scientific cognition. In the **Southwestern German School of Neokantianism**, epistemology was, roughly speaking, transformed into a theory of **value.**

ETHER, CALORIC (*Äther, Wärmestoff*). Starting with his **pre-critical** period, Kant suggested at a number of points in his writing career that some hypothetical **matter** or other (fire-matter, magnetic matter, caloric) could be employed as an explanatory principle in natural philosophy. However, it was not until he started compiling the notes that later became known as the *Opus Postumum* that he began working out the possible functions and properties of such a matter in any detail. In his last work, Kant forged the terms 'ether' and 'caloric,' which he almost invariably treated as synonyms, into key concepts of his project of a transition from the **metaphysics** of nature to **physics**.

His recourse to ether may have been reinforced by the revolution effected in **chemistry** by Antoine Laurent de Lavoisier (1743–1794), though Kant eventually made much wider and more speculative use of the term than Lavoisier had ever envisaged. Similarly to the famous French chemist, Kant attempted to explain the differences between the three states of matter (solid, liquid, gas) by reference to caloric. However, for him, ether was not an empirical entity, rather it was an **a priori concept** that helped to extend the conceptual realm into the empirical one. Ether was meant to provide philosophical foundations for science in a way that the concepts of the *Critique of Pure Reason* and even of the *Metaphysical Foundations of Science* could not do, because they were too formal and insufficiently specific.

Kant attributed characteristics to ether by means of which he was then able to explain various phenomena of nature. He claimed that ether was imponderable, incoercible, present in the whole universe, and that it penetrated all substances; moreover, it was supposed to remain in the same place, though being subject to a permanent oscillatory motion. Kant assigned several functions to this hypothetical matter: as possessing internal oscillatory motion it could guarantee that the lever arm required for weighing would remain rigid, it could account for cohesion, for the original forces of **attraction** and repulsion, also for the continuity of the world; by proclaiming that it provided the ground for perpetual movement, Kant tied it to the modal **category** of **necessity**. Eventually, Kant was no longer content with treating ether as merely hypothetical, and he then attempted to prove, in a **transcendental deduction**, that ether is a necessary condition of the possibility of **experience**, and thus objectively valid.

The concept of ether enjoyed some credence in the science of the 18th and 19th centuries, though in a different form from Kant's. Eventually, the concept was given up, when it was realized that it was fictitious.

ETHICAL SOCIALISM. **Hermann Cohen**'s conception of state and society, as it was presented mainly in his *Ethik des reinen Willens* (1904, 2nd ed. 1907), was strongly linked to Kant's practical philosophy, in spite of the fact that Kant himself was an advocate of a laissez-faire, libertarian system of government. There is a number of points of connection. On a general level, Cohen, in a Kantian vein, emphasized the role of the ethical ideal and downplayed the significance of actually existing social and political conditions, especially as they manifested themselves in their economic form. The true concept of socialism was for Cohen the ethical one. This prompted him to distance himself from Karl Marx's materialism, as he considered the latter's notion that mankind's struggle for improvement is a product of economic conditions to be self-contradictory.

On a more specific level, Cohen explicitly referred to Kant's version of the categorical **imperative** as it is stated in the *Groundwork of the Metaphysics of Morals:* "Act so that you treat humanity, whether in your own person or in that of another, always as an end and never as a means only." This led him to stress that a worker was never to be treated as a commodity. In addition, he derived the motivation for his idea of a cooperatively constituted government and society from Kant's remarks on the "systematic union of different rational beings through common laws" and from his expression "realm of ends." Furthermore, as Cohen fully accepted Kant's emphasis of the central role that **freedom** was to play in ethics, he correspondingly stressed the importance of freedom for social and political thought.

Cohen's differences with Kant can be traced to other influences on him, for example, to the socialism of **Friedrich Albert Lange**, and especially to the Messianic tradition of **Judaism**. The latter led Cohen to claim that politics was to look neither to the present nor to a glorious past, but rather to the future eternal continuation of the effort to realize morality. Similarly, Cohen envisioned that the primary role of freedom was to guarantee the future realization of humanity. *See also* MARBURG SCHOOL OF NEOKANTIANISM; NEOKANTIANISM.

ETHICS, MORAL PHILOSOPHY. In the *Critique of Pure Reason*, Kant divided systematic philosophy from **pure reason** into a **metaphysics** of nature and a metaphysics of morals. The latter pertains to "that which should be" (A 840/B 868) and contains principles of reason that "determine action and omission **a priori** and make them necessary" (A 841/B 869). This discipline, also called by Kant "pure moral philosophy" or "pure morals," comprises the rational part of ethics, while the **empirical** part is labeled "practical" or "moral anthropology" (Ak 4, p. 388; Ak 6, p. 217). Pure moral philosophy seeks the ground of obligation of moral precepts "not in the nature of the human being or in the circumstances of the world into which he is placed, but a priori merely in **concepts** of pure reason" (Ak

4, p. 389) as "the principles of a possible pure will" (p. 390). Such philosophy aims at a **universal** and necessary practical **law** that determines the **will** of every rational being.

In his *Metaphysics of Morals*, Kant distinguished ethical and juridical legislation. Both make a given **action** a **duty**, but only in the former is the duty at the same time the **incentive** of the action, while in the latter duty does not belong to the concept of a law (Ak 6, pp. 218–19). On this difference between morality and legality, Kant grounds the division of the metaphysics of morals as a "system of the doctrine of duties" into a doctrine of **virtue** and a doctrine of right (p. 379). While the doctrine of right is concerned with duties that are based on "external legislation," the doctrine of virtue (*ethica*) deals with duties that do not stand under external laws. This distinction has far-reaching consequences; owing to it, Kant may be considered as the founder of a liberal legal and political theory.

Kant rejected all claims that the foundation of morals requires the idea of **God** and that the compliance with duty demands religious motivation. However, he thought of morals as leading to religion, since morals is oriented toward the **highest good**, which can be attained only on the supposition of the existence of God and of the immortality of the **soul**.

Around 1880, there was a noticeable increase in interest in Germany in ethics and, along with it, in the ethics of Kant. In the **Marburg School of Neokantianism**, the focus was, on the one hand, on the problem of the transition from **epistemology** to ethics and therefore on the methodological relationship between these first two parts of the system, and, on the other hand, on the interpretation of the categorical **imperative** in terms of **ethical socialism**. In addition, **Hermann Cohen** criticized Kant's separation of law and morals, conceiving of ethics as the realm of the principles of law. In the **Southwestern German School of Neokantianism, Bruno Bauch** attempted to found ethics on the philosophy of **value**. Leonard Nelson, who took up **Jakob Friedrich Fries**'s interpretation of Kant, also criticized the separation of the duties of law from the duties of **virtue**; he distinguished the doctrine of right from the doctrine of virtue or ethics in a strict sense of the word by claiming that the former is concerned with the demands of the legal order of a society rather than with actions of individuals. *See also CRITIQUE OF PRACTICAL REASON; GROUNDWORK OF THE METAPHYSICS OF MORALS.*

EVIL (*das Böse*). In his *Critique of Practical Reason*, Kant distinguished between physical ill (*Übel*), which is related to "the sensory state of the **person**," and moral ill or evil (*Böses*), which has to do with the **will** or with **actions**. A thing cannot be called 'evil'; only "the manner of acting, that is,

only the **maxim** of the will, and consequently the acting person" may be
held to be such (Ak 5, p. 60). Evil does not, therefore, endanger the natural
order. It gains relevance only in the course of Kant's discussion in his *Religion within the Limits of Mere Reason* of the question why humans act
according to evil maxims rather than in conformity to the categorical imperative. Kant claims that such failure must be attributed to **freedom** rather
than to sensory instinctive nature. The acceptance of good maxims is based
on the original predisposition of human nature toward **good**, the acceptance
of evil maxims on the natural propensity toward evil. If the propensity toward evil is to count as morally relevant, it must not be conceived as innate,
but must be viewed as brought upon us by ourselves. Kant answers his
question by declaring the propensity to be a nontemporal intelligible deed
(*peccatum originarium*). This 'natural' and yet not natural (because it is our
own fault) propensity toward evil is called the radical (*wurzelhaft*) evil in
human nature (pp. 31–32). Its origin in reason remains inexplicable for
Kant. Its consequence is that people invert the "moral order," that is, they
subordinate the moral law to self-love. Not self-love, inclination, or sensibility as such are morally evil, it is rather the assessment of them as positive
in relation to moral **autonomy** under the law that is evil. To be a good person one must not only develop the predisposition toward good, one must
also combat evil, since the latter is characterized precisely by the fact that
one does not *will* to resist the inclinations that tempt one to transgress
against moral law (pp. 57–58).

EXISTENCE (*Dasein, Existenz, Sein*). See ACTUALITY, BEING.

EXPERIENCE (*Erfahrung*).   In the 18th century, the traditional complex
of the different meanings of 'experience' underwent a thorough change.
The notion of "being experienced," that is, possessing a trove of knowledge
amassed in the course of a person's life or in the development of a culture
increasingly lost importance for epistemology and was replaced by the interest, on the part of intellectuals, in situations in which one could *make*
experiences. Thus for Kant, the experiences of foreign countries, peoples,
and cultures related in travel reports provided the foundation for his
ethnographically and ethnologically oriented attempt to gain knowledge of
humans (*Anthropology from a Pragmatic Point of View*, *Physical Geography*). While for the young Kant still working within the framework of the
Leibniz-Wolff school, 'experience' at least initially stood for the exemplary knowledge of the particular and was therefore subsumed under the
expression "historical experience," the emphasis gradually began to shift

toward the notion of 'experience' in the sense of a process of acquiring knowledge by means of observation and experiment (B xiii).

Although in his **critical** epistemology, Kant admits that from a temporal point of view (psychological genesis) all human **cognition** commences with sensible experience (sensation, perception), he nevertheless emphasizes that cognition must contain, next to the **matter** of **sensation**, also a nonempirical **form** without which it would have no objective **validity**. More precisely, experience qua empirical cognition consists of a connection (synthesis) of the **manifold** given by sensibility, a **synthesis** that is performed by the **understanding** in a **judgment**. While Kant in his **pre-critical** *Inaugural Dissertation* still localized the synthetic function in the logical employment of the understanding rather than in a real one (§ 5), in the *Critique of Pure Reason* he grounded the form of cognition in the **transcendental** rules of **pure thinking** of an object (A 55/B 80). The manifold brought by these rules (**categories, principles of pure understanding**) under a **unity** is the **object** of experience. The relationship between experience and its object is determined by the supreme principle of synthetic judgments: "The conditions of the possibility of experience in general are at the same time conditions of the possibility of the objects of experience" (A 158/B 197).

Unlike synthetic judgments a priori, judgments of experience (synthetic judgments **a posteriori**) possess only a comparative **universality**. In addition, Kant characterizes them as **contingent** (B 3–4): although the manifold of sensations, intuitions, or perceptions is necessarily connected in experience (B 218; P, § 22), such a necessity does not entail the material necessity of the existence of an empirically cognized object (A 226/B 279), since experience tells us only "what there is, but not that it must be thus and not otherwise" (A 1). In the *Prolegomena*, Kant distinguishes the objective validity of the judgments of experience from the merely subjective validity of the judgments of **perception** (§§ 18ff.).

The pre-critical Kant conceived of inner experience as "an immediately evident consciousness" (in the sense of **René Descartes**'s notion of intuition), claiming that it could help to supply, in a Newtonian spirit, the method in metaphysics. In the first *Critique*, he fully abandoned this idea. As all other experience, inner experience has an a priori component and presupposes above all the **transcendental unity of apperception** (cogito). Kant joins to this rejection of **empiricism** a refutation of material **idealism** by proving that inner experience cannot claim priority over outer experience in founding cognition and the certainty of cognition (B 274ff.). The illusion of this priority is demolished by the insight that the immediate self-certainty of the '**I think**' includes no (inner) experience and therefore no cognition.

The empirical consciousness of my self is rather the determination of what is given in inner intuition by self-affection (B 68).

Kant's analysis of experience serves not only as a foundation for a nonempirical epistemology but also as a **critique** of **metaphysical** claims. Kant stresses repeatedly that a priori cognition is possible only of objects of **possible experience** (B 166; P, § 57). In addition, he insists that there is only one experience (just as there is only one space and one time), "in which all perceptions are represented as in thoroughgoing and lawlike connection" (A 110). While in the first *Critique* Kant regarded the question "how are synthetic judgments a priori possible?" as the guide to the critique of metaphysics (B 19), in his later years he claimed that it was the question "how is experience possible?" that represented the highest task of **transcendental philosophy** (Ak 20, p. 275). Based on this, Kant then attempted to develop a theory of scientific experience.

Hermann Cohen presented his interpretation of Kant's theoretical philosophy under the label *Kant's Theory of Experience* (1871, 2nd ed. 1885), arguing that Kant had discovered a new concept of experience and that he had delivered with the *Critique of Pure Reason* a "critique of experience" (p. 3) that had clarified the possibility of experience in a transcendental investigation. Cohen conceived of metaphysics as consisting of nothing but the problem of how scientific experience was possible. While for Kant experience comprises both the matter of sensible sensations and a form that originates in our own faculty of cognition, Cohen's theory of experience concentrates only on form and situates all reality in possible experience. Cohen identified experience with mathematical science, considering the latter, however, not as empirical, but as a priori cognition. Under the heading of a transcendental theory of experience, he then included only the conditions of the validity of a priori cognition. He canceled the sensible, material component of experience, integrating it, at the same time, into a determination through form. Cohen grounded this expansion of the a priori into the realm of the absolutely empirical in his interpretation of the principle of the **"Anticipations of Perception."**

EXPOSITION (*expositio, Erörterung*). Since Kant did not think that **definitions** in **philosophy** were possible, he attempted to supply alternative methods for explicating and denoting the contents of a given **concept**. One such means was provided by the term exposition, by which he understood "the distinct **representation** of that which belongs to a concept" (A 23/B 38). However, he made significant use of this term only in connection with the concepts of **space** and **time** in the second edition version of the **Transcendental Aesthetic** in the *Critique of Pure Reason*. Here, he distinguished between a **metaphysical** exposition as the distinct representation of that which belongs to an **a priori** concept (A 23/B 38), and a **transcendental** exposition that explains a concept as a **principle**, leading to the "insight into the possibility of other **synthetic cognitions** a priori" (B 40).

EXTENSION (*Ausdehnung*). Unlike **René Descartes**, Kant made no great use of this concept in his epistemology, while in his philosophy of science he placed it squarely behind the much more central concept of **force**. This is apparent in his first **pre-critical** piece *Thoughts on the True Estimation of Living Forces* (1749), in which Kant rejected the Cartesian conception that **bodies** are defined by their extension, and defended instead the Leibnizian notion that force is present in bodies before extension (§ 1). In his further writings on physics or its conceptual foundations, such as the *Monadologia Physica* (1756), the *Metaphysical Foundations of Natural Science*, and the *Opus Postumum*, Kant consistently maintained the theory that physical entities, be they physical monads, **matter**, or bodies, occupy space not simply because of their extension but because of the forces of **attraction** and repulsion.

- F -

FACT (*factum, Faktum, Tatsache*). Kant used the Latin *'factum'* and its two German renditions more or less interchangeably. Unfortunately, although he employed these words only a limited number of times in his writings, his usage was not completely consistent, perhaps because in each instance he was attempting to prove some rather specific point. One place at which Kant employed all three words is at the beginning of the "**Transcendental Deduction**" in the *Critique of Pure Reason*. Here, he explained his aims in the deduction by drawing attention to the juridical distinction between the questions *quid juris* and *quid facti;* while the former concerns the lawfulness or the entitlement of a legal claim, the latter has to do just with the fact (*Tatsache*). In philosophy, *quid juris* pertains to the justification of **cognition**, *quid facti* to its genesis: one inquires after the fact (*Faktum*) from which our possession of a given **concept** has arisen. Kant was here contrasting his own attempt to prove the legitimacy of the **categories** with empiristic epistemology, especially as he ascribed it to **John Locke** (A 84-85/B 116-17).

More or less unrelated to this meaning of 'fact' as the genesis of cognition is Kant's assertion in the *Critique of Practical Reason* that there exists a fact of **pure practical reason**. Because the consciousness of the fundamental **moral law** can neither be denied nor be derived from antecedent data of reason nor yet based on any pure or empirical **intuition**, Kant calls such consciousness a "fact of reason" (Part 1, Bk. 1, Ch. 1, § 7). Some clarity, but also additional confusion, is introduced by the third place at which Kant discusses facts (*res facti, Tatsachen*), namely, in the *Critique of Judgment* (§ 91). Here, he defines facts as "**objects** for concepts whose objective reality can be proved." He mentions three examples of such facts. First, there are mathematical properties of magnitudes in geometry. Although this is more or less clear, given that, as Kant himself points out, such properties "are capable of an **a priori** presentation for the theoretical use of reason," some residual uncertainty persists in regard to the relation of this passage to the *Prolegomena*, where Kant assumes the same fact that a priori propositions in **mathematics** (and **natural science**) exist, without, however, explicitly speaking of facts (§§ 6, 14). Second, this time more or less in keeping with the usage in the "Transcendental Deduction," Kant claims that things that can be exhibited in **experience** may count as facts. And third, he states that the "**idea** of **freedom**" is a fact, whose reality is exhibited by the practical laws of pure reason and, in accordance with these, in real acts, and therefore in experience. This is clearly at some odds with the explication of the "fact of practical reason," though a link is provided by Kant's claim that the consciousness of moral law is inseparably connected with the consciousness of the freedom of the will (CPrR, Part 1, Bk. 1, Ch. 1, § 7, Deduction, no. 1).

One of the most important characterizing features of the **Marburg School of Neokantianism** was the attempt to ground epistemology by reference to the fact of science (*Faktum der Wissenschaft*). Instead of seeking the given in sensations, **Hermann Cohen** focused on the given in the laws of mathematical science, pointing to Kant's claim in the *Prolegomena* (§ 2) and in the second edition of the *Critique of Pure Reason* (B 14–18) that synthetic judgments a priori really do exist in mathematics and physics. This fact then provided Cohen with his starting point in working out his version of the **transcendental method**. However, Cohen rejected Kant's fact of pure practical reason. **Paul Natorp** supplemented in his own system the fact of science with facts of culture (*Kulturfakta*) such as morality, art, and religion, on which he then built his systematic philosophy of culture. In doing this, he interpreted the fact as a *fieri* in order to underscore that cognition is an infinite task or **problem**.

FACULTY (*Fakultät*).   Following an old tradition dating back to the founding of the universities between the 15th and 17th centuries, most German universities in the 18th century were divided into the higher faculties of theology, law, and medicine and the lower faculty of philosophy. Teaching positions in the higher faculties were usually more prestigious and better remunerated than their philosophical counterparts. Philosophy generally served as a propaedeutic and still tended to be considered as a mere maidservant of theology. Especially in his piece *Conflict of the Faculties*, Kant argued that the higher faculties were dependent on the government, and that it was the task of the philosophical faculty to stand above them, to promote the critical spirit, and to protect the truth.

FACULTY (*Vermögen, Fähigkeit, Kraft*). Much of Kant's critical philosophy was based on the premise that the **mind** possessed different powers or faculties, each of which had different functions. In the *Critique of Pure Reason*, Kant claimed that **sensibility** was the lower faculty of **cognition** (*Erkenntnisvermögen*), while **understanding**, **judgment**, and **reason** comprised the higher faculties (A 130/B 169). The functions that correspond to the latter three are, respectively, the production of concepts, judgments, and inferences. Kant strongly linked these powers with his **architectonic**. Sensibility was dealt with almost exclusively in the "**Transcendental Aesthetic**," the understanding and judgment in the "**Transcendental Analytic**," and reason in the "**Transcendental Dialectic**." Only loosely connected with this, Kant discussed in the *Critique of Judgment*, in addition, the relationship of these powers to the faculties of the soul (*Seelenvermögen*), also labeled as faculties of the mind (*Vermögen des Gemüts*). Here, he linked the understanding to the faculty of cognition, judgment to the faculty of pleasure and pain, and reason to the faculty of desire. The first one deals with **nature** and produces natural law, the second deals with **art** and produces aesthetic judgments, and the third deals with **morals** and produces moral law.

Objections have been raised against such a compartmentalization of the human mind on Kant's part, especially in view of the fact that he never greatly bothered to justify it. One may defend him by pointing to the fact that he is not suggesting that we split up the human mind, only that we assign different capabilities to it. These positions are to some extent reflected in the debates about the proper way to translate his writings into English or French. Thus, for instance, there has been some dispute among Kant scholars whether *Kritik der Urteilskraft* should be translated as *Critique of Judgment, Critique of the Faculty of Judgment,* or *Critique of the Power of Judgment*. The shorter rendition has the disadvantage of allowing the possibility that individual judgments are at stake, the second of suggesting a compartmentalization of the human mind beyond Kant's intentions, the third of being insufficiently technical and precise, since the word 'power' has numerous connotations that completely miss the target. Of course, any of these is acceptable as long as one is sufficiently aware of what Kant meant. *See also* SYSTEM.

FAITH. *See* BELIEF.

FEELING *(Gefühl)*. Kant defines feeling as the "capacity for having **pleasure** or pain in a representation" (MM, Ak 6, p. 373). The experience of this feeling is not linked to any insight into an **object**; rather, it is only the **subject** that feels pleasure or pain within himself. Kant labels the representations that are related to the subject in this fashion 'aesthetic' (CJ, Ak 5, p. 204). Such a conception of feeling (of the beautiful) is present already in his **pre-critical** piece *Observations on the Feeling of the Beautiful and the Sublime*, where Kant assumes that pleasure and displeasure are not really caused by the characteristics of the external things that excite them, but that they repose on the feelings experienced by each person (Ak 2, p. 207).

From the feeling of the **beautiful** as a disinterested satisfaction, Kant distinguishes **moral** feeling, or, referring to Francis Hutcheson, moral sense. In the further pre-critical writing *Inquiry Concerning the Distinctness of the Principles of Natural Theology and Morality*, Kant opposes cognition to feeling as the sensation of the good (Ak. 2, p. 299). On the one hand, this moral feeling provides the will with its universality and thus functions as a capacity of reason, on the other hand, it is a basic fact that cannot be deduced from principles of reason.

Kant retained this notion of moral feeling until he developed the conception of the categorical **imperative** as a material **law** of reason. But once he replaced moral feeling by (practical) reason (p. 395), he reduced feeling to its merely sensible and empirical character. In his critical period, Kant therefore rejected moral feeling when it was claimed to serve as the ground of moral judgment, though he accepted it when it was viewed "as the subjective effect that the law exercises on the **will**" (GMM, Ak 4, p. 460, see also p. 442), allowing it to be integrated into the "respect for moral law" (CP, Ak 5, p. 80). This respect is a positive feeling produced by the moral law itself, is thus not of empirical origin, and is the only feeling that is cognized a priori (p. 73).

Hermann Cohen founded his **aesthetics** on "pure feeling," which he grasped as the third direction of consciousness next to thinking and willing. With this conception, however, he did not envisage the psychological conditions of the production and reception of **art**, but only the specific manner of artistic 'production.' **Paul Natorp** differed by introducing productive fantasy as the organ of artistic creation and by claiming that aesthetic feeling only accompanies the creation of art, rather than constituting it. On the other hand, Natorp understood feeling in the sense of an immediate self-experience without an object to lie at the origin of **religion**, which, however, prompted Cohen to object.

FICHTE, JOHANN GOTTLIEB (1762-1814). After becoming familiar with Kant's philosophy in 1790, Fichte visited Kant in Königsberg during the following year. In 1792, Kant supported the publication of Fichte's anonymous *Versuch einer Kritik aller Offenbarung* (*Attempt at a Critique of all Revelation*). The piece was widely thought to contain Kant's own philosophy of religion, but once Kant revealed the identity of the true author, Fichte's scholarly reputation was established. Already in 1794, Fichte succeeded to **Karl Leonhard Reinhold**'s professorship at the University of Jena. Also in 1794, Fichte published his *Grundlage der gesamten Wissenschaftslehre* (*Foundation of the Complete Doctrine of Science*), in 1797 the two *Einleitungen* (*Introductions to the Doctrine of Science*), and, starting with 1801, several new versions of the doctrine of science.

Just as Reinhold, Fichte understood his philosophy, that is, "Doctrine of Science" or "Science of Science," as **criticism**, thinking that he was adhering to the spirit, if not the letter of Kant. However, Kant openly distanced himself from Fichte's doctrine of science by stressing that all criticism indeed had to follow not just the spirit, but also the letter of his own writings (Ak 12, pp. 370–71). Fichte especially disapproved of the fact that Kant had taken the 'given' in space and time as his point of departure; he himself sought the foundations in an act of positing by the self, a positing that he labeled a 'deed of action' (*Tathandlung*). As his further attempts to establish the highest principle of the doctrine of science demonstrate, Fichte had deviated already with his original formulation ("the self originally and absolutely posits its own being," *Grundlage*, § 1) from Kant's concept of the pure self as an "original **apperception**" (B 132). Fichte nevertheless wished to continue maintaining that there was complete accord between his own and Kant's system. He thus had to deny especially the fact that Kant had based experience on something different from the self, and he therefore interpreted the thing, which according to Kant **affects** the mind, as a "mere thought," stressing instead the power of the self.

Although **Hermann Cohen** distanced his own philosophy from that of Fichte, he nevertheless on a number of occasions expressed his esteem for the latter's development of Kant's thought and even showed himself to be influenced by Fichte in certain points, such as in his treatment of the principle of identity. Fichte played a more important role in the **Southwestern German School of Neokantianism**, namely, in **Wilhelm Windelband**'s conception of criticism that went beyond Kant, and in Emil Lask's sketch of a logic of concept-formation in the philosophy of history.

FINALITY. *See* PURPOSE (*Zweck*); PURPOSIVENESS (*Zweckmässigkeit*).

FORCE (*Kraft*). A fundamental concept in Kant's philosophy of science throughout his life, one which played an important role in many of his writings. Kant's first publication, *Thoughts on the True Estimation of Living Forces* of 1749, was intended as a resolution of the so-called *vis viva* controversy, namely, the dispute between the Cartesians and the Leibnizians whether the formula mv or mv^2 was the correct measure of force. Kant attempted to combine the Cartesian quantitative-physical account with the Leibnizian qualitative-metaphysical one, but he became dissatisfied with his effort as he became aware of the fact that his own solution was riddled with problems and that both the Cartesian and the Leibnizian accounts of force were insufficient. This possibly induced Kant to turn more strongly (and permanently) to **Newtonian** physics. Subsequently, Kant came to rely on the forces of **attraction** and repulsion. This is prominent in his *Universal Natural History and Theory of the Heavens* of 1755, where he attempted to explain the origin of the solar system by the joint influence of these two forces. In the *Monadologia Physica* (1756), Kant explained **matter** in terms of physical monads as points occupying space by means of the forces of attraction and repulsion. In his *Attempt to Introduce Negative Magnitudes into Philosophy* (1763), Kant introduced the distinction between logical and real opposition, and, in the process of doing so, frequently used forces to illustrate the latter.

Forces played a prominent role in the *Metaphysical Foundations of Natural Science*, where Kant called attraction and repulsion 'original' and 'fundamental,' explaining matter in terms of them in order to avoid **atomism**. On the basis of his 'dynamical' theory of matter, he then dealt with additional moving forces in the section "Mechanics," employing these in his derivation of Newton's laws of motion. Kant introduced yet other, more specific forces in his *Opus Postumum* in order to account for more particular physical phenomena. Here, he also attempted to account for forces by resorting to the **concept** of **ether**.

Throughout his philosophical career, Kant's concept of force, with the possible exception of the piece of 1749, shows remarkable stability. This is especially true of attraction and repulsion. Kant claimed certain basic characteristics for them from early on, retaining these only with slight modifications. Thus, he apparently always held forces to be capable of increasing or diminishing in infinitesimally small steps, though he did not express this thought explicitly at any great length until after he introduced the concept of intensive **magnitudes** in the "**Anticipations of Perception**" in the *Critique of Pure Reason*.

Kant also always showed at least some awareness of the problem of our cognition of forces. Possibly drawing a clue from Newton's famous refusal to speculate on the cause of the force of gravity (*hypotheses non fingo*), Kant consistently declared that the fundamental forces were inscrutable and that only their effects were known to us. In the *Inaugural Dissertation*, for instance, he emphasized that forces must be given in experience and that their possibility or impossibility cannot be decided a priori (§ 28), retaining this position in the first *Critique* (A 207/B 252, A 770–71/B 798–99). Kant's clearest admission of the problematic nature of the epistemological status of the fundamental forces occurred in the *Metaphysical Foundations*, where he treated them as part of a merely hypothetical explanation of matter. Prior to this, in his pre-critical writings, as well as subsequently, in the *Opus Postumum*, Kant displayed a tendency to treat the two forces as certain.

FORM. Although Kant, in a general statement on form and **matter** in the chapter dealing with the "**Amphiboly** of the Concepts of Reflection," appears to treat the two concepts more or less on a par, defining matter as that which is to be determined and form as that which effects the determination, the latter plays by far the more important role in his **critical philosophy**. Unlike matter, which he claims is given in **impressions** of **sensibility**, Kant regards form, in general, as provided by the subject. The quintessence of his **epistemology** lies in his contention that **experience** and **cognition** are possible only thanks to the fact that their forms, namely, the forms of **intuition** (**space** and **time**) and the forms of the **understanding** (**categories** and **principles of pure understanding**), are given **a priori**. Kant rejects the claim of rationalism that the form of cognition or of experience consists of **innate ideas**, and he equally rejects the position of **empiricism**, according to which form is abstracted from experience and is, therefore, a posteriori. Instead, he maintains that form, that is, the a priori intuitions and concepts, determines the order of **appearances** by making possible a synthesis of the data provided by the sensibility.

Kant's philosophy of **science** is marked by the same concern with the a priori contribution of the subject, namely with formal laws, that is, with the most basic conceptual presuppositions of science. It is the latter that he lays down in his *Metaphysical Foundations of Natural Science* and later attempts to expand on in the so-called *Opus Postumum*.

Kant's **moral** philosophy too is based on the notion of the supremacy of form, which he identifies with moral law. Paying heed only to form means acting in accordance with **reason** and its moral commands. Such form stands in contrast to **inclinations** and emotions, which Kant regards as the sensible matter of human motivation. It is only by determining the **will** by the form and by desisting from being determined by the matter that one can be said to act in a moral way. In **aesthetics**, form again plays a crucial role; it is what makes the quality of judgments of taste possible. Here too one must disregard matter.

Attempting to grasp all cultural achievements (language, myth, science, etc.) as expressions of a basic mental function, **Ernst Cassirer** introduced the concept of "symbolic form" or "symbolic formation," which he defined as the "energy of the mind by which a meaningful mental content is linked to a concrete sensible sign and innerly assigned to this sign."

FORMS OF INTUITION. *See* INTUITION; SPACE; TIME.

FREE WILL. *See* DETERMINISM.

FREEDOM (*Freiheit*). In his *Critique of Pure Reason*, Kant addresses the issue of freedom mainly in order to prove that this concept is not contradictory and that it can therefore serve as the foundation for his **ethics**; the latter will then be based on the presupposition of practical freedom. For Kant, freedom is the idea or the concept of reason of an unconditioned beginning of a "series of conditions of the appearance" (A 334/B 391). He is not concerned with a temporal beginning, but with a spontaneous effect (action), by virtue of which "a series of appearances that runs according to natural laws" begins from itself. Kant calls this free **causality** "transcendental freedom" (A 446/B 474). Such a causality can be ascribed only to a fictitiously thought "intelligible cause" (A 537/B 565) that stands outside the series of **appearances** and is not subjected to time, although its effects are located in the temporally determined world of appearances. Kant attributes such a causality to the **thing-in-itself** as its "intelligible character"; the thing-in-itself is then thought as an "acting subject" (*causa noumenon*) (A 539/B 567).

For Kant, this assumption of an unknown intelligible causality out of freedom gains its plausibility and sense from his notion of the duality of **humans**. The human being is conscious of itself as a part of nature, as it appears, and in its pure **apperception** as a rational being, whose intelligible causality manifests itself in the **imperatives** to which he is submitted in his practical existence (A 546–47/B 574–75). Kant thus finds the solution to the problem of freedom in his concept of the human being: the intention of the theory of transcendental freedom is realized in such a way that the human being's pure self-consciousness is thought as determined by an **ought** that does not occur in **nature**.

However, the real possibility or even actuality of freedom is not proved by this transition from transcendental to practical freedom. In other words, with "freedom in the practical understanding," Kant is presupposing more in his ethics than just the transcendental freedom whose logical possibility (noncontradictoriness) he claims to have proved. The "objective reality" of freedom emerges only from his analysis of moral **law**: freedom turns out to be the "*ratio essendi*" (ground of being) of moral law, moral law to be the "*ratio cognoscendi*" (ground of cognition) of freedom (CrPR, Ak 5, pp. 3–4). By labeling the consciousness of moral law a "**fact** of reason" (p. 31), Kant implicitly determines the ground of cognition of freedom as a factual one and as incapable of any further rational insight. That means that we can have insight into freedom as the necessary presupposition of the possibility of moral law, but not into the possibility of this presupposition itself (GMM, Ak 4, p. 461; CrPR, Ak 5, p. 46).

Kant radically separates practical freedom from natural lived experience in which human willing and acting occur; he thus develops the meaning of freedom not in regard to natural humans, but in regard to rational beings. The latter's freedom is initially determined purely negatively as a freedom from something; the content of the freedom to do something is gained by the rational being only by a thinking self-determination that, in the sense of practical philosophy, consists of the **autonomy** of the **will**, which is a law for itself (Ak 4, p . 440). *See also* DETERMINISM.

FRIES, JAKOB FRIEDRICH (1773–1843). Distancing himself emphatically from those speculative, idealistic thinkers who claimed that they were surmounting Kant's philosophy, Fries understood himself as a true, if not uncritical Kantian. In his book of 1805, *Wissen, Glauben und Ahndung* (*Knowledge, Belief, and Conjecture*), he modified central concepts of Kant's theoretical philosophy: belief as the "necessary conviction out of mere reason" aims at ideas in which it seeks the 'eternal'; conjecture as the mediating power between knowledge and belief is the teleological conception of "the eternal order of things in the finitude of nature."

In his further work *Neue* (2nd ed.: *oder anthropologische*) *Kritik der Vernunft* (*New (or Anthropological) Critique of Reason*) of 1807 (3 vols.; 2nd ed. 1828–31), Fries claimed that Kant in his *Critique of Pure Reason* left unexplained how **cognition a priori** can itself be cognized, that is, what the status of **transcendental** cognition was. As this last ground of all cognition, Fries identified the non-cognizable immediate activity of reason that was already present in all cognition. The observation of our own inner life, including reflection, which Fries explicates in his "anthropological critique of reason," finds this original spontaneity of reason always only in connection with the sensible given, never in isolation. The distinction between 'empirical' reflection and immediacy replaces Kant's distinction between **experience** and reason.

While Rudolf Otto (1869–1937) used Fries's position as the basis for his own philosophy of religion, Leonard Nelson (1882–1927) founded a genuine Neo-Friesianism. In his *Über das sogenannte Erkenntnisproblem* (*On the So-Called Problem of Cognition*) of 1908, Nelson declared that the investigation of the objective validity of cognition as it was carried out in **Neokantianism** was impossible, because no criterion of the objective validity of cognition could be provided without falling into an infinite regress. Against the threat of skepticism he introduced, in keeping with Fries, the distinction between immediate cognition and a mediate one that was based on principles.

FUNCTION. Kant used the word 'function' in a solely mathematical sense during his **pre-critical** period (Ak 1, p. 83), and he spoke of bodily functions a number of times throughout his writing career (e.g., Ak 2, p. 364; Ak 9, p. 463). In the *Critique of Pure Reason*, however, he narrowed down the meaning of the term to signify chiefly the "**unity** of the act of ordering different representations under one common representation" (A 68/B 93). Such a unity is central to his theory of **concepts**, and, accordingly, he claims that "concepts rest on functions." In addition, **judgments**, being composed of concepts, are said to be "functions of unity among our representations." Kant exploits this close relationship between judgments and concepts in order to derive, in the so-called metaphysical **deduction**, all of "the functions of the understanding," that is, the **table of categories**, from an exhaustive exhibition of "the functions of unity in judgments," that is, from the so-called **table of judgments** (A 69/B 94). He justifies this step again by reference to 'function,' namely, by claiming that the same function that gives unity to different representations in a judgment also gives unity to the category. This explains why there are as many categories as there are logical functions of all possible judgments in the table of judgments (A 79/B 104–5). The derivation of the categories as a step from formal **logic** to **transcendental logic** represents a crucial component of Kant's epistemology: while the functions of formal logic are merely the form of our thinking in general, the categories are the forms of **a priori cognition** and thus the condition of possible **experience**. However, if the categories are applied beyond the bounds of experience, that is, without reference to an object given in **intuition**, they too are then worth no more than merely logical functions (A 239/B 298).

- G -

GENIUS. By the time Kant in his *Critique of Judgment* (1790) took recourse to the concept of genius as the subject and the creative ground of the fine **arts**, the reception in Germany of French and British theories of genius as well as the romantic cult of genius of the *Sturm und Drang* period were long a thing of the past. However, Kant introduced the concept not as an echo of a fashion, but as an element of his own conception of the fine arts. The latter must be *considered* as **nature**, even if one is conscious of them as arts. The artist is then a genius because it does not suffice to just learn the rules of artistic creation, rather one must possess "the inborn predisposition of the mind (*ingenium*) by which nature gives the rule to art" (Ak 5, p. 307).

In his *Anthropology from a Pragmatic Point of View*, Kant also characterized genius in terms of the creative imagination. The "mystical name" genius is applied to artistic talent, since talent is impossible to explain or to learn (Ak 7, pp. 224–25). From the conviction that imitation is not the foundation of the fine arts, a conviction that at the end of the 18th century was generally accepted, Kant concludes that prominent scientists, for example, **Isaac Newton**, cannot be called geniuses, given that their discoveries ultimately do not differ from what can be acquired "with effort by means of imitation" (Ak 5, p. 308).

GEOGRAPHY. Kant lectured on geography during his whole academic career starting with the summer term of 1756; his general intention was to provide his students with an idea of their place in the world. Along with his lectures on anthropology, this was a popular course, less concerned with first principles than with empirical laws; both of these courses were practically oriented, entertaining, and better attended than their counterparts on **logic** or **metaphysics**. In spite of the fact that he had never traveled much anywhere, Kant was able to draw on his immense erudition, and benefit from his ability to present the material in a lively fashion. As is apparent from the published announcements of his courses and from the lecture notes of his students (Ak 9, pp. 151–436), Kant took into consideration a number of definitions and divisions of geography. According to one of the most complete, physical geography was defined as the general outline of nature, and the claim was made that it served as the foundation for all other types of geography, namely, mathematical geography, concerned with the shape, size, and motion of the earth; moral geography, whose task it was to deal with the different morals and characters of people in different parts of the world; political geography, concerned with the relation of political laws to the physical features of a country; mercantile geography, which dealt with the subject of trade in surplus products; theological geography, investigating the influence of the physical characteristics of an area on the theological principles adopted by its inhabitants (pp. 164–65).

GOD. In his published writings, Kant consistently presupposed and even openly advocated a rational belief in God. He was always highly critical of all claims of direct insight into God on the part of the mystics, whom he tended to regard as religious fanatics. This position is well illustrated in the *Dreams of a Spirit-Seer* (1766), in which he attacked the Swedish visionary Emmanuel Swedenborg. However, in spite of this element of continuity, a significant shift in Kant's thought did occur. In his **pre-critical** pieces, his standpoint could be described as deistic. At this stage, he attempted to prove God's existence though he did distance himself from the traditional version of the ontological argument. In his **critical** period, he realized that all proofs of God's existence were fallacious and he attempted to show that faith in God could not rely on demonstrations of God's existence (for example, B xxx). Nevertheless, Kant held that faith could be rational if God were treated only as an **ideal** of pure reason and if, as such, it was restricted to the **moral** sphere. Kant integrated this rational belief in God into his moral philosophy by claiming in the *Critique of Practical Reason* that the idea of God could serve as a **postulate** for the sake of completing (though not grounding) morality.

In the *Critique of Judgment* and in his writings on the philosophy of history such as the "Idea for a Universal History with a Cosmopolitan Purpose" (1784) and the "Conjectures on the Beginning of Human History" (1786), Kant discussed the notion of the **purposiveness** of the world, vaguely suggesting that there may have been some sort of a divine plan at play in the development of mankind. However, biographical research on Kant has repeatedly voiced the opinion that in his later years Kant did not much believe in anything and that his remarks on rational religion were included in his writings solely for the benefit of the uneducated masses.

In his ethics, **Hermann Cohen** assigned to the idea of God the task of guaranteeing the realization of morality among humans, rejecting, however, all essential determinations of God (such as person or mind). In his philosophy of religion, Cohen tied God explicitly to the correlation with humans;

God was then to assume responsibility for individual morality in the sense of freeing a person from sin.

GOD, PROOFS OF THE EXISTENCE OF (*Gottesbeweise*). At a number of places in his writings, most prominently in the last chapter of the "**Transcendental Dialectic**" of the *Critique of Pure Reason* entitled "Ideal of Pure Reason," where he deals with rational theology, Kant discusses three arguments for the **existence** of God. The most important of these was for him the ontological argument as it was developed by Anselm of Canterbury and then employed by **René Descartes, Gottfried Wilhelm Leibniz**, and others (though Kant repeatedly attributed it to Descartes alone). This proof is based solely on an analysis of the concept of God; it claims that it would be contradictory to deny the existence of a perfect being, since existence is among the predicates included in perfection. Kant criticized this argument already in his **pre-critical** pieces *Nova Dilucidatio* of 1755 (Prop. 6) and *The Only Possible Ground of Proof for a Demonstration of the Existence of God* of 1763 (Part I, Consideration 1) on the grounds that existence was not a predicate and that it could therefore not be inferred from the mere **idea** of God. However, in both of these writings Kant went on to present his own version of the ontological argument, attempting to prove God's existence by resorting to the concept of possibility. He started out by claiming that the inner possibility of things presupposed something existing, without which there would be no material for thought and therefore also not for the possible. He then proceeded to demonstrate by a number of complicated steps that this existing something had to be God. In the *Critique of Pure Reason*, he then not only repeated his earlier criticism of the traditional version of the ontological argument, he now rejected all versions of such arguments, including his own.

What Kant called the "cosmological argument" was based on the contingency of the existence of the world, which requires a necessary ground. This proof, first introduced by Thomas Aquinas, had been utilized by **Christian Wolff** and his followers. In the chapter "Ideal of Pure Reason" Kant states it in the following form. "If something exists, then an absolutely necessary being also has to exist. Now I myself, at least, exist; therefore, an absolutely necessary being exists." Kant identifies a number of 'dialectical' and therefore untenable presumptions in the argument. Thus, one may not infer from the contingent to a **cause** outside the world of sense; one may not infer from the impossibility of an infinite series of causes to a first cause; reason may not complete this series by doing away with every condition, since without such conditions there can be no concept of **necessity**; uniting the logical possibility of a concept of all **reality** with its **transcen-**

dental possibility would require a principle of the feasibility of such a synthesis, which, however, can be had only within **experience**.

Kant seriously entertained the physicotheological argument or argument from design in his pre-critical period, starting with the *Universal Natural History and Theory of the Heavens* of 1755; he restated it at some length in *The Only Possible Ground* (Part II). This argument was very popular in the 18th century and circulated in different versions. Kant rejected claims that particular cases of **purposiveness** in nature were proof of God's being and defended instead the assertion that God's existence was manifest only from the general nomological order of the universe. Kant realized early on that this argument could only be persuasive, but that it lacked in geometrical rigor and could therefore not produce apodictic necessity. This was also the case with the so-called moral proof of the existence of God presented in the *Critique of Judgment* (§ 87): there can be only a moral ground for the assumption of a final end of the world, and from this assumption "in accordance with the concepts of practical reason" can be inferred merely by reflective judgment a "moral being as the author of the world" (§ 88).

In the chapter "Ideal of Pure Reason," Kant concludes his critique by claiming that the best that the cosmological and physicotheological proofs could achieve is to demonstrate the existence of some necessary and purposive being. However, not only would this not be God in the desired sense of the word, but, more importantly, Kant was convinced that neither of the arguments proves even this limited goal. They therefore presuppose the ontological argument, and since that is unsound as well, we must give up all hope of attaining **cognition** of God's existence.

GOOD (*Gut*). Kant distinguishes between, on the one hand, good as it is opposed to evil in itself and that is good "in itself and unconditionally," and, on the other hand, a mere conditional or comparative good (Ak 8, p. 282) that may serve as the means to an end. "Practical good," according to Kant, determines the **will** "objectively, that is, from grounds that are valid for every rational being as such"; it is opposed to the **agreeable**, which "influences the will only by means of feeling" (Ak 4, p. 413; CJ, Ak 5, pp. 205ff.).

From the British moral sense philosophers, Kant accepts the conception that the good must be determined by its relation to the **subject**, which is motivated by it to perform good **actions**. However, he bases this relation not on a **feeling**, but on **pure reason**, which, as practical, is itself the ground of the good. This means that no material determination of the good is presupposed. The concept of the good as the necessary object of the faculty of desire (Ak 5, p. 58) arises only from a determination of the will by a practical principle or **law** of reason; good refers "to actions, not to the person's state of feeling," and "absolutely good" or "absolutely **evil**" can be called "only the way of acting, the **maxim** of the will, and consequently the acting **person** himself . . . but not a thing" (p. 60). Absolutely good is a will that submits itself at all times to the immediately determining practical law of reason (p. 62). When, on the other hand, human well-being is at stake rather than the good, then the determination of the will rests on an end that is not commanded by reason, even if one may seek to attain it by the best possible means.

In his *Religion within the Boundaries of Mere Reason*, Kant distinguishes a natural inclination of humans to evil from the "original predispositions to the good in human nature." The latter is subdivided into, first, a physical-mechanical self-love (for self-preservation, for the propagation of the species, for community with other human beings), second, a physical-rational self-love that involves comparison with others for which reason is required, and, third, respect for the moral law as an incentive to the will (Ak 6, pp. 26–28).

GROUNDWORK OF THE METAPHYSICS OF MORALS. In this foundation of his **ethics**, Kant saw it as his task to discover and describe "the supreme principle of morality." The work (temporarily) replaces a foundational effort that was entitled "critique of pure practical reason" (Ak 4, pp. 391–92). The book, which appeared in 1785, is divided into three sections. Kant begins by assuming that "all humans are capable of moral insights thanks to their reason, he then seeks the supreme principle of morality, and deals, finally, with the concept of **freedom** in the course of his discussion of a transition to the "**Critique of Practical Reason**." In the First Section, he develops the key concepts and theories of his moral philosophy, especially those of the good **will** and of **duty**. In Section Two, he determines the **law**, the compliance with which characterizes the good will and thus morality, as the categorical **imperative**. As he further shows, this imperative is not imposed on the will by an outside agency, but it is the will itself that subjects itself to it. Kant labels this act of self-legislation **autonomy**. With autonomy, the freedom of the will of all rational beings is presupposed. On the basis of his discussion in Section Three of the **idea** of freedom, Kant concludes that **practical reason** may *think* itself into an intelligible world of freedom, but that it cannot *explain* how freedom and thus also the categorical imperative are possible (Ak 4, pp. 458ff.).

The work exercised a strong influence and helped to spread the acquaintance with Kant's critical philosophy among a wider public. Along with the *Critique of Practical Reason*, it is still plays an important role in today's ethical discourse.

- H -

HAPPINESS (*Glückseligkeit*). The difference between luck (*fortuna*) and happiness (*beatitudo, felicitas*) is leveled by the German word '*Glück*'; however, Kant in his terminology abides by this distinction by separating '*Glück*' (in the sense of '*fortuna*' as the favor of fate) from '*Glückseligkeit*' (as the experience of a fulfilled life that overrides particular events). For the **pre-critical** Kant, just as for **Gottfried Wilhelm Leibniz** and **Christian Wolff**, happiness consists in **perfection**. In contrast, the critical Kant refuses to describe morality with this concept (GMM, Ak 4, p. 443). But, above all, he abandons the notion that the **will** and moral **action** should be determined by happiness as a goal. Kant defines happiness as the "satisfaction of all our **inclinations** (extensive, with regard to their manifoldness, as well as intensive, with regard to degree, and also protensive, with regard to duration)" (A 806/B 834). Happiness is for the human being "his own last natural **end**" and is, as such, unattainable, but it is not his "final end" (*Endzweck*), as which the human being must posit himself independently of **nature** (CJ, Ak 5, pp. 430–31). For one thing, the human being's own nature prevents him from reaching the goal of happiness, for another, happiness is a wavering and arbitrary representation, and is thus unsuitable for determining the will in accordance with moral **law**.

Nevertheless, Kant recognizes that the wish to be happy is necessarily present in every rational, yet finite being. But as each individual with his or her subjective **feelings** of **pleasure** and pain has different ideas of happiness, this latter can, objectively viewed, be only a **contingent**, not a necessary practical principle of the determination of the will (CrPR, Ak 5, p. 25). The subjection of the will under moral law has, therefore, as its goal not happiness, but the **dignity** to be happy. The problem that not everyone who is worthy of happiness is also really and truly happy is the subject matter of the **postulates** of practical reason.

In his doctrine of virtue in the *Metaphysics of Morals*, Kant establishes it as a **duty** to advance the happiness of others, though he does not admit any parallel obligation to further one's own physical happiness (Ak 6, p. 388).

HEAUTONOMY. *See* AUTONOMY, HEAUTONOMY, HETERONOMY.

HEGEL, GEORG WILHELM FRIEDRICH (1770-1831). For Hegel, Kant's philosophy is already a historical artifact; nevertheless, his confrontation with Kant permeates his whole work. Hegel admits that with Kant's philosophy, **thinking** becomes concrete, that is, it is understood as self-determining and thus as free; he criticizes Kant for failing to demonstrate being in self-consciousness (*Lectures on the History of Philosophy, Werke*, 20 vols., Frankfurt 1969-1970, here vol. 20, pp. 331-32). Although he counts Kant's concept of **synthetic judgments a priori** among the greatest achievements of Kantian philosophy (*Science of Logic I, Werke*, vol. 5, p. 240), he criticizes the execution of this idea, reproaching Kant for subsisting in "psychological idealism" with which Kant was then unable to attain true objectivity. In summary, he declares that Kant's philosophy is a complete philosophy of the **understanding** that dispenses with **reason** (*Werke*, vol. 20. p. 385).

Already in his writings from his time in Jena (1801-1807), Hegel sees "a twofold spirit" in Kant's philosophy, especially as the latter is presented in the *Critique of Judgment:* according to Hegel, Kant shows in the reflection of the understanding the efficacy of the great idea of reason but, at the same time, he again extinguishes this idea (*Werke*, vol. 2, pp. 268-69). In his *Glauben und Wissen* (*Belief and Knowledge*), Hegel claims that Kant's, Friedrich Heinrich Jacobi's, and **Johann Gottlieb Fichte**'s philosophies are all equally characterized by the absolute opposition of the finite and the infinite (p. 294); he regards the first two as being committed to finitude as an absolute and to a belief in an absolute beyond (p. 333). Hegel presents a thorough discussion of Kant's theoretical philosophy in his *Encyclopedia of the Philosophical Sciences in Outline* (3rd ed., 1830, §§ 40ff.). As far as practical philosophy is concerned, Hegel praises both Kant and Fichte for making "the essence of law and of duty and the essence of the thinking and willing subject absolutely one" (*Werke*, vol. 2, pp. 469-70), criticizing them, however, for remaining on the standpoint of the ought (*Lectures on the Philosophy of Religion, Werke*, vol. 16, p. 219).

HEIDEGGER, MARTIN (1889-1976). In the second, never completed part of *Being and Time*, Heidegger intended to discuss "Kant's theory of schematism and time as a precursor of the problem of temporality." In connection with his work on this topic, Heidegger composed an interpretation of the *Critique of Pure Reason*, which he published in 1929 under the title *Kant and the Problem of Metaphysics*. Here, he understood Kant's work as a grounding of **metaphysics**, a grounding that was concerned with the possibility of ontology. From this point of view, he assigned primacy to (receptive) **intuition** as an element of finite cognition over **thought** and he expressed his preference for the first edition version of the "**Transcendental Deduction**" over the second edition version. He thought he could prove that the transcendental imagination was the hidden root of intuition and thought, a view from which Kant himself had recoiled. While he neglected **space**, Heidegger worked out the relation of the imagination to **time**, even identifying **pure sensibility** with time and time with the '**I think**.' In the preface to the fourth edition of his book (1973), Heidegger recanted, admitting that his 'violent' interpretation was in fact an 'over-interpretation.' His later pieces on Kant's philosophy (*Kant's Thesis about Being*, 1961; *What Is a Thing*, 1962) are based on a different approach to Kant; Heidegger now attempts to situate Kant's texts more within their historical context.

HELMHOLTZ, HERMANN (1821–1894).   One of the most important scientists of the 19th century and a precursor of **Neokantianism**, Helmholtz was famous largely for his experimental work in physiology and physics as well as for his contributions to mathematics and the theory of music. He became concerned with the relationship between Kant's epistemology and the physiology of sense **perception** already during his student years; he thought he was in agreement with Kant that all **cognition** of **reality** must derive from **experience**. He claimed that the physiology of perception had proved empirically what Kant had attributed to the structure of the mind, namely, that our perception is determined just as much by the nature of our senses as by outer **objects**. Accordingly, we have no immediate perception of outside objects, but must deduce their nature from our **sensations**, which are their effects. Just as for Kant, the **causal principle** for Helmholtz was not an empirical one, but had to be considered as a law of our **thought** given to us prior to all experience. Later, Helmholtz would classify the causal principle as a hypothesis. In his mature theory of perception, he maintained that the senses do not provide isomorphic images of things, but merely (symbolic) signs. Based on the latter, we arrive at the true ideas of things by learning how to use the signs to govern our motions and actions. In addition, Helmholtz showed that visual experience of non-Euclidean **space** was possible, thus seriously challenging Kant's conception of Euclidean geometry as the **a priori form** of **outer sensibility**.

HERDER, JOHANN GOTTFRIED (1744–1803).   Although initially a student of Kant, Herder eventually drifted more toward the counter-Enlightenment, stressing the supernatural, the particular, and the local rather than **reason**, the universal, and the **cosmopolitan**. Three main points of contact with Kant are noteworthy. 1) Herder's notes from Kant's lectures from ca.

1764 have survived and provide a valuable source for reconstructing Kant's thought at that time. 2) In 1785, Kant wrote fairly unfriendly reviews of the first two volumes of Herder's *Ideen zur Philosophie der Geschichte der Menschheit* (1784–1785), accusing Herder of a lack of philosophical precision and of arguing in analogies. After this, the relationship between the two philosophers turned sour. 3) In his late work *Verstand und Erfahrung* (1799), which contains an attack on Kant under the heading *Eine Metakritik zur Kritik der reinen Vernunft*, Herder stressed that a proper understanding of language not only as a historical phenomenon, but also as both sensuous and intellectual would have discouraged Kant from splitting the **mind** into **sensibility** and **understanding** and from introducing other dichotomies.

HETERONOMY. *See* AUTONOMY, HEAUTONOMY, HETERONO-MY.

HIGHEST GOOD (*höchstes Gut*).   Taken separately, neither **happiness** nor morality or virtue (with which the worthiness to be happy is given) constitute the "complete **good**" for rational beings; they can do so only in conjunction (A 813/B 841). While virtue as the highest condition of all happiness must be the "supreme good," it is only "happiness distributed in exact proportion to morality" that constitutes the complete or "highest good" (Ak 5, pp. 110–11).

It is the highest good of the intelligible **world** that for Kant presupposes a "highest original good," that is, the idea of **God** as the ideal of the highest good (A 814/B 842). Whether and how its attainment may be expected by human beings who submit their **will** completely under moral **law** is the subject of Kant's reflections and of subsequent debates. The problem arises from the ambiguity of his answers to the question of the role that the highest good is supposed to play in moral motivation. If one claims that in dealing with the issue of motivation Kant was consistent in his rejection of all ethical eudaimonism, then it must be explained how he can connect the promotion of the highest good with the adherence to moral law (Ak 5, p. 114). A possible link is suggested by his identification of the highest good with the final end of morality (Ak 5, p. 129; Ak 6, pp. 6–7), which would be reached in a morally perfect world. However, this conception remains unproblematic only as long as Kant does not contaminate the idea of moral perfection (holiness) with the question of its attainment; here, he places the infinite progress of moral endeavor under the premise of an infinitely continuing existence that may be secured only by hypostatizing the highest good to God.

In his ***Anthropology from a Pragmatic Point of View***, Kant identifies the "highest moral and physical good" of humans with "moral happiness." It does not arise out of a mixture of physical and moral good, but out of the struggle between the inclination to well-being and virtue, a struggle in which the principle of the former is restricted by the principle of the latter (Ak 7, p. 277).

HISTORY (*Geschichte*). As a general phenomenon of the Enlightenment in the 18th century, theologically permeated universal history was superseded by a history of humankind understood as the process of civilization. The increasingly common collective singular 'history' (*Geschichte* or *Historie*) corresponded to the conception of one humankind as the subject matter of history. To the new "philosophy of history" (the expression was minted by Voltaire), the task was assigned to discover, among the large number of historical facts, universal principles that guide historical development.

On the basis of his critical examination of **Johann Gottfried Herder**'s writings on the plan and development of history, Kant considered it possible that a "regular course" in the history of the human species could be discovered, a course that results from the complete and **purposeful** unfolding of the natural talents of humans and that leads to the establishment of a civic society based on law, and, beyond that, of a **cosmopolitan** state of **peace** between nations. The motivating force behind this development is, according to Kant, the antagonism of the "unsociable sociability," that is, the tendency of humans to both socialize and isolate themselves.

To this new understanding of history corresponds a new assessment of the value of philosophy or of the science of history. While the acting subjects, individuals and nations, are not aware that they are following a plan of **nature**, Kant claims for his idea of a philosophy of world history that it not only grounds history on this plan, but that it also fosters this plan and thus expedites the progress toward the end of history (Ak 8, pp. 17–31). In spite of his optimism, Kant makes the caveat that the progress toward a better future manifests itself only as an increase of legality, not of morality (Ak 7, p. 91).

Hermann Cohen and **Paul Natorp** no longer founded their philosophy of history on natural teleology, and opted instead for the ethical "law of the ought." Similarly to Kant, Cohen regarded law as the "vehicle of history." His messianic interpretation of the course of history was not apocalyptically colored, but expressed only the 'eternal' task to work toward a state of peace, thus linking the concept of history to his **ethical socialism**.

With their logically grounded concept of history and with its distinction from the equally logically grounded concept of nature, **Wilhelm Windelband** and **Heinrich Rickert** greatly influenced the methodology of history and the notion that history is the field of culture and of values.

HÖNIGSWALD, RICHARD (1875–1947). As a student of **Alois Riehl**, Hönigswald developed a **transcendental philosophy** that was characterized by far greater resort to realist elements than was generally accepted in **Neokantianism**. He emphasized that the conditions of the **possibility** of the given were to be sought not merely in pure principles but also in reality. In addition, he wished to include the investigation of the role of the **subject** in **philosophy**, and not just in **psychology** as the Neokantians generally did, insisting that all **cognition** is possessed by individuals.

HOPE. Toward the end of his **pre-critical** piece *Dreams of a Spirit Seer*, Kant points out that the weight of rational arguments depends on whether they are placed on the scale of hope or of unprejudiced justification. Although committed to unbiased deliberation, Kant cannot and will not abolish the "bias of the balance of the understanding" that arises with the hope that not everything is over with death (Ak 2, pp. 349–50, 373). He emphasizes the experience we make that the hoping person has a privileged approach to questions of life after death.

Hope has for Kant a relevance both for his philosophy of **history** and for his philosophy of religion. The question, "What may I hope" (A 805/B 833), which aims at the future realization of the moral **ought**, concerns, on the one hand, the historical progress toward a "general cosmopolitan state" (Ak 8, p. 28); **Hermann Cohen** linked this expectation to the messianic hope in **Judaism**. On the other hand, hope is directed at **happiness**. The legitimacy of this hope for happiness, that is, for "the state of a rational being in the world in the whole of whose existence everything goes according to his wish and will" (Ak 5, p. 124), arises for Kant strictly out of the fact that the individual has made himself worthy of happiness by his conduct or has demonstrated "unremitting endeavor to make himself worthy of happiness" (A 809–10/B 837–38). The suggestion of a necessary connection between this endeavor and the fulfillment of this hope is itself the object of a hope that hinges on the premise that the highest **reason** not only commands morality, but that it also guarantees the realization of the connection in **nature** (A 810/B 838). Kant explicitly remarks that hope implies the step to religion (Ak 5, p. 130), but in his writings on this topic, he more often resorts to the concept of **belief**. He thus turns the affective disposition of hope into a mode of a metaphysical cognition of the eternal.

HUMAN BEING (*Mensch*). For Kant, the human being belongs to two **worlds**: on the one hand, he is an **appearance** in the sensible world, and has, as such, an empirical character, that is, he is part of the causal chain of **nature**; on the other hand, the human being is for himself an intelligible object or a rational being (**noumenon**) that in its actions is independent of nature and thus free (A 539–41/B 567–69, A 544–47/B 572–75). With this concept of the human being, Kant provides the specifics of his solution of the problem of **freedom** and its application to experience (A 546/B 574).

Kant attributes it to a plan of nature that humans developed all their talents and thus achieved **culture**; in this process, nature utilized the antagonism of the "unsociable sociality" (Ak 8, pp. 20–21). However, human reason developed fully only within the species, not in the individual. Moreover, the moral perfecting that should result in a general law-abiding civil society as well as in a **cosmopolitan** state of **peace**, has by far not yet been reached (pp. 22ff.).

The human being is the "lord of nature" because he is the only earthly being that can set **ends** for himself, and, in this sense, he is also in his destiny the last end of nature. However, viewed as such, the human being still remains trapped in nature (CJ, Ak 5, p. 431). If the human being wishes to conceive himself as the final end, that is, place himself in relation to an end that suffices for itself independently of nature, he must define himself as a moral being whose existence is his own end (p. 435). As such a "*homo noumenon*," a human is a **person** (Ak 6, pp. 434–35). See also HISTORY; MIND (*mens, Gemüt*); OUGHT (*Sollen*); SOCIABILITY, SOCIALITY (*Geselligkeit*).

HUME, DAVID (1711–1776). After the middle of the 18th century, Hume achieved a great deal of fame throughout Europe for his writings on history as well as social and political philosophy. He also attained some disrepute for his critique of religion and for his epistemological views. His *Treatise of Human Nature* (1739–1740) and the shorter but more elegant *Enquiry Concerning Human Understanding* (1748, translated into German in 1755) examined our cognition of **causality** as well as of **substance**, the **self**, and other key philosophical notions. In spite of the fact that Hume, for example, never denied the reality and importance of causality, he was generally taken as a skeptic; other aspects of his philosophy tended to be overlooked.

Although Kant disagreed with a number of fundamental tenets of Hume's thought, he appreciated the fine points of his philosophy much better than most of his contemporaries, and there was possibly no philosopher who exercised a greater amount of influence on him than Hume. The early reactions to the *Critique of Pure Reason* may indeed have been deeply mistaken in their emphasis of the proximity of Kant's philosophy to Hume's **skepticism**, but they were by no means purely accidental. Kant had come into contact with Hume's writings during his **pre-critical** phase sometime in the late 1750s. Hume's views would have confirmed him in his endeavor to distance himself from the kind of **metaphysics** practiced in the so-called **Leibniz-Wolff** school, a metaphysics that was dominant in Germany at that time. At the end of both his *Attempt to Introduce the Concept of Negative Magnitudes* (1763) and his *Dreams of a Spirit-Seer* (1766), for instance, there are passages in which Kant repeats the gist of Hume's argument against classifying causality as an **a priori** rational **concept**, though he does not mention Hume explicitly. Later, Kant must have forgotten the import of Hume's lesson, given that he claims in the *Inaugural Dissertation* (1770) that causality is indeed an a priori rational concept that enables us to know **things-in-themselves**.

Around 1772, Kant was evidently reminded of the significance of Hume's analysis once again, since he began to rethink not only the concept of causality, but of the other **categories** as well. This reminder is mentioned in a famous passage in the introduction to the ***Prolegomena***, where Kant claims that the recollection of Hume had awakened him from his dogmatic slumber. Kant's main answer to Hume's analysis of causality was provided in the Second **Analogy** in the *Critique of Pure Reason*, though Kant also stressed in a number of other places that generalizing Hume's problem and thus discovering the **categories** was crucial to his solution. He admitted that Hume was right that such concepts cannot be derived by conceptual analysis, but claimed that he was mistaken in concluding that any of them were therefore the product of habit. Kant, in the end, reproached Hume with overlooking the potential of a solution that turned out to be no less than one of the centerpieces of his own critical philosophy, namely, the thesis that the categories owe their a priori character to their function as the conditions of the possibility of **experience**.

In his pre-critical ethics and aesthetics, Kant favored Hume's theory of moral sense with its emphasis of feeling at the expense of reason, but during the second half of the 1760s, he began to question and eventually rejected this view, opting instead for the highly rationalistic **moral philosophy** typical of his mature thought.

HYPOTHETICAL. *See* CAUSALITY; IMPERATIVE, CATEGORICAL AND HYPOTHETICAL.

- I -

I THINK (*cogito, ich denke*). Kant considers the proposition 'I think' as an act of apperception, under which the manifold of **intuition** is synthesized in one consciousness. Without such an act, the given **representations** would not be grasped together in a consciousness, that is, thinking would not belong to it (B 137). In this fashion, the 'I think' is a vehicle of all concepts; it is itself a **transcendental concept**, which, moreover, precedes and makes possible all other transcendental concepts, also containing "the form of every **judgment** of **understanding** whatever" (A 348/B 406). Thus, the 'I think' expresses the act of determining my **existence**, though only of my existence as an **appearance**, since my existence always remains only sensibly determinable. This last point has far-reaching consequences for Kant's theoretical philosophy, since the determination through transcendental concepts of my existence merely as an appearance ultimately restricts the use of the **categories** to empirical **intuition** (B 429).

Aside from ascribing these functions to the 'I think,' Kant also discusses its epistemological status. He claims that the 'I think' expresses an indeterminate empirical intuition, though it is given neither as an appearance nor as a noumenon, but as something that exists. 'I think' is an empirical proposition, even though the I is not an empirical representation; rather, it is purely intellectual, as it belongs to thinking in general. However, without any empirical representation, the act I think would not occur; the empirical is only the condition of the application of the pure intellectual faculty (B 423). Although Kant claims that 'I think' already contains the proposition 'I exist,' it nevertheless remains nothing but a formal condition and it would be ill-conceived to attempt to infer from it properties of the **soul** such as substantiality and, ultimately, **immortality**. *See also* PARALOGISMS; TRANSCENDENTAL UNITY OF APPERCEPTION.

IDEA. Kant restricted the term 'idea' essentially to the realm of **reason**, claiming to be using it in a similar fashion as **Plato**. He criticized philosophers such as **John Locke, George Berkeley,** and **David Hume** for employing it in a more general sense to include, for example, sensory perceptions. Ideas for Kant extend beyond possible **experience**, and are thus sharply distinguished from **concepts** of the **understanding**. They seek a higher order than do the concepts of the understanding, they aim at the "**totality** of conditions," that is, at the unconditioned (A 322/B 379), or, as Kant puts it in the *Prolegomena*, at "the collective **unity** of all possible experience," without, however, being themselves part of experience (§ 40). Ideas do not serve to determine an **object**; rather, they can represent objects only indirectly; they are only heuristic and not ostensive concepts (A 670-71/B 698-99). In other words, when used correctly, that is, on the basis of a critique of the human cognitive faculties, ideas are employed only in a regulative and not in a **constitutive** manner; this is Kant's technical way of setting them apart from the concepts of the understanding. In themselves, ideas are not contradictory. But their misuse leads to contradictions or to pseudo-demonstrations, or, in Kant's parlance, to **dialectic** and **transcendental illusion**. This occurs when one loses sight of the fact that they are not constitutive, or, in other words, when one treats them as if they could produce **cognition**. Kant discusses the generation of three specific **transcendental ideas**, namely, the psychological, the cosmological, and the theological, that is, soul, world, and God. He attempts to derive these out of logical inferences, in a similar fashion as he derives the **categories** of the understanding out of the logical structure of judgments. He claims that there are precisely three ideas of reason, because there are only three species of relation, namely, the categorical synthesis in a **subject** (yielding the soul), the **hypothetical** synthesis of the members of a series (yielding the world), and the **disjunctive** synthesis of the parts in a system (yielding God) (A 323/B 379).

While ideas in theoretical philosophy, when properly used, serve to suggest to the understanding the possibility of a higher order, in practical philosophy, the corresponding ideas of the **immortality** of the soul, of the **freedom** of the will and of **God** become **postulates** of practical reason. Aside from this, Kant introduces the expression "**aesthetic** ideas" in his *Critique of Judgment*. He reiterates his claim that ideas cannot directly lead to cognition, but explains this limitation somewhat differently than for the ideas of reason: aesthetic ideas do not lead to cognition because of their character as **intuitions** of the **imagination** for which a concept can never be discovered (§ 57).

IDEAL. Though unimportant in Kant's epistemology, the conception of ideas of which no **cognition** could be attained but which can serve as archetypes in various ways played an important role in different parts of his philosophy. Kant defined an ideal as an individual thing that is determined by an **idea** of **pure reason**; while the latter gives the rule, the former "serves as the original image for the thoroughgoing determination of the copy." It was with some justification that Kant claimed that ideals amounted to what **Plato** called ideas in the divine understanding, namely, "the most perfect thing of each species of possible beings and the original ground of all its copies in appearance." (Leaving aside the fact that it was not Plato, but only one part of the Platonist tradition that located ideas in the divine understanding.) Generally less concerned with the creative power of archetypes, Kant instead insisted that ideals, as **regulative** principles, are useful in **morals**, where, for example, the ideal of the Stoic sage serves as "an indispensable standard of reason" (A 568–70/B 596-98). In his **aesthetics**, Kant speaks of the archetype of **taste** or ideal of the **beautiful** that is based on "reason's indeterminate idea of a maximum," and that "cannot be represented by **concepts**, but only in an individual presentation," and that is therefore an ideal of the **imagination**. Kant claims that such an ideal of beauty cannot be vague beauty, but that the beauty here required must be "fixed by a concept of objective **purposiveness**." He thinks that only humans are susceptible of an ideal of beauty, since of all beings only the human being has the purpose of his existence in himself. In the end, the ideal of human beauty concerns only the human shape insofar as the latter is an expression of morality (CJ, § 17).

Already in his last **pre-critical** piece, the *Inaugural Dissertation* of 1770, Kant identified the most perfect ideal with **God**. Continuing in this vein in the last chapter of the "**Transcendental Dialectic**" of the *Critique of Pure Reason*, Kant went on to deal with God under the heading of the "Ideal of Pure Reason," though here he greatly enlarged the scope of his discussion by including his critique of the proofs of God's existence. Later on, in the "Doctrine of Method," he called God in the sense of the morally most perfect being "the ideal of the highest good," thus presaging the use of the concept of God as a **postulate** in the *Critique of Practical Reason* (A 810-11/B 838-39).

Hermann Cohen borrowed the concept of the ideal from aesthetics, where it referred to the being of a work of art, and applied it to morality, whose ideal reality consists of the process of perfection; the 'eternity' of this historical process is guaranteed by the idea of God.

IDEALISM. Kant maintained that only one form of idealism was tenable, namely, his own **transcendental idealism**, and, starting with his *Inaugural Dissertation* of 1770 (§ 11), he exerted a great deal of effort to distance himself from all other idealistic philosophies. In the appendix to the *Prolegomena*, he claimed that the previous kinds of idealism were characterized by the credo that all **cognition** gained through the **senses** is illusory, while **truth** is to be had only in the **ideas** of the **pure understanding** and pure **reason**; he contrasted this conception with his own idealism, which he held to be its exact reverse. In the famous "Refutation of Idealism," added to the second edition of the *Critique of Pure Reason* in order to again emphasize his rejection of "material idealism," Kant distinguished between the "problematic idealism" of **René Descartes** and the "dogmatic idealism" of

George Berkeley. While perfunctorily dismissing the latter as the false claim that **space** was a property of **things-in-themselves,** he produced a complicated **transcendental argument** to refute the latter, claiming that inner experience, which was indubitable, was possible only on the assumption of outer experience and therefore of outer **objects.**

ILLUSION (*Schein*). It was one of the central tenets of Kant's theoretical philosophy that we have no **cognition** of **things-in-themselves,** but only of how these appear to our cognitive faculties. But it was equally crucial for him to maintain that appearances do permit objective cognition, and he thus denied that they could be termed illusory. Kant ascribed such a mistaken conception to **George Berkeley,** explaining that it was caused by taking **time** and **space** for properties inherent in things-in-themselves, rather than recognizing them to be the **forms** of our **sensibility** (B 69–71). Another kind of error to which Kant applied the label was "dialectical illusion." He subsumed under this heading two somewhat different, if related, kinds of misuses. One of these arises from the attempt to reach cognition of **objects** on the basis of general **logic;** such logic in fact deals only with the formal conditions of judging and can yield no content of cognition (A 60–2/B 84–86). The second, for Kant far more significant kind of dialectical illusion is produced by attempting to apply the **pure concepts** of the **understanding** beyond the bounds of **experience.** This, termed "**transcendental illusion,**" is the subject of the **Transcendental Dialectic** of the *Critique of Pure Reason.* Both types of dialectical illusion arise when no object is given in **intuition,** and when one disregards this fact.

IMAGINATION (*Einbildungskraft*). Following a general tendency in the 18th century, Kant recasts, both in his **epistemology** and in his **aesthetics,** the function of the imagination (*facultas imaginandi*) in a new and positive fashion. As "the ability to represent an object in **intuition** even when it is not present" (B 151), imagination belongs to **sensibility.** From an empirical or psychological point of view, imagination connects in this reproduction of **representations** the sensibly given in accordance with the laws of **association.** However, insofar as **spontaneity** is involved in such a synthesis, imagination includes a productive element. In his *Anthropology from a Pragmatic Point of View,* Kant distinguishes productive imagination as the power of the "original presentation" of an absent object from reproductive imagination, whose function consists of a presentation that is merely derived from an earlier empirical intuition (Ak 7, p. 167). In his epistemology, Kant assigns to (productive) imagination a specific connecting **a priori** function, which he labels "figurative **synthesis**"; its task is to a priori determine **intuitions** in accordance with the **categories** (B 152). The product of this imagination is the transcendental **schema** of a concept of the understanding (A 140/B 179).

In his **aesthetics**, Kant explains the representation of a beautiful object, which pleases generally without a concept, in terms of the free play of the imagination and the understanding (Ak 5, p. 217). The judgment of taste is based on the "free lawfulness" of the "productive and autonomous" imagination (pp. 240–41).

IMMANENT. *See* TRANSCENDENT.

IMMORTALITY (*Unsterblichkeit*). In keeping with tradition, Kant held immortality, next to God and freedom, to be one of the three proper ends of investigation in **metaphysics**. In opposition to the rational **psychology** of **Christian Wolff** and many of his followers, Kant argued that the immortality of the **soul** could not be demonstrated by syllogistic means; any attempt to do so would only produce **paralogisms**, that is, fallacious inferences. However, if reason is unable to prove immortality, it is equally incapable of disproving it, leaving open the possibility that immortality may be thought as an **idea** of **practical reason**: one may be **morally** certain of a future life. In the *Critique of Pure Reason*, Kant denies that such a presupposition could be separated from the obligation that pure reason imposes on us, and in the *Critique of Practical Reason*, he develops this point further by classifying immortality as a "**postulate** of pure practical reason."

IMPENETRABILITY (*Undurchdringlichkeit*). In keeping with his dynamical theory of **matter**, according to which matter is explained in terms of the original **forces** of **attraction** and repulsion rather than by recourse to **extension** or atoms, Kant defined impenetrability already in his **pre-critical** piece *Physical Monadology* (1756) as a force (repulsion), by means of which matter maintains its spatial extension and offers resistance to other matter (Ak 1, p. 482). In his major **critical** work on philosophy of science, the *Metaphysical Foundations of Natural Science*, Kant continued to hold impenetrability to be the effect of the force of repulsion, claiming now that it was a fundamental property of matter, a property that enables our senses to cognize matter as something **real** in space (Ak 4, pp. 499, 508). Although in this work, he also discussed and admitted as a possible alternative the so-called mechanistic explanation of matter, following which matter is comprised of atoms and the void, and impenetrability is a consequence of the hardness of atoms, Kant expressed his clear preference for the dynamical theory. In the *Opus Postumum*, he then radicalized his objections against absolutely hard atoms and the void, and rejected the atomistic theory as completely untenable, thus establishing repulsion again as the only basis of impenetrability. In the pre-critical piece *Dreams of a Spirit-Seer* (1766), Kant also briefly considered the notion that the presence of the soul in the body could be explained along the lines of physics, namely, by recourse to impenetrability. However, he quickly abandoned this idea, since he found it contradictory that an impenetrable soul could exist in the same place as an impenetrable body.

IMPERATIVE, CATEGORICAL AND HYPOTHETICAL. Under an imperative, Kant understands the formula of a **command**, that is, "an objective **principle**, insofar as it is necessitating for a **will**" (Ak 4, p. 413; see also Ak 5, p. 20). Depending on the degree of obligation, he distinguishes between a hypothetical and a categorical imperative, further dividing the former into problematical and assertoric. While a problematical imperative is an imperative of skill that demands actions necessary in order to attain some possible end, an assertoric imperative concerns an actual end that must be presupposed in all human beings, namely, "the end of **happiness**"; this end can be attained by selecting the appropriate means with prudence. The categorical imperative, on the other hand, commands an action as objectively necessary without reference to any end that is to be attained. It concerns not the **matter** of or the consequences of an **action**, but only the **disposition** out of which an action occurs, and is insofar an apodictic and practical principle, that is, a **law** (Ak 4, pp. 415–16). While there are many hypothetical imperatives, there is only one single categorical imperative, for which, however, Kant finds a number of different formulations. The first one is: "act only in accordance with that **maxim** through which you can at the same time will that it become a universal law" (Ak 4, p. 421; see also Ak 5, p. 30); the second one places the end of all moral willing into the rational being as an end in itself (Ak 4, p. 429); the third expresses the idea of a **will** that submits to its own universal legislation (pp. 435–36).

For **Bruno Bauch**, the moral principle in its relationship to the subject does not exist only as an imperative, but assumes three forms. As a "demand of essence," it is related to the actions of the subject in their dependence on the character, commanding that the subject become a personality. As a "demand of the will," it is identical with Kant's categorical imperative and his principle of **autonomy**. As a "demand of effectiveness," it aims at the performance of a certain duty. Here, Bauch reinterprets Kant's teachings on the hypothetical imperatives. He is concerned with imperatives whose realization is dependent on individual circumstances, that is, laws shaped by cultural factors that provide norms for the realization of the categorical demand of the will in real actions. What is hypothetical in these demands is not merely their validity but also their realization, which depends on individual powers and capabilities.

Even more pointedly than Kant, Leonard Nelson stressed the principle of autonomy by disallowing all hypothetical imperatives in practical philosophy. He treated these as mere technical rules and therefore as theoretical propositions with only a surreptitious claim to obligation. Although he distinguished the moral valuation of an action from the question whether someone received what was legally his due, he did not consider it necessary to formulate two imperatives, one for virtue or disposition and one for law, because he thought that moral law yields a unified principle of the two cases.

IMPRESSION (*Eindruck*).   Kant used this word frequently, designating with it the input of raw data by the **senses**, data that were devoid of all **a priori** elements. In his **critical** period, Kant held that impressions arise when we are **affected** (*affiziert*) by things. Although such 'sensations,' 'sense-data,' 'impressions,' or 'ideas' played prominent roles in the philosophies of Kant's more empiricist-oriented predecessors **John Locke, George Berkeley,** and **David Hume,** Kant himself never explicitly discussed impressions, presumably owing to the fact that he considered them to be insufficient for producing **cognition.** However, in spite of the fact that he focused his epistemological investigation overwhelmingly on the a priori components, Kant always preserved some role for the senses, thus steering clear of pure **idealism.** This was the case even in his so-called *Opus Postumum*, in which he significantly extended the scope of the a priori, without, however, completely eliminating impressions.

INCENTIVE (*Triebfeder*).   The German word "*Triebfeder*" was originally employed to designate the mainspring of a clock, but was then transferred, under the influence of the French materialists of the 18th century, to descriptions of living beings, including humans. Kant used it in his **ethics,** referring with it to impulse in animals and to **interest** in rational beings (Ak 5, p. 79). Because of the human **freedom** that he presupposed in his moral philosophy, Kant held that an incentive could lead to an **action** only when it was made into a **maxim** (Ak 6, p. 24).

In his lectures on ethics and in the *Groundwork of the Metaphysics of Morals*, Kant made the distinction between incentive as the "subjective ground of desire," and motive as the "objective ground of volition" (Ak 4, p. 427), but he later gave it up. Within this early distinction, the concept of incentive was restricted to subjective motivation determined by material ends; in the ***Critique of Practical Reason***, incentive is then defined as the "subjective ground of determination of the will," and it now applies to the "will of a being whose reason does not by its nature necessarily conform with the objective law" (Ak 5, p. 72) and who, therefore, in distinction to the divine will, encounters moral **law** as an **ought**. The search for subjective incentives of moral action does not, prima facie, appear to stand in any immediate relation to moral law. Kant solves the problem of how a sensible being can be motivated by practical **reason** by attributing to moral law itself the effect of an incentive. This effect consists in an a priori cognizable **feeling** that is expressed, on the one hand, negatively and painfully in the exclusion of all **inclinations** from the moral determination of the **will**, and, on the other hand, positively in the **respect** for moral law.

In his "Doctrine of Virtue," Kant repeatedly refers to the "general ethical command: 'act in conformity to duty out of **duty**'," thus aiming to establish moral law as the sole incentive (Ak 6, pp. 391–93, 446).

INCLINATION (*Neigung*).   Under inclination, Kant understands a "habitual sensible desire" (Ak 7, p. 251; Ak 6, p. 212). When one is subjected to an inclination, one's faculty of desire is dependent on sensations, for example, on the experience of pleasure, and one thus betrays a need (Ak 4, p. 413n.). Closely related is the concept of propensity (*Hang, propensio*), which Kant defines as the "subjective ground of the possibility of an inclination (habitual desire, *concupiscentia*)" (Ak 6, p. 28).

When dealing with the foundation of morality in **practical reason**, Kant presupposes the opposition between **nature** and **virtue** and, accordingly, he discredits inclinations as "always burdensome to a rational being" and even as "blind and servile"; they change, they grow, and yet they "always leave behind a still greater void than one had thought to fill" (Ak 5, p. 118). A **will** that is determined by inclinations can never be moral. Acting out of **duty** and acting out of inclination contradict each other even when the objects to which duty and inclination refer are the same. It is essential for the determination of the will by moral **law** that it occur without the effect of sensible incentives and, even more drastically, that all inclinations be rejected insofar as they could be opposed to moral law (p. 72).

The most powerful and internal inclination in humans is the one to **happiness** (Ak 4, p. 399). Kant does not reject this inclination and its fulfillment by excluding it from morality altogether; he declares natural inclinations "considered as such" to be good, but he demands that they be tamed by prudence in order that the goal of happiness not remain unattained because of a conflict of different inclinations (Ak 6, p. 58). By aiming at such "ends of inclination" (Ak 4, p. 396), we submit our conduct to the rational rules of prudence.

Against the attempt of Friedrich Schiller (1759–1805) to harmonize duty and inclination in the concept of grace, Kant introduced the notion of an "inclination to duty," though he retained the distinction of the two concepts (Ak 6, p. 23n.). However, he admitted that one could speak of a "sense-free inclination" as the effect (not cause) of a pure interest of reason (p. 213).

INCONGRUENT COUNTERPARTS (*inkongruente Gegenstücke*). Any two symmetrical, three dimensional objects that are identical in their internal relations, but are distinguished by an "inner difference" so that "the surface enclosing the one object cannot possibly enclose the other" (Ak 2, p. 382); for example, a right winding and a left winding sea shell or a right hand and a left one. As his thinking on **space** evolved, Kant utilized such cases to defend two different positions. In his **pre-critical** piece "Concerning the Ultimate Ground of the Differentiation of Directions in Space" of 1768, he employed incongruent counterparts to argue against the conception of **Gottfried Wilhelm Leibniz** that space consists of the external relations between parts of matter, and in favor of **Isaac Newton**'s theory of absolute space: the fact that we are able to distinguish between such objects cannot be owing to the mutual relations of their parts, but must be due to the reference that such objects have to absolute space (pp. 382–83).

However, only two years later in his *Inaugural Dissertation*, Kant rejected Newton's scheme and used incongruent counterparts to defend his own conception of space as the **a priori form** of **intuition**. Kant now emphasized that such objects could only be distinguished on the basis of intuition and not by conceptual means, that is by **sensibility** and not by the **understanding** (§ 15). He used this case twice in his **critical** writings, in the *Prolegomena* (Ak 4, p. 286) and in the *Metaphysical Foundations of Natural Science* (Ak 4, p. 484), though not in the *Critique of Pure Reason*. There has been much speculation about the reasons for this omission, ranging from Kant's alleged awareness of the weakness of this argument to the more plausible point that the first *Critique* is supposed to follow the synthetic rather than the **analytic method** and is therefore allowed to base its arguments only on the powers of the human cognitive faculties, but not on **facts**.

INDIVIDUAL. *See* PERSON.

INDUCTION. Unlike the empiricists, who tend to hold induction in high esteem, Kant did not regard the conclusion from the many to the all or from the particular to the **universal** to be of any great value as far as the requirements of **transcendental philosophy** were concerned.

He considered induction to be mere empirical **cognition** that was **contingent** and thus incapable of **necessity** and universality (A 196/B 241); it could yield only empirical certainty, that is, only "comparative universality" (A 24, A 91/B 124), and could therefore not serve as the basis of certain cognition such as is required in **mathematics**, in **pure** science, or in **metaphysics**.

INERTIA (*Trägheit*). Kant regarded inertia along with permanence in the quantity of matter and equality of action and reaction as part of **pure** natural science (B 21n.). More precisely, in the ***Metaphysical Foundations of Natural Science***, he identified inertia as the second law of (pure) mechanics. As such it corresponded, on the one hand, to the second analogy (**causality**), on the other hand, to **Isaac Newton**'s first law of motion. In his explanation of the wording of the law ("all alteration of matter has an external cause"), Kant placed the stress on 'external.' He considered inertia as an important characteristic of **matter**, one which excluded the possibility that matter could act on the basis of its own inner determinations; the inertness of matter meant for Kant its lifelessness. If matter was therefore to change its state of **motion**, the cause would have to come from the outside. Together with permanence, inertia guaranteed in Kant's view the possibility of **natural science**, while hylozoism would spell its demise (Ak 4, pp. 543–44). Kant assumed a **force** of inertia only during his **pre-critical** period (Ak 1, p. 243), but rejected this widely accepted Newtonian notion in his **critical philosophy** of science, arguing that not only was it a contradiction of terms, but that it also misleadingly suggested that a moving body would have to use up a part of its motion to overcome the inertia of a body at **rest**, a notion that in its turn would lead to the mistaken idea that motion in the world would diminish. Kant preferred to think of the resting body as moving with an infinitesimally small velocity and thus as exercising resistance not thanks to its inertia, but thanks to its motion (Ak 4, pp. 550–51).

INFINITY (*Unendlichkeit*). With his acceptance of the **continuity** of **space** and **time**, Kant also admitted that they both consisted of an infinite number of parts. In the same way, he could grant that **reality**, as a continuous **magnitude**, was susceptible to infinite **degrees** (A 209/B 254). In general, Kant had no problems with infinity in its mathematical sense. He found it unobjectionable to speak of drawing a line to infinity, also of the descent from one pair of parents without end; Kant characterized such progressions as proceeding from a condition to the conditioned. However, when a conditioned is given, we can only progress toward the unconditioned, but we can never attain it, in fact, we cannot even know whether it exists or not. We cannot regress to infinity, we can only continue to regress indeterminately. This is the lesson taught by the **antinomies** of **pure reason**. It applies, for example, in regard to the concept of the **world**, which is not given as an **intuition** and about which we cannot, therefore, determine whether it is finite or infinite. In other words, infinity, be it the infinitely small or infinitely large, cannot be applied to **objects** beyond **experience**, even if reason demands that we unceasingly seek the next member of a given series, all the way to infinity. Infinity in this sense can serve only as a **regulative idea**.

Kant returns to the subject of infinity in its regulative (practical) usage at the end of the *Critique of Practical Reason*, where he emphasizes the value of morality. He claims that the contemplation of "the immeasurable magnitude of worlds upon worlds . . . annihilates my importance as an animal creature," but that the contemplation of the **moral law** within us infinitely raises our worth as it reveals a "life independent of all animality" (Ak 5, p. 162).

For **Georg Wilhelm Friedrich Hegel**, Kant's concept of infinity fell under the heading "bad infinity," that is, the never to be completed progression of finite determinations. Hegel opposed to this bad infinity the concept of the truly infinite, which is not only opposed to the finite but which also transcends this opposition. The problem of infinity was further pursued in mathematical and scientific discussions at the end of the 19th century. Aside from the actual infinite in Georg Cantor's set theory, the interest was focused on the **continuum** and on the grounding of the infinitesimal calculus. *See also* ANTICIPATIONS OF PERCEPTION.

INNATE IDEAS (*angeborene Ideen*). Although a certain similarity between Kant's conception of the **a priori** and the notion of innate ideas as it was defended, for instance, by **Gottfried Wilhelm Leibniz** is undeniable, Kant himself in his critical philosophy always rejected the latter. Already in his last **pre-critical** piece, the *Inaugural Dissertation* of 1770, Kant claimed that neither the **concepts** of the **understanding** nor the concepts of **time** and **space** were innate. Instead, he maintained that such concepts were based on and derived from the laws of the mind (§§ 8, 15). In the *Critique of Pure Reason*, Kant avoided speaking about laws of the mind as the basis of concepts, but he did retain the quintessence of his earlier position. His clearest statement on innate ideas comes in his piece *On a Discovery whereby any New Critique of Pure Reason is to be Made Superfluous by an*

Older One of 1790, in which he defended his position against the charge made by Johann August Eberhard that the *Critique* was inferior to the philosophy of Leibniz. Here, Kant explained that it was not the concepts that were innate, but rather the ground in the subject of the **forms** of **intuition** of space and time and of the **synthetic unity** of the **manifold** in concepts. Owing to this ground in the subject, incoming **impressions** would then prompt the cognitive power to produce a representation of an object (Ak 8, pp. 221–23).

INNER SENSE (*innerer Sinn*). Kant's label for the power by means of which the mind intuits itself and its inner states. The concept of "inner sense" had a long history before Kant, appearing, for example, in **John Locke**'s thought as the bearer of the ideas of reflection. However, by embedding the concept into his **transcendental philosophy**, Kant transformed it considerably. He distinguished inner sense from an outer one, through which we represent to ourselves **objects** as outside us. While holding that the **form** of the latter was **space**, he maintained that the form of the former was **time**, meaning that everything that belongs to the inner determinations can be represented only in terms of temporal relations (A 22–23/B 37). Because all **representations** belong to inner sense, regardless of whether they arise through the influence of external or inner causes or whether they originate **a priori** or empirically (A 98–99), inner sense is more encompassing than outer sense and is therefore called "the sum of all representations" (A 177/B 220), or, alternatively, "the only totality in which all of our representations are contained" (A 155/B 194).

Since Kant generally denied that we have any **intuition** or **cognition** of the **soul** as an object, he stressed that inner sense too is incapable of intuiting the soul. He supported the claim that I can intuit myself only as I appear by advancing a complicated argument that traded on the distinction between inner and outer sense: from the fact that we can represent time, the form of inner sense, only in spatial terms, for example, by drawing a line, that is, in terms of the form of outer intuition, it is evident that "we must order the determinations of inner sense in time in the same way as we order those of outer sense in space"; if we then admit that our cognition of objects by means of the determinations of outer sense is possible only insofar as we are externally affected, then we must also concede that we intuit ourselves through inner sense only as we appear and not as we are (B 156). In other words, both inner and outer sense present us only with intuitions of appearances and not of **things-in-themselves**.

Tied to Kant's conception of inner sense as '**receptivity**' (A 145/B 185) was his further distinction between inner sense and apperception. He claimed that inner sense contained only the form of and a manifold of intuition, maintaining that the latter was not synthesized by inner sense and that it therefore contained no *determinate* intuition at all. Such a **synthesis** was effected by the **transcendental unity of apperception**, which "applies to the manifold of intuitions in general, and, prior to all sensible intuition, under the name of the **categories**, to objects in general." In other words, the unity of apperception produces synthesis by affecting inner sense (B 153–55). See also SENSE (*Sinn*).

INTELLIGIBLE WORLD. *See* WORLD.

INTERACTION (*Wechselwirkung*). *See* COMMUNITY.

INTEREST. Inspired by his reading of Francis Hutcheson, **Jean-Jacques Rousseau**, and Christian Garve, Kant was the first German-writing author to use the concept of 'interest' in an all-encompassing manner to deal with problems in theoretical and practical philosophy as well as in aesthetics. He frequently relied on the concept to mediate between **sensibility** and **reason**. For the realm of speculative reason, Kant spoke of reason's own interest that is based on a propensity of its nature to attain the **systematic** whole of cognition. Out of this 'speculative interest' there arise **maxims** of reason that find their expression in the **regulative principles** of the employment of reason (A 666/B 694). However, in regard to the final purpose of rational thought, a **practical** interest of reason plays a far more prominent role than the speculative one (A 797–98/B 825–26). The speculative and the practical interests of reason are united in three questions: "1) What can I know? 2) What should I do? 3) What may I hope?" (A 804–5/B 832–33).

In his moral philosophy, Kant makes it plain that there can be interest only for beings that both possess reason and are finite (Ak 5, p. 79). When reason assumes the form of interest, it becomes practical, that is, "a cause that determines the **will**" (Ak 4, p. 459n.) or an **incentive** of the will (Ak 5, p. 79). A finite rational being can take either a **pure** interest, dependent merely on the practical principle of reason; or it can determine its will empirically out of a "pathological interest in the object of an action" or "on the presupposition of a special feeling of the subject" (Ak 4, pp. 413n., 459–60n.), that is, it makes its practical use of reason dependent on sensibility. However, even for pure interest, Kant stresses that the validity of moral **law** does not depend on it, but precedes it (pp. 460–61).

In his *Critique of Judgment*, Kant characterizes **aesthetic** judgment as a 'disinterested' one: he denies for it both the "interest of the senses" and the moral "interest of reason." In defining interest here as the 'satisfaction' that "we connect with the representation of the existence of an object," Kant is placing interest into a relationship with the faculty of **desire**, either as it involves empirically a satisfaction in the **agreeable** or morally a **pure** satisfaction in the **good**; such an interest cannot provide the ground of the contemplative aesthetic judgment that is indifferent to the existence of its object (Ak 5, pp. 204–10). However, it is possible to link to it secondarily and indirectly both an empirical (social) and an intellectual (moral) interest in the **beautiful**. Kant connects the latter to natural beauty and proclaims that the immediate interest in it is a mark of a "good soul" (Ak 5, pp. 296–303).

INTUITION (*Anschauung*). Very roughly, this term refers to data provided by **sensibility**, data without which our **concepts** would be empty and without which there would be no **cognition** at all. The English translation is misleading, as it includes mystical connotations that were completely foreign to Kant, who restricted the term to its sensible meaning. Resorting to 'intuition' derives all of its justification from Kant's own Latin rendering of the word as *intuitio*. However, 'intuition' has become the accepted standard, and attempts at alternate translations have fared poorly.

Kant introduced the distinction between intuitions as the products of sensibility, and concepts as the products of the **understanding** already in his *Inaugural Dissertation* of 1770, and he retained it throughout his **critical philosophy**. Intuitions provide our cognition with an immediate relation to **objects**, they are particular, and the subject is passive in receiving them (**receptivity**). Concepts, on the other hand, are discursive, general, and symbolic, and the subject is active in synthesizing them (**spontaneity**). Kant strongly insisted on the separate nature of these two faculties of the mind and of their products, stressing, nevertheless, their equal value; famous in this regard is his statement that "thoughts without content are empty, intuitions without concepts are blind" (A 51/B 75). He claimed that this conception enabled him to occupy an intermediary position between the rationalists, who accepted only the understanding and denigrated the data of sensibility as merely confused concepts, and the empiricists, who emphasized sensibility at the expense of the understanding. Kant did not consider the gap between the two faculties to be a serious difficulty, addressing the question of bridging it in his chapter on "**Schematism**."

Kant divides intuitions into three types. First, empirical intuition is related to objects through **sensation**; one may speak here of the **matter** of **appearances**. Second, **pure** intuition is the pure form of sensibility and functions as the **form** of appearances; pure intuition is devoid of all sensation, only extension and form remain. Kant identifies **space** and **time** as the only two pure forms of sensible intuition. Finally, Kant also described an intellectual or original intuition, through which the **existence** of objects would be given. However, he rejected the notion that finite beings such as humans could possess intellectual intuition already in the *Inaugural Dissertation* (§ 10, see also B 72). The distinction between empirical and pure intuition is crucial to Kant's theoretical philosophy in a number of respects. It enables him to defend a theory in which the status of raw empirical data is safeguarded, yet it also allows him to present such data as already somehow structured and thus amenable to cognition. With his conception of pure intuition, Kant can explain how an **a priori**, apodictically certain **mathematics** is possible, and, based on the fact that pure intuition as the form of sensibility is present in all appearances, he can then explain how mathematics necessarily applies to all objects of **experience**, and thus how a mathematical **physics** is possible.

Kant's theory that sensibility and the understanding are the two roots of human cognition (A 15/B 29) and, along with it, his view that intuitions and concepts are of equal importance for cognition have often been criticized and transformed. Two diametrically opposed positions in this regard were defended by **Hermann Cohen** and **Martin Heidegger**. While the former in his *Logik der reinen Erkenntnis* of 1902 completely abandoned, on the basis of his interpretation of the principle of the **Anticipation of Perception**, the dualism of intuition and thought, attempting to ground the objective validity of cognition without any recourse to empirical or pure intuition, the latter in his *Kant and the Problem of Metaphysics* of 1929 declared intuition to be the essence of "finite human cognition," and held the "reinterpretation of cognition as judgment (thought)" to be a transgression against the spirit of the Kantian critique. *See also* SYMBOL.

- J -

JUDAISM.   One must keep separate Kant's comments on Judaism, his good personal relations with distinguished Jewish scholars, and his influence on the Jewish Enlightenment (Haskala). In his *Religion within the Boundaries of Mere Reason*, Kant argued that the followers of the Jewish religion had no access to "the interior of the **moral** disposition" (Ak 6, p. 79), since their faith amounted to, at least originally, only "a collection of merely statutory laws," that is, coercive laws imposed on the individual (125). Accordingly, Kant viewed the union of the different "religious sects" in an enlightened, pure, morally based religious faith as the "euthanasia of Judaism." The great influence that his critical philosophy had exercised on the Jewish Enlightenment in the generation after Moses Mendelssohn may be surmised from the fact that he was able to quote the recommendation made by Lazarus Bendavid, who had commented on Kant, to "openly accept the religion of Jesus" (Ak 7, pp. 52–53).

Hermann Cohen counteracted Kant's 'outrageous' conception of Judaism by working out the "inner relation" of Kant's philosophy to Jewish prophesy in theology, ethics, and in the philosophy of history. In distinction to Kant, he underscored the contribution of Judaism to the ongoing development of Christianity ("Innere Beziehungen der Kantischen Philosophie zum Judentum"; "Inner Relations of Kant's Philosophy to Judaism," 1910).

JUDGMENT (*Urteil*). Given that Kant considered that all thinking basically occurred in the form of judging, it is hardly surprising that judgment plays a crucial role in his philosophy, both in the sense of a logical (formal or transcendental) operation or proposition and in the sense of the faculty or power of the mind to judge. However, Kant clearly separates these two meanings; he never identifies the "faculty (or power or capacity) of judgment" (*Urteilskraft*) with the act of judging or its result (*Urteil*).

In theoretical philosophy, judging involves determining whether something is or is not (A 131/B 170). Kant offers various definitions that differ from one another in accordance with the varying role that judgment plays in his **architectonic**. The most general definitions of judgment are offered in the context of his discussion of formal **logic**; here the emphasis is on **unity**. Thus he says that a judgment is the mediate **cognition** of an **object**, that is, the **representation** of a representation of it, and "all judgments are accordingly functions of unity among our representations" (A 68–69/B 93–94). In his *Logic*, he similarly defines a judgment as "the representation of the unity of consciousness of different representations or the representation of the relations of different representations insofar as these constitute a **concept**" (§ 17).

However, judgments are crucial to Kant's project of presenting an **a priori** set of concepts or principles as a foundation of epistemology. The key question here is stated in terms of 'judgment,' namely, "how are synthetic judgments a priori possible" (B 19, 73). One important step in the solution is Kant's derivation of the **categories** from the **table of judgments** in the so-called **metaphysical deduction**. This involves the step from general logic to **transcendental logic**, or, in terms of the type of judgments that are concerned, the transition from analytic judgments a priori to synthetic judgments a priori. In connection with the latter, Kant needs to stress the necessity that arises from the application of the categories, that is, the fact that the relation that is involved is objectively valid. Thus, here he defines a judgment as the way of bringing "given cognitions to the objective unity of apperception" (B 141–42). In the *Critique of Pure Reason*, Kant invariably ties **objective** cognition to judgment. His famous distinction in the *Prolegomena* between judgments of **experience** that are objective and judgments of perception that are not objective is therefore misleading, since in the language of the first *Critique* the latter do not qualify as judgments at all.

Hermann Cohen's *Logik der reinen Erkenntnis* (*Logic of Pure Cognition*) was meant to provide a philosophical grounding of mathematical and scientific cognition in an open system of judgments. Cohen grasped judgments as ways of thought with which the categorical elements of the cognition of an object (reality, space, time, number, law, and so forth) could be produced without recourse to a-logical factors. A judgment was then understood as a unity of separation and connection. In contrast, **Paul Natorp** developed a system of basic logical functions, not of judgments or principles. Natorp then arrived at the constitutive moments of concept and judgment by deducing them from this system.

In the **Southwestern German School of Neokantianism**, judgment was dealt with primarily in view of the valuation implicit in the claim of the truth of a synthesis of representations. However, the younger authors of the School differed in their assessment of the importance of judgment for objective cognition. While for **Bruno Bauch** judgment, next to concept and method, amounted to the fundamental "structural form of truth" and for Jonas Cohn epistemology was in its core a theory of judgment, for Emil Lask the logic of judgments took second place behind the logic of objects, which was centered on the categories and not on judgments. *See also* ANALYTIC AND SYNTHETIC JUDGMENTS.

JUDGMENT, FACULTY OF (*Urteilskraft*). Taking a clue from the terminology of Alexander Gottlieb Baumgarten, according to whom a specific *facultas dijudicandi* could be concerned either with the objects of logic or of the senses (or of taste), Kant considers the faculty of judgment (also translated as "power of judgment") to be one of the higher cognitive faculties of the mind, placing it between the **understanding** and **reason**. The understanding, as the "faculty of rules" (A 126, A 132/B 171), is as such not capable of establishing a link between the rules and their application. For this to be accomplished, the faculty of judgment is required, as the "faculty of subsuming under rules, i.e., of determining whether something stands under a given rule or not" (A 132/B 171). This talent (Kant speaks of 'mother-wit') cannot be learned, it can only be practiced (A 133/B 172). From the point of view of **transcendental philosophy**, Kant subsequently expounds a "Doctrine of the Faculty of Judgment," the task of which is to show how a rule that is implied in a concept of the understanding may be applied to **intuitions (Schematism)** (A 135–36/B 174–75).

In the *Critique of Practical Reason*, Kant develops a "Typic of Pure Practical Judgment" with which he wishes to resolve the difficulty that the practical **law** of reason as a "law of freedom" has to be applied to **actions** in the sensible world that belongs to nature. The subsumption of such actions under the categorical **imperative** cannot be carried out with the aid of a sensible schema, but only on the basis of a law that functions, in the form of a law of nature, as a *type* of moral law (Ak 5, pp. 67–70).

While working out the systematic unity of his critical philosophy in the *Critique of Judgment*, Kant related the cognitive power of the faculty of judgment as an a priori principle to the feeling of pleasure and pain. In this fashion, he also gained the foundation for a solution to the problem of the universal validity of **aesthetic** judgments. In distinction to the subsumption of the particular under a given general treated in the first two *Critiques*, a process that Kant considered to be the work of the determinant faculty of judgment, he now describes a faculty of judgment that attains the general by taking a given particular as its point of departure. This he calls the reflective faculty of judgment (Ak 5, p. 179). When the reflective faculty of judgment is involved, one must, unlike in the case of the determinant one, inquire after the principle of the passage from the particular to the general. According to Kant, reflective judgment itself provides this principle by assuming the formal **purposiveness** of nature in its empirical laws. In this way, the search for the unity of nature in the manifold of the empirical laws appears as a meaningful project.

Roughly distinguished, the aesthetic faculty of judgment is linked to subjective purposiveness, while the teleological faculty of judgment in the narrow sense of the word is tied to the objective purposiveness of nature.

Johann Wolfgang Goethe followed Kant, though not uncritically, in employing in his scientific studies the concept of an intuitive faculty of judgment. **Jakob Friedrich Fries**, on the other hand, in his most important work *Neue oder anthropologische Kritik der Vernunft* of 1807, brought the procedure of the reflective judgment into proximity to induction. In the 20th century, Hannah Arendt attempted to interpret the critique of aesthetic judgment as providing a background to political philosophy. Jean-François Lyotard discovered in the reflective faculty of judgment a form of generalization that corresponds to the heterogeneity of the types of discourse.

JURISPRUDENCE. *See CONFLICT OF THE FACULTIES;* RIGHT (*Recht*).

- K -

KINGDOM OF ENDS (*Reich der Zwecke*). Kant introduced this expression in his ***Groundwork of the Metaphysics of Morals*** as a label for the union of autonomous rational beings under common laws. The kingdom of ends is marked by the following characteristics: 1) Its members are **ends** in themselves, that is, **persons** who can never be fully used as means; 2) the **moral laws** that connect them are grounded in **pure reason** and are therefore strictly **universal**; the laws are not imposed on the members of the kingdom, but the members pass them onto themselves, that is, they legislate them and address them to themselves; the laws determine both the ends in themselves and the proper ends of each rational being, thus connecting these beings into a systematic whole. The kingdom of ends is an ideal (Ak 4, p. 433), which mankind is morally obligated to realize. However, each person must cooperate in this undertaking (p. 439).

Kant integrated into his conception various topical notions of the philosophical and theological traditions. Thus, for example, the customary concepts "kingdom of grace" and "kingdom of nature" provide the background for his own concepts of "kingdom of ends" and "kingdom of nature," concepts that Kant placed both in opposition and in analogy to each other (pp. 436ff.). The two kingdoms resemble one another in that each of them has a lawful constitution, they are set apart by the specific type of their lawful determination (self-imposed versus externally necessitated). The whole of **nature** can be regarded as a 'kingdom' only insofar as it "is related to rational beings as its end" (p. 438). In the *Critique of Judgment*, Kant claims that the use of the reflective **faculty of judgment** produces the regulative "idea of the whole of nature as a system in accordance with the rule of ends" (Ak 5, p. 379), an **idea** that then leads to an ethicotheology in which **God** is not only thought of as "the legislative sovereign in a moral kingdom of ends," but is also adorned with all his traditional attributes (p. 444).

Hermann Cohen saw in Kant's "kingdom of ends" the archetype of his own ideal of a community of autonomous beings, an ideal that he viewed as an "ethical reform idea" and that he opposed to the existing governmental politics of power and class society. In accordance with his **ethical socialism**, he emphasized that the Kantian moral law in the kingdom of ends could be realized only if the person of the laborer was finally recognized as an end in itself. He rejected the religious connotations of the "kingdom of God" by stressing that the realization of the "kingdom of ends" would have to be sought in politics.

KNOWLEDGE (*Wissen*). *See* COGNITION (*Erkenntnis*).

- L -

LANGE, FRIEDRICH ALBERT (1828-1875). One of the precursors of the **Marburg School of Neokantianism.** Lange's fame was based on his work in education, social reform, and political writing; he became a professor in Marburg in 1872. He helped to shape the movement by endorsing in the two volumes of his celebrated *Geschichte des Materialismus* (2nd ed. 1873-1875), a work that went through at least 10 editions, Kant's theoretical philosophy. He interpreted Kant from the point of view of contemporary theories of the physiology of sense perception, maintaining that our **experience** is determined by our psycho-physical structure. With this position, Lange set himself apart both from objectivist materialism and from speculative **metaphysics,** which he dismissed as a play with words (*Begriffsdichtung*). Recognizing the need to accommodate questions about the meaning of life, he admitted a world of **ideas** in Kant's sense of the word as a complement to the realm of **appearances.** In order to emphasize this addition of a world of values to the world of being, he coined the expression "standpoint of the ideal." Nevertheless, Lange did not consider that ideas could enter theoretical philosophy, but claimed that they would only be useful for edification in **religion** and **art** or for motivation to moral conduct; he felt that in their latter function they had been depicted in an exemplary way in Friedrich Schiller's (1759-1805) poetry.

Lange was also greatly concerned with social problems, especially with the wretchedness of workers during industrialization. In his major publication devoted to this topic, *Die Arbeiterfrage in ihrer Bedeutung für Gegenwart und Zukunft beleuchtet* (*The Problem of Workers in Its Significance for the Present and the Future Elucidated*) (1865), a book that went through at least seven editions, he interpreted such desolation in a social Darwinian manner as a consequence of the general struggle for existence. As a solution, he proposed a type of democratic socialism. He attacked Karl Marx's theory of history and of revolution, stressing the need for a more factual approach to the contemporary situation and for an examination of the consequences and side-effects of revolutions. This led him to advocate a pragmatic approach to improving the lot of the workers. Lange's social philosophy exercised a powerful impact on **Hermann Cohen's** notion of **ethical socialism.** The personal acquaintance of the two philosophers, and Cohen's gratefulness to his mentor also led him to adopt significant elements of Lange's epistemology.

LAW (*Gesetz*). Unlike **rules**, all laws, both theoretical and practical, are objective, universal, and necessary. Kant considered the **principles of pure understanding** to be the supreme, pure laws of **nature**. As products of the understanding, the pure laws serve to order **appearances** and to structure and to make possible empirical **cognition**. In its function as the source of these laws, the understanding acts as the legislator of nature, or, more specifically, of the formal **unity** of nature.

Particular laws are particular determinations of the pure laws of the understanding; they stand under them and in accordance with them, though they cannot be derived from them. They can be discovered only by recourse to particular experience (A 127–28; B 165). Kant was acutely aware of the fact that even the particular laws carried with them "an expression of necessity," though they tended to seem accidental to the understanding (A 159/B 198; CJ, Introduction), and he repeatedly attempted to explain the possible foundations of this necessity. One approach he followed was to subordinate the particular laws to more encompassing wholes, the coherence of which would guarantee that each particular law would be endowed with a greater amount of certainty. Kant explored this approach in the "Appendix" to the "**Transcendental Dialectic**" and again in the "Introduction" to the *Critique of Judgment*, suggesting in both cases that **regulative** principles of reason or the principle of **purposiveness** could help to order the particular laws and thus provide them with some measure of necessity. This approach, however, labored under the disadvantage that such principles for the ordering of laws were only subjectively valid. Kant explored another line of attack in the *Metaphysical Foundations of Natural Science*, and, being dissatisfied with the results, again in the so-called *Opus Postumum*. In these works, he extended the categories first into the realm of **matter** and **motion**, later also into the realm of the relations of motive **forces**. The laws that he was concerned with were initially mainly the laws of **physics**, later also those of **chemistry** and biology. Though the latter approach to ground the necessity of particular laws may have seemed to Kant the most promising one, he never completed the task; whether this was due to the inherent difficulty involved or simply due to Kant's own old age is unclear.

Laws also played a central role in Kant's practical philosophy. Here, Kant considered **reason**, specifically practical reason, to be the source of such laws, which he labeled the laws of **freedom**. Unlike the laws of nature, which deal with that which does happen, the laws of freedom only command what **ought** to happen (A 802/B 830). Among the laws of practical reason, Kant then distinguished between **moral** laws, which are derived on the basis of the categorical **imperative**, and juridical laws. While the latter refer only to an external use of freedom, the former refer both to the external and the internal use of freedom (Ak 6, p. 214). The different aspects of Kant's concept of law were taken up by the **Neokantians**. In the theoretical philosophy of the **Marburg School**, the concept underwent an inflationary expansion: The **transcendental** principles, that is, **Hermann Cohen**'s "laws of thought" and **Paul Natorp**'s "original law" of the synthetic unity, were labeled as 'laws' as were the 'objects' of experience, in which the manifold of appearances is brought to a unity. Cohen recognized a 'judgment' or a category of law, which implies that he regarded laws of nature as products of **thought**. The understanding of law as a **function** was promoted, beyond Natorp, by **Ernst Cassirer** in his *Substanzbegriff und Funktionsbegriff* of 1910. Cassirer also presented a finely worked out interpretation of the relationship between law and **fact** and between general and particular laws. In his book on the theory of natural laws (*Das Naturgesetz*, 1924), **Bruno Bauch** placed the logical presuppositions of natural laws into the system of the categories and determined these laws correspondingly as a general complex of categories that is filled with empirical content.

LEIBNIZ, GOTTFRIED WILHELM (1646–1716).   While Leibniz's present-day fame rests on his achievements as a universal genius who made notable contributions to a number of fields of learning, having, for instance, invented, at roughly the same time as **Isaac Newton**, but independently of him, the calculus, much of his early impact in philosophy was largely due to his monadology. Many of the ideas from the monadology were taken up almost immediately by other thinkers, first and foremost by **Christian Wolff**. However, Leibnizian philosophy was used selectively and a significant part of what was chosen was transformed and integrated into the various philosophical systems of his successors. The school of thought that arose from this effort of rethinking Leibniz is generally referred to as the Leibniz-Wolff (or Leibnizian-Wolffian) school. Since it dominated much of German academic philosophy commencing with the 1720s and continuing well into the second half of the 18th century, it is no wonder that the young Kant was also heavily influenced by it. Much of his **pre-critical** writings could, in fact, be classed under the heading of the Leibniz-Wolff school, though his attitude toward it was, from the first, always a critical one. Kant, for example, never accepted the idea of the preestablished harmony, a notion central to Leibniz (Ak 1, pp. 412, 415; Ak 2, pp. 390, 409), and he also rejected Leibniz's conception of windowless monads that are not causally related among each other (Ak 1, p. 415). From early on, Kant further rejected the traditional ontological argument for the existence of

God as it was first stated by Anselm of Canterbury, subsequently developed by Leibniz and then accepted by his followers (Ak 1, pp. 394–95; Ak 2, pp. 72–77). However, since the young Kant did adopt many of the tenets of Leibnizian thought, it may be fairly stated that much of his **critical philosophy** was the result of a long process of increasingly distancing himself from the Leibniz-Wolff school, and along with it, from his own earlier positions, even if many elements were not simply discarded, but were retained in a transformed shape. Thus, for instance, in regard to the dispute of the freedom of the will versus **determinism**, the young Kant defended the Leibnizian-Wolffian conception against Christian August Crusius (1715–1775), one of the major critics of the school (Ak 1, pp. 401–5), before proceeding in the *Critique of Pure Reason* to develop his own, highly original answer to the problem based on his **phenomena-noumena** distinction (third **antinomy** of pure reason). Another such crucial step concerned the theory of the **transcendental aesthetic.** Kant initially adhered to Leibniz's notion that **space** and **time** are nothing but external relations between objects, but rejected this view in 1768 in order to defend Newton's conception that space was absolute, before arriving in 1770 at his own theory that space and time are the forms of **intuition.**

Perhaps the most significant break with the Leibniz-Wolff school involved the gradual rejection of the claim that logical **analysis** of concepts offered the only possibility for discovering truth. This part of the process of weaning himself away from Leibnizianism may be traced as far back as the *Nova Dilucidatio* of 1755, in which Kant refused to unreservedly accept the principles of contradiction and of sufficient reason as the first starting points of philosophy. This was followed by numerous further small steps. One may mention the claim, defended in the *Attempt to Introduce Negative Magnitudes into Philosophy* of 1763, that there is not only a logical contradiction in philosophy but also a real one. This process ultimately culminated in Kant's discovery of the **synthetic judgments a priori.** Also very important was Kant's rejection in the *Inaugural Dissertation* of the claim of the Leibniz-Wolff school that sensible data are merely confused **concepts** of the **understanding** (§ 7), and the corresponding elevation of **sensibility** to a separate and equal **faculty** of the **mind.** In the first *Critique*, Kant retained the distinction between the two faculties, calling it now **transcendental** rather than merely logical (A 44/B 61). The most explicit and concerted rejection of Leibniz in the first *Critique* occurred in the chapter on the "**Amphiboly** of Concepts of Reflection," in which Kant criticized Leibniz's rationalism, specifically his error ('amphiboly') of treating concepts of reflection such as 'identity' and 'difference' or 'inner' and 'outer' as if they were attributes of **things-in-themselves**. Within the framework of this criticism, Kant also rejected Leibniz's claim of the universal validity of his celebrated principle of the identity of indiscernibles, restricting it instead to the realm of concepts and excluding it from the realm of appearances.

In the 1790s, Kant saw himself confronted with Leibniz on two more occasions. The first time, he was provoked by Johann August Eberhard's (1739–1809) charge that the critical philosophy not only represented no advance on Leibniz but that it was, in fact, inferior to it. In his reply, *On a Discovery whereby any New Critique of Pure Reason is to be Made Superfluous by an Older One* (1790), Kant did not so much attack Leibniz as he accused Eberhard of misunderstanding both the main tenets of the critical philosophy and the main doctrines of Leibniz, namely, the principle of sufficient reason, the monadology, and preestablished harmony. Kant ended up claiming that his *Critiques* in fact agreed with a correct understanding of Leibniz. However, in his draft (composed ca. 1793–1794) of a response to the prize question proposed by the Berlin Academy in 1791, "What Real Progress has Metaphysics Made in Germany since the Time of Leibniz and Wolff?" Kant was far more critical of Leibniz. He called preestablished harmony the "most peculiar fiction in philosophy" and assigned the philosophy of Leibniz and Wolff to the first and lowest stage of **metaphysics**, namely, the dogmatic one. He claimed that the school initiated by these two philosophers had attempted to demonstrate unknowable teachings, ones that his own critical philosophy had shown to be tenable only as matters of moral conviction.

The more that **Hermann Cohen** and **Paul Natorp** distanced themselves from Kant's dualism of intuition and thought, the more they approached Leibniz's philosophy. With his infinitesimal calculus, Leibniz proved for Cohen the productive power of thought. And Natorp found in Leibniz an important instance of the logical nature of the mathematical. But it was only with **Ernst Cassirer**'s book *Leibniz' System in seinen wissenschaftlichen Grundlagen* (*The Scientific Foundations of Leibniz's System*) of 1902 that a comprehensive interpretation of Leibniz was presented by one of the Neokantians. Just as Bertrand Russell and Louis Couturat in their works on Leibniz that were published almost at the same time (1900 and 1901), Cassirer defended the view that it was the logical principles that were the roots of Leibniz's thought. However, unlike Russell and Couturat, Cassirer understood 'logic' in the **Neokantian** sense of a theory of the principles of scientific cognition. Cassirer's *Leibniz* can therefore be seen as providing the historical underpinnings of Cohen's *Logik der reinen Erkenntnis* (1902).

LIE (*Lüge*). Kant held every kind of lie to be morally reprehensible, even the so-called white lies or lies out of necessity. To promise something while intending to break the promise may possibly be prudent in view of the consequences of such conduct, but can never count as being in accordance with **duty**. The **maxim** to lie in a certain case can never be made into a universal **law**, because such a justification of lying would undermine the credibility of every promise and even the possibility of a lie, and would therefore be self-destructive (Ak 4, pp. 402–3). According to the doctrine of virtue in the ***Metaphysics of Morals***, a lie is the "greatest violation of a human being's duty to itself" as a moral being (Ak 6, p. 429); in the early lectures on moral philosophy, however, lying was still treated within the framework of duties toward others (Ak 27/1, pp. 444ff.). While answering criticism from Benjamin Constant, Kant argued anticonsequentialistically that even the possible positive consequences of a lie, for example, preventing a crime, cannot justify the suspension of the precept of reason to be truthful ("On a Supposed Right to Lie from Philanthropy," Ak 8, pp. 423–30). **Johann Gottlieb Fichte** confirmed Kant's strict proscription of lying, but held that moral and ultimately even physical resistance in order to prevent a planned crime was morally prescribed.

LIEBMANN, OTTO (1840–1912). One of the precursors of **Neokantianism**, Liebmann became famous for his first book *Kant und die Epigonen* (1865). Here, he claims that the entire post-Kantian philosophy is an exercise in futility due to its preoccupation with the **thing-in-itself**, that is, with a topic that Kant had already proven to be no better than trying to square a circle. The book stimulated renewed interest in Kant in part thanks to Liebmann's motto "back to Kant," which he repeated mantra-like at the end of each chapter, and which was to become the rallying call for the Neokantians. In his further publications *Über den objectiven Anblick* (*On the Objective Sight*) (1869) and *Analysis der Wirklichkeit* (*Analysis of Reality*) (1876, 2nd enlarged ed. 1880), Liebmann adhered to his own motto by pursuing the project of a critical **metaphysics**. This involved specifying the subjective factors of empirical cognition and included a discussion (fated to forever remain merely hypothetical) of the absolute foundation of things and of their cognition.

LIFE (*Leben*). In the context of his natural philosophy, Kant, taking a stance against hylozoism, distinguishes life from lifeless **matter** by assigning **desire** to it, which he defines as the "inner principle of a substance to alter its state" (Ak 4, p. 544). He follows the epigenetic theory of Johann Friedrich Blumenbach in the debate about a life-force, and differentiates the "merely mechanical formative power that is present in all matter" from the "formative drive" in organized (organic) bodies (CJ, Ak 5, p. 424). In his practical philosophy, Kant defines life as the "power of a being to act according to laws of the faculty of desire" (CrPR, Ak 5, p. 9; see also MM, Ak 6, p. 211). The value of human life is not linked to enjoyment, we must rather seek it by acting "**purposively** and independently of **nature**" (CJ, Ak 5, p. 434); it consists of our consciousness that we must adhere to duty (Ak 11, p. 433).

LIMIT. *See* BOUNDARY.

LIMITATION. *See* NEGATION; REALITY.

LOCKE, JOHN (1632-1704). In Germany in the 18th century, Locke's epistemology and political philosophy exercised an appreciable amount of influence, though they did not play the same dominant role there as they did in Britain and France. Kant interpreted Locke as a proponent of a pure **empiricism**, that is, of a philosophy that supposedly accepted only **representations** derived from the **senses**, but that was incapable of properly accommodating the **pure concepts** of the **understanding** on which Kant built his own critical epistemology. Kant contrasted Locke's position with that of the rationalists **René Descartes** and **Gottfried Wilhelm Leibniz**, and attempted to find a middle ground, thus seeking to avoid the errors while retaining the positive aspects of both of the extremes. Kant agreed with Locke that all **cognition** starts with **experience** and that we have no innate ideas, but he criticized him for investigating only the genesis of cognition and not its legitimacy. He accused Locke of mistakenly thinking that the concepts of the understanding were derived from experience rather than that they served as the conditions of the possibility of experience. In addition, Kant claimed that Locke was inconsistent and ended up venturing beyond the bounds of experience when he tried to prove the existence of **God** and the immortality of the soul (B 127-28, A 854/B 882). Here, Kant was not totally accurate, since Locke attempted to prove only the former, but not the latter.

Kant summed up his critique of Locke in the section entitled "**Amphiboly**," in which he attacked both the empiricists and the rationalists. He accused Locke of having 'sensitivized' the concepts of the understanding, that is, of having interpreted them as empirical or abstracted concepts of reflection (A 271/B 327). This criticism, and along with it, much of Kant's view of Locke, is not completely justified, since it assumes that

Locke, who divided ideas into those of sensation and of reflection, conceived of the latter as derived from the former, whereas, in fact, Locke claimed that we could arrive at simple ideas by reflecting on the operations of our mind. Since Kant's own view that a priori cognition is derived from the laws governing our mind bears a certain amount of resemblance to Locke's teachings, the distance between the two thinkers was not as drastic as Kant had pretended, even if Locke had neither elaborated his notion nor did he place it at the center of his philosophy as Kant had done.

As a relatively minor point of criticism, Kant also took issue with the inappropriate use of the term 'idea' on the part of certain unnamed philosophers; he likely had primarily Locke and **George Berkeley** in mind. He claimed that they employed the word in an overly general sense so as to include sensory perceptions (A 319–20/B 376–77).

LOGIC. The discipline of formal (or general) logic enjoyed a high standing for Kant and served as a model of an established science, a model that **metaphysics** was in some way supposed to emulate (B viii). On such logic, Kant lectured regularly during his whole teaching career; his own notes as well as the notes taken by some of his students have been published (Ak 9, Ak 24). However, Kant was also acutely mindful of the limitations of formal logic. Against the tendency of the **Leibniz-Wolff** school to deduce all knowledge by means of logical analysis, he began to stress already in his **pre-critical** writings, especially in the *Attempt to Introduce the Concept of Negative Magnitudes into Philosophy* of 1763, the distinction between logical and real relations, generally emphasizing the greater importance of the latter.

At the outset of the critical period, this distinction matured into the distinction between general and **transcendental logic**. Kant divided the former into pure and applied, and defined general applied logic as containing "the rules of the use of the **understanding** under the subjective empirical conditions that **psychology** teaches" (A 53/B 77). Far more important for his critical project was, however, pure general logic, which "abstracts from all content of **cognition**," that is, from all objects and "considers only the logical form in the relation of cognitions to one another, that is, the **form** of **thinking** in general" (A 55/B 79). On the basis of this characterization, Kant labeled pure general logic, that is, classical logic, as *formal* logic; historically, he was the first one to do so. Kant regarded such logic, which he knew only in its Aristotelian, that is, syllogistic, version, as complete.

Kant's main innovation was his transcendental logic. Kant offered various definitions of this discipline and spelled out various points of contrast with general logic. According to one such basic determination, transcendental logic has to do "with the laws of the understanding and reason insofar as they are related to objects **a priori**" (A 57/B 81-82); it does not, therefore, abstract from all content of cognition, though it contains only the a priori elements of this content. The difference between general and transcendental logic is also directly linked to the difference between the **table of judgments** and the **table of categories**, since the former is part of general logic, while the latter serves as the basic tool of transcendental logic. Furthermore, transcendental logic has as its matter the **manifold** of a priori **intuition**, and as its subsequent task the pure **synthesis** of this manifold (A 76-77/B 102).

In German idealism, Kant's transcendental logic was taken, against Kant's antimetaphysical and antiontological intention, as the point of departure for a speculative, metaphysical logic, in which the forms of thought and of being were dialectically identified (see **Georg Wilhelm Friedrich Hegel**'s *Science of Logic* of 1812-1816). This was opposed by **Jakob Friedrich Fries** and Eduard Beneke, who attempted to found logical laws on philosophical anthropology and psychology, respectively. Toward the end of the 19th century, a dispute arose between the proponents of so-called 'psychologism' and thinkers such as Gottlob Frege and Edmund Husserl, who, inspired by Bernhard Bolzano, claimed that logical laws are valid independently of psychological facts. In **Neokantianism**, logic was largely identified with theoretical philosophy, that is, with epistemology and theory of science. This "logic of cognition" was the successor to Kant's transcendental logic, though the Neokantians integrated formal logic into it; the table of judgments no longer provided the guiding thread for the discovery of the basic functions (categories, judgments) of cognitive thought. But only **Heinrich Rickert** and Emil Lask utilized the expression "transcendental logic" in a productive way in their philosophies.

LOVE (*Liebe, eros, amor*). Kant distinguishes between pathological and practical love; the former consists of **sensation** or **incentive** and cannot be commanded, the latter is, as benevolent conduct (*amor benevolentiae*), subject to the **will**, which in its turn stands under the **law** of **duty** (Ak 4, p. 399; Ak 6, pp. 401, 449). Good **actions** carried out from love and benevolence cannot as such be considered **moral**, because they are independent of a **command**, and are thus ultimately done out of **pleasure**. On the other hand, the biblical command to love God and one's neighbor demands "respect for a law that commands love"; such love is then not a matter of personal choice. According to Kant's interpretation, God's commands must be followed *gladly* and the duties toward one's neighbor must also be fulfilled *gladly*. However, only the *striving* for this **disposition** can be commanded, since doing something *gladly* cannot be a duty (Ak 5, p. 83). **Respect** is a prerequisite of true love, although Kant admits that in view of human imperfection, love is a necessary complement when duty is actually followed. In the Part "Doctrine of Virtue" in the ***Metaphysics of Morals***, Kant works out, on the basis of the maxim of practical benevolence, particular "duties of love" toward other human beings (Ak 6, pp. 450ff.). Ideal friendship is here defined as "the union of two **persons** through equal mutual love and respect" (Ak 6, p. 469).

Love of life and sexual love are deemed by Kant to be nature's ends that aim at the preservation of the individual person and of the human species (Ak 6, p. 424). But he disparages sexual love as love "in the narrowest sense of the word" that has nothing in common with moral love, because it is the carnal enjoyment of another person (Ak 6, p. 426). It derives its moral justification solely from its purpose, which can be attained only in marriage.

Kant's treatment of love stimulated a new philosophical analysis of the concept; for his immediate followers, this went hand in hand with their radicalization of his teachings on subjectivity. On the one hand, there was the leap from a transcendental self to a loving one (**Johann Gottlieb Fichte, Friedrich Wilhelm Joseph Schelling**), on the other, there was an effort to overcome the duality of the sensible and rational self in the name of love (Friedrich Schiller, Wilhelm von Humboldt). Among the Neokantians, it was especially **Hermann Cohen** who presented reflections on love in his ethics and aesthetics. However, he refused to interpret love as an affective foundation of virtue, and he placed the virtues of honor and dignity above those of love. He nevertheless based his aesthetics on pure feeling that he determined as the love of the nature of human beings.

- M -

MAGNITUDE (*Grösse*).   Magnitude is a property of all **appearances**, since all appearances stand under the categorical **synthesis**, and the **mathematical categories**, both **quantity** and **quality**, have to do with magnitude. In addition, magnitude is the **concept** under which the **understanding** subsumes all **intuitions** in **space** and **time**, thus making the application of mathematics to **experience** possible. Kant distinguished between extensive magnitudes, discussed in the "**Axioms of Intuition**," and intensive magnitudes, dealt with in the "**Anticipations of Perception**." The former arise on the basis of the categories of quantity, the latter on the basis of quality. However, outside of the context of these two mathematical principles of the understanding, Kant generally referred with the term 'magnitude' only to extensive magnitude, defining it at one point as "a determination of how many times a unit is posited in a thing," claiming that this "how-many-times is grounded on successive repetition, thus on time and the synthesis (of the homogeneous) in it" (A 242/B 300).

As Kant considered both extensive and intensive magnitudes to be **continuous**, he claimed that all appearances were continuous (A 170/B 212). In the case of extensive magnitudes, their continuity was based on the fact that space and time are continuous, that is, that between any two points in space or time there are again spatial or temporal parts, the points being mere boundaries. For intensive magnitudes, the **reality**, that is, **degree** of a **perception** could be diminished by infinitesimally small steps until it would reach zero, at which point, reality would no longer be reality, but negation. The discipline that dealt with magnitudes first and foremost was, for Kant, unsurprisingly, **mathematics**. Here, he thought that magnitudes could be constructed not only in arithmetic and geometry but also in algebra, namely, by means of a symbolic construction (A 717/B 745).

Kant takes up the concept of magnitude again in the *Critique of Judgment*, in the course of his discussion of the **sublime**, which he defines as something "absolutely large" or as "that in comparison with which everything else is small" (§ 25). This definition compels Kant to consider what magnitude in aesthetic terms means. In this connection, he distinguishes between the mathematical determination of size by means of numbers or signs (as in algebra), and the nonmathematical estimate of the magnitude of all objects of nature, an estimate he considers to be **aesthetic**. Such an estimate is expressed by reflective **judgments**, and it is in this fashion that we judge whether something is sublime or not (§ 26).

MAIMON, SALOMON (1753–1800). While Friedrich Heinrich Jacobi and Gottlob Ernst Schulze leaned in their examination of Kant's **criticism** on the philosophy of **David Hume**, Maimon took in his own interpretation and further development of the critical philosophy far more strongly elements of the **Leibniz-Wolff** school into consideration. Maimon criticized as illusory the common notion of the **things-in-themselves** that **affect** us, assigning to things-in-themselves, nevertheless, a positive signification: he identified **cognition** of them with the completeness of the cognition of appearances. According to Maimon, in a completely cognized object, nothing is given any longer, everything is thought; the dualism of **appearance** and **thinking** is overcome in complete thinking or in a complete idea. However, Maimon admitted that this was possible only for an infinite **understanding**. He explained the difference between the two sources of cognition by pointing to the difference between a finite understanding and an infinite one, and he therefore linked the **categories** and **ideas** differently than Kant did. In his theory of the "transcendental differentials" of the infinite understanding, Maimon held that the particular contents of experience arise out of the differentials (and in accordance with the "law of determination") and may be justified on their basis. This theory was subsequently elaborated by **Hermann Cohen** in his "principle of the infinitesimal method."

MANIFOLD (*Mannigfaltiges*). Kant's expression for the essentially unstructured multitude of data given to us by our **sensibility**; according to his view, every **intuition** contains a manifold (A 97). A manifold is a consequence of our being **affected** by things, that is, it is the result of the **receptivity** of our cognitive powers. Manifolds alone do not constitute **cognition**, in fact, even our awareness that a manifold is a manifold is not provided by our sensibility, but requires the prior awareness, produced by the **understanding**, of the **unity** and the multiplicity of the manifold. Cognition arises when the understanding adds **form** to the manifold. This process, labeled by Kant the **synthesis** of our understanding, is central to his epistemology and is described at some length in the "**Transcendental Analytic.**"

Kant distinguishes between empirically given manifolds and ones that are given **a priori**. Although the latter are supposed to serve as the basis of the synthesis that yields the **categories**, Kant does not adequately explain the characteristics that such manifolds should have. Presumably, it would include only **pure** a priori intuitions, that is, temporal (A 99) and perhaps also spatial relations. However, as such relations would follow the rules of **mathematics** and thus require an act of the understanding, such manifolds would apparently fail to fulfill the requirement of being unstructured multitudes given to our receptivity. Moreover, Kant does not explain, and it is otherwise not clear, how the categories are supposed to arise out of such a priori given manifolds.

It is, incidentally, doubtful whether Kant really thought that unsynthesized manifolds actually existed. It is more likely that he viewed them as a philosophical construct, as a tool for philosophical analysis.

MARBURG SCHOOL OF NEOKANTIANISM. Something in the manner of a "school of thought" began to develop in Marburg in 1898–1899 with the granting of doctorates to Albert Görland (1869–1952) and **Ernst Cassirer** (1874–1946). Soon after, the school began to attract attention not only from the German academic community but also from the wider European one. The characterizing mark of the school was provided by its reliance on the **transcendental method** and by the ensuing **critical idealism** as these had been developed by the 'heads' of the school **Hermann Cohen** and his younger colleague **Paul Natorp**. The distinguishing mark of critical idealism was the epistemological rearrangement of the relationship between **intuition** and **thought**, a restructuring carried out by Cohen in the 1880s. Cohen admitted a 'given' only in relation to a conceptual **function**. While Natorp retained this position, Cohen in his systematic philosophy after 1900 fully abandoned the notion of cognitive input stemming from **sensibility** in favor of the claim of the epistemological sovereignty of pure 'productive' thought, thus maintaining that cognition was totally produced by thought. This turn went hand in hand with the integration of central elements of Leibnizian philosophy.

Among the younger philosophers who studied in Marburg the most prominent were Nicolai Hartmann (doctorate in 1907), Wladyslaw Tatarkiewicz (1909), Dimitrij Gawronsky (1910), and Heinz Heimsoeth (1911). The great significance of Marburg at this time is further attested by the fact that José Ortega y Gasset and Boris Pasternak were students there. The school essentially lasted until 1912, when Cohen left for Berlin and his teaching chair was assumed by the experimental psychologist Erich Jaensch. The sole publication of the school were the eight volumes (often consisting of several separate parts) of the *Philosophische Arbeiten* that appeared between 1906 and 1915.

MATERIALISM. By the time Kant came to compose his critical works, a number of early modern philosophers had advanced materialistic doctrines, for example, Thomas Hobbes, the French Materialists (La Mettrie, Helvétius, d'Holbach), or Joseph Priestley. However, with the exception of Priestley, whom he apparently considered as an empiricist rather than as a materialist, Kant did not discuss any of the materialist thinkers. Nor did he deal with materialism at any appreciable length, dismissing it (or rather: his own version of it) in a few cursory remarks. In the *Prolegomena*, he called materialism a psychological concept "unfit for any explanation of **nature** and which moreover confines reason in practical respects" (§ 60). The point of this is made clearer in the chapter on **"Paralogisms"** in the *Critique of Pure Reason*, where Kant offhandedly rejects materialism along with dualism and spiritualism, maintaining that such theories illegitimately take us into the realm of **things-in-themselves** of which we can have no **cognition** (A 379; B 419–20). This also clarifies his statement in the preface to the second edition of the first *Critique*, according to which **criticism** severs the root of materialism (B xxxiv): since we always have to do only with **appearances**, we can have no justification for reducing everything to matter taken as a thing-in-itself. The **Neokantians** were in full agreement with Kant in their rejection of materialism as the metaphysical opposite of spiritualism. **Hermann Cohen** correspondingly denied that the historical materialism of Karl Marx could provide an adequate foundation of political socialism, grounding the latter as an **ethical socialism** in an "idealism of ethics."

MATHEMATICAL AND DYNAMICAL CATEGORIES, PRINCIPLES, AND IDEAS. Kant employs his highly technical distinction between mathematical and dynamical as it pertains to different kinds of concepts only in three very specific contexts. The terms 'mathematical' and 'dynamical' in this usage have no immediate connection to mathematics or dynamics: neither do these concepts serve as the **principles** of the two disciplines nor do they directly account for their respective possibility. In fact, one of the mathematical principles (Anticipations) turns out to serve in the *Metaphysical Foundations of Natural Science* as the basis of the science of dynamics. Two of the uses of the distinction are closely related (**categories** and **principles of the understanding**), the third one (**ideas**) stands somewhat apart.

Kant claimed that the categories of **quality** and **quantity** were "concerned with **objects** of **intuition** (pure and empirical)," while those of **relation** and **modality** were "directed at the **existence** of these objects (either in relation to one another or to the **understanding**)" (B 110). He labeled the first two categories and the corresponding principles of the understanding, namely, the **axioms of intuition** and the **anticipations of perception**, mathematical, while calling the second two categories and the corresponding principles, the **analogies of experience** and the **postulates of empirical thinking in general**, dynamical. In regard to the principles of the understanding, Kant offered three different explanations of the distinction, none of which is fully clear. First, he demarcates the mediate, that is, **discursive** certainty of the dynamical principles from the immediate, that is, intuitive certainty of the mathematical ones (A 161–62/B 201). He is apparently concerned with stressing that the mathematical principles have to do with objects as they are primarily given to intuition, while the dynamical ones primarily have to do with objects as they are thought to exist in space and time.

Kant's second explanation is given in a footnote added to the second edition version and is simply too brief to be of much help. He claims that the **synthesis** involved in mathematical principles is that of the homogeneous that does not necessarily belong together, while the synthesis in the case of the dynamical principles is that of the inhomogeneous that necessarily belongs together, such as accident and **substance** or effect and **cause** (B 201-2). More promising is the third explanation, in which Kant links the mathematical principles with **constitutive** and the dynamical ones with regulative use. This is helpful, provided one remains aware of the fact that the distinction between constitutive and regulative is here not made in respect to **experience** as is the case in most of the other passages of the first *Critique* where it occurs, but in respect to **appearances**. Kant seems to be suggesting in this context that mathematical principles permit the application of mathematical **construction** to certain aspects of existence, that is, they teach how intuition and the real in perception can be "generated in accordance with rules of a mathematical synthesis," while the dynamical principles do not allow any construction of existence, since they "concern only the relation of existence" (A 178-79/B 221-22). It should be added that the whole distinction between mathematical and dynamical principles is anyway only of subservient importance in Kant's epistemology, since he himself admits that in both cases there is complete certainty (A 160-61/B 200).

Of greater significance for his whole philosophical system is Kant's distinction between mathematical and dynamical ideas, or strictly speaking, the distinction between mathematical and dynamical cosmological ideas. Kant claims that in the two mathematical **antinomies** all the theses and the antitheses are false, because they involve assertions about things beyond the **limits** of our **cognition**. However, in the case of the dynamical antinomies, all theses and antitheses may be true if restricted to their proper sphere of validity.

MATHEMATICS. For Kant, mathematics was a science containing apodictically certain propositions, a science that could thus serve as a model for **metaphysics** (*Prize Essay*, Consideration 1; P, Part 1; B x-xi). In addition, however, Kant also presented his own highly original philosophy of mathematics, which is commonly labeled as intuitionism, owing to the fact that it is based on Kant's conception of **time** and **space** as **pure intuitions**. Kant denied that mathematics could be based on a mere examination of **concepts** and that it could therefore proceed analytically, by resorting to the principle of contradiction, as **logic** does. Rather, Kant famously declared that "mathematical **judgments** are all **synthetic a priori**" (B 14). In the case of arithmetic, which arises out of the **a priori** intuition time, simple additions such as 7 + 5 = 12 may appear to be analytic, but are, in fact, synthetic, as we cannot arrive at the sum by analyzing the two other numbers: we must go beyond their concepts and resort to intuition, representing the numbers by fingers or points. The case of geometry, which arises out of the a priori intuition space, is no different. One cannot, for example, arrive at the principle that "the shortest line between two points is the straight one" by analyzing the concept of a straight line, but one must again make recourse to intuition (B 16). Kant admits that there are some **analytic** propositions in geometry, such as a = a or (a + b) > a, but denies that they are true **principles** and claims that even these must be exhibited in intuition in order to be of any use in mathematics (B 17). Algebra, too, resorts to construction in intuition, characterized by Kant as symbolic construction, in distinction to the ostensive one in used geometry (A 717/B 745).

Kant distinguished the **method** of mathematics from that of philosophy already in his **pre-critical** period, most notably in the *Prize Essay* of 1763/1764. Here, as later also in the **Critique of Pure Reason**, Kant stressed that mathematics begins with **definitions**, but that philosophy can only hope to arrive at definitions in the end (Consideration 1, § 3; A 730/B 758). The distinction between the two disciplines is then discussed at some length in the first *Critique:* while philosophy is **cognition** from concepts, mathematics is cognition from the **construction** of concepts; "philosophical cognition considers the particular only in the universal, but mathematical cognition considers the **universal** in the particular . . . yet nonetheless a priori," thanks to the fact that the rules of construction, which apply regardless of the manner of presenting the concept in intuition, guarantee universality (A 713–14/B 741–42). Philosophy cannot thus prove that, for example, the three angles of a triangle are equal to two right angles, since it can only examine concepts, whereas a mathematician proves the case by construction (A 716/B 744). Only mathematics, not philosophy, contains axioms and proceeds by demonstrations. However, according to Kant's conception, mathematics is not based on axioms. These occur rather only in geometry, but not in arithmetic. As examples of geometric axioms Kant offered: "between two points only one straight line is possible" and "two straight lines do not enclose a space" (A 163–65/B 204–5).

Kant's theory that mathematics is based on the a priori forms of all intuition space and time makes it possible to explain both the certainty of mathematics and its applicability to **objects** of **experience**. Kant thought that if mathematics were a product of the **understanding**, as, for example, **René Descartes** had held, there would be no guarantee that it would be applicable to empirical objects. If, on the other hand, mathematics were abstracted from the relations of empirical objects, as Kant claimed would have followed from **Gottfried Wilhelm Leibniz**'s conception of space, then there would be no guarantee that mathematics would be anything more than an empirical discipline, devoid of certainty.

In the 19th and early 20th centuries, intuitionism in the philosophy of mathematics went into abeyance. This became especially pronounced with, on the one hand, the advent of logicism after the publication first of Gottlob Frege's (1848-1925) *Grundlagen der Arithmetik* in 1884 (*Foundations of Arithmetic*, trans. J. L. Austin, 2nd ed. 1980) and then of Bertrand Russell's and A. N. Whitehead's similarly oriented *Principia Mathematica* (2nd ed. 1925-1927), as well as with, on the other hand, the rise of formalism following the publication of David Hilbert's (1862-1943) *Grundlagen der Geometrie* in 1899 (*Foundations of Geometry*, trans. L. Unger, P. Bernays, 1971). However, although these movements were essentially anti-Kantian, they did take Kant's philosophy of mathematics as their point of departure. Moreover, intuitionism has since been resurrected by L. E. J. Brouwer (1881-1966) and others, though in a different form than Kant's early version of it.

Among the **Neokantians**, philosophical contributions to the discussion of the foundations of mathematics were made by **Paul Natorp, Ernst Cassirer**, and Jonas Cohn. In his attempts to work out an (epistemo)logical grounding of mathematics, Natorp concentrated especially on the theory of numbers. Cassirer dealt with, among other things, the dispute concerning the formalistic versus intuitionist grounding of mathematics as well as the paradoxes of set theory. In his book *Voraussetzungen und Ziele des Erkennens* (*Presuppositions and Goals of Cognition*) of 1908, Cohn focused his investigation of mathematical theory on the problem of construction, which he regarded as the basic problem of mathematical cognition.

MATTER. In his **pre-critical** writings, Kant considered matter mainly in the sense of the physical material of the world. Thus, for instance, in the *Universal Natural History and Theory of the Heavens* of 1755, he attempted to explain the solar system and the rest of the universe by postulating a basic matter that was then formed by the **forces** of **attraction** and repulsion into stars and planets.

In the section "On the **Amphiboly** of the Concepts of Reflection" in the *Critique of Pure Reason*, he linked matter as the determinable with **form** as the determination. This pair of **concepts** constituted the last of the four sets of the so-called concepts of reflection. Kant's point was that at the most abstract level, matter as the determinable in general and form as its determination gained a transcendental signification, "since one abstracts from all differences in what is given and from the way in which that is determined." In this most general sense, matter amounts to the components in every being, while form is the way in which these components are connected (A 266/B 322).

However, next to matter as a concept of reflection, Kant also retained the less abstract, more specific concept of matter as the material of the universe. While in his pre-critical writings, especially in the *Physical Monadology* (1756), Kant explained matter in terms of physical monads, during his critical period he resorted only to forces; in the *Metaphysical Foundations of Natural Science*, a work largely devoted to matter, he claimed that the explanation of matter in terms of **atoms** and the void was inferior to the one based on attraction and repulsion, in the *Opus Postumum* he then dismissed atomism as wholly impossible. Kant therefore held matter to be impenetrable thanks to the force of repulsion, he also ascribed to it the capability of being compressed infinitely, and he held it to be infinitely divisible, that is, **continuous**. As further basic characteristics of matter, he listed the law of the conservation of the quantity of matter and he emphasized that matter was **inert**, that is, not endowed with thought or desire or an ability to move on its own, as he held it to lack inner determinations; the inertness of matter implied for Kant its lifelessness (Ak 4, p. 544).

MAXIM.   In his theoretical philosophy, Kant understands under "maxims of reason" subjective principles that arise out of the interest of **reason** in a systematic **unity** of **cognition** (A 666/B 694). However, the concept plays a far greater role in his **ethics**. Here, it denotes the subjective principle of the **will** that is determined objectively by moral **law** (Ak 4, pp. 400-1; Ak 5, p. 19). *See also CRITIQUE OF PRACTICAL REASON.*

MECHANICS.   *See METAPHYSICAL FOUNDATIONS OF NATURAL SCIENCE.*

METAPHYSICAL DEDUCTION. *See* DEDUCTION.

METAPHYSICAL FOUNDATIONS OF NATURAL SCIENCE.   Kant's major work on the philosophy of science, published in 1786. The 'Preface' contains a number of philosophically significant reflections on science. Kant gradually narrows down what counts as genuine science: he first excludes all disciplines lacking systematic order, then all "empirical sciences," calling these "historical natural doctrines," and, finally, from the remainder, that is, from the "rational disciplines," he eliminates **psychology** and **chemistry**. On the one hand, these lacked a **pure**, that is, a **metaphysical** part that was to be based on **reason** and that was to be apodictically certain, on the other hand, they were not composed of principles amenable to mathematical treatment. In the end, only **physics** qualified as a science in the full sense of the word.

To establish the first metaphysical principles of physics, Kant applies the **categories** to the **concept** of **matter**, thus arriving at the four chapters of his book: 1) Phoronomy (based on the categories of quantity) considers matter only insofar as it is the **motion** of a point through space. More of less corresponding to our kinematics, this part deals largely with the addition of motions as it is represented by the addition of vectors. 2) Dynamics (quality) considers matter insofar as it fills space. There are two competing theories to explain how this occurs, namely, the so-called mechanical one, based on **atoms** and the void, and a dynamical one, based on the two forces of **attraction** and repulsion. Kant opts for the latter, mainly because he thinks it difficult to account for absolute void and the absolute impenetrability of atoms. 3) Mechanics (relation) considers matter insofar as it has moving forces. Here, Kant first treats the problem of assessing the quantity of matter, before he presents three laws of mechanics that are strongly linked to the **analogies of experience** and more loosely to **Isaac Newton**'s laws of motion. 4) Phenomenology (modality) considers the motion of matter insofar as it can be an object of experience. Each of its three propositions determines the modality of motion in respect to each of the previous chapters: rectilinear motion of matter as opposed to the motion of relative space is a merely possible predicate (phoronomy), circular motion is a real predicate (dynamics), and the motion of a body in respect to another body requires necessarily the equal and opposite motion of the latter (mechanics).

The book did not gain any great immediate acclaim. However, Kant's greater emphasis on **space** at the expense of **time** in the second edition version of the *Critique of Pure Reason*, which came out just one year after the *Metaphysical Foundations*, may have been inspired by his work on the philosophy of science, given that his occupation with matter and motion would have led him to a greater appreciation of the importance of space. Several years after the publication of the *Metaphysical Foundations*, Kant became convinced that the work still left a gap in the critical philosophy, a lacuna that was to be closed by a conceptual transition from the foundations of physics to physics itself. Kant's notes pertaining to this task form the so-called *Opus Postumum*. *See also* BODY.

METAPHYSICS. In general, Kant considered metaphysics, roughly defined as the system of all **a priori cognitions**, to be the most exalted of all the disciplines of human knowledge, though he was often highly critical of it. Much of his philosophical writing is devoted to cleansing metaphysics of its untenable doctrines and to assuring it of a solid foundation that would forever set it on a secure course. The latter part of this intention is nicely expressed by the full title of the *Prolegomena to Any Future Metaphysics that will be Able to Come Forward as Science*. Originally, Kant derived his conception of what metaphysics was largely from the so-called **Leibniz-Wolff** school. In keeping with that tradition, he divided metaphysics, even in his critical period, into an ontology, which, during this phase, he identified with **transcendental philosophy**, rational **psychology**, rational **cosmology**, and rational **theology**.

Kant's misgiving vis-à-vis metaphysics date already to his **pre-critical** period. Thus, in the 'Preface' to *The Only Possible Argument in Support of a Demonstration of the Existence of God* of 1763, Kant compares metaphysics to a dark ocean without shores and without lighthouses (Ak 2, p. 66), though he still indulges in almost unimpeded metaphysical speculation. In the almost simultaneously composed *Prize Essay* (1763/1764), he became even more critical, but sought, in addition, to reform metaphysics by clarifying the relationship between its method and that of **mathematics**, and by finally suggesting that **philosophy** was to use as its axioms material **principles**. Realizing in his *Dreams of a Spirit-Seer* (1766) that this proposal was not practicable, Kant became abusive of metaphysics and of its proponents, but did suggest for the first time that metaphysics ought to concern itself with ascertaining the **limits** of human **reason** (Ak 2, p. 368). This subsequently ripened into the project of the **critique of pure reason**, a project characterized by the recognition that the old metaphysics was doomed to failure, because it dogmatically made assertions about **things-in-themselves**, assertions that result in contradictions (**antinomies**) and, more generally, in **transcendental illusion**.

Metaphysics can become a **science** that is as secure as mathematics and **physics** only by examining the a priori conditions of possible **experience** and by restricting its cognitive claims to the realm of **appearances**. However, aside from this metaphysics in a narrow sense of the word, for which Kant reserved the label "metaphysics of nature," he also called the science of pure **morals**, a science based on no empirical conditions, the "metaphysics of morals" (A 841/B 869). With these two expressions, informed by his claim that metaphysics has as its two objects **nature** and **freedom**, he replaced the Aristotelian distinction between theoretical and practical philosophy.

The **Neokantians** did not share Kant's aim of providing a new foundation of metaphysics as a science; there was no place for metaphysics in their philosophy. After World War I, there was a resurgence of metaphysical weltanschauung in Germany, which influenced the interpretations of Kant. *See also* LANGE, FRIEDRICH ALBERT; ONTOLOGY.

METAPHYSICS OF MORALS. Under this title, Kant combined in one volume two of his works that both appeared in 1797, namely, the *Metaphysical First Principles of the Doctrine of Right* and the *Metaphysical First Principles of the Doctrine of Virtue.* The book presents a systematic exposition of the **metaphysics** of the practical employment of **pure reason** (A 841/B 869) on the basis of the *Critique of Practical Reason.* In his 'Introduction,' Kant analyzes the key concepts that pertain to the human **faculty** of **desire** (feelings of pleasure and pain, inclination, faculty of choice, wish, will), and he defines the preliminary concepts of the metaphysics of morals (freedom, imperative, permitted/prohibited, obligation, and so forth). His basic distinctions are those between juridical and ethical legislation, legality and morality, external and internal legislation, duties of right and duties of virtue.

Kant commences the first part with a general characterization of the doctrine of **right** (*Ius*) as "the sum of those **laws** for which an external legislation is possible" (Ak 6, p. 229). He then proceeds to a definition of right and to the formulation of the general principle of right and of a juridical law, before presenting an exposition of private right. Under this title, he deals with the right to private property and the conditions for the acquisition of private property; under "right to a thing" he subsumes personal right and contract right. At the end, he takes up public right (right of a state, right of nations, cosmopolitan right).

The doctrine of **virtue** is concerned with those duties that do not stand under external laws (p. 379). In the first division, "The Doctrine of the Elements of Ethics," Kant divides the **duties** of virtue into duties to oneself and duties to others. The perfect duties to oneself, which all stand under the command to know oneself, are duties toward oneself either as an animal being (self-preservation) or as a moral being (truthfulness, liberality, self-respect). The duties to others consist in **love** and **respect**. In the second division, "The Doctrine of the Methods of Ethics," Kant discusses the problems of exercising moral reason in the theory and practice of duties (teaching and ascetics). *See also* ETHICS.

METHOD. The significance of method for Kant is immediately apparent from his definition of it as "a procedure in accordance with **principles**" (A 855/B 883); given that Kant did not think that anything at all could be achieved in philosophy and science without seeking and following principles, **rules**, or **laws**, it is clear that method had to assume a central position in his whole undertaking. This is also suggested by Kant's assertion in the preface to the second edition of the *Critique of Pure Reason* that the whole book is "a treatise of method" (B xxii). The importance of method is both underscored and undermined by the fact that next to a "Doctrine of Elements" there is a "Doctrine of Method" included in all three *Critiques* as well as in Kant's *Logic*. However, the "Doctrines of Method" are generally not very methodological; they include disparate reflections on the preceding parts of the works, deal rather unsystematically with the form of the different disciplines, and offer seemingly haphazard comparisons between them. Moreover, there is no great consistency between the "Doctrines of Method" in the different works. In the first *Critique*, Kant defines the transcendental doctrine of method as "the determination of the formal conditions of a complete **system** of **pure reason**" (A 707-8/B 735-36), however, in the *Critique of Practical Reason*, the doctrine of method of practical reason is designed to deal only with the problem of how moral law influences the human mind and action. Not surprisingly, in Kantian scholarship, the "Doctrines of Method" are generally not treated nearly as extensively as are the "Doctrines of Elements."

Among the various remarks on method within and outside of the sections entitled "Doctrine of Method," Kant presents a number of important distinctions. He thus contrasts the naturalistic method with the scientific one, claiming that the former relies merely on common understanding, while the latter is systematic. Kant is dismissive of the naturalistic method and concerns himself only with the scientific one, subdividing it into dogmatic, skeptical, and critical (A 855/B 883). The dogmatic method is exemplified by the **Leibniz-Wolff** school and is characterized by its insufficiently critical stance toward the capabilities of reason. Kant identified the skeptical method with **David Hume**, and viewed it as a corrective for the errors of the dogmatics, setting it apart from **skepticism** itself, which he regarded as an insufficiently critical rejection of all certainty of cognition. The critical method was Kant's own project of the **critique of pure reason**, aimed at overcoming the two prior positions by examining the boundaries and limits of the human cognitive faculties.

Another important distinction, one which had occupied Kant already in his **pre-critical** writings, was between the method of **philosophy** and that of **mathematics**. In a similar vein, Kant distinguished the method of cognition out of pure reason as the critical method (A 712/B 740) from the method of natural science.

The **Marburg Neokantians** interpreted Kant's theoretical philosophy methodologically and developed it into a "methodical idealism" (**Hermann Cohen**). Especially **Paul Natorp** emphasized that in philosophy, unlike in science, it is not the results that matter, but the process of attaining cognition; he thus determined philosophy as method, that is, as a cognition-grounding process of thought. *See also* ANALYTIC METHOD.

MIND (*mens, Gemüt*). Kant used this term mostly as a generic expression for the mental powers or faculties of the human subject. 'Mind' may then be variously divided into a **receptivity** (that is, **sensibility**) and **spontaneity** (that is, **understanding**) (A 50/B 74), into the **faculties** of **cognition**, **pleasure** or pain, and desire, or, more specifically, into "sensation, consciousness, imagination, memory, wit, the power to distinguish, pleasure, desire, etc." (A 649/B 677). Occasionally, 'mind' also signifies the entirety of all **representations**, or, more precisely, the faculty of combining representations. Aside from this, Kant also sometimes employed the word in the sense of consciousness. *See also* PSYCHOLOGY; SOUL; TRANSCENDENTAL UNITY OF APPERCEPTION.

MODALITY. In general, modality does not determine an **object**, which is already determined by the other groups of categories, but concerns the relation of the object to the cognitive faculties of the subject. Modal categories are derived from the modality of **judgments**, where Kant is concerned with general rather than with **transcendental logic**. True to his overriding notion of modality, Kant states even at this level that modality contributes nothing to the content of a judgment, which is provided by quantity, quality, and relation. Modal judgments only determine the "value of the copula in relation to thinking in general." There are three kinds of such judgments, namely, problematic ones, in which "one regards the assertion or denial as merely possible," assertoric ones, in which "it is considered actual (true)," and apodictic ones, in which "it is seen as necessary" (A 74/B 100). In his *Logic*, Kant explains the difference between these three types of judgment in terms of our consciousness of the mere possibility, actuality, or necessity of the act of judging (Ak 9, p. 108). In the *Critique of Pure Reason*, he apparently also adhered to this model, defining apodictic judgments as ones that are combined with "the consciousness of their necessity" (B 41). Kant conceived a kind of progression in judgments from **possibility** to **actuality** to **necessity**, claiming that one first judges something problematically, then assumes it assertorically as true, and finally asserts it to be necessary and apodictic. He therefore speaks in this context of "moments of thinking in general" (A 76/B 101).

The modal **categories** derived from the judgments are possibility—impossibility, existence—nonexistence, and necessity—contingence. Again, Kant stresses that they "do not augment the concept to which they are ascribed, but express only the relation to the faculty of **cognition**" (A 219/B 266). The conditions of the application of the modal categories are set down first in the chapter on **schematism**, where Kant explicates the schemata of modality on the basis of how possibility, actuality, and necessity relate to **time** (some time, determinate time, all times), subsequently in the chapter dealing with the **postulates of empirical thinking in general**, in which he deals with the conditions of the empirical use of the modal concepts. The role of modality in Kant's philosophy of **physics** is discussed in the *Metaphysical Foundations of Natural Science* under the heading "Phenomenology." Here, Kant considers the **motion** of **matter** insofar as it can be an object of experience. As the possible, he specifies at this level rectilinear motion of matter as opposed to the motion of relative space; as the actual, circular motion; and as the necessary, the motion of a body in respect to another body.

In his *Logik der reinen Erkenntnis* (1902), **Hermann Cohen** dealt with modality under the heading "Judgments of Method"; he was motivated by the critical intention of assessing the value and the scope of the categorical laying of foundations of scientific cognition.

Paul Natorp interpreted in his *Die logischen Grundlagen der exakten Wissenschaften* (1910) Kant's theory of modality in such a way that it comprised three steps in which scientific cognition is attained: cognition with the value of the merely possible (hypothesis), the established fact, and the necessary according to a law. He conceived of the second step as a procedure of progressive determination that provisionally ends with a 'fact.' Actuality as an "absolute fact," that is, as a completed determination, remains an everlasting **problem** (*Aufgabe*). In the "General Logic" of his late work, Natorp then, on the one hand, placed the modal categories at the head of his development of the basic structure of thinking, and, on the other hand, modified their order by shifting actuality as the all-round determination behind necessity as the one-sided and progressive determination.

MORAL WORLD. *See* KINGDOM OF THE ENDS; WORLD.

MORALITY. *See* DIGNITY; DISPOSITION; DUTY; *GROUNDWORK OF THE METAPHYSICS OF MORALS*; PERSON; VIRTUE.

MORALS. *See* ETHICS.

MOTION (*Bewegung*).   An important concept in Kant's philosophy of **physics**, though it generally did take second place behind the concept of **force**, owing to the fact that Kant tended to regard motion as a mere external attribute of the state of a **body**, and that he viewed this attribute as often determined precisely by force. In his **critical philosophy**, Kant stressed that motion was not a **pure concept** such as **time** and **space**, but that it was an empirical datum, namely, the "perception of something movable" (A

41/B 58). In this sense, the concept of motion was only secondary to the pure concepts; for instance, it was possible only through the representation of time (A 31/B 49). Hand in hand with this conception went Kant's repeated emphasis that motion could not be given as the effect of an unknown **thing-in-itself**, but only as an **appearance** of the influence of such an unknown cause on our senses. For this reason, motion could not be the subject of a pure science such as geometry. However, Kant also distinguished from such a motion of a physical body, motion "as an action of the subject." While the former could not belong to geometry, the latter did, and Kant even claimed that it was part of **transcendental** philosophy. What he had in mind here, was not the motion of an object of physics, but rather the **synthesis** of the **manifold** in space, that is, a "description of a space" as "a pure act of the successive synthesis of the manifold in outer intuition in general by productive imagination" (B 155). Motion in the sense of the motion of an object played an important role in the *Metaphysical Foundations of Natural Science*, since Kant claimed that **matter**, the subject of the work, could be known only thanks to motion, for it is only through motion that the senses can be affected. Consequently, Kant's application of the **categories** to matter relied heavily on the concept of motion, and each of the four determinations of matter is stated in terms of the concept of motion (Ak 4, pp. 476–77).

- N -

NATORP, PAUL (1854–1924). Together with **Hermann Cohen**, Natorp was the founder of the **Marburg School of Neokantianism**. His epistemology, based on the concept of function, was informed by Kant's **transcendental logic**, and, more specifically, by the latter's notion of synthetic **unity**. Natorp conceived of this unity as a basic relation between the one and the manifold, claiming that its unfolding would yield the law governing the process of **cognition**. These leading ideas were already present in his work *Platos Ideenlehre* (1903), in which he interpreted Platonic ideas as laws rather than as entities of any kind. In his further book *Die logischen Grundlagen der exakten Wissenschaften* (*The Logical Foundations of the Exact Sciences*) of 1910, he developed the notion of the basic relation into a system of logical functions, the **categories**, which, according to him, served as the epistemological foundation of **mathematics** and **physics**. In his *Allgemeine Psychologie nach kritischer Methode* (*General Psychology in Accordance with the Critical Method*) of 1912, Natorp described the subjective, psychological elements of cognition on the basis of their exact correlation to the previously gained objective elements of cognition, thus establishing an original form of philosophical **psychology**. Natorp did not consider that the transition from **epistemology** to **ethics** would be burdened by any serious difficulties, given that he maintained that an **ought** was inherent in cognition. In his ethics (*Sozialpädagogik*, 1899), which he understood as a theory of the practical ought, Natorp distinguished three degrees of the realization of this ought: drive, which in the struggle with matter takes on the form of labor; choice or will, with which desire concentrates on something; rational will, which follows the unconditional ought. In his *Religion innerhalb der Grenzen der Humanität* (*Religion within the Limits of Humanity*) (1894, 2nd ed. 1908), Natorp attempted to integrate religion into his **system**, claiming, unlike Cohen, that religion was based on **feeling**. Later, Natorp's thought became increasingly mystical, without, however, fully abandoning the earlier rational, critical positions.

NATURAL SCIENCE (*Naturwissenschaft*). In the "Preface" to his **Metaphysical Foundations of Natural Science**, Kant includes under the heading of "the study of nature" (*Naturlehre*) natural history, **psychology, chemistry**, and **physics**. However, strictly speaking, only the last mentioned qualifies for him as a science in the full sense of the word, since only physics is capable of a thorough mathematical treatment, and, perhaps even more important, since it contains a **pure** part. It is thus no accident that in the course of his discussion of the question "how is pure natural science possible?" in the *Critique of Pure Reason*, Kant identified natural science with physics (B 17–18, 20). Kant described the metaphysical foundations that such a science requires at a number of levels. In the most formal sense, all science must fall under the **categories**, which in a second step are schematized and yield the **principles of pure understanding**; these in their turn are applied to **matter** and **motion** and yield the *Metaphysical Foundations* themselves. On the other hand, Kant hardly touched on the empirical portion of natural science, claiming that it contains only empirical laws, though, unlike his idealist followers, he never suggested that one could dispense with this part.

In the unfinished **Opus Postumum**, Kant attempted to work out yet another level of concepts that were to serve as the pure part of science, this time, however, concerning himself with the transition from the metaphysical foundations of science to physics itself. As a further novelty, Kant was now increasingly willing to entertain chemical theories, perhaps because he became aware of both the foundational potential and the improved possibility of mathematical treatment that were implied in Antoine Laurent de Lavoisier's new chemistry.

NATURE. In his **critical philosophy**, Kant did not refer with the term 'nature' to any entity existing independently of humans, reserving it primarily for the order and regularity, produced by our own **understanding**, of **appearances**. He thus insisted that it was the understanding that provided the "legislation for nature," and that "without the understanding there would be no nature at all, that is, no **synthetic unity** of the manifold of appearances in accordance with rules" (A 126). Under such legislation, Kant understood the **a priori** concepts and laws, namely, the **categories** and the **principles of the understanding**, perhaps also the propositions presented in the *Metaphysical Foundations of Natural Science*. When Kant speaks of a "unity of nature," he has therefore primarily a unity of rules in mind, a unity that amounts to "a necessary, i.e., a priori certain unity of the connection of appearances" (A 125, A 216/B 263). Nature in this **transcendental** sense does not encompass the specific, empirical laws of nature. Requiring data from the **sensibility**, such laws do not originate in the **pure** understanding, and Kant accordingly describes them as "only particular determinations of the pure laws of the understanding" (A 127–28). Kant labels this conception of nature *"natura formaliter spectata,"* that is, nature in a formal sense, distinguishing it from *"natura materialiter spectata,"* that is, nature in a material sense. While with the former he stresses the dependence on the pure concepts and principles of the understanding, with the latter he denotes only the sum total of all appearances, bracketing out the question of the connection of the appearances (B 163–65). Within this latter sense of nature, Kant further distinguished an extended and a thinking nature (Ak 4, p. 467).

It is from nature in its formal sense that Kant also distinguished, more or less in passing, the concept of the **world**; unlike nature, which Kant in this context labeled as "a dynamic whole," the world is no legitimate object of **cognition** and is the subject matter of the **antinomies** of pure reason (A 418–19/B 446–47). In addition, Kant distinguishes such a nature, which stands under the determination of the categories and which is the legitimate object of cognition, from the **idea** of "nature in general." This **regulative** idea of an unlimited series is used as a rule for explaining given appearances **as if** the series were infinite (A 684–85/B 712–13), and Kant speaks here accordingly of a regulative principle of the unity of nature (A 693/B 721). The **purposiveness** of nature is likewise only a regulative idea. Kant emphasizes that it cannot be used to prove the existence of **God** and that the contrary case is also not acceptable, namely, explaining the order and purposiveness of nature by a resort to God (A 772–73/B 800–1).

One of the most important distinctions that Kant draws within his critical philosophy is that between the realm of nature and the realm of **free-**

dom, a distinction that later played an equally prominent role in **Neo-kantianism**. The human being as a being of the senses belongs to the realm of nature, and is, as such, determined, submitted to the **necessity** of nature, that is, to the **causality** of nature or to the **laws** of nature; this aspect is the subject matter of the **metaphysics** of nature. The human being as a rational being is part of the realm of freedom or of a supersensible nature, submitted to the causality of freedom, and thus to **moral** law; this aspect is the subject matter of the metaphysics of freedom. The relationship between the two realms is taken up first in the third antinomy in the *Critique of Pure Reason* and the discussion is continued in the other two *Critiques*. In addition, in his *Critique of Judgment*, Kant attempts to reconcile, under the heading maxims of reflective **judgment**, mechanical explanations of nature with the conception of a teleologically organized nature (§§ 70–71).

In his philosophy of **history**, Kant operated with a concept of nature that acts purposefully, though without the knowledge of humans, to develop humankind's talents toward a final goal.

NECESSITY (*Notwendigkeit*). Necessity is the third of the **categories** of **modality**, and as such it is derived from apodictic **judgments**. Kant describes the necessity of a judgment in terms of an inseparable connection with the **understanding** (A 76/B 101). From the necessity of judgments, where one is still at the level of logical necessity, Kant then advances to the problem of the application of the categories, first under the heading **schematism**, where he defines the schema of necessity as "the existence of an object at all **times**" (A 145/B 184), then under the heading of the third **postulate of empirical thinking in general**. According to the third postulate, "that whose connection with the actual is determined in accordance with general conditions of experience is (exists) necessarily" (A 218/B 266). As Kant explicitly stresses, what is here involved is material necessity rather than merely **logical** one. It cannot be cognized merely from **concepts**, but only "from the connection with what is perceived in accordance with general **laws** of **experience**." Kant is greatly concerned with linking this law to **causality**, stating that we cognize only the necessity of the effects whose causes are given. He therefore speaks of the hypothetical necessity of everything that happens, or conversely, he classifies as **a priori** the proposition that nothing in nature happens by accident. Such laws ground **nature** (A 226–28/B 279–81).

Kant's strict separation of logical necessity from the necessity of existence also figures prominently in his critique of the ontological argument for **God**'s existence. Kant claims that the necessary existence of God cannot be proven from mere concepts, and this ultimately leads him to conclude that the unconditionally necessary being cannot be **cognized** at all, but can only be thought.

Necessity is crucial for Kant's **transcendental philosophy**, if only because necessary cognition is supposed to serve as its basis. One may view such necessity as ultimately founded in the **transcendental unity of apperception**, as Kant himself seems to suggest in the first edition of the *Critique of Pure Reason* (A 106–7); one may also consider the necessity of such cognition to be grounded in the fact that it provides the necessary conditions of the possibility of experience.

Kant recognized several different kinds of necessity. Aside from necessity in the realm of nature, he accepted a practical necessity in the realm of **morals** as well as a necessity pertaining to the judgment of **taste** in the realm of **aesthetics** (CJ, § 18).

NEGATION. In his **pre-critical** piece *Attempt to Introduce Negative Magnitudes into Philosophy* (1763), Kant distinguished negation that is a consequence of a real opposition (privation) from negation that is simply a lack (defect, absence), illustrating the distinction with the case of a nonmoving body: its rest comes about either as the result of one force canceling out an opposite force or in virtue of the fact that there is simply no force involved (Ak 2, pp. 177–78).

In Kant's **critical philosophy**, negation is, along with **reality** and limitation, one of the **categories** of **quality**; it is derived from negative **judgment**. Kant considers it necessary to separate within **transcendental logic**, though not within formal **logic**, infinite judgment from affirmative and negative judgment. In infinite judgment, a logical affirmation is made by means of a negative predicate (for example, immortal) (A 72/B 97). Merely logical negation that pertains to the copula and not to the content of a concept is capable of only preventing error (A 709/B 737). The category of negation must be understood as "transcendental negation," that is, as "nonbeing in itself." It is opposed to "transcendental affirmation," that is, to the category of reality with which "a something" is thought, "the concept of which in itself already expresses a being." A determinate negation is, according to Kant, possible only when it is grounded on the opposed affirmation. Negative concepts are therefore always derived. If one assumes the "All of reality," then all true negations will be "nothing but limits" of this All without their own positive meaning (A 574–76/B 602–4).

Arguing against Christoph Sigwart, who in his logic followed Kant's position, and defining negation as a judgment about an attempted or completed positive judgment, **Wilhelm Windelband** claimed that negative judgment contained its own element of factual **validity**. **Heinrich Rickert** distinguished the negation of an existing something that results in a mere not-something, from the negation of a value that gives rise to a mis-value (*Unwert*) as another something. At the same time, he denied **Paul Natorp**'s thesis that the original meaning of negation comes down to otherness. **Hermann Cohen** interpreted infinite judgment as a process of thought in the production of a something by means of the original negation of a preceding something. The application of this process in science is exemplified by the production of the concept of the intensive out of the negation of the extensive by Galileo or Gottfried Wilhelm Leibniz.

NEOKANTIANISM. Inspired by Kant, though generally adhering more to the spirit than to the letter of his work, especially during its later phase, in which a number of Neokantians developed their own systems of philosophy, this movement became dominant at a number of German universities. The origin of full-blown Neokantianism is usually dated to the 1860s, its demise to the first decades of the 20th century, when it was gradually displaced by anthropological philosophy (with its emphasis on the real subject as opposed to an abstract one) as well as by the philosophy of life, and when it was severely disrupted by the advent of national socialism. The movement arose in response to **materialism**, naturalism, and post-Kantian German **idealism**, often displaying strong ties to positivism, especially in the early period. Initially, it had a dual goal: to guarantee the scientific status of philosophy by undertaking a priori epistemological analysis of the principal philosophical concepts, and to ascribe to philosophy the role of a guide, a role that could not be fulfilled by any of the specialized scientific disciplines.

The number of thinkers who have been labeled Neokantians is large, their affiliations were manifold. Following a suggestion of Alois Riehl (1913), one should consider as Neokantians authors who, thanks to their study of Kant, succeeded in advancing philosophy beyond its past achievements. One such thinker was **Charles Renouvier**, the main representative of French Neokantianism. His major work, the *Essais de critique générale* (1854–1864), is marked by an antimetaphysical phenomenalism, by a theory of the **categories** that is based on **relation** and that is critical of positivism as well as by his claim that there is **freedom** within the realm of **appearances**. Also undisputed is the existence of an Italian Neokantianism. Its main proponents were Carlo Cantoni, whose comprehensive work *Emanuele Kant* (1879–1884) greatly contributed to the acquaintance with Kant's philosophy in Italy, Felice Tocco (1845–1911), Giovanni Cesca (1859–1908), and Filippo Masci (1844–1923). The main representatives of Neokantianism in Germany were **Hermann Cohen**, **Alois Riehl**, and **Wil-**

helm Windelband. Historiographically, it has become accepted practice to identify only two major schools, the **Marburg School** (Cohen, **Paul Natorp**) and the **Southwestern German School** (Windelband, **Heinrich Rickert**, Emil Lask, Jonas Cohn, **Bruno Bauch**). Although in the course of time, the differences between these parties became increasingly pronounced, the schools did share a common program based on the following tenets: Philosophy is centered around a theory of scientific **cognition**, cognition that it considers as exemplary. It is the task of this theory to analyze by means of reflection the conditions of the **validity** of cognition. Determining the legitimate ground of valid scientific cognition (*quaestio juris*) is carried out from the beginning from the point of view of the **system**; philosophy must then also consider the conditions of moral action and aesthetic experience. Cognition is not treated in regard to a real **subject** or to the relationship subject-**object**. If the epistemological subject is not abandoned completely, it is used merely as the epitome of the **principles** of validity. All ontological determinations are reduced to a consideration of the conditions of validity, especially as the latter pertain to scientific cognition. This last point constitutes the quintessence of **critical idealism**, a position that demarcates the two schools from, among others, the critical realism that was advocated by Alois Riehl. The latter's realistic interpretation of Kant, especially as it was subsequently developed by Oswald Külpe (1862–1915), is therefore often not counted as part of Neokantianism. The Neokantians became engaged in different areas of philosophy; aside from their interpretations of Kant, they contributed to epistemology and methodology of science (Natorp, **Ernst Cassirer**, Windelband, Rickert), philosophy of law (Rudolf Stammler, Lask, Max Salomon), ethics (Cohen), philosophy of religion (Cohen, Natorp), and, in the end, philosophy of culture. They also wrote extensively on the history of philosophy (Windelband, Cassirer).

   While at the beginning of the 20th century the Marburg School increasingly turned to the philosophy of **Gottfried Wilhelm Leibniz** rather than to that of Kant, the Southwestern School tended after 1910 in various ways toward Neo-Hegelianism. Rickert claimed that the general end of the historical phenomenon of Neokantianism arrived in 1924 with the death of Alois Riehl. Be that as it may, Rickert's own later writings certainly cannot be considered as part of Neokantianism in a strict sense of the term. This is even more the case in regard to some of the younger authors whose philosophical development led them outside of the scope of their schools. Cassirer departed from Neokantianism with his *Philosophy of Symbolic Forms* (1923–1929), Nicolai Hartmann with his *Metaphysik der Erkenntnis* (1921), Heinz Heimsoeth with his ontological interpretation of Kant in the

1920s, Jonas Cohn with his *Theorie der Dialektik* (1923), Siegfried Marck with his *Die Dialektik in der Philosophie der Gegenwart* (1929-1931), Richard Hönigswald with his *Grundlagen der Denkpsychologie* (1921), and Bruno Bauch with his several later writings. Claims of a "Younger Neokantianism" must therefore be taken with reservations.

NEWTON, ISAAC (1642-1727). Owing mainly to his two major works on science, *Philosophiae Naturalis Principia Mathematica* (1687) and *Opticks* (1704, 4th ed. 1730), Newton became highly influential in the European intellectual scene in the 18th century. Not only did his views guide and inspire much work in natural philosophy, his physics was also seen as a paradigm of successful intellectual endeavor, and his method won wide acclaim and emulation. His philosophical convictions in a stricter sense of the word were known to the educated public largely from the correspondence between Samuel Clarke, Newton's mouthpiece, and **Gottfried Wilhelm Leibniz** (*A Collection of Papers which Passed between the Late Learned Mr. Leibnitz and Dr. Clarke, in the Years 1715 and 1716*, published in 1717).

In Germany, Newton's thought initially encountered considerable resistance from the Leibniz-Wolff school, but Kant became an adherent, if not an uncritical one, from early on. In his *Universal Natural History and Theory of Heavens* (1755), he accepts the basics of Newtonian physics, but attempts to extend them in their scope. Thus he seeks to account for the origin of the universe on principles of Newtonian science and he rejects any resort to supernatural intervention when it comes to explaining the workings of the planetary system; Newton himself had seen the workings of the divine hand in both areas. In his *Prize Essay* of 1763/1764, Kant not only recommends Newton's physics as an exemplary specimen of genuine science, he also suggests that Newton's analytic-synthetic **method** ought to be applied to **metaphysics**. In his "Concerning the Ultimate Ground of the Differentiation of Directions in Space" (1768), Kant argues against Leibniz's conception of relational **space** and in favor of Newton's absolute space, though he was to give up the latter theory soon after in the *Inaugural Dissertation* of 1770, advancing instead his own critical conception of space as the **form** of **intuition**; here, he also embarked on a methodological path that had little in common with Newton.

There are numerous explicit and implicit references to Newton in the *Critique of Pure Reason* and in the *Metaphysical Foundations of Natural Science* (1786). Conspicuous are the strong ties between the **analogies of experience** from the first *Critique*, the three laws of mechanics from the *Metaphysical Foundations*, and Newton's three laws of motion. However,

Kant also criticized Newton by contending that physics required first of all metaphysical foundations and not mathematical ones. In spite of that, Newton continued to play an important role in Kant's writings on theoretical philosophy, including in the *Opus Postumum*. *See also* PRE-CRITICAL WRITINGS.

NOTHING (*Nichts*). Kant takes up the **concept** of nothing apparently largely for the sake of the completeness of the **system** at the end of the **Transcendental Analytic** in the *Critique of Pure Reason* (A 290–92/B 346–49). Under the guidance of the **categories**, he distinguishes four meanings of the term 'nothing' as it relates to the concept of the **object** in general. He thus arrives at 1) an object of thought (*Gedankending, ens rationis*), which he defines as "an empty concept without an object" (examples: **noumena**, new fundamental **forces**); 2) the "concept of the absence of an object" (*nihil privativum*) (examples: shadows, cold); 3) an imaginary being (*ens imaginarium*), that is, an "empty intuition without an object" such as **space** and **time**; 4) the *nihil negativum*, the impossible, an "empty object without concepts" (example: a rectilinear figure with two sides). These differentiations owe much to the scholastic tradition, especially to Scotist ontology with its distinction between *nihil negativum* and *nihil privativum*, distinctions that Kant himself had introduced and discussed in his **pre-critical** piece *Attempt to Introduce Negative Magnitudes into Philosophy* of 1763 (Ak 2, pp. 171ff.).

Hermann Cohen also contrasted 'something' and 'nothing,' desisting, however, from the attempt to seek the origin of 'something' in an impossibility (*Unding*) that would signify the contradiction of 'something.' Rather, he considered 'nothing' to be a merely methodical detour that is followed in order to arrive at the corresponding 'something' (*Logik der reinen Erkenntnis*, pp. 84ff.). *See also* NEGATION.

NOUMENON. In accordance with the meaning of this word as "that which is thought," Kant does not refer with 'noumenon' directly to **things-in-themselves**, but rather to things as they are thought by **pure understanding**. He thus labels noumena variously as "beings of the understanding" (B 306, A 254/B 310) or, in the *Prolegomena*, as "pure beings of the understanding" or "beings of thought" (§ 45). On the whole, Kant's use of the term 'noumenon' is complicated. Straightforward and in keeping with the philosophical tradition is the fact that Kant contrasts noumena with phenomena. In the *Critique of Pure Reason*, this famously occurs in the third chapter of the "Analytic of Principles," that is, of the second book of the **"Transcendental Analytic."** However, the distinction between phenomena and noumena goes back to the **pre-critical** *Inaugural Dissertation* (§ 3), even if there Kant still held that noumena could be cognized by the understanding, since he still believed that the understanding could grasp things as they were in-themselves. After giving up this assumption in his **critical philosophy**, he then held that noumena could only be thought, but not cognized. At the root of this conception lies his distinction between the positive and negative use of the concept of noumenon. Kant defined noumenon in a negative sense as something that is not an object of our **sensible intuition**, while noumenon in a positive sense would have signified an object of a nonsensible intuition. Since, however, as Kant repeatedly stresses, we do not have such an intellectual intuition, we have no insight into the possibility of noumena, we cannot **cognize** them, and our understanding extends beyond sensibility only problematically. In epistemology, we can use the term 'noumenon' only in a negative sense, as a **boundary** concept. The implication Kant draws from this is that the **categories** do not apply to noumena, since they are limited to sensible intuition; there is therefore no determinate **object** for noumena, and the latter are not the concepts of an object, but only an expression of the question of whether there may be objects beyond the bounds of our sensible intuition, a question that Kant declares to be unsolvable. In the *Prolegomena*, Kant, in addition, calls the **transcendental ideas**, namely, the psychological, cosmological, and theological ideas, noumena. Here, he maintains that noumena are what **reason** seeks when it looks for a final condition of an otherwise unlimited series of conditions, and that this activity of reason seduces the understanding to a **transcendent** and hence illegitimate use (B 307–8, A 254–55/B 310–11, A 287–89/B 343–45; P, §§ 33–34, 45).

However, Kant did admit a positive employment of the term, though only in **moral** philosophy. Since noumena may be thought, Kant claimed that **freedom** of the **will** was a noumenon and he used the expression *'causa noumenon'* to indicate the idea of a **causality** of freedom (Ak 5, p. 49). A noumenal self was then one that could never be cognized, but only thought, and it could be thought **as if** it were not subject to natural causality, but endowed with freedom. *See also* APPEARANCE.

NUMBER.   In the course of expounding his philosophy of **mathematics**, Kant also reflected on the philosophical foundations and on the philosophical significance of numbers, putting these subsequently to various uses in his theoretical philosophy. In the *Critique of Pure Reason*, Kant defined number as "a **representation** that summarizes the successive addition of one (homogenous) unit to another," or, in other words, as "the **unity** of the synthesis of the manifold of a homogeneous intuition in general" (A 142–43/B 182), in the *Prolegomena*, more simply, as the successive addition of units in time (§ 10). The addition of numbers is then characterized as the "synthesis of that which is homogeneous (of units)" (A 164/B 205). Although generating numbers and counting are processes that take place in **time** and thus in **pure intuition**, they also require an act of the **understanding**, namely, a **synthesis**. Thanks to this latter characteristic, Kant subsumes the concept of number under the **category** of allness (B 111). Kant uses number in his chapter on **schematism**, where it serves as the pure schema of **magnitude** (*quantitas*) (A 142/B 182). Moreover, Kant claims, without offering much of an explanation, that number makes it possible to construct the concepts of space and time as quanta (A 720/B 748).

- O -

OBJECT (*Ding, Gegenstand, Objekt*). Kant uses the three German terms more or less interchangeably. Periodic attempts to distinguish *Ding*, *Gegenstand*, and *Objekt* have not been found convincing. In accordance with Kant's **Copernican Revolution**, our **cognition** of objects is not owing to the fact that it conforms to them, since then we could not explain how we can cognize anything about them **a priori**, but, rather, the objects conform to the **concepts** of the **understanding** (B xvii). We cannot therefore cognize how objects are apart from their relationship to our **mind**, or, in Kant's words, the **thing-in-itself** remains unknowable for us. An object of cognition is constituted by synthesizing the **manifold** of **intuition**, that is, by applying the **categories** to it and thus by producing a unified lawful connection, which *is* the object of cognition. The application of the universally valid categories ensures that this connection is likewise universally valid; for this reason, object cannot be explained by recourse to subjective psychological processes. Although the connection does not exist apart from the **synthesis** on the part of the subject, it is, nevertheless, objective and empirically real.

In the *Critique of Practical Reason*, Kant also speaks of the concept of an object of **pure practical reason**, defining it as "the idea of an object as an effect possible through **freedom**," that is, as "the relation of the **will** to the **action** whereby it or its opposite is brought into being." He further claims that the only objects of practical reason are those of the **good** and the **evil** (Part 1, Bk. 1, Ch. 2).

OBJECTIVE.   Kant contrasts objective and subjective in two different ways. First, in the technical sense of his own **critical philosophy**, objective is grounded in the subjective. Objective is valid **necessarily and universally**, that is, for all subjects of **cognition**, and, at the same time, it also pertains to objects of possible **experience**. However, this 'objective' is based on the subjective forms of **sensibility** and on the subjective conceptual apparatus grounded in the **transcendental unity of apperception**. Both of these components are involved in the process of cognition by providing the necessary conditions of the **validity** of objective judgments. In an important sense, therefore, this 'subjective' also has to do with universal validity.

In a second way, Kant contrasts objective and subjective more or less in accordance with common usage. Objective then again designates the necessary and universal, but subjective now only pertains to certain subjects or is valid only in certain limited ways. Relations that are objectively valid, that is, relations for which Kant in the first *Critique* reserves the label **judgments**, arise on the basis of the "principles of the objective determination of all representations." On the other hand, relations of representations of only subjective validity arise, for instance, on the basis of the laws of **association** (B 142). A similar distinction between objective and subjective is famously made in the *Prolegomena*, though here Kant generously includes under the label judgments also subjectively valid relations. He thus contrasts the objectively valid "judgments of experience" with the only subjectively valid "judgments of perception" (P, § 18). In accordance with the **Copernican Revolution** and with the above remarks, it would appear to be evident that using the terms 'object' or 'objectivity' to refer to **things-in-themselves** should, for Kant, count not just as misleading but as downright erroneous, given that the subjective conditions that are necessary for objectivity are missing. Kant more or less confirms this (e.g., A 242–47/B 299–303), but does, unfortunately, on occasion resort to such unwarranted language (e.g., P, § 19).

In the *Critique of Practical Reason* and the *Groundwork of the Metaphysics of Morals*, Kant speaks of an objective determination of the **will** by the categorical **imperative** or of the objective validity of the moral **law**. Objective here is used again in the sense of universal, that is, always necessary or valid for all rational beings. It is opposed to subjective in more or less the second sense outlined above: as subjective, Kant now considers the motivation from **inclination**, which, of course, cannot be universal.

ONTOLOGICAL PROOF OF THE EXISTENCE OF GOD. *See* GOD, PROOFS OF THE EXISTENCE OF.

Gottfried Wilhelm Leibniz (1646–1716)

David Hume (1711–1776)

Immanuel Kant around 1755. Drawing by Duchess Keyserling

University of Königsberg in the 18th Century

Immanuel Kant around 1768. Study by Becker

Immanuel Kant's house in Königsberg

Immanuel Kant in 1784. Engraving by Townley

Immanuel Kant in 1789. Drawing by Schnorr von Carolsfeld

Kant around 1790

Immanuel Kant around 1798. Drawing by Puttrich

Hermann Cohen (1842–1918)

Paul Natorp (1854–1924)

ONTOLOGY. In his lectures on metaphysics in 1765/1766, Kant still taught that ontology was "the science of the more general properties of all things" (Ak. 2, p. 309; see also Alexander Gottlieb Baumgarten, *Metaphysica*, 4th ed., 1757, § 4). In the *Critique of Pure Reason*, however, he claims that he is replacing such an ontology, "which presumes to offer **synthetic a priori cognitions** of things in general" (A 247/B 303), with a transcendental analytic of the **pure understanding**. While describing his critical system of philosophy later on in the *Critique* (A 845–46/B 873–74), he does use the term 'ontology' along with the expression "**transcendental philosophy**" as a designation of the first part of the **metaphysics** of nature, without, however, giving any credit to traditional ontology (Ak. 8, p. 190). In his answer to the prize question raised by the Berlin Academy of Sciences in 1791, "What Real Progress has Metaphysics Made in Germany since the Time of Leibniz and Wolff?" Kant upholds his new position, according to which ontology is transcendental philosophy that "contains the conditions and first elements of all our a priori cognition" (Ak 20, p. 260).

A so-called ontological interpretation of Kant became prominent in the 1920s in Germany. It owed its origin to the work of Heinz Heimsoeth and its main proponents were **Martin Heidegger**, and later Gottfried Martin and Ottokar Blaha. These authors stressed for various reasons the metaphysical implications of Kant's thought, especially the ontological grounding of a new conception of the person and of the world.

OPUS POSTUMUM. In the 'Preface' to his *Critique of Judgment* of 1790, Kant claimed that the project of **critical philosophy** was completed with that work; however, a short time later, he must have become acutely aware that there still remained a conceptual gap between the foundations of physics as he laid them down in his *Metaphysical Foundations of Natural Science* (1786) and **physics** itself. The notes he started compiling in 1796 in order to close this lacuna and on which he continued working until 1803, that is, as long as his health permitted, offer various titles for this project; "Transition from the Metaphysical Foundations of Natural Science to Physics" is perhaps the most appropriate one, given that, at least initially, Kant sought to extend the critical, **a priori** conceptual scheme further into the realm of the empirical than he had in 1786. However, the work as a whole is difficult to interpret as it drifts to subject matters that have little in common with the title, also because one cannot rely on any **architectonic** as a guide. Additional problems are caused by sloppy spelling and grammar as well as by an inconsistent use of terminology. The notes comprise countless sketches ranging from a few words to a few pages; these various drafts in different stages of completion deal with a given topic, then skip to the next, only to return to the original theme later on.

In the beginning, Kant was clearly concerned with finding notions that would have provided the conceptual structure for a philosophical account of physical bodies. He attempted to construct an elementary system of motive **forces** organized under the guiding thread of the **categories**, but, at least initially, usually did not get beyond **quality**. Subsequently, the sketches take up the concept of **ether**, with which Kant tried to explain various phenomena of physics, even presenting a **transcendental deduction** to prove that ether is the necessary condition of possible **experience**. Toward the end of his life, he turned to topics of practical philosophy and to problems raised in the 'Introduction' to the *Critique of Judgment* such as **purpose, God, freedom**, or **autonomy**.

The whole work was deemed unfit for publication shortly after Kant's death and was not edited in its entirety until 1936–1938, when it appeared as volumes 21 and 22 of the *Akademieausgabe*. Lately, this effort has come under criticism for a number of reasons, one of them being the fact that the different parts of the manuscript were published in random order rather than in the (presumed) sequence in which Kant had composed them. Given the chaotic nature of the work, it is no surprise that the commentators differ widely on many issues. There is, for instance, profound disagreement as to what form the completed work would have assumed. While attempts were undertaken to reconstruct the work, claiming it as essentially unified, other interpretations hold the notes to be mere reflections leading in unforeseen directions, manifesting the development of Kant's thought, but not permitting any conclusions as to the possible nature of the finished product. Nevertheless, there is some measure of agreement today that Kuno Fischer's severe judgment (1860), holding the work to be a product of senility, is mistaken, and the last several decades have witnessed increased interest in the work; this is evidenced by the increasing number of interpretations and translations into different languages such as Spanish, Italian (both 1983), French (1986), and English (1993). *See also* APPEARANCE OF APPEARANCE; ATOM; ATTRACTION; BODY; IMPENETRABILITY; PERCEPTION.

ORGANISM. Kant was concerned with providing cogent explanations of organisms throughout his philosophical career. Already in 1755, in his **precritical** piece *Universal Natural History and Theory of the Heavens*, he admitted that organisms could not be readily explained by mechanical laws, and that one would therefore be more easily able to account for the origin of the solar system than for a caterpillar (Ak 1, p. 230). Kant realized that organisms as organized systems of parts that support each other, that is, in which each part seems to exist and function for the sake of the other parts and of the whole, would have to be explained by recourse to **purposes** and ends. Although he sometimes equated organisms with machines, especially when the latter were qualified as natural machines, he far more frequently maintained that machines were an inferior kind of organism, since they possessed only motive **forces** but not formative ones (CJ, § 65; Ak 21, p. 186).

During his pre-critical period, especially in his piece *The Only Possible Ground of Proof for a Demonstration of the Existence of God* of 1763, Kant explored the possibility that purposively organized organisms could be considered as proofs of a divine design of nature. However, in his most concerted effort at dealing with organisms and with organized nature in the course of his discussion of **teleology** in the *Critique of Judgment* (§§ 65ff.), Kant dwelt on the fact that certain entities (such as a blade of grass, § 77) could be explained only by teleological laws, and he argued that there was no conflict between teleological laws and mechanical ones.

ORGANON.   Prior to Kant, the term was used as a label for the collection of the Aristotelian logical works, while Francis Bacon attempted to reorganize all human knowledge under the title *New Organon*. Kant employed the term only sparingly. In his *Logic*, he described an 'organon' as instructions or a set of rules for producing a certain piece of **cognition**, insisting, however, that the object of the cognition be known in advance. He claimed that **mathematics** was an organon, "as a science that contains the ground of the extension of our cognition in respect to a certain use of reason." Since **logic** abstracted from the content of cognition, its object could not be known in advance, and it was therefore not to be categorized as an organon, except perhaps in the weak sense that it served to appraise and correct our cognition rather than extend it. Instead, Kant preferred to classify logic as a **canon** (Ak 9, p. 13). In the *Critique of Pure Reason*, Kant focused on the aspect of organon that involved the illegitimate expansion of cognition and objected to the characterization of philosophy as an organon, stressing that **reason** has the inevitable tendency to illegitimately seek cognition beyond the bounds of possible **experience** (A 63/B 88; A 795/B 823).

ORIGIN (*Ursprung*).   In his *Religion within the Boundaries of Mere Reason*, Kant defined the (first) origin as the "descent of an effect from its first cause," distinguishing, on the basis of this definition, between "origin according to **reason**" and "origin according to **time**." Under the former he understood a cause that is not connected with the corresponding effect in time, while with the latter he referred to the natural cause of a temporal event (Part I, Sect. IV, Ak 6, pp. 39–40). This distinction opens up a new realm for dealing with the question of origin, a domain located between **metaphysics** and empirical **psychology** or anthropology. Situating himself within this realm in the course of his discussion of the origin of **cognition** in the *Critique of Pure Reason*, Kant contrasts a temporal beginning with a nontemporal one (B 1) and, corresponding to this, draws the distinction between a subjective and an objective origin of cognition. In the "**Transcendental Logic**," he subsequently separates the empirical origin of cognition in sense **impressions** from an **a priori** origin that cannot be attributed to things (B 80–81). However, Kant frequently speaks of 'origin' only in connection with his discussion of the a priori conditions of cognition. Such an a priori origin is placed partly in the psychological faculties of cognition (understanding, reason, and so forth), partly in the logical form of **judgment** or of the inferences of reason. In Kant's **transcendental philosophy**, the clarification of the question of the origin of cognition culminates in the claim that "the **understanding** is the origin of the general order of nature" (P, § 48).

The term 'origin' gained great prominence in **Neokantianism**. For **Hermann Cohen**, the true origin of things was grounded by Kant's category of **reality**; Cohen understood the construction of the finite out of the infinitesimally small as the paradigm-case of the production of reality. In his *Logik der reinen Erkenntnis*, Cohen departed from Kant's grounding of cognition in sensibility and the understanding and attempted to prove that cognition originates solely in **thought**. To think the origin of cognition means to prove that cognition is the product of a laying of foundations (in the Platonic sense of a hypothesis, that is, a standard of truth); Cohen emphasized that origin can always only be found in a laying of foundations (*Grundlegung*), never in absolute foundations (*Grundlage*). **Paul Natorp** interpreted Cohen's 'origin' as the concept of the synthetic unity of the manifold, rather than as the activity (production) of the mind in the way that Cohen grasped 'origin.'

OUGHT (*Sollen*). Applies to humans as beings that belong both to the realm of **sensibility** and to the realm of **reason**. Reason produces moral **law** which would be automatically binding for all beings that belonged solely to the realm of reason; whatever that law dictated would automatically be willed by such beings. Humans, however, are also motivated by desires or **inclinations** produced by their sensibility that are in conflict with moral law, so that they must attempt to overcome these desires, and the moral law does not automatically motivate them. Thus the moral law is an

imperative, with which an ought and not a wish (*Wollen*) is expressed (Ak 4, pp. 453–54; Ak 5, p. 20).

Against **Georg Wilhelm Friedrich Hegel**'s criticism, **Hermann Cohen** stressed the significance of the ought for an adequate understanding of a **will** that is determined by moral law. Cohen therefore attributes to the ought a being that differs from the being of nature, and he claims that the reality of this being of the ought is proved by the existence of juridical law. **Paul Natorp** grounded the transition from theoretical to practical philosophy in the ought. He achieved this by interpreting the Kantian theory of ideas as a "logic of the ought," that is, by grasping the progress of **cognition** as an infinite **problem** (*Aufgabe*), which ought to be fulfilled and which thus effects the transition to the "practical ought."

In contrast, **Heinrich Rickert** shifted the ought into the center of his theory of cognition: the general object of cognition is itself a "transcendent(al) ought" that is recognized in a judgment.

OUTER SENSE (*äußerer Sinn*). *See* INNER SENSE; SPACE.

- P -

PAIN. *See* PLEASURE AND PAIN (*Lust und Unlust*).

PARALOGISM. Kant was greatly concerned with dismantling the traditional discipline of rational **psychology**, which aimed to prove that the **soul** was immaterial, simple, numerically identical at different times, and thus, ultimately, incorruptible and **immortal**. He set out to accomplish this task in the first chapter of the **Transcendental Dialectic** of the *Critique of Pure Reason* under the heading "Paralogisms of Pure Reason." Basically, he argued that the proponents of rational psychology illegitimately attempted to extend the notion of the self beyond the realm of **experience** and that their 'proofs' therefore amounted to nothing but dialectical **illusion**. Unlike a logical paralogism, which is a syllogism with a fallacious form regardless of the contents, a **transcendental** paralogism goes astray because of a transcendental ground that misleads us into drawing a false inference. Since it is ultimately the nature of human **reason** that is responsible for the fallacy, the resulting illusion is unavoidable, though it may be resolved and thus defused (A 341/B 399).

Key to Kant's position is a proper understanding of the expression '**I think**.' He regards it as solely the **form** of the **transcendental unity of apperception** on which every experience depends; the 'I think' therefore functions only as a subjective condition of possible **cognition** in general. Kant provides various general formulations of his underlying idea that we are entitled only to a formal self from which it is illegitimate to infer a substantive one. Thus he claims, for instance, that the error of his opponents consists in taking the 'I think' as a concept of a thinking being in general (A 354). Alternatively, he suggests that it is illicit to infer "from the transcendental concept of a subject that contains nothing manifold . . . the absolute unity of this subject itself," since we have no concept of such a subject at all (A 340/B 398).

Taking the **categories** as his guide, Kant identifies four paralogisms that attempt to demonstrate the substantiality, simplicity, numerical identity, and ideality of the soul. All his refutations, both in the first edition version and in the somewhat simplified second edition one, follow a similar pattern. Against substantiality, for example, he argues that it is illegitimate to conclude from the formal proposition 'I think' that the soul is therefore a substance, since such an inference lies beyond the bounds of experience (A 350). Against identity, he argues that although it is undisputably true that our consciousness possesses an identity at different times, this is only "a formal condition of my thoughts and their connection," a condition from which we are in no way entitled to infer "the numerical identity of my subject" (A 363).

PASSION. *See* AFFECT.

PEACE (*Friede*). Perpetual peace was the goal already of Kant's theoretical philosophy: when all philosophical controversies are resolved by a **critique** of **reason** that acts as a court of justice, then reason moves from the state of **nature** to the lawful state of peace (A 751-52/B 779-80). This is possible because, as Kant repeated in 1796, the idea of **freedom** or **autonomy** is not subjected to conflicts of opinion. However, the prospect of this perpetual peace among philosophers is not affirmed by a peaceful philosophy resting on its presumed laurels, but by an armed one, even if it is not in a state of war (Ak 8, pp. 416-17).

As far as political theory is concerned, Kant's book *Toward Perpetual Peace* of 1795, whose title follows Abbé Castel de St. Pierre's *Traité de la paix perpétuelle* of 1713, not only discusses political measures for the preservation of peace but spells out, in an innovative fashion, the preconditions of universal peace in human society. Among these preconditions, Kant specifies a federative union of free countries and a republican constitution within each of the countries. To work toward peace is a moral **duty**, because peace represents the only lawful state based on the adherence to moral **law**, both between countries and between individual human beings; war is subject to the veto of moral **practical reason** (MM, Ak 6, pp. 354-55).

While **Johann Gottlieb Fichte** and Jean Paul accepted Kant's thinking about peace, **Georg Wilhelm Friedrich Hegel** rejected it. Within the context of his discussion of the messianic conception of universal peace, **Hermann Cohen** rendered Kant's ideas more precise by adding his interpretation of the peace of the soul as a religious virtue.

PERCEPTION (*Wahrnehmung, Perzeption, perceptio*). Compared with his predecessors **John Locke, George Berkeley, David Hume**, and **Gottfried Wilhelm Leibniz**, Kant accorded to perception a relatively minor role. His remarks on perception are not always consistent. In the standard English translations of the *Critique of Pure Reason*, this problem is compounded by the fact that the two German words and the Latin one are all rendered as 'perception.' Though Kant himself confused the issue by identifying both of the German terms with the Latin *'perceptio'* (for example, P, § 20 and A 320/B 376-77), there is good reason for claiming that *Perzeption* and *Wahrnehmung* should be held apart.

In Kant's most common characterization of perception (*Wahrnehmung*), the presence of **consciousness** is stressed. Representative is his determination of perception as **sensation** or **appearance** accompanied by consciousness (A 120); one may attribute the identification in the *Prolegomena* of perception with empirical intuition (§ 10) to carelessness. Helpful is Kant's statement that perception has sensation as its **matter** and appearances as its **objects** (A 165-67/B 207-8). Perception in this sense stands in an intermediate position between mere sensation and **cognition** or **experience**. Given that it is always classified as empirical, for example, as an "empirical consciousness," it can become **experience** only if a **concept** of the **understanding** is added, that is, if perceptions are synthesized by the understanding. Perceptions as such are therefore not subject to any **a priori** conceptual determination, and it is possible to 'anticipate' only one property of perceptions, namely, the fact that the sensations in them must possess an intensive **magnitude** ("**Anticipations of Perception**").

In the first *Critique*, Kant uses the word *'Perzeption'* only once, when he presents a cognitive ladder of some key concepts. In this context, perception (*Perzeption*) means **representation** with consciousness and is divided into sensation and cognition. The identification of perception (*Perzeption*) with either sensation or cognition obviously contradicts Kant's remarks on *'Wahrnehmung.'* The absence at this place of the word *'Wahr-*

nehmung,' which would have to be positioned between sensation and cognition, is, in fact, conspicuous (A 320/B 376-77).

In the *Prolegomena*, Kant famously, and controversially, distinguished between judgments of perception (*Wahrnehmungsurteile*), which are linked by the understanding only subjectively, and judgments of experience, which are linked by the understanding **objectively** (§ 20). It has been argued by many commentators that the expression "judgments of perception" is contradictory, given that in the *Critique of Pure Reason* Kant described perceptions as not standing under any concept of the understanding, a characteristic that would preclude them from being directly combined into judgments.

In the course of his attempt to bridge the gap between philosophy of **natural science** and **physics** in the so-called *Opus Postumum*, Kant became increasingly concerned with finding concepts that would structure not just experience but also perception. Although he still operated with the same definition of perception as in the first *Critique* (appearance with consciousness) (for example, Ak. 22, pp. 32, 325, 366, 420, 611), Kant now employed expressions such as "possible perceptions" or "system of perceptions," and he spoke of the need to present an a priori list of perceptions for the sake of experience (Ak 22, pp. 22, 32, 387). He thought that this structuring function would be fulfilled by the concepts of the relations of motive **forces**, and he introduced a number of expressions (such as self-**affection** or **appearance of appearance**) to convey the idea that it is the subject that places these formal elements into perception.

PERFECTION (*Vollkommenheit*). In the pre-Kantian philosophical tradition, the concept of perfection was employed in ontology, ethics, and aesthetics both in the qualitative sense of 'inner' perfection and in the quantitative sense of 'external' perfection. Kant's discussion in his **pre-critical** piece *An Attempt at Some Reflections on Optimism* of absolute and relative perfection (Ak 2, pp. 30-31) is still situated within the context of the old scholastic metaphysics. Kant breaks with this type of philosophy when he rejects the transcendental concepts "unity, truth, and good (perfect)" in their old sense of fundamental ontological attributes of things, replacing them, within the framework of his **transcendental logic**, with the "criteria of all **cognition** of all things in general." He carries out this transition by relating the concepts of unity, truth, and perfection to the three **categories** of **quantity** in their application to heterogeneous elements of cognition. Perfection then means "qualitative completeness" or the **totality** of a **concept** (B 113-15).

From this theoretical meaning, Kant distinguishes a practical one, according to which perfection is the "fitness or adequacy of a thing for all sorts of ends" (CrPR, Ak 5, p. 41; see also MM, Ak 6, p. 386). When perfection becomes the determining ground of the **will**, then the latter is subjected to a previously given **purpose** and is thus guided, from a moral point of view, by an empirical principle, not by a formal one of reason (Ak 5, p. 41). Nevertheless, in his theory of **virtue**, Kant includes the fostering of one's own (not of someone else's) perfection among those purposes that are at the same time **duties** (Ak 6, pp. 386-87).

In distinction to the scholastic philosophy of **Christian Wolff** who understood pleasure as the sensible representation of the perfection of an object (Ak 20, p. 226) and who, correspondingly, grasped the aesthetic feeling of the beautiful as a pleasure that promotes moral feeling, Kant radically separated in his *Critique of Judgment* perfection from **beauty**, which is experienced only in the feeling of **pleasure** (p. 228). Perfection is "objective inner purposiveness," but beauty is thought as the merely formal subjective purposiveness of an object, not as its objective purposiveness (Ak 5, pp. 227-28).

In his *Logic*, Kant still moved along scholastic paths when he distinguished between the logical and aesthetic perfection of cognition, that is, between the correspondence of a cognition to an object according to universally valid laws, and its correspondence, grounded in the sensibility of humans, to a subject ('beauty') (Ak 9, pp. 36-37). These reflections are partially of a **pre-critical** character and combine epistemological considerations with aesthetic and rhetorical ones (Ak 16, pp. 99ff.).

In post-Kantian philosophy, the concept of perfection strongly receded into the background. **Johann Gottlieb Fichte**'s demand in his *Vorlesungen über die Bestimmung des Gelehrten* for perfecting the human being to infinity finds a late resonance in **Hermann Cohen**'s explication of the "ethical ideal" into its three components: perfection, perfecting, and the imperfection of perfecting.

PERSISTENCE (*Beharrlichkeit*). See SUBSTANCE.

PERSON. Ontologically speaking, the human being is, for Kant, a person insofar as he is "conscious of the numerical identity of his self at different times" (A 361). It would be a mistake, however, to attempt to deduce from this definition the claim that a person (soul) is an absolutely persisting **substance**.

In Kant's thought, the concept of 'person' gains its full relevance only in his **ethics**. Here, the distinction between persons and things is important.

While in practical contexts the latter have only a relative value as means, the former are objective ends; they are beings "whose existence is in itself an end" and who possess an absolute worth (GMM, Ak 4, p. 428). This qualification is not gained on the basis of natural attributes of humans, but on the basis of morality (pp. 434-35), since 'personality' consists of the "freedom and independence from the mechanism of the whole of **nature**" (CrPR, Ak 5, p. 87). Unlike things, persons as subjects of **actions** are capable of responsibility (Ak 6, pp. 26, 223). *See also* DIGNITY; VALUE.

PHENOMENOLOGY. *See METAPHYSICAL FOUNDATIONS OF NATURAL SCIENCE.*

PHENOMENON. *See* APPEARANCE; NOUMENON.

PHILOSOPHY. Kant provided a number of clues as to what he understood by 'philosophy,' also offering various related distinctions, but advancing no dominant explicit definition. In one important sense, philosophy for Kant roughly coincided with the **critique of pure reason**. This is strongly suggested by his comment that philosophy, except for the history of philosophy, cannot be learned, and that one can only acquire the ability to philosophize, that is, one can learn to conduct an investigation into the sources of the general **principles** of **reason**. At almost the same place in the first *Critique*, however, Kant apparently entertained a wider conception. He distinguished philosophy according to its scholastic concept from philosophy in accordance with its cosmopolitan concept (*Weltbegriff*). With the former, he most likely had the view of the **Leibniz-Wolff** school in mind, a view that he would not have regarded as fully satisfactory; as its end he admitted only the systematic unity of **cognition**. The latter he characterized as "the science of the relation of all cognition to the essential **ends** of human reason (*teleologia rationis humanae*)" (A 839/B 867), stressing that only this concept gives dignity and absolute value to philosophy and calling such a philosophy a doctrine of wisdom (*Weisheitslehre*) (A 837-39/B 865-67).

In addition, Kant distinguished philosophy from other disciplines, most often from **mathematics**, which he characterized as the cognition from the **construction** of concepts; the appropriate **method** in philosophy then consisted of cognition from concepts. He also drew a number of distinctions within philosophy itself. In place of the Aristotelian division into theoretical and practical philosophy, he adopted the one into philosophy of nature and philosophy of morals (A 840/B 868), or, more frequently, into **metaphysics** of **nature** and metaphysics of **morals**. This accorded better with his view that the two objects of philosophy are nature and **freedom**. Taking recourse to the Stoics, he added, in the 'Preface' to the *Groundwork of the Metaphysics of Morals*, logic to the branches of philosophy, defining it as formal cognition occupied with only the **form** of the **understanding** and of reason, and opposing it to material cognition that has to do with definite objects and the laws to which these are subject; here again he identified as such laws those of nature and freedom. Finally, he distinguished between pure and empirical (applied) philosophy, though there is no doubt that he regarded only the former as the real prize to be won. See also SYSTEM; TRANSCENDENTAL PHILOSOPHY.

PHORONOMY. See *METAPHYSICAL FOUNDATIONS OF NATURAL SCIENCE*.

PHYSICO-THEOLOGY. See GOD, PROOFS OF THE EXISTENCE OF.

PHYSICS. Although Kant made no direct contribution to physics itself, he had an excellent grasp of the subject and he made some important reflections on the philosophical status of its laws. In his first **pre-critical** book *Thoughts on the True Estimation of Living Forces* (published in 1749), Kant attempted to resolve the dispute between the Cartesians and the Leibnizians as to the correct measure of **force** (mv or mv^2). In his subsequent writings, he became more strongly attached to Newtonian physics, to which he eventually attempted to provide the philosophical foundations in the *Metaphysical Foundations of Natural Science*. Kant retained a lively interest in physics and in the question of its conceptual foundations throughout the whole of his adult life, setting out in his unfinished last piece of writing, the *Opus Postumum*, to account for the necessity of particular laws of physics.

Kant also considered physics as an instance of a well-established discipline that could serve as a model for **metaphysics**. He thought that physics owed its success to the fact that it contained a **pure** part that enabled the researcher to deal with empirical data on a rational basis; neither would the scientist let the data dictate to him nor would he allow himself any flights of fancy. In a much quoted passage from the preface to the second edition of the *Critique of Pure Reason*, Kant discussed the examples of Galileo and Evangelista Torricelli to argue that **reason** must approach nature with principles and with experiments devised on the basis of these principles (B xii–xiii). The pure part of physics contains **synthetic a priori judgments** as **principles**, for example, conservation of the quantity of matter, or equality of action and reaction; Kant viewed these principles as grounded in the **principles of the understanding** (B 17–18, B 128, A 846/B 874).

PLATO. There is some measure of agreement on the part of the scholarship that Kant read Plato extensively only in 1769 and that his acquaintance with Plato's thought possibly exercised an influence on the *Inaugural Dissertation* of 1770. Here, Kant, for instance, sharply distinguished for the first time between **phenomena** and **noumena**. During his **critical** period, Kant's attitude toward Plato was marked both by criticism and by praise. Kant objected that Plato had built his philosophy solely within the realm of **reason** without sufficient regard to the fact that his usage of the word 'idea' failed to provide a guarantee of a congruence between ideas and **experience**, if only because ideas did not serve as the key to possible experience in the way that the **categories** did. According to Kant, Plato allowed reason to indulge in ideal explanations of natural **appearances** and neglected the physical investigation of them. But most of all, Kant was bothered by the fact that Plato did not examine the epistemological foundations of his philosophy, in other words, that he failed to engage in a critique of the human cognitive faculties in the manner that Kant himself set out to do. He thus accused Plato of having said more than he had known, of having indulged in "an exaggerated expression," and of having deduced his ideas in a mystical way.

However, Kant did admit that Plato had stressed that our **cognition** feels a higher need than just the spelling out of appearances and he did find Platonic ideas highly useful for practical philosophy. He emphasized that the idea of **virtue** was a concept of reason, an archetype, and that instances of it in experience could only serve as examples, never as archetypes. In the same vein, he approved of the idea of the Platonic republic, that is, of "a **constitution** providing for the greatest human **freedom** according to **laws** that permit the freedom of each to co-exist with that of others," labeling it a "necessary idea." As in the case of virtue, he found the practicability of the idea to be only of secondary importance, expressing the hope, however, that approximating to the idea of the ideal constitution would lead to the diminution of the need for punishment. Kant also claimed to be in agreement with Plato in regard to the assertion that **teleological** order (for example, in a plant, an animal, or in the whole order of nature) was possible only in accordance to ideas (A 5/B 9, A 313–17/B 370–75, A 472/B 500). It should finally be noted that under the heading 'Plato' Kant presented less the historical person than a broadly accepted form of Platonic philosophy whose origins date back to antiquity.

In **Neokantianism**, Plato assumed a far more significant role than he had ever played for Kant; in fact, the movement has often been branded "Platonic Kantianism" or "Kantian Platonism." Not only did its main representatives, **Hermann Cohen**, **Wilhelm Windelband**, and **Paul Natorp**, each compose a special work on Plato (*Platons Ideenlehre und die Mathematik*, 1878; *Platon*, 1900; *Platos Ideenlehre*, 1903, 2nd ed. 1921), they also made countless references to Plato throughout their other work. This interest in Platonic ideas may be traced to Hermann Lotze's (1817–1881) book *Logik* (1874), in which an idea is interpreted not as an existing entity, but as something that is true and valid, that is, as an affirmative judgment. Both Cohen and Natorp grasped the Platonic idea as a hypothesis, not, however, in the sense of a supposition that is to be proved or disproved by empirical facts, but rather in the sense of a standard of truth, that is, of a justification of a concept. Such an idea then serves as the foundation of the cognition of the nomological order of being, that is, as a **transcendental a priori**.

PLEASURE AND PAIN (*Lust und Unlust*). Pleasure and pain stand to each other in real opposition, not in a logical one. They are like gain and loss, not like gain and a lack; pain is a "negative pleasure" (Ak 2, pp. 180–81; Ak 7, p. 230). At the outset of the second part of his *Anthropology from a Pragmatic Point of View*, which deals exclusively with the feeling of pleasure and pain, Kant contrasts enjoyment (sensible pleasure) with pain (sensible displeasure), treating them both in a similar fashion. In view of this symmetry, he can often limit himself to an explication of pleasure. This he divides into sensible and intellectual, the former further into enjoyment (pleasure of the senses) and taste (pleasure of the imagination, that is, "contemplative pleasure or inactive delight," Ak 6, p. 212), the latter into pleasure from presentable concepts and pleasure from ideas (Ak 7, p. 230).

Kant defines the general concept of pleasure as the "representation of the agreement of an object or of an action with the subjective conditions of life" (CrPR, Ak 5, p. 9n.). According to the 'Introduction' to the *Critique of Judgment*, the systematics of philosophy is based on the three basic faculties of the soul: the feeling of pleasure and pain is situated between the **faculty** of **cognition** and the faculty of **desire** and is assigned to the **faculty** of **judgment**, which stands in the middle between the **understanding** and **reason** (Ak 5, pp. 177–78, 198). Unlike sensation, pleasure is a purely subjective, noncognitive element of the representation of an object; pleasure forms the basis of an **aesthetic** judgment by way of a resort to the formal **purposiveness** of an object (pp. 189, 193).

The relationship of pleasure and the faculty of desire yields "practical pleasure." When pleasure is the cause of a desire, then the latter has the character of a habitual **inclination**; pleasure then represents an "interest of inclination." When, on the other hand, pleasure follows desire, then it is an "intellectual pleasure" or a "non-sensible inclination" out of a pure interest of reason (MM, Ak 6, pp. 212-13). When it is the pleasure derived from the actuality of an object that determines the faculty of desire, then the latter is subjected only to an empirical principle, not to a universally valid practical **law** (CrPR, Ak 5, pp. 21-22). In Kant's view, pleasure and pain cannot therefore ground a morality that is binding for all rational beings.

POSSIBILITY (*Möglichkeit*). Given that the concept of possibility played a central role in the philosophy of the **Leibniz-Wolff** school, it is not surprising that the **pre-critical** Kant concerned himself with this concept as well. In the *Nova Dilucidatio* (1755) and then again in *The Only Possible Ground of Proof for a Demonstration of the Existence of God* (1763), he attempted to prove God's existence on the basis of the concept of possibility, by arguing that the inner possibility of things presupposed something existing, without which there would be no material for thought and therefore also not for the possible. By a series of complicated steps he then tried to demonstrate that this existing something had to be God. Though in his critical period Kant rejected all such arguments, he did then draw on a distinction that he first started exploring in his early years, namely, the one between real and logical possibility. This was discussed especially in the piece *Attempt to Introduce Negative Magnitudes into Philosophy* (1763).

In the *Critique of Pure Reason*, Kant first introduces possibility in the **table of judgments** within the group "modality of judgments" under the heading 'problematic.' In such judgments, "one regards the assertion or denial as merely possible" (A 74/B 100). Moving from general **logic** to **transcendental logic**, Kant then derives the **category** 'possibility – impossibility,' and, advancing to the question of the applicability of the categories, he arrives at the **schema** of possibility. This he defines in temporal terms as "the agreement of the synthesis of various representations with the conditions of **time** in general, thus the determination of the representation of a thing to some time" (A 144/B 184). Subsequently, possibility emerges as the first **postulate of empirical thinking in general**: "whatever agrees with the formal conditions of experience (in accordance with intuition and concepts) is possible" (A 218/B 265). Recalling his pre-critical attempts to establish the difference between logical and real possibility, Kant here stresses the fact that concepts for which real possibility is claimed must not only satisfy the criterion of noncontradiction, but must in addition either provide the conditions of the possibility of **experience** or be given in experience.

The concept of 'possibility' also plays an important role in Kant's rejection in the **"Transcendental Dialectic"** of the traditional arguments for the existence of **God**. Again falling back on the distinction between logical and real possibility, Kant now charges that the arguments fail to prove anything, because real possibility cannot be demonstrated by showing that a concept is noncontradictory, but must have some foundation in actual existence.

POSSIBLE EXPERIENCE (*Mögliche Erfahrung*). Although Kant in his **critical philosophy** used both the term 'experience' and the expression "possible experience," there is a tendency on the part of some Kantians and Kant scholars to emphasize either the one or the other. By stressing that Kant's **epistemology** is a theory of possible experience rather than just experience, one underscores the importance of the **formal** elements in Kant's philosophy, that is, of the **categories** and the **principles of pure understanding**; under 'experience' one will then tend to understand **science** or scientific experience. Conversely, by placing the emphasis on experience rather than on possible experience, one opens up the field for interpretations that primarily deal with everyday experience and that tend to ignore science.

POSTULATES. Certain unproven propositions that play a crucial role for Kant both in his epistemology, under the heading of **postulates of empirical thinking in general**, and in his **moral** philosophy. But though postulates may be ultimately indemonstrable, Kant criticizes the practice in philosophy of arbitrarily advancing, under the title of a postulate, an unproven proposition without any justification, claiming that this makes it permissible to introduce even nonsensical claims that are then not open to **critique**. He therefore stresses that some sort of justification or '**deduction**' is required when a postulate is employed. Generally speaking, if something is certain and something else is the necessary condition of it, then this latter entity may be postulated even if it cannot be demonstrated or cognized.

Postulates were used mainly in **mathematics**, and Kant himself points to the similarities in the use of postulates here and in philosophy. In mathematics they describe a procedure: "the practical [that is, experimental, not moral] proposition that contains nothing except the synthesis through which we first give ourselves an object and generate its concept." As he explains, when we already possess (as a priori and necessary) the concept of a circle we can then postulate that it may be drawn with a given line from a given point on a plane. Such a proposition cannot be proved, since it lays down precisely the procedure that generates the concept.

In practical philosophy, what one postulates is a certain **object** rather than an action; moral **laws** necessarily presuppose the existence of this object as "the condition of the possibility of their binding force." This being the case, the existence of the object is postulated rightfully, though, as Kant stresses over and over, only practically, that is, without any cognitive claim involved (A 232-34/B 285-87, A 633-34/B 661-62, Ak 5, pp. 12n., 122). In the *Critique of Practical Reason*, Kant then identifies three such postulates: **immortality**, **freedom**, and the existence of **God**. These derive, respectively, from "the practically necessary condition of a duration adequate to the perfect fulfilment of the moral law," "from the necessary presupposition of independence from the world of sense and of the capacity of determining one's will by the law of an intelligible world," and "from the necessity of the condition for such an intelligible world to be the highest good, through the presupposition of . . . the existence of God" (Ak 5, p. 132).

POSTULATES OF EMPIRICAL THINKING IN GENERAL (*Postulate des empirischen Denkens überhaupt*). The three postulates **possibility, actuality**, and **necessity** are those **principles of pure understanding** that specify the conditions for the empirical application of the **modal** categories of possibility, existence, and necessity. Such **postulates** are 'subjectively' synthetic, since they add to the concept of a thing "the cognitive power whence it arises and has its seat," without, however, providing any information about the **object** (A 233-34/B 285-87). What is crucial from the point of view of Kant's **transcendental philosophy** is the fact that the postulates are of **transcendental** use, that is, they are part of the apparatus that specifies the necessary conditions of **experience**, and thus go beyond merely logical employment.

Kant began to realize the significance of some such difference already in his **pre-critical** period, especially in his piece *Attempt to Introduce Negative Magnitudes into Philosophy* (1763), in which he for the first time argued for the distinction between real and logical usage of concepts. One major consequence of this new understanding of the modal concepts was to limit their use to the empirical realm and to disqualify any talk of possible worlds or of the cognition of a necessary being. How far Kant had moved beyond the thinking of the Leibniz-Wolff school on this issue is apparent from his claim that the extension of possible objects is the same as that of actual and even necessary ones. **Gottfried Wilhelm Leibniz**'s theory that our actual world had been created as the best out of an infinite number of other possible worlds amounted for the critical Kant to nothing but unwarranted speculation.

POWER. *See* FACULTY (*Vermögen, Fähigkeit, Kraft*).

PRACTICAL REASON (*Praktische Vernunft*). For Kant, **pure** reason is practical when it proves "its reality and that of its concepts by deed" (CrPR, Ak 5, p. 3; see also B ix–x). The distinction between pure practical and speculative (theoretical) **reason** refers to the different uses of one and the same reason (GMM, Ak 4, p. 391). When reason is viewed as "the **faculty of principles**" (Ak 5, p. 119), its speculative employment strives to attain the highest principles **a priori** of the **cognition** of **objects**, while its practical use aims at an a priori determination of the **will** by a "causality of **freedom**" that is proper to reason. Unlike in its cognitive function, reason in its practical employment determines the will immediately and **constitutively**, so that Kant regards practical reason and the will (as the faculty to act in accordance with principles) as identical (Ak 4, p. 412; Ak 6, p. 14). For human beings, however, the will does not follow the **laws** of reason necessarily, because it is submitted to subjective **inclinations**, so that, for humans, the laws assume the character of **imperatives** or **commands** that coerce the will (Ak 4, p. 413).

In this sense, practical reason has its own "original principles a priori" into which theoretical reason has no insight (Ak 5, p. 120). Under principles (*Grundsätze*) of practical reason, Kant understands "propositions that contain a general determination of the will, having under it several practical rules." Within this class of principles, Kant distinguishes the merely subjectively valid **maxims** from the **objective** practical laws that are valid for the will of every rational being (p. 19). Practical principles that originate in a material determining ground of the will do not count among the practical laws. The highest practical principle of the "basic law of pure practical reason" is the categorical imperative. Acting in accordance with it means that one subjects one's will exclusively to the pure form of the law (pp. 30–31).

PRE-CRITICAL PHILOSOPHY. Before the publication of the first edition of his *Critique of Pure Reason* in 1781, Kant had written 30 so-called pre-critical texts, dealing with a wide variety of subjects ranging from earthquakes to the human races, from the aging of the earth to syllogisms. Although the designation pre-critical is in general applied collectively to all of the texts, in conformity to the fact that they stem from the period before Kant underwent his critical turn, that is, before he adopted his version of the **Copernican Revolution**, strictly speaking, only those texts with a philosophical content are genuinely pre-critical; the others fall outside the scope of the labels pre-critical/critical.

The (philosophical) pre-critical texts are characterized by an adherence to the metaphysical tradition of the so-called **Leibniz-Wolff** school, though Kant's attitude toward the main tenets of this tradition was, from the beginning, marked by a certain amount of distance, becoming increasingly skeptical as time progressed. Kant's own misgivings may have been accentuated by his contact in the 1750s with the thought of **Jean-Jacques Rousseau** and **David Hume**. The following writings are worthy of special mention. Kant's first piece, *Thoughts on the True Estimation of Living Forces* (published in 1749), was intended as a resolution of the dispute between the Cartesians and the Leibnizians on the correct measure of force, a dispute that concerned the question which of the formulas mv or mv^2 was the correct one. As in some of his later pre-critical and especially in his **critical philosophy**, Kant here attempted to mediate between two seemingly irreconcilable positions, presenting a proposal that, however, turned out to be worthless for deciding the debate. In his *Universal Natural History and Theory of the Heavens* (1755), Kant attempted to combine Newtonian **physics** with the physico-theological argument for the **existence** of God, thereby hoping to improve both on **Isaac Newton** and on the standard versions of the argument from design: his universe was built on the basis of the physical **laws** inherent to **matter**, and it required no divine intervention in order to be sustained. Newton was hereafter to play an important role in Kant's theoretical philosophy.

The *Nova Dilucidatio* (1755) was more heavily dependent on the Leibniz-Wolff tradition than any other of Kant's works, though Kant did question the central role played by the principle of contradiction in the philosophy of his predecessors. As the basic principles of **cognition**, he presented identity, contradiction, succession, and coexistence, presaging with the last two the **principle** of **causality** of his later philosophy. In addition, he defended a compatibilist notion of human **freedom**, a notion that he was to greatly refine in the *Critique of Pure Reason*.

In *The Only Possible Ground of Proof for a Demonstration of the Existence of God* (1763), Kant rejected the traditional ontological argument by claiming, as he was to do in his critical phase, that **existence** was not a predicate, and presented his own version of the proof based on the concept of **possibility**. He attempted to link this argument to the physico-theological one by claiming that possibility was identical with the essence of matter and with its divinely legislated properties, thus further developing the conception presented in the earlier *Universal Natural History*.

Kant's doubts about traditional metaphysics became more clearly apparent in his prize essay *Inquiry Concerning the Distinctness of the Principles of Natural Theology and Morality* (1763/64), where he proposed a new method for philosophy by clarifying the relationship between the procedures of **mathematics** and **metaphysics**. He claimed that philosophy was to rely, in analogy to Newton's physics, on certain inner experience, that is, on immediate evident consciousness, and he suggested that philosophy was to use as its axioms material principles, an example of which he provided in his *Attempt to Introduce Negative Magnitudes into Philosophy* (1763). Here, the idea of real rather than logical contradiction is introduced and the problem of the real ground and thus of causality is stated.

In the *Observations on the Feeling of the Beautiful and the Sublime* (1764), Kant turned to a discussion of **aesthetics**. Unlike in his critical work in this area, he was at this point still far more strongly dependent on the notion of '**feeling**,' being under the possible influence of the moral sense theory of Shaftesbury (1671–1713) and Francis Hutcheson (1694–1746).

In the heavily satirical *Dreams of a Spirit-Seer* (1766), Kant attacked both the mystical visions of Immanuel Swedenborg (1688–1772) and some of the tenets of the metaphysical tradition, especially those relating to the concept of the **soul** and to the mind-body problem. Increasingly, Kant conceived metaphysics not as a study of **being** but as a study of the **limits** of human **cognition**.

The critical turn actually commenced with the inaugural dissertation *On the Form and Principles of the Sensible and the Intelligible World* (1770). Here, Kant distinguished between the **sensible** and the **intelligible world**, criticizing the tradition for having confounded these realms. Under the heading sensible, he presented the conception of **space** and **time** as the **forms** of **sensibility**, a conception that heralds the theory presented in the "**Transcendental Aesthetic**" of the *Critique of Pure Reason*. In addition, by ascribing numerous errors of his predecessors to their confusion of the two realms, Kant anticipated his critical theory of the **antinomies** of reason. At this stage though, he accounted for such missteps by claiming that sensibility encroached on the understanding, rather than by holding that the concepts of the understanding were used illegitimately beyond the limits of sensibility.

However, in 1770, Kant still had no useful notion of the function of the understanding and of reason (which he did not even hold to be distinct) and he spent a good part of the next decade working this out. Owing to the seemingly disparate character of the pre-critical texts as well as to the fact that Kant later essentially repudiated them, abandoning many of the ideas developed in those writings, the early period of his work has received far less attention from the scholarship than has the critical phase. Nevertheless, a large number of pre-critical conceptions were utilized by Kant in his later years, although usually in a more restrained form as **postulates** or as **regulative ideas**, for example, the existence of God or **purpose**. *See also* AS-

TRONOMY; ATOM; ATTRACTION; BODY; DETERMINISM; EX-
TENSION; FORCE; IMPENETRABILITY.

PRINCIPLE (*Grundsatz, Prinzip, Principium*). Frequently employed terms
in Kant's philosophy. They occur in a number of different contexts and
their meaning varies correspondingly, sometime denoting the same as **law**,
at other times presupposition, yet at others **maxim**. In addition, Kant often
used them in a rather nontechnical sense, for example, as any guiding notion or idea that allows a systematic ordering of data.

Although the two German words and the Latin one are customarily
translated with the same term into English, an argument could be made for
rendering '*Grundsatz*' differently from the other two words. When speaking in a technical sense, Kant reserved '*Grundsatz*' for, on the one hand,
the so-called principles of **practical reason**, and, on the other, for the **principles of pure understanding**, further differentiating within the latter between **constitutive** and regulative as well as between mathematical and
dynamical principles. The expression "principles of pure understanding,"
though adopted in the English translations of the *Critique of Pure Reason*
by J. M. D. Meiklejohn, Norman Kemp Smith as well as Paul Guyer and
Allen W. Wood, poses serious problems when confronted with Kant's explication of the role of reason in his introduction to the "**Transcendental
Dialectic**." Here, Kant made a point of denying that the **understanding**
could be a faculty of principles (*Prinzipien*), declaring that it is "the faculty
of the unity of appearances by means of rules," while **reason** is the faculty
of principles, or, more specifically, "the faculty of the unity of the rules of
understanding under principles" (A 302/B 359). Barring principles (*Prinzipien*) from the understanding is a consequence of Kant's definition of principles in a strict sense as synthetic propositions from concepts and of his
accompanying claim that the understanding cannot yield such principles (A
301/B 357-58).

There is less justification for insisting on the distinction between
'*Grundsatz*' and '*Prinzip*' in contexts in which Kant is not relying on any
strict definition of 'principle.' This is the case when he admits that one may
call all universal propositions principles (*Prinzipien*), since he claims that
this involves only a loose, comparative sense of the term principle. A similar situation arises with respect to mathematical axioms (for example, there
can be only one straight line between any two points): these may be called
principles, but Kant restricts such usage only to those cases that can be subsumed under them (A 300-1/B 356-57). No serious problem of conflicting
translation arises in regard to Kant's use of 'principle' in the *Critique of
Judgment*. Here, he discusses the distinction between **transcendental** prin-

ciples and metaphysical ones. He defines the former as those principles "by means of which the universal **a priori** condition under which alone things can be **objects** of our **cognition** at all is represented," while the latter "represent the a priori condition under which alone objects, whose concept must be given empirically, can be further determined a priori." In accordance with these definitions, Kant then classifies the principle of the **purposiveness** of nature as transcendental, and the principle of practical purposiveness as metaphysical, because "the concept of a faculty of desire as a will must still be given empirically" (Second Introduction, V). Finally, it must be added that Kant himself suggested in his *Logic* that the words *'Grundsatz'* and *'Prinzip'* may be used as synonyms (§ 24).

PRINCIPLES OF PURE UNDERSTANDING (*Grundsätze des reinen Verstandes*). Kant claimed that these principles flowed out of the **categories**, to which they therefore correspond. However, unlike the categories, the principles of pure understanding stand under clearly specified sensible conditions (discussed first under the heading **Schematism**) and are therefore directly applicable to **experience** and to the **objects** of experience (A 136/B 175). These principles are **synthetic judgments a priori,** they are necessary and universal and they contain the ground of all other synthetic judgments. They are not grounded in higher **cognitions,** but provide the **form** of all experience and the form of all objects of experience. Though not themselves part of **mathematics,** they make the principles of mathematics possible and, though not themselves part of science, they stand above all particular scientific laws. In this way, they make **nature** possible and are its highest laws. Through them, **appearances** are ordered and become objective experience. Thanks to them, we are able to distinguish objective experience from **illusion** or from mere subjective sequences of representations.

Just as Kant divides the categories into mathematical and **dynamical** ones, so he separates the principles of pure understanding into mathematical and dynamical ones. Among the former he counts the **Axioms of Intuition** and the **Anticipations of Perception,** while the latter consist of the **Analogies of Experience** and the **Postulates of Empirical Thought in General.** In his philosophy of **physics,** presented in the *Metaphysical Foundations of Natural Science*, Kant again takes up these principles, applying them, however, to the additional sensible condition of **matter,** thus rendering them more particular.

PROBLEM (*Aufgabe, Problem*). Kant speaks of problems chiefly in the "**Transcendental Dialectic,**" thus remaining within the topical dimension

of the concept of problem, even if elements of its mathematically methodological meaning are still present. The **ideas** of **reason** are labeled as problems because it is questionable whether their **object** can be cognized *in
concreto;* in this sense, Kant calls the cosmological ideas the "four natural
and unavoidable problems of reason" (A 462/B 490). In discussing the resolution of these problems, Kant assigned to the concept of problem a new
meaning. He declared the resolution of the problem whether and how the
unconditioned can be cognized, to be a 'task,' characterizing such a task as
a problem (A 508/B 536). This concerns especially the problem of the systematic **unity** of our **cognition**, a unity that is not "given in itself, but only
as a problem"; Kant calls this problematic assumption of a **universal rule**
the "hypothetical use of reason" (A 647/B 675). In the "Transcendental Dialectic," Kant uses the terms 'problem' and 'problematic' as opposites of 'axiom' and 'constitutive' or 'apodictic,' whereas in the "**Transcendental Analytic**" the two terms are distinguished from **assertoric judgments**.

   Hermann Cohen and **Paul Natorp** used 'problem' not as a dialectical
concept but as an epistemological one. They regarded as genuine the problem of turning appearances into objects by recourse to laws; it was to be
resolved by the **transcendental method**, whose first step consists in trans-
forming the presupposed **fact** of science into the 'problem' of identifying
the conditions of the validity of scientific cognition. The examination of
these conditions is primarily concerned with the object of cognition, so that
Natorp regarded the object as the problem, while Nicolai Hartmann claimed
that being fulfilled this role.

   In view of the massive and uncontrolled use of the term 'problem' at
the beginning of the 20th century, Hartmann attempted in his *Grundzüge
einer Metaphysik der Erkenntnis* (*Essentials of a Metaphysic of Cognition*)
of 1921 to differentiate between "posing a problem," "the situation of a
problem," and "the contents of a problem." The problem of epistemology
reached its apex for him in the movement from the given to the problematic, a movement he called, in Aristotelian fashion, aporetic. In the place of
"constructive systematic thought," he then substituted the "searching problematic thought." In their criticism of the subjectivist transformation on the
part of existential philosophy of the concept of 'problem,' **Heinrich Rickert** and **Richard Hönigswald** defended the scientific conception of 'problem,' according to which problems were to be understood as "instances of
objective meaning."

   By orienting himself on the systematic division of problems into theoretical and axiological ones, **Wilhelm Windelband** sketched a program of
a new form of philosophical historiography that followed the history of
philosophical problems; he carried this out in his *History of Philosophy* of

1892. He was aware of the fact that the "eternal problems" of philosophy depended on cultural and individual factors, so that no necessity could be assumed for the historical sequence in which such problems occurred.

PRODUCTIVE IMAGINATION. *See* IMAGINATION.

PROLEGOMENA TO ANY FUTURE METAPHYSICS THAT WILL BE ABLE TO COME FORWARD AS SCIENCE. This work is essentially an abbreviated and somewhat simplified version of the *Critique of Pure Reason.* Published in 1783, it was prompted in part by a hostile and in many points erroneous review of the first edition of the *Critique,* a review that appeared in the *Göttingische Anzeigen von gelehrten Sachen* of 1782, and that was written by two proponents of the so-called popular philosophy, Christian Garve (1742-1798) and Johann Georg Heinrich Feder (1740-1821). Kant's title clearly demonstrates his concern with preparing the ground for a well founded **metaphysics,** that is, with presenting a propaedeutic that will not and, indeed, cannot be superseded because it is based on an examination of the human cognitive powers. Unlike the *Critique,* which follows the synthetic method that proceeds from **reason** itself, the *Prolegomena* follow the **analytic** (regressive) **method** that assumes certain **facts** as if they were given, namely, the existence of **a priori** propositions in mathematics and science, and that then proceeds (regresses) to investigate the conditions under which alone such facts are possible.

The book is divided into three main parts. The first one, dealing with the question "How is Pure **Mathematics** Possible?" corresponds to the "**Transcendental Aesthetic,**" the second one, entitled "How is Pure **Science** Possible?" treats similar subject matter as the "**Transcendental Analytic,**" and the last one, called "How is Metaphysics in General Possible?" parallels the "**Transcendental Dialectic.**" Although all the parts of the *Prolegomena* are shorter than their corresponding counterparts in the *Critique,* some of them are truncated conspicuously, such as the section dealing with the **principles of the understanding,** and there are some key conceptions that are completely omitted, such as the **transcendental unity of apperception.** However, in return, there are a number of passages in the *Prolegomena* that are remarkable for various reasons. In response to the review of the first edition of the first *Critique,* Kant makes a point of explaining his version of **idealism,** pointing out that his "**transcendental idealism**" is a 'critical' or a 'formal' one that does not place the real **existence** of **objects** in doubt. Much quoted is also Kant's claim in the "Introduction" that it was the recollection of **David Hume** that interrupted his dogmatic slumber. It is in part due to this remark that the extent and the timing of

Hume's influence on Kant are subject to much scholarly debate. Yet another much discussed topic is the distinction between "**judgments of perception**" and "**judgments of experience**," a distinction that Kant does not make in the *Critique*. *See also* BERKELEY, GEORGE.

PROOF (*Beweis*). Kant discussed the different kinds of proofs that were appropriate to the different disciplines mainly at the end of the section on "The Discipline of Pure Reason" in the "Doctrine of Method" of the *Critique of Pure Reason* (A 782–94/B 810–22). Here, he focused largely on the proofs of **synthetic judgments a priori** and of **transcendental** propositions. His first basic distinction was between proofs in **mathematics**, which may properly be called **demonstrations** as they proceed from the **construction** of **concepts** and are therefore apodictically certain, and proofs in **philosophy**, which are acroamatic or **discursive** (A 734/A 762). Within philosophy, he then distinguished between the proof of the **categories** and the **principles of pure understanding**, on the one hand, and that of the **ideas of reason**, on the other. The former proceeds by showing that such concepts and principles are the necessary conditions of the possibility of **experience**; Kant called this kind of proof a **transcendental deduction**. Ideas of reason cannot really be proved, though it may be shown that they may be legitimately employed as **regulative** principles of the systematic unity of the understanding; any other proof of the ideas of reason would be illegitimate, that is, **dialectical**, as Kant had previously shown in the "**Transcendental Dialectic**" in regard to the attempts to prove the **immortality** of the soul (**paralogisms**), the validity of **cosmological** ideas (**antinomies**), and the existence of **God** (**ideal** of pure reason).

Kant laid down three general rules for transcendental proofs. First, one must consider "whence one can justifiably derive the principles on which one intends to build and with what right one can expect success in inferences from them." With this proviso, Kant wished to stress that we must approach the proofs of the pure concepts and principles of the understanding differently from the proofs of the ideas of reason. Second, only one proof of each transcendental proposition is possible. Kant justified this by claiming that every transcendental proposition "proceeds solely from one concept and states the synthetic condition of the possibility of the object in accordance with this concept." Third, such proofs can only be ostensive, never apagogic. Kant laid down the difference between these two kinds of proof in his *Logic*, explaining that the ostensive or direct proofs prove a truth from its grounds, while the apagogic or indirect ones prove the truth of a proposition from the falseness of its negation (Ak 9, p. 71). Kant maintained that apagogic proofs are not admissible in disciplines in which there is the danger of subreption, that is, of mistaking the subjective in our representation for the objective, since they then only lead to dialectical **illusion**. Here, he was thinking above all of the ideas of pure reason: asserting something of an idea may be just as false as asserting its opposite, so that it would be impossible to prove the truth of one of the predicates by proving the falseness of its negation. Apagogic proofs are admissible in mathematics and they could also be used in **science**, since observations will guard against error, though Kant thought that such proofs would not play any significant role in empirical inquiries. *See also* TRANSCENDENTAL METHOD.

PROPENSITY (*Hang*). *See* INCLINATION.

PSYCHOLOGY. Next to **theology** and **cosmology**, psychology was one of the three divisions of Special **Metaphysics** for a number of the philosophers of the so-called **Leibniz-Wolff** school. Departing more or less radically from his predecessors, Kant in his critical period distinguished between three types of psychology. Empirical psychology was for him a part of applied **philosophy**, which did not belong to metaphysics. He considered it as a species of the physiology of **inner sense** that consisted of observations on the play of our thoughts and on the natural **laws** of the thinking self. As such, it was restricted to **experience** (A 347/B 405–6) and was expounded by Kant mainly under the heading 'anthropology.' Although Kant was clearly very interested in this discipline, he denied that it could reach the status of a rigorous **science**; in the 'Preface' to the *Metaphysical Foundations of Natural Science*, he argued that **time**, the form of inner sense, did not lend itself in any significant way to mathematical treatment because of its one-dimensionality, and because of the fact that the very process of observing the subject tends to alter it. Empirical psychology could thus never yield more than a "natural description" (*Naturbeschreibung*) of the soul and could not hope to be more than a mere 'historical' discipline.

Rational psychology, on the other hand, would be a branch of metaphysics, striving to teach apodictically about thinking beings in general, and dealing with properties such as the simplicity and the persistence of the **soul** (A 347/B 405–6). However, as Kant argued at great length in the chapter on the **Paralogisms** of Pure Reason, such cognition of the soul is unattainable. He thus concluded that rational psychology was not a doctrine that might provide us with an addition to our self-consciousness but only a **discipline**, setting impassable **boundaries** for **reason** (B 421).

Third, one could speak of a **regulative** use of psychology: one avoids the misuse of psychology, the paralogisms, by taking the psychological

idea as a heuristic rather than as an ostensive concept. One does not attempt to show how an **object** is constituted, but only how we ought to seek the connection of objects in general. 'Soul' then signifies nothing but the schema of a regulative concept, and we will connect all appearances of our mind only **as if** the mind were a simple substance. Kant may also have identified a fourth kind of psychology, namely, a critical one describing the legitimate transcendental role of the self in cognition. Although he devoted a great amount of attention to this topic in the **Transcendental Deduction** of his *Critique of Pure Reason*, he did not apply the label psychology to this task. *See also* TRANSCENDENTAL UNITY OF APPERCEPTION.

PURE (*Rein*). Kant uses the term 'pure' to indicate that something is separate from or independent of **experience**, that is, devoid of all elements of **sensation**. He thus distinguishes a pure **cognition** from an empirical one. Pure is closely linked to **a priori** (and thus to **universal** and **necessary**), but at a crucial point in the first *Critique* Kant does suggest that pure is in some sense even more distanced from the empirical, namely, when he explains that the sentence "Every alteration has its cause" is a priori but not pure, since the concept of alteration can only be derived from experience (B 3). The title of his main work, *The Critique of Pure Reason*, suggests a project that investigates the nonempirical foundations of all cognition. Within the framework of this undertaking, Kant uses the adjective 'pure' extensively to qualify both the **faculties** of the mind that he examines, for example, **reason**, **understanding**, and the products or functions of those faculties, namely, **representation**, **form**, **intuition**, **apperception**, **concept**, **cognition**, **consciousness**, **synthesis**. In addition, in the *Metaphysical Foundations of Natural Science*, he discusses the "pure part of **natural science** (*physica generalis*)" which serves as the conceptual basis of physics. In the *Critique of Practical Reason*, Kant speaks of a pure **will** that is independent of all empirical determination, that is, that is determined only by pure reason. In general, pure reason in ethics is concerned only with moral **good** and **evil**. Kant contrasts it with instrumental reason, which is concerned with the means of attaining **happiness** and is then only an aid to **sensibility**.

PURE REASON (*Reine Vernunft*). **Reason** when it is completely separated from all elements of **sensibility**. As such, it is the source of the **ideas** of reason and, in the realm of morals, of the moral **law** and the **postulates** of pure practical reason. In the latter sphere it is opposed to instrumental reason, which serves only as an aid to sensibility. *See also* PURE.

PURE UNDERSTANDING (*Reiner Verstand*). The **understanding** when it is completely devoid of all elements of **sensibility**. As such, it serves as the source of the **categories** and the **principles of the understanding** and thus forms one of the pillars of Kant's **transcendental philosophy**. It is opposed to, on the one hand, a 'common' or 'healthy' understanding, which is presumably not **pure** and which Kant declares to be insufficient for the purposes of philosophy, and, on the other hand, an understanding that could **intuit**. Although Kant at a number of points entertains the notion of such an understanding, in which "all of the **manifold** would at the same time be given" (B 135; see also P, § 34), he invariably stresses that this is not the kind of understanding given to us; we must remain content with a **discursive** understanding rather than an intuitive one.

PURPOSE (*Zweck*). 'Purpose' or 'end' is Kant's label for final cause; it is defined as the "concept of an object insofar as it at the same time contains the ground of the actuality of this object" (CJ, Ak 5, p. 180). One may think, for example, of the representation of a work of art that the artist has in her mind, a representation that she will subsequently realize.

In the tradition of Aristotelian ethics, the distinction was made between technical purposes and practical ones. In the case of the former, the end of an action is external to its products or consequences, in the case of the latter, the end is internal to the action's products or consequences. Kant defines in his **ethics** a practical end as that which "serves the **will** as the objective ground of its self-determination," distinguishing subjective ends that originate in **desire** from objective ones that have motives shared by all rational beings; in the latter case, formal ends are involved. An unconditionally valid **practical principle**, the categorical **imperative**, cannot strive to attain material ends, because these are always only relative. The ground of an unconditional determination of the will can only be provided by an end that is inherent in the rational being, that is, by the latter as "an end in itself." Kant thus famously proclaims: "the human being and in general every rational being exists as an end in itself" (GMM, Ak 4, pp. 427–28).

In his search for a guiding thread to the **history** of humankind that proceeds according to a plan, Kant attributes an intention, and thus the pursuit of ends, also to **nature** (Ak 8, pp. 17ff.). What this is supposed to mean when one is to avoid a relapse into creation theology is explained in the *Critique of Judgment*. With the **faculty** of **judgment**, Kant interprets nature as **art**, and introduces a cluster of expressions centered around "technique of nature," with which he ascribes to nature, by analogy, a "causality in accordance with ideas"; this enables him to account for organic life in spite of our inability to explain the latter in terms of mechanical causality

(Ak 5, p. 390). His supposition of an "intentional technique" of nature is controversial. Expanding the problem to the whole of nature leads to the question of the final end. Kant defines this as "that end which needs no other as the condition of its possibility" (p. 434). As he stresses, there is no being in nature that could claim to be such a final end (p. 426). Only the human being regarded as a noumenon and standing under moral law may be viewed as a final end of the world, since moral law prescribes, in accordance with the concept of the final end, an unconditioned end (pp. 435, 448–49).

PURPOSIVENESS (*Zweckmässigkeit*). For the critical Kant, the **idea** of **God** means that one regards the **world** under the **regulative** principle of the purposive **unity** of things and thus secures for it the highest systematic unity (A 685ff./B 713ff.). In the discerning view of the *Critique of Judgment*, purposiveness is a **concept** of reflection with which the "need of the **understanding**" is satisfied, though only in a subjective manner, to assume the unity of **nature** in the infinite manifold of empirical **laws** (CJ, Ak 5, pp. 183–84). As Kant puts it, "nature is represented through this concept **as if** an understanding contained the ground of the unity of the manifold of its empirical laws" (pp. 180–81).

This purposiveness, with which Kant ascribes to nature a 'technique' beyond mechanics (Ak 20, p. 204), is a formal one. Kant replaces the traditional metaphysical presupposition, that nature itself is purposefully organized with a principle of the **faculty of judgment**, namely, with a heuristic principle that merely expresses a need and an expectation in our research of nature. While in the experience of the **beautiful** he assumes formal subjective purposiveness, that is, a purposiveness without an end (Ak 5, p. 301, see also 219ff.), that is, a correspondence between the represented **object** and the faculty of **cognition**, the teleological view of natural appearances according to means-ends relations is concerned with objective material purposiveness. In a teleological judgment, natural products are assessed as ends, namely, as the effects of conceptual causes. Kant distinguishes external purposiveness (usefulness or beneficial effects) as we attribute it to natural processes from inner purposiveness (**perfection**) (§ 63); the latter pertains to "organized beings" (**organisms**), that is, to so-called natural ends which Kant characterizes as organized and self-organizing beings (§ 65) that are the cause and effect of themselves (§ 64).

From a more general point of view, the faculty of judgment with the concept of a purposiveness of nature achieves the transition from the causality of nature to the determination of its final end by **practical reason** (Ak 5, p. 196).

- Q -

QUALITY. A highly technical term for Kant, used as the title of the second group of the categories. In the *Critique of Pure Reason*, Kant first discussed the quality of a **judgment**, which concerns the question whether the predicate is attributed to the subject or opposed to it. In respect to quality, judgments can be affirmative, negative, or **infinite**. In an affirmative judgment, the subject is thought under the sphere of a predicate, in a negative judgment, the subject is thought outside the sphere of the predicate, and in an infinite judgment, the subject is placed in the sphere of a concept that lies outside the sphere of another concept (Ak 9, pp. 103–4). From these types of judgments, Kant derived the three **categories** of quality, namely, **reality**, **negation**, and **limitation**, placing them together with the categories of quantity under the heading "**mathematical categories.**" The application of the categories to **appearances** is discussed first in reference to the corresponding **schema**, namely, **degree**, subsequently to the corresponding **principle of pure understanding**, that is, the "**Anticipations of Perception.**" The latter guarantees **a priori** the applicability of intensive **magnitudes** to sensations.

In the *Metaphysical Foundations of Natural Science*, Kant expounded under the heading 'quality' theories of **matter**, opting for a dynamical explanation based on the two original **forces** of **attraction** and repulsion. In the *Opus Postumum*, Kant then mainly sought to formulate, under quality, the more specific conceptual foundations of the laws governing the states of matter (solid, liquid, gas) and their changes, attempting to account for these phenomena by introducing the concept of **ether**.

In the *Prolegomena*, Kant also mentioned the distinction introduced by Galileo and advocated, among others, by **John Locke**, but subsequently rejected by **George Berkeley** and **David Hume**, between primary and secondary qualities. However, his main purpose here was to refute the charge of **idealism** raised against him after the publication of the first edition of the *Critique of Pure Reason:* since holding the secondary qualities of heat, color, and taste to be mere appearances does not qualify anyone as an idealist, so considering the primary qualities of extension, place, and space to be appearances does not justify the label of idealism either (§ 13, Remark II). *See also* TABLES OF JUDGMENTS AND CATEGORIES.

QUANTITY. The general heading of the first group of the **categories**. In the *Critique of Pure Reason*, Kant first discusses the quantity of a **judgment**, which, according to his conception, depends on how the subject is fully or partially included in or excluded from the notion of the predicate.

In respect to quantity, judgments can be **universal**, particular, or singular. In a universal judgment, the sphere of a concept is included within the sphere of another concept, in a particular judgment, only a part of a concept is included, and in a singular judgment, a concept that has no sphere is included as a part in the sphere of another (Ak 9, p. 102). From these types of judgments Kant then derived the categories of **unity**, plurality, and allness, placing them together with the categories of **quality** under the title "**mathematical categories.**" Kant discussed the applicability of the categories to **appearances** first under the label 'Schematism,' identifying **number** as the schema of quantity, then under the heading **principles of pure understanding**, which in the case of quantity are the "Axioms of Intuition." These guarantee **a priori** the applicability of extensive **magnitudes** to empirical objects.

In the *Metaphysical Foundations of Natural Science*, Kant treated under quantity the **motion** of **matter** considered as a point, explaining compound motion by means of the addition of vectors. In the so-called *Opus Postumum*, Kant then examined the presuppositions required for determining the quantity of matter by means of weighing, explaining the functioning of a balance by recourse to the concept of **ether**.

Aside from this, Kant rejected the traditional distinction between **mathematics** as the discipline concerned with quantity and **philosophy** as the discipline concerned with quality, accounting for the difference instead by claiming that the former proceeds by the **construction** of concepts, while the latter is the rational **cognition** from **concepts** (A 713–15/B 741–43). *See also* TABLES OF JUDGMENTS AND CATEGORIES.

QUID FACTI, QUID JURIS. *See* FACT.

- R -

RATIONALISM. *See* EMPIRICISM.

REALISM. Kant's preferred label for his own critical philosophy was "**transcendental idealism**," an expression with which he wished to stress his contention that we can cognize only **appearances** and not **things-in-themselves** and that our **pure cognition (space, time, categories)** provides the necessary conditions of the possibility of **experience**. Kant contrasted this position with transcendental realism, which he held to be the illegitimate doctrine that our representations present things as they are in themselves or that they are identical with them. He claimed that such a doctrine would ultimately lead to the denial of the **reality** of empirical objects, thus resulting in the equally illegitimate empirical idealism. His own transcendental idealism, on the other hand, would safeguard the reality of empirical objects and would therefore be compatible with empirical realism (A 369; A 491/B 519).

REALITY (*Realität*). Contrary to what Norman Kemp Smith's translation of the *Critique of Pure Reason* occasionally suggests (for example, B xxv), reality for Kant does not lie beyond the realm of **appearances**, nor does Kant ever contrast reality with appearance. Kant places reality prior to **negation** and **limitation** (combination of reality and negation) as the first of the **categories** of **quality**. The **function** of **judgment** that corresponds to it is affirmation, so that Kant claims that reality is a determination "which can be thought only through an affirmative judgment" (A 246). He designates with reality (*realitas phaenomenon*) a something whose concept "in itself indicates a being (in time)" (A 143/B 182). He therefore understands the category of reality as the qualitative determination of **being**, a determination that qualifies the **object** of **cognition** as a thing (*Ding, Sache, res*). In the background stands a scholastic definition, according to which *realitas* is the true positive determination of a thing or its affirmative predicate. However, while the scholastics also considered actuality (existence, *Wirklichkeit, existentia, actualitas*) to be a *realitas* that forms the complement to essence and that is the thoroughgoing intrinsic determination of a thing (Alexander Gottlieb Baumgarten, *Metaphysica*, 4th ed., Halle, 1757, §§ 36, 66), Kant separates reality and **actuality**: "Being [that is, existence] is not a real predicate" (A 598/B 626).

In addition, Kant's usage of the category of reality is restricted by the exigencies of his **critical philosophy**. Under the sensible conditions of human **cognition**, one may create a generally affirmative predicate of **things-in-themselves** (*realitas noumenon*), but such a predicate is only fictitious and cannot be attributed in a judgment, contrary to what Kant himself had held in his **pre-critical** *Inaugural Dissertation* (1770). That no cognition can be gained with the mere concept of reality is also true of the idea of the "All of reality" (*omnitudo realitatis*). For the critical Kant, "reason only grounded the thoroughgoing determination of things in general" on such an idea of all reality, "without demanding that this reality should be given objectively, and itself constitute a thing" (A 580/B 608). The latter, however, will turn into a false claim, if this idea is hypostatized to a thing that is thoroughly determined through itself (*ens realissimum*).

Kant's remarks on the category of reality (*realitas phaenomenon*) are ambiguous and have led to different interpretations. On the one hand, the principle of the "**Anticipations of Perception**" suggests that 'reality' is the conceptual form of the determination of intensive **magnitudes**, but not also of the positing of the qualitative being of the thing, given that the only a priori cognition that **sensation** allows is, as Kant stresses, its measurable intensity or continuity in time: the real *has* a **degree** (B 207). On the other hand, Kant defines the pure function of the understanding 'reality' as that "to which a sensation [that is, "the effect of an object on the capacity for representation" (A 19/B 34)] in general corresponds" (A 143/B 182), or, alternatively, he insists that what constitutes the matter (material), that is, "the reality in appearance (corresponding to sensation), has to be given" (A 581/B 609). It has therefore been suggested that a distinction must be made within Kant's concept of the category of reality between an apprehensive-synthetical form of *quality* and a categorical-synthetical form of *intensity*, and that the pure something must be grasped as a third a priori form of given next to **space** and **time** (Anneliese Maier, *Kants Qualitätskategorien*, 1930). Contrary to this suggestion, **Hermann Cohen** had already in 1883 proposed an interpretation that explicitly aims to move beyond Kant. Cohen saw in Kant's concept of reality the connection of the a priori of a pure something with the a priori of intensity. He claimed, unlike Kant, that with this conceptual function of the qualitative determination of magnitude the real is generated in thought (*Das Prinzip der Infinitesimal-Methode*, § 18).

The expressions "empirical reality" and "objective reality" signify the **validity** of pure concepts. The complement of the "empirical reality" (that is, objective validity) of space and time is their "transcendental ideality" (that is, the denial that they are applicable to objects of reason) (B 44, 52), while the complement of the proof of the "objective reality" or 'validity' of the pure concepts of the understanding (that is, the proof of their relation to objects) is the recognition that they are 'empty' in their merely logical usage. The proof in the "**Transcendental Deduction**" of the objective reality of the categories applies also to the category of reality.

REASON (*Vernunft*). Kant uses this term in two different senses. In the more encompassing one it stands for all the higher **faculties** of the **mind** and includes the **understanding**. It is in this sense that the project of the **critique of pure reason** is conceived, namely, as an examination of the cognitive powers of the human subject. In a more restricted sense, reason is one of the three major faculties of the human mind; it is then distinguished from **sensibility** and the understanding. This division of the powers of the **mind** yields the organization of the major part of the *Critique of Pure Reason*, the "Doctrine of Elements," into its main divisions "**Transcendental Aesthetic**," which deals with sensibility, "**Transcendental Analytic**," which deals with the understanding, and "**Transcendental Dialectic**," which has reason as its main topic. Kant was greatly concerned with delineating reason in the narrow sense of the word from the understanding, labeling the latter as "a faculty of **unity** of **appearances** by means of rules" and the former as "the faculty of the unity of the rules of understanding under **principles**"; reason applies neither to **experience** nor to an **object**, but to the understanding (A 302/B 359). And while the understanding produces **constitutive** concepts and moves within the bounds of experience, reason ventures beyond experience. It then produces either **transcendental illusion**, when it is misled into seeking **cognition**, or, if it restricts itself to **thinking**, it legitimately serves either as a guide for the understanding or as the faculty of the moral realm. It then contains regulative principles or **ideas** within the sphere of theoretical philosophy as well as the principle and the **postulates** of pure practical reason within moral philosophy. *See also CRITIQUE OF PRACTICAL REASON.*

RECEPTIVITY. A major characteristic of human **sensibility**, opposed by Kant to the **spontaneity** of the **understanding**. Kant defined sensibility as "the receptivity of our mind to receive **representations** insofar as it is affected in some way" (A 51/B 75). He held that the receptivity of the **subject**, that is, the capacity to be affected by **objects** "necessarily precedes all **intuitions** of these objects," and, by thus claiming that the form of sensible intuition lies in the subject and its receptivity, he explained how the **form** of all **appearances**, that is, **space** and **time**, can be given in the mind **a priori** (A 16/B 42).

RECIPROCITY (*Wechselseitigkeit*). *See* COMMUNITY.

RECOGNITION. In the 1781 first edition version of the "**Transcendental Deduction**" of the *Critique of Pure Reason*, Kant introduced the conception of a threefold **synthesis** in order to describe the action of the **understanding** on the **manifold** of the **sensibility**, an action that is essential for **cognition**. Kant's technical labels for taking up, going through, and combining the manifold (A 77/B 102-3) were "synthesis of **apprehension** in **intuition**," "synthesis of **reproduction** in the **imagination**," and "synthesis of recognition in the **concept**," also called the unity through transcendental apperception (A 95).

After the synthesis of the apprehension grasps the manifold and the synthesis of reproduction retains it, the third synthesis unifies it and brings it to a concept. Kant speaks here of the "one consciousness that unifies the manifold" and of a "consciousness of **unity**." Thus, for instance, if I am to cognize the concept of a **number**, I must, when I count, cognize the generation of the multitude of units, which hover before me, through the successive addition of one to the other, that is, I must become conscious of the unity of the synthesis in order to arrive at the concept. Concepts play a crucial role in this account because Kant conceives of them as **rules** that unite, or, in his own words, concepts contain a "unity of rule," and such unity of rule determines every manifold. The particulars of Kant's argument are riddled with problems, since he introduces two conceptions that both present their own special difficulties, namely, the notion of the "**transcendental object = X**" and that of the "**transcendental unity of apperception.**" The gist of the matter amounts to the fact that Kant, on the one hand, relates recognition to an **object**, claiming that our cognitions must necessarily agree with each other in relation to an object, that is, "they must have that unity that constitutes the concept of an object" (A 104–5). On the other hand, he claims that a **necessity** is involved, and that this must have a transcendental ground, namely, the unity of consciousness, or, in technical terms, the transcendental unity of apperception. And, so the argument continues, the latter "is at the same time a consciousness of an equally necessary unity of the synthesis of all appearances in accordance with concepts" (A 108). Ultimately, by way of the unity of apperception, the **categories** are brought into play, and they then serve as the ground for the recognition of the manifold, that is, this synthesis must proceed in accordance with the categories (A 125).

In the completely revamped second edition version of the "Transcendental Deduction" of 1787, Kant employed neither the term recognition nor the conception of the threefold synthesis. However, as his notes from as late as 1797 indicate, he had not abandoned the notion of such a process, integrating it into a sketch of the whole of his critical philosophy (Ak 18, pp. 682–85).

REFLECTION. *See* AMPHIBOLY.

REGULATIVE PRINCIPLES. *See* CONSTITUTIVE AND REGULATIVE PRINCIPLES.

REINHOLD, KARL LEONHARD (1758–1823). Having spent his childhood in Vienna, Reinhold was educated at a college of the Barnabite Order. After 1780, he felt increasingly torn between his duties toward the order and his commitment to the Enlightenment with the Illuminates and Freemasons. In 1784, he escaped to Weimar, where he was supported by Christoph

Martin Wieland. In the journal *Teutsche Merkur*, edited by Wieland, Reinhold published, starting in 1786, his *Briefe über die Kantische Philosophie* (*Letters on Kantian Philosophy*), in which he showed himself to be a staunch Kantian and with which he significantly contributed to the spread of Kantianism in Germany. In 1787, he became a professor of philosophy at the University of Jena, after 1794 he taught in the then Danish city of Kiel.

During his time in Jena, he published his *Versuch einer neuen Theorie des menschlichen Vorstellungsvermögens* (*Essay on a New Theory of the Human Power of Representation*) (1789) and his *Beyträge zur Berichtigung bisheriger Missverständnisse der Philosophen* (*Contributions to a Correction of Previous Misunderstandings of Philosophers*) (1790, 1794). In these works, he presented an ameliorated **critique of reason**, one that was founded on a unified highest **principle** that Reinhold called the "law of consciousness." According to this principle, the representation in consciousness by the subject must be separated from the object and the subject, and must be related to them both. With this principle, Reinhold prepared the ground for later post-Kantian systems of philosophy. However, while in 1797/1798 he was still willing to accept the critical development of his "elementary philosophy" by **Johann Gottlieb Fichte**, Reinhold parted from Fichte after 1800 with his objectivist turn toward "logical realism," and, after 1805, he completely abandoned German Idealism by increasingly focusing on the philosophy of language.

RELATION (*Relation, Verhältnis*). In its primary use, 'relation' is the title of the third group of the categories. In the *Critique of Pure Reason*, Kant first deals with the relation of **judgments**, claiming that in this respect judgments can be categorical, hypothetical, or disjunctive; such judgments assert, respectively, a relation between a subject and a predicate, between ground and consequence, or "between the divided **cognition** and all the members of the division" (A 73/B 98; Ak 9, p. 104). From these types of judgments Kant derived the **categories** of inherence and subsistence, causality and dependence, and community, placing them together with the categories of **modality** under the heading "**dynamical categories**."

The applicability of the categories is guaranteed by schematizing them; for relation the three **schemata** are "persistence of the real in time" (substance), "the real upon which, whenever it is posited, something else always follows" (causality), and the simultaneity of the determinations of one substance with those of another in accordance with a general rule (reciprocity, community). The corresponding **principles of pure understanding** in the case of relation are the three **analogies of experience**, namely, sub-

stance, causality, and **community.** In the *Metaphysical Foundations of Natural Science*, Kant discussed under relation chiefly a modified version of **Isaac Newton**'s laws of **motion.** In the so-called *Opus Postumum*, he then attempted to explain the conceptual presuppositions of the cohesion of **matter** by recourse to the notion of the relation of motive **forces** and to the concept of **ether.** *See also* TABLES OF JUDGMENTS AND CATEGORIES.

RELIGION. *See* CHRISTIANITY; CHURCH; GOD; JUDAISM; *RELIGION WITHIN THE BOUNDARIES OF MERE REASON;* REVELATION; THEOLOGY.

RELIGION WITHIN THE BOUNDARIES OF MERE REASON. The work consists of four parts. The Berlin censorship granted permission to print only the first one, which then appeared in the April 1792 issue of the journal *Berlinische Monatsschrift*, but rejected the second piece, inducing Kant to publish all parts as a book. As Kant wrote in a letter to Carl Friedrich Stäudlin on May 4, 1793, the work is devoted to answering the question "What may I hope for?" Kant sought the response in his own attempt to unify the Christian religion with **practical reason** (Ak 11, p. 429), criticizing, on the one hand, the major Christian dogmas, and assigning, on the other, to a Christianity reduced to rational **faith,** the function of grounding, if not morality itself, then at least the respect for the authority of moral **law.**

The first piece develops the theory of radical **evil** that is founded on a propensity to evade, by yielding to egotistical **inclinations,** the determination of the **maxims** of action by the categorical **imperative,** so that a "reversal of incentives" results. The original "predisposition to **good**" can be restored by means of a "revolution in the **disposition**" (Ak 6, p. 47), namely, by the resolution to be moral solely out of **duty.** As Kant argues in the second piece, religion offers aid in this task by interpreting Jesus as a personified archetype of moral perfection. In the third piece Kant construes the idea of the Kingdom of Heaven as a **regulative principle** of action, a principle that demands that we leave the ethical state of nature of the permanent struggle between good and evil. The fourth piece contains severe criticism of false church services and of priestcraft in a **church** based on, from a moral point of view, merely arbitrary divine precepts. The publication of the book brought Kant into conflict with the Prussian censorship, but the work was successful with the learned public, going through several reprints and new editions in quick succession.

RENOUVIER, CHARLES (1815–1903). The main representative of **Neo-kantianism** in France (*Essais de critique générale*, 1854–1864). Starting with **relation**, Renouvier produced a doctrine of the **categories** that was critical of positivism, and he developed an antimetaphysical phenomenalism. Renouvier attributed **freedom** to the phenomenal world, in which it manifests itself as the activity of thought, so that already the claim of freedom is classified as a free act. Abandoning Kant's distinction between theoretical and practical **reason** allowed Renouvier to deal with the problem of moral freedom without recourse to a noumenal world. He admitted moral law as an immediate imperative of a free consciousness, maintaining, however, that such an imperative can be adhered to only in a society based on solidarity.

REPRESENTATION (*Vorstellung*). The generic term for designating the determinations of the **mind**. As representations Kant labels everything from the "color red" to the '**I think**' that accompanies all other representations. In the *Critique of Pure Reason*, Kant presents a hierarchical classification of representations in which the role of the genus is assumed by "representation in general." Under it stand: **perception** (*Perzeption, perceptio*) as a representation with consciousness, **sensation** as a perception that refers to the subject as a modification of its state, and **cognition** as an objective perception. Cognitions are then divided into **intuitions** and **concepts**, the latter are further subdivided into **empirical** and **pure**. Pure concepts that originate in the **understanding** are called notions, and concepts that go beyond the possibility of **experience** are **ideas** (A 320/B 376–77). With this use of 'representation' and with the accompanying hierarchy Kant was reacting against the employment of the word 'idea' as the generic label for the contents of the mind, an employment made, for example, by **John Locke**; instead, Kant wished to restrict idea only to the **faculty** of **reason**.

The English rendering 'representation' owes its justification to the fact that Kant added the Latin '*repraesentatio*' to the German '*Vorstellung*.' However, the translation is somewhat misleading in that it may be seen to be suggesting that there must be something that is represented, which, however, was not Kant's intention. For that matter, the German word is not totally felicitous either, since it also connotes the conjuring up of images, and this too does not correspond to Kant's intentions, at least not in any central way. Both the German expression and its English rendering must therefore be taken strictly as technical terms.

REPRODUCTION. In the first edition version of the "**Transcendental Deduction**" of the *Critique of Pure Reason*, Kant described the action that the **understanding** has to perform on the **manifold** given by the **sensibility** in terms of a threefold **synthesis**. This process, by which **cognition** is generated, consists of taking up, going through, and combining the manifold (A 77/B 102–3), or, in technical terms, of carrying out a "synthesis of **apprehension** in **intuition**," then a "synthesis of reproduction in the **imagination**," and finally, a "synthesis of **recognition** in the **concept**" (A 95).

The synthesis of apprehension allows us no more than to grasp the manifold in a successive fashion. If cognition is ever to result on such a basis, we must subsequently be capable of retaining our **representations** in order to arrive at some kind of a (preliminary) whole. Kant offers some examples in order to explain this point. When we draw a line in thought or when we think of a certain time span, we grasp the representations successively, and we would lose them if they were not reproduced by the imagination. Kant distinguishes between empirical laws of reproduction and association in the imagination and their corresponding **transcendental principles**, claiming that the former must necessarily be grounded in the latter, namely, in a pure transcendental synthesis of the imagination. Kant then calls the corresponding power of the mind the transcendental faculty of the imagination. Together with the syntheses of apprehension and recognition it constitutes the transcendental ground for the possibility of all cognition (A 100–2).

For reasons that are not completely clear, Kant employed in the completely revamped second edition version of the "Transcendental Deduction" of 1787 neither the term reproduction nor the conception of the threefold synthesis. Perhaps he wished to avoid creating the impression that he was describing a merely psychological process rather than giving account of the transcendental conditions of cognition. Be this as it may, his notes from as late as 1797 indicate that he had not dropped the notion of such a process, which he attempted to integrate into a sketch of the whole of his critical philosophy (Ak 18, pp. 682–85).

REPRODUCTIVE IMAGINATION. *See* IMAGINATION.

REPULSION. *See* ATTRACTION, REPULSION.

RESPECT (*Achtung*). The only moral **feeling** that Kant admits in his **ethics** (Ak 5, p. 75). As such it pertains to moral **law**, but not as its foundation or as its criterium; rather, respect is caused by the moral law in the subject as a "representation of a worth that infringes upon my self-love" (Ak 4, p. 401). In this way it provides the **incentive** to adopt the law as one's **maxim**. *See also CRITIQUE OF PRACTICAL REASON*.

REST (*Ruhe*). Throughout his writing career, Kant admitted only a very limited concept of physical rest. He rejected the notion of absolute rest already in his **pre-critical** piece *Thoughts on the True Estimation of Living Forces* (1749), claiming that a body otherwise at rest should be regarded as moving in respect to another body that was moving toward it. In his *New Conception of Motion and Rest* (1758), he then introduced a rather peculiar conception of rest, arguing that rest was in fact infinitesimally small **motion**. In his **critical philosophy** of science, specifically in the ***Metaphysical Foundations of Natural Science***, Kant then rendered this definition somewhat more precise by claiming that rest was a motion with infinitesimally small velocity in a finite amount of time. Kant explained his preference for such a conception on the grounds that it made mathematical construction possible (Ak 4, p. 486). However, his definition did entail some unusual consequences, compelling him, for example, to reject the otherwise widely accepted notion of a **force** of **inertia**.

REVELATION (*Offenbarung*).   Although Kant clearly distinguished between, on the one hand, the different forms of rational **theology**, and, on the other, revelation theology, he maintained that biblical revelation could be interpreted only in accordance with the standard of the practical rules of a **pure** rational religion. The divine nature of revelation can be cognized by us only thanks to the "**God** in us," that is, thanks to the moral concepts of our human **reason** (Ak 7, p. 48). This position was the source of contention between the post-Kantian theological schools of 'Rationalism' and 'Supranaturalism.' In arguing for the existence of a supra-natural revelation, the latter made recourse to Kant's claim that human reason was incapable of judging divine communication. *See also* BELIEF.

REVOLUTION.   Kant understood under 'revolution' large scale changes in science, in metaphysics, and in morals, though mainly, as a political concept, the term signified for him all encompassing alterations in the constitution of a government. The "revolution in the way of thinking" in mathematics and science (B xi) served him as a model for the projected "revolution in metaphysics" (B xxii).

Kant basically welcomed the French Revolution because it led to a republican form of government, which he thought would promote the progress of humankind toward **peace**. And he regarded the widespread approval of the revolution as an expression of the moral legitimacy of the self-determination of a nation that chose such a form of government (Ak 7, p. 85).

On the other hand, Kant declares political revolutions to be illegitimate because they are illegal. Refusing to submit under the general legislative will of the sovereign completely destroys the rule of law (Ak 6, pp. 319-20). Even where the latter enjoys only a limited legitimacy, it is still preferable to anarchy (Ak 8, p. 373). However, Kant establishes it as a **duty** of the politician to work toward the state of law, that is, to aim at reforms in a legal manner, and to interpret revolutions, "when they are produced by nature," as a "demand by nature" to bring about a libertarian "legal constitution" (Ak 8, p. 373).

In the 1860s, faced with the newly minted "proletarian issue," Friedrich Albert **Lange** propounded a similar position as Kant, advocating both support for and mitigation of a revolution by a critique of social evils and their pragmatic remedy. In the same vein, **Hermann Cohen** defended "efforts for the reform of law and government" against the Marxist theory of revolution.

RICKERT, HEINRICH (1863-1936). Successor to **Wilhelm Windelband** as the leading proponent of the **Southwestern German School of Neokantianism.** Following his predecessor, Rickert was also chiefly concerned with the concept of **value,** even claiming that epistemology was "a science of theoretical values." Further developing Windelband's distinction between nomothetic (scientific) and idiographic (historical) cognition, Rickert claimed that in the former the empirical component is neglected, the individual character of reality is lost, and the concepts become, with increasing abstraction, divorced from reality. Only in the latter kind of cognition does one approach reality, so that history may be called the "true science of reality." Rickert's most prominent student was Emil Lask (1875-1915), but he also exercised considerable influence on Max Weber. *See also* VALIDITY.

RIEHL, ALOIS (1844-1924). The major representative of the so-called realistic **Neokantianism.** In his most important work, *Der philosophische Kriticismus und seine Bedeutung für die positive Wissenschaft* (1876-1887), he analyzed empirical **cognition** in order to identify its rational a priori elements. He interpreted Kant's *Critique of Pure Reason* as already having provided a sort of a foundation of a scientific **philosophy,** claiming that such a philosophy was possible only as **epistemology.** Accordingly, Riehl attempted to work out a theory of scientific cognition, that is, a theory of the conditions that guarantee that cognition has a 'real' significance. Owing to the fact that he acknowledged that the 'real' elements of cognition represent the given, his position is labeled "critical realism"; it stands in contrast to the "**critical idealism**" of mainstream Neokantianism, which tended to the claim that the given was to be sought not in **sensibility** but in the facts of **pure** science. It should, however, be stressed that Riehl's realism did indeed deserve the modifier 'critical,' as he emphasized that perceived things are not identical with **things-in-themselves**. In distinction to the **Marburg School**, which followed the line **Descartes-Leibniz**-Kant, he adhered to the line **Locke-Hume**-Kant. Riehl's most important student was **Richard Hönigswald**.

RIGHT (*Recht*). Kant's answer to the question "What is right?" aimed at a normative concept of right. He distinguished between the question of which right (*ius*) applied in which place and the question of what is right (*iustum*), and he sought the general criterion with which one could recognize what is right (*iustum*) and what is wrong (*iniustum*) (MM, Ak 6, p. 229). Nevertheless, Kant also demanded for the concept of right a link between *ius* and *iustum*, that is, between the legal and the right. His argumentation took the early modern tradition of natural law as its point of departure, though Kant then made a turn toward rational right by searching for the roots of judgments on right or wrong in "mere reason." However, this 'moral' concept of right concerned only the external relation between persons as responsible subjects and their external freedom to do or omit doing something independently of the compelling power (*Willkür*) of others; not at stake was the inner or moral **freedom** to determine oneself independently of one's own **incentives** and needs.

The concept of right that was based on **reason** was as follows: "right is the sum of the conditions under which the choice of one can be united with the choice (*Willkür*) of another in accordance with a universal law of freedom" (p. 230). One can use this concept for deciding whether juridical laws are right, that is, whether the choice or the actions of different humans under these laws do not contravene the **law** of freedom. How does the "general law of freedom" realize this rational grounding of juridical laws? The idea of the latter is to secure freedom from the power of others. These laws can achieve this task only when they contain a limitation that forbids the employment of this freedom in such a way that someone else's freedom is interfered with. But this is possible only if the limitation is general, and this in turn is possible only on the basis of laws that are binding for everyone. Juridical laws then contain the conditions under which someone may use his freedom (that is, freely do or omit doing what he wants) without hindering the freedom of someone else. According to Kant, such a legal system, which is directed at a common life in freedom, is inconceivable without coercion (p. 231).

ROUSSEAU, JEAN-JACQUES (1712–1778). In his "Notes" on his own *Observations on the Feeling of the Beautiful and the Sublime* of 1764, Kant admitted that he had learned from Rousseau to honor humans as such, instead of respecting them only for their intellectual capabilities (Ak 20, p. 44). For Kant, Rousseau was a teacher of human morality.

Kant's intensive examination of Rousseau began around 1762, after the appearance of the *New Heloise* (1761), the *Social Contract* (1762), and *Emile* (1762). As was the case with other thinkers whose notions Kant adopted, he appropriated ideas from Rousseau by immediately integrating them into his own thought. Important for Kant's philosophy of **history** were the idea of the perfectibility of the human species, which Rousseau had developed in his *Second Discourse* (1755), and the reflections on how **culture** must proceed if there is to be a reconciliation of nature and culture, reflections that Kant found in Rousseau's other above-mentioned writings (Ak 8, pp. 116–17). However, Kant did not found his **ethics** on any empirical study of man; Rousseau provided him with the key term **'freedom,'** but not with the principle of the **autonomy** of the **will**. And there remain fundamental differences in their political theories and philosophy of law, especially in regard to the distinction between law and morality as well as the division of powers in government.

RULE (*Regel*). Kant repeatedly describes the **understanding** as a "faculty of rules." By this he means that the **synthesis** of **appearances** or of **perceptions** by the understanding occurs according to rules that constitute the conditions for the unification into concepts in one consciousness. Kant focuses here on the rules a priori as the conditions of necessary unification (P, § 23). As these unifying conditions consist of the categorical **unity**, Kant identifies rule and **category**, depicting, at the same time, the category as "a general condition of rules" (A 135/B 174). The **principles of pure understanding** serve then as the "rules of the **objective** use" of the categories (A 161/B 200).

In Kant's **ethics**, rule, **law**, and **imperative** stand in a close relationship to one another. In general, a practical rule prescribes an **action** as the means to attain an intended effect (CrPR, Ak 5, p. 20). Even the practical law (the categorical imperative) may be labeled as a "practical rule" (p. 31). However, Kant cautions not to confuse the second formulation of the categorical imperative with the "golden rule," which he refuses to classify as a universal law (GMM, Ak 4, p. 430). In moral qualifications of actions, moral law functions as a "rule of judgment," that is, as a criterion for the assessment (*Beurteilung*) of actions in regard to their morality (Ak 5, p. 69).

Kant uses the expression "practical rule" far more frequently to designate empirically derived precepts and to distinguish the latter from moral law (Ak 4, p. 389). Accordingly, he characterizes hypothetical imperatives as practical rules, that is, as "rules of skill" (Ak 5, p. 25), "rules of art," and "rules of prudence" (CJ, Ak 5, p. 172).

- S -

SCHELLING, FRIEDRICH WILHELM JOSEPH (1775-1854). The early Schelling first followed **Johann Gottlieb Fichte**, but under the influence of Baruch Spinoza he soon thrust out beyond subjective idealism, attempting to establish his own brand of "natural philosophy" (*Naturphilosophie*) next to the Kantian **transcendental philosophy**. He expanded Kant's question concerning the subjective conditions of objective **cognition** into the idea of the **absolute**, which contained both Spinoza's absolute object and Fichte's absolute subject: the absolute develops as an objective subject-object (nature) into a subjective subject-object (spirit), which is within itself able to construct nature. In this "doctrine of nature" of the human spirit, natural and transcendental philosophy enjoy equal rights and are both members of the system of philosophy.

Aside from the general borrowings from Kant's theoretical philosophy on the basis of Fichte's thought, Schelling argued in his *Philosophische Briefe über Dogmatismus und Kriticismus* (*Philosophical Letters on Dogmatism and Criticism*) of 1795 that deciding between the two systems would be possible not on the basis of theoretical, but of practical philosophy, that is, out of the "freedom of the spirit." A specific criticism of Kant occurs in the "natural philosophy," in which Schelling searches for the unity behind the duality of the forces of **attraction** and repulsion, a duality that Kant himself had considered to be basic. Also important for Schelling were Kant's reflections on the teleological explanation of nature in the *Critique of Judgment* (§§ 74ff.).

SCHEMATISM. Kant considered the **understanding** and the **sensibility** to be essentially heterogeneous faculties, and their respective products (concepts and intuitions) to be separated by gaps. However, following a key notion of his, expressed by the sentence "thoughts without content are empty, **intuitions** without **concepts** are blind" (A 51/B 75), **cognition** could be had only if concepts and intuitions were both involved. Kant claimed that combining concepts and intuitions and thus bridging the gaps was to be effected by mediating schemata. The most important of these schemata in Kant's philosophy were the **transcendental** ones that would ensure the applicability of the **categories** to **objects**. Kant dealt with such a schematism in the first chapter of "The Transcendental Doctrine of the Power of Judgment" or the "Analytic of Principles," obviously regarding the task to be anything but trivial, given that the categories were concepts derived from the logical structure of judgments and as such clearly radically different from **appearances.** Kant proposed that "time-determinations" would yield the required schemata, which would be **pure,** intellectual, and sensible. He resorted only to **time** and not to **space,** arguing that time was the more encompassing form of every sensible intuition, while space was only the form of outer intuitions. Time is homogeneous with the category thanks to its universality, and it is homogeneous with appearances because it is contained in every empirical **representation** of the **manifold.** Kant claimed that the schemata were products of the **imagination,** but, as he stressed, they were not images but general procedures, that is, **rules** of the imagination. As the schema of the categories of **quantity** he assigns **number,** of the categories of **quality** he designates **degree.** The schemata of the categories of **relation** are "persistence of the real in time" (**substance**), "the real upon which, whenever it is posited, something else always follows" (**causality**), and the simultaneity of the determinations of one substance with those of another in accordance with a general rule (reciprocity, **community**); of the categories of **modality** "the agreement of the synthesis of various representations with the conditions of time in general" (**possibility**), "the existence at a determinate time" (**actuality**), and "the existence of an object at all times" (**necessity**) (A 142–45/B 182–84).

Kant stressed that while schematizing the categories realizes them, that is, makes their application to objects and the cognition of objects possible, it also restricts their use to the conditions of sensibility. Conspicuous about the chapter on schematism is its brevity, especially in comparison with the lengthy discussion of the **principles of pure understanding.** This seems to suggest that schematism was for Kant only an intermediate, if highly necessary, step, and that it is only in the following chapter on the "Principles of Pure Understanding" that the application of the categories is fully explicated. That Kant is here dealing with more specific principles than the schemata is evident from the fact that space (as a more specific form) is introduced (especially in the second edition version of the chapter).

In the *Opus Postumum*, schematism again plays a mediating role. Kant was here concerned with the transition from the **metaphysical foundations of natural science** to **physics** and he thought that this could be effected by means of the concepts of moving **forces.** He thus introduced the expression "schematism of moving forces, insofar as it can be thought a priori," suggesting that this was to serve as the first step of the transition. In keeping with the basic intention of the transition project of the *Opus Postumum*, according to which the material is to be increasingly subjected to the formal, Kant speaks of a subsumption of appearances under the **law** of **perceptions** (Ak. 22, pp. 265, 487, 491, 494).

SCHOPENHAUER, ARTHUR (1788–1860). In his work, Schopenhauer dealt with nearly all aspects of Kant's philosophy, though he did so mostly critically and with a certain measure of irony. On the basis of the first edition of the *Critique of Pure Reason*, which he preferred to the second edition, Schopenhauer understood the phenomenal world as a totality of representations that are connected according to the law of sufficient reason; however, he interpreted the **thing-in-itself** that provided the foundation of the representations as **will**. As Schopenhauer explained in his main work *Die Welt als Wille und Vorstellung* (*The World as Will and Representation*) of 1819, he grasped the will as a basic incentive whose manifestations he sought in inorganic and organic nature and even in humans. He discussed the differences from and the similarities to Kant in the appendix to his main work ("Critique of Kantian Philosophy"). The first half of the piece *Über das Fundament der Moral* (*On the Foundations of Morals*) of 1841 is devoted to a scathing criticism of Kant's **ought**-based ethics, whose "a priori soap bubbles" Schopenhauer regarded as nothing but theological morals in disguise.

SELF (*Ich*). *See* PSYCHOLOGY; SOUL; TRANSCENDENTAL UNITY OF APPERCEPTION.

SELF-CONSCIOUSNESS (*Selbstbewusstsein*). *See* PSYCHOLOGY; SOUL; TRANSCENDENTAL UNITY OF APPERCEPTION.

SENSATION (*Empfindung*). The **matter** of **perception** or the matter of **intuition**. Kant calls it "the effect of an **object** on the capacity for representation, insofar as we are affected by it" (A 20/B 34). Sensation is the result of the subjective reaction of **receptivity** to an object, so that it concerns only the **subject** and the modification of its state. Sensation is never cognized **a priori**, and, accordingly, the term '**pure**' excludes sensation. If sensation is the matter of perception, and the pure **form** is provided by **space** and **time**, then sensation is that in our **cognition** that makes it **a posteriori**, that is, that makes it empirical intuition (A 42/B 59–60). Since sensation is not an objective **representation**, that is, "in it neither the intuition of space nor that of time is to be encountered," it has no extensive **magnitude**, but an intensive one (A 165/B 208). Given, however, that sensation is indispensable for cognition, since **existence** is given only through sensation, it is called the real of the appearances. As such sensation can vary between **reality** and negation = 0 by "a continuous nexus of many possible intermediate sensations" (A168/B 210). Although all sensations are given a posteriori, "their property of having a **degree** can be cognized a priori" (A 176/B 218). *See also* ANTICIPATIONS OF PERCEPTION.

SENSE (*Sinn*).   In his *Critique of Pure Reason*, Kant distinguished in a philosophically important manner between an **inner sense** and an outer one, but left the treatment of the senses to the philosophically less rigorous *Anthropology from a Pragmatic Point of View*. Here, after declaring that the senses neither confuse us nor rule over the understanding nor deceive us (§§ 9–11), he divides sensibility into sense and imagination, defining the former as "the faculty of intuition in the presence of an object," while the latter functions without an object. Kant's distinction in the *Anthropology* between an inner and an outer sense is more closely related to everyday language than it is to his **transcendental philosophy**. Kant now explains that while through outer sense our body is affected by external things, through inner sense it is affected by the mind. He adds as a third division an "interior sense" (*innwendiger Sinn*) to account for the feelings of pleasure and pain (§ 15). Subsequently, Kant introduces further divisions. The senses of bodily sensation split into "vital sensation" and "organ sensation." The former are heat, cold, shudder, and horror, the latter are the five senses, of which touch, sight, and hearing are characterized as more objective than subjective, while taste and smell are deemed to be more subjective than objective (§§ 16–21).

SENSIBILITY (*Sinnlichkeit*).   Kant introduced this as a separate power of the mind in the *Inaugural Dissertation* of 1770, departing with his conception from the **Leibniz-Wolffian** view that sensible data are merely confused concepts of the understanding (§ 7). He retained the separation between sensibility and the understanding in the *Critique of Pure Reason*, calling now, however, such a distinction **transcendental** rather than merely logical (A 44/B 61). Sensibility is the faculty of **intuitions**, and as such it is distinguished both from the **understanding** (**concepts** and **principles**) and from **reason** (**ideas**); each of these faculties has its own **forms** or laws and it is the task of the project of the examination of our cognitive powers to identify these forms and principles as well as to determine what they are and how they function in the cognitive process. Kant defined sensibility as "the capacity (**receptivity**) to acquire **representations** in the way in which we are affected by objects" (A 19/B 33). Sensibility is thus the receptive (passive) faculty, unlike the understanding, which is marked by **spontaneity** (activity). Through sensibility, **objects** are given to us. In fact, this is the only way in which we can receive objects; in contrast, through the understanding, objects are thought. Kant insisted on a strict separation of the functions of the two faculties, but this did not preclude cooperation between them. Indeed, for the sake of **cognition** there was no alternative but for the two faculties to combine their powers; as Kant pointed out, the determination of an object can occur only in the combination of sensibility and the understanding (A 258/B 314). The role of mediating between the two faculties was then played by the transcendental **schemata**. The **forms** of sensibility were the pure forms of intuition **time** and **space**, and the field of study that deals with the principles of **a priori** sensibility is the "**Transcendental Aesthetic**."

In his practical philosophy, Kant understood under sensibility mainly the sensible instincts that were a hindrance to moral action, and he opposed sensibility to the **autonomy** of **practical reason**.

SENSIBLE WORLD. *See* WORLD.

SKEPTICISM. Kant held skepticism to be an ultimately untenable position, but one which was highly valuable in combating dogmatism and thus in preparing the ground for his own version of **criticism**. He regarded dogmatism as a blind, unexamined trust in the human cognitive faculties, and spoke of it as a first step on the road to **transcendental philosophy**. Skepticism represented for him then a second step, a useful resting place, though not a dwelling site (A 761/B 789). In this context, Kant distinguished between the skeptical method and skepticism itself. He was appreciative of the former as highly useful for criticism and as a cure for the dogmatic. He described it as a suspension of judgment, as a provisional treatment of claims as uncertain, as a process of seeking to uncover the ground of misunderstandings. All the while, the skeptical method was characterized by the hope of arriving at the truth. Kant admitted that it was suited only to transcendental philosophy and not, for instance, to **mathematics**, experimental **science**, or **morals**. In the course of his **critique** of epistemology Kant, explicitly referred to the skeptical method especially while discussing the **antinomies** of pure reason (A 485-86/B 513-14). Skepticism, on ·the other hand, was to be superseded, since it treated everything as **illusion** and yet insisted on distinguishing **truth** and illusion, a distinction for which it lacked an adequate criterion. Kant viewed skepticism as pernicious since it undermined all **cognition** (A 423-24/B 451-52; Ak 9, pp. 83-84). He conceived of his own critique as a third step and also as a middle ground between the two extremes; this is the sense of his remark in the preface to the second edition of the *Critique of Pure Reason*, according to which criticism severs the root of skepticism (B xxxiv). Kant regarded **David Hume** as the main proponent of skepticism or at least he thought that Hume's philosophy inevitably led to skepticism (B 127–28, A 764/B 792).

SOCIABILITY, SOCIALITY (*Geselligkeit*). Kant employed the German *'Geselligkeit'* first of all as a label for the inclination of human beings to socialize, an inclination that occurs in conjunction with the opposite inclination to isolate oneself. He regarded this antagonism, which he described with the famous expression "unsociable sociality," as a means used by **nature** to develop in the course of history the talents of the human species on their path to cultivation, civilization, and moralization (Ak 8, pp. 20–21). Second, the term denotes sociality, as it was, for instance, prescribed in the casuistic compendium on manners of the Freiherr von Knigge (*Über den Umgang mit Menschen*, 1788). Kant examines the corresponding rules in his **Anthropology from a Pragmatic Point of View** in connection with the leading idea of his philosophy of **history**. Beyond that, he also points to an aesthetic aspect of sociality, when he grants that sociable entertainment during a good meal is beneficial to the junction of good-living and virtue and thus to humanity. Even if the rules of a tasteful banquet cannot really be compared with moral laws, "nevertheless, everything that fosters sociality is . . . a robe that advantageously clothes virtue" (Ak 7, pp. 277–82).

SOUL (*Seele*). Kant struggled with the concept of soul and with the problem of its relation to the **body** in the **pre-critical** writing *Dreams of a Spirit-Seer* (1766), in which he rejected a number of positive characterizations of immaterial substances, but where he was left with the resilient difficulty of having to explain phenomena such as life. In the *Critique of Pure Reason*, he maintains that we cannot cognize the soul as it is in itself, but are only acquainted with it as it appears in **inner sense**. Thus, it is impossible for us to know whether the soul is a **substance** endowed with **immortality**, though it is possible for us to think this. Kant considers rational demonstrations of the substantial nature of the soul as mistaken attempts on the part of **psychology** to extend our **cognition** beyond the realm of **experience**, and he calls such fallacious arguments **paralogisms**. He admits that the self indeed possesses attributes such as simplicity or identity, but he does not ascribe these to any substantial soul, considering them instead to be merely formal properties of the **I think**. Kant also claims that on the basis of his **critical philosophy** he can easily avoid having to deal with the mind-body problem, that is, with the riddle plaguing especially Cartesian-type philosophies of how two radically different substances can interact. By viewing **matter** as just a representation in inner sense and not as some different substance outside us, the problem is reduced to a description of how representations in inner sense are conjoined with the modifications of our outer sensibility, that is, how the soul and matter are conjoined with one another according to constant **laws** so as to be connected into one experience (A 385–86).

SOUTHWESTERN GERMAN SCHOOL OF NEOKANTIANISM. Also known as the Baden School. Its origins date to the 1890s; its main representatives were Wilhelm **Windelband** and **Heinrich Rickert**, its most important predecessors Kuno Fischer (1824–1907) and Hermann Lotze (1817–1881). Fischer's influence was owing to his depiction of Kant in his work on the history of recent philosophy (*Immanuel Kant,* first 1860), in which he examined the connection between the Kantian and the post-Kantian, idealistic, philosophy, thus conveying **Johann Gottlieb Fichte**'s conceptions to the **Neokantians.** Lotze contributed, on the one hand, the concept of **validity,** by means of which he distinguished the **reality** of propositions or truths from the reality of **being,** processes, and persistence (*Logic,* 2nd ed., 1880, sect. 316–18). On the other hand, he introduced the concept of **value** into idealistic **metaphysics** by declaring in his work *Metaphysics* (1841) that the metaphysical ground of being was the **good** or **absolute purpose.** Later, he expanded this ethical foundation into a more encompassing one that was based on a general theory of values. The "world of value" was supposed to function as a methodological premise in the search for the cognition of reality, a search that was to be conducted by resorting to the "world of the forms." To values he attributed the status of objective ideality, restricting, however, the reality of values as well as that of Platonic ideas to their validity. Lotze's attempt was later clarified by Windelband's and Rickert's distinction between "ideal being" and "non-real validity."

The relationship of the Baden School to Kant was characterized by Windelband's motto of 1883, "understanding Kant means going beyond him"; from the outset, any recourse to Kant's thought was going to serve the purpose of further developing his philosophy. Kant's conception of method was retained, but his critical philosophy was, following Lotze, transformed into a doctrine of validity and amplified so as to cover all cultural phenomena. The Baden School philosophers also extended their examination of the principles of theoretical validity to their own philosophical ('meta-theoretical') propositions (see Emil Lask's *Logik der Philosophie,*

1911), thus addressing the question of the "ultimate foundation" (*Letztbegründung*). The problem of theoretical validity was focused on the relationship of **cognition** and the cognized **object** in a **judgment**. There was general agreement within the school that the determination of cognition and the determination of the object were linked but independent; there were debates in regard to the details. They also shared the notion that cognition was based on theoretical values; in this they differed from the **Marburg School** philosophers, who held that cognition was based on object-producing **principles** of thought. The Baden Neo-Kantians maintained that judgment as the claim of the truth of a **synthesis** of ideas included a valuation; the value predicates true or false express approval or disapproval. They also stressed that a philosophical examination of the objectivity or general validity of valuing could be carried out only by means of another "valuation of the valuations." Windelband anchored such valuations, in analogy to Kant's **transcendental consciousness**, in a valuing "normal consciousness."

The philosophers of the Baden School publicized their conceptions in numerous books; commencing with 1910, they also published the journal *Logos*.

SPACE (*Raum*).   There is no exaggeration involved in calling Kant's conception of **time** and space truly revolutionary. Next to the **concepts** and **principles** of the **understanding** and the **ideas** of **reason**, the teachings on space and time jointly constitute one of the three main pillars of Kant's **critical philosophy**. Kant needed several decades to arrive at his own conception of space. In his **pre-critical** writings, he adhered mostly to Gottfried Wilhelm **Leibniz**'s view of space as the order of external relations between objects. This was to change radically in 1768, when Kant abandoned Leibniz in favor of Isaac **Newton**, arguing in his essay "Concerning the Ultimate Ground of the Differentiation of Directions in Space" that space must be **absolute**, since otherwise we could not distinguish the so-called **incongruent counterparts**. However, only two years later, Kant presented his own theory of space as the **form** of **sensibility** in his *Inaugural Dissertation*, a theory whose essence he was to retain for the rest of his philosophical career. The differences between the version of 1770 and the one of the *Critique of Pure Reason* are relatively minor; the main one is caused by the altered status of the understanding and its newly defined relation to sensibility: while in the earlier work Kant still supposes that sensibility is responsible for ordering the data, in his mature philosophy he assigns this function solely to the understanding.

Most of Kant's final theory of space is presented in the "**Transcendental Aesthetic**." Here, he claims that space is not given empirically, but is an **a priori** form of **intuition**, that is, it is subjective, though subjective not in the sense of varying from person to person, but in the sense of not being a property of **objects** as they are apart from their relation to humans. In spite of its subjective nature, space is fully real (that is, objectively valid) and is necessarily a property of objects, though not as they are in themselves, but only as appearances, that is, space is not a property of **things-in-themselves**. Kant combines these three main points (subjectivity, objective validity, and necessity) in the expression that space and the objects in it are "empirically real but transcendentally ideal." The properties of space form the basis of the principles of geometry, which owes its a priori status to the a priori status of space, given that geometry expresses the manner in which we *must* intuit things.

Although Kant treated time and space both in the *Dissertation* and in the "Transcendental Aesthetic" in parallel fashion, assigning to each point by point almost identical properties, the use he subsequently made of the two forms of intuition did diverge significantly. Based on the consideration that time, as the form of **inner sense**, is more encompassing than space, Kant initially assigned to it a more prominent function. However, his own development of a philosophy of science as well as his wish to answer the charge that the first edition of the first *Critique* presented an **idealism** in the manner of **George Berkeley**, led Kant to accord a greater role to space in the second edition of the *Critique*. One important general tendency here was to argue that without a determinate spatial order there could be no determinate order in time. This is prominent in the new version of the "**Transcendental Deduction**," where the **transcendental unity of apperception** provides the **unity** not only of temporal data, as in the first edition rendering, but also synthesizes space (B 154–56); it is, furthermore, famously reflected in the newly added sections "Refutation of Idealism" (B 274–79) and "General Note on the System of Principles" (B 288–94). In the *Metaphysical Foundations of Natural Science*, Kant makes it clear that only space with its three dimensions can serve as the foundation of a true science, namely, **physics**; time's one-dimensionality fails to provide a comparable basis for **psychology**. *See also* CONSTRUCTION; CONTINUITY; DIMENSIONS OF SPACE; INFINITY; MATHEMATICS.

SPONTANEITY. Kant refers with this term mostly to our capacity to produce **representations**, a capacity that serves as the basis of all **concepts**. He speaks mostly of the spontaneity of the **understanding**, far less frequently of the spontaneity of the productive **imagination** (B 151–52) or of the spontaneity of the **transcendental unity of apperception** (B 132). He contrasts spontaneity with the **receptivity** of **sensibility**; the former is determining, the latter the determinable. Kant claims that it is legitimate to ascribe spontaneity to the productive imagination, in spite of the fact that the imagination in general belongs to sensibility, since this attribution is restricted to only one act of the imagination, namely, to its performance of a transcendental **synthesis** that pertains merely to the unity of apperception. Kant also distinguished a spontaneity of the understanding that produces concepts from a spontaneity of **reason** that produces ideas. On the basis of the latter, Kant was able to associate spontaneity with **freedom** and thus secure a foundation for his **ethics**, though in his writings on the latter he does not rely on the concept of spontaneity.

STATE (*Staat*). The standard translation of '*Staat*' by the Kant scholarship is 'state,' though often, 'government' would far better accord with common English usage. Kant defined state (*civitas*) as "a union of a multitude of human beings under juridical **laws**" (MM, Ak 6, p. 313). If instead of focusing on this relationship of the people to the state, one were to concentrate on the relations of the people among each other as they stand under juridical laws, then one would use the expression "civil state" (*status civilis*). The concepts 'citizen,' "civil state," and "civil constitution" concern primarily the "*homo politicus*," and not the human being as a natural being, or as a being endowed with possessions (*bourgeois*), along with its social class.

For explaining the foundation of the state, Kant resorts to the early modern construct of the social contract. He then argues that the state should have a republican constitution, because only such a constitution "issues from the idea of the original contract, on which all rightful legislation of a people must be based." Essential to the republican constitution is the separation of the executive and legislative powers; in addition, it reposes on three principles: "the freedom of the members of a society (as individuals)," "the dependence of all (as subjects) on a single common legislation," and the "law of the equality of all (as citizens of a state)" (Ak 8, pp. 349–50). In the *Metaphysics of Morals*, Kant combines the second and third principles, and adds "civil independence" as a new third one (Ak 6, pp. 314–15), with which he restricts what counts as a citizen: it may not be a child or a woman, and he must be "his own master (*sui iuris*)," that is, "possess some property that supports him" (Ak 8, p. 295). Only a citizen in this narrow sense of the word (*citoyen*) is empowered to participate in passing legislation. The united will of the people has the power to legislate; for Kant, this is the will of the totality of those men who are capable of expressing their own will, because they are socially not dependent on the power of others. Accordingly, Kant distinguishes, on the one hand, those who benefit from the protection of the laws and who stand under the already existing public laws as free and equal (*Schutzgenossen*), from, on the other hand, the actual 'citizens,' who, in addition, have the right to legislate.

On the question of the right of resistance against a despotic government, Kant expresses himself very reticently. He does defend the "freedom of the pen," but this then is for him the only permitted means of standing up for people's rights (Ak 8, p. 304). He allows a "negative resistance" by the representatives of the people in parliament (Ak 6, p. 322), but rejects, out of principle, resistance even against a tyrannical ruler, "on the pretext that he abused his authority (*tyrannis*)" (p. 320).

While in Kant the distinction between state and society exists only in a preparatory stage, **Hermann Cohen** in his writings on ethics commented on their relationship against the background both of **Georg Wilhelm Friedrich Hegel**'s philosophy of law and of the contemporary discussion of the concepts. Cohen recommended Kant's **"kingdom of ends"** as a guide for a cooperatively structured state as well as for an ethically reformed society. Society functioned for Cohen as a mediating entity between state and individual; on the one hand, from an empirical point of view, society represented economic life, on the other, when viewed as an ideal social order that served for formulating the demand for material justice, it provided the foundation of **ethical socialism**. *See also* REVOLUTION.

STRAWSON, PETER F. (1919–). British logician and metaphysician who 'rethought' a number of Kantian themes, incorporating them into his own philosophy, especially as it was presented in his classic work *Individuals: An Essay in Descriptive Metaphysics* (1959). At a time when metaphysics was in disrepute, Strawson formulated his program of "descriptive metaphysics" as an attempt to capture the fundamental structure of our instinctively held beliefs; this approach bore considerable resemblance to Kant's theoretical philosophy. Although his idea of a conceptual scheme is more empiricist than Kant's corresponding conception, given that it discards the notion of the **synthetic a priori**, there are other, closer points of contact. The most prominent of these is Strawson's theory of an individual as a primitive, underived, and irreducible notion, a notion that bears affinity to Kant's concept of the **transcendental unity of apperception**. In *The Bounds of Sense* (1966), his own interpretation of the *Critique of Pure Reason*, Strawson attempted to downplay the significance of Kant's **transcendental idealism**, trying to demonstrate that other positions of the **critical philosophy** would be largely unaffected.

SUBJECT. *See* PSYCHOLOGY; SOUL; TRANSCENDENTAL UNITY OF APPERCEPTION.

SUBJECTIVE. *See* OBJECT; OBJECTIVE.

SUBLIME (*Erhabenes*). Kant examines the sublime in its own **analytic**. Just as the **beautiful**, it pleases in itself; just as 'beautiful,' the label 'sublime' provides no information concerning the objective character of objects (CJ, Ak 5, p. 244). Satisfaction with the sublime, unlike that with the beautiful, is not playful, it is serious; it consists of ideas of **reason**, which are evoked by the "negative **pleasure**" that we experience while viewing chaotic nature (for example, a stormy ocean) (Ak 5, p. 245). The feeling of the sublime keeps the objects of metaphysics present in a "feeling of the spirit" (*Geistesgefühl*) (Ak 5, p. 192). Kant distinguishes two forms of the sublime. The mathematical sublime is 'absolutely' or "beyond all comparison" large (Ak 5, p. 248; see also Ak 2, p. 215), and the corresponding disposition of the mind leads to a "super-sensible substratum" of **nature** (Ak 5, pp. 255–56). The **dynamical** sublime has to do with the fearful power of nature, to which we feel inferior, and yet from a nonsensible perspective superior, because the representation of the possible threat to our physical existence by natural powers makes us aware that we are not only vulnerable natural beings, but that, in addition, we have a moral vocation that elevates us above nature (Ak 5, pp. 261–62).

While Friedrich Schiller (1759–1805) (*Vom Erhabenen*, 1793), under the influence of Kant, and **Johann Gottfried Herder** (*Kalligone*, 1800), in opposition to Kant, developed their own conceptions of the sublime that were based on art, **Georg Wilhelm Friedrich Hegel** shifted the concept of the sublime from aesthetics to the philosophy of **religion**. The concept has been genuinely resurrected only in the 1980s, when especially Jean-François Lyotard made explicit recourse to Kant and linked the sublime to the postmodern theory of reason.

SUBSTANCE. As the first **category** of **relation**, substance in Kant's **critical philosophy** is part of the conceptual apparatus that constitutes the necessary conditions of the possibility of **experience**. Largely bypassing the varied employment of the concept on the part of the philosophical tradition, Kant makes fairly specific use of the term 'substance.' He does, however, make a point of rejecting as meaningless a number of conceptions of substance that were outside the scope of our experience. He thus distances himself from Leibniz's notion of substance as a monad precisely because such a conception has nothing to do with experience, but is an object of

pure understanding (A 265–66/B 321–22); in the chapter on the "Paralogisms of Pure Reason," he denies that the **soul** is a substance; finally, he
rejects the notion of a substance that would be persistently present in **space**
without filling it, that is, the conception of an intermediary substance between **matter** and **thought** (A 222/B 270).

Aside from occasionally using 'substance' in fairly customary,
straightforward ways, Kant accepts from general **logic** the notion of substance as the subject of a proposition of which things are predicated. In his
most technical employment, Kant ties substance to the unchangeable or to
persistence. The latter two usages are reflected in his definitions. As a logical subject: substance is "that which is subject absolutely, the last subject,
that which does not as predicate presuppose another subject" (Reflection
5295, Ak 18, p. 145); "the concept of a substance means the last subject of
existence, i.e., that which itself does not in its turn belong to the existence
of another as a predicate" (Ak 4, p. 503). Persistence forms the core of the
following definitions: substance is "the unchangeable in existence in which
alone the succession and simultaneity of appearances can be determined in
regard to time" (A 144/B 183), "the ultimate subject of the changeable . . .
that which persists . . . the substratum of everything that changes" (A 205/B
250), "the persistent object of sensible intuition" (A 772/B 800).

The category of substance is derived from categorical judgments, that
is, the categorical relation of subject to predicate. The sole distinguishing
mark of such judgments that Kant mentions is that only two **concepts** are
involved (A 73/B 98). He sheds some light on this, when he employs the
case of substance in his explanation of how all the categories determine the
order of concepts in judgments. In judgments, it is left open which of two
concepts will be subject and which predicate and it is the category, here
that of substance, namely, "Inherence and Subsistence," which determines
the order. One will therefore not say "something divisible is a body" but
rather "all bodies are divisible" (B 128–29).

It is in the schematization of the category of substance that Kant introduces the temporal notion of persistence. The **schema** of substance is thus
said to be the "persistence of the **real** in **time**," that is, something that "en-
dures while everything else changes" (A 144/B 183). 'Persistence' plays a
central role also in the "First Analogy," Kant's most extensive discussion
of substance. Notable here is, in addition, the development from the first to
the second edition. The principle of the persistence of substance in the A-
version plays on the traditional distinction between a substance that remains and its accidents that change: "All **appearances** contain that which
persists (substance) as the **object** itself, and that which can change as its
mere determination, i.e., a way in which the object exists." In the B-version

of the principle, Kant drops the distinction between substance and accident and moves explicitly toward the law of the conservation of **matter** by taking up quantitative considerations: "In all change of appearances substance persists, and its quantum is neither increased nor diminished in nature." Another important change in the B-version involves the inclusion of space; Kant now claims that in order to exhibit something that persists corresponding to the concept of substance, we need an **intuition** in **space** (B 291). In his proof of the principle of the "First Analogy," Kant argues that temporal relations and, therefore, all **alterations** are possible only in that which persists. Since our **apprehension** is always successive and since we cannot perceive time itself, there must be a substratum of everything real, and this, Kant claims, is substance. It is only thanks to substance that appearances can be determined in a possible experience (A 182–89/B 224–32).

In the *Metaphysical Foundations of Natural Science*, the concept of substance turns up at two different locations. In the 'Dynamics,' Kant resorts to substance more or less incidentally while explaining his dynamical theory of matter and showing that matter is infinitely divisible. Here, he first defines material substance as that in space which by itself is movable, explaining that matter is the subject of everything in space that may be considered as belonging to the existence of things. Based on this, he then continues with the claim that all parts of matter will also be substances, thus opening up the possibility of dividing matter indefinitely (Ak 4, 502–3). More in keeping with the systematic intent of his critical treatment of substance is his "First Law of Mechanics" which is by his own admission derived from the "First Analogy," namely, from the proposition that no substance arises or perishes in natural alterations. In the *Metaphysical Foundations*, he modifies this into an overt version of the law of conservation of matter, stating that "in all alterations of bodily nature, the overall **quantity** of matter remains the same" (Ak 4, 541).

SYMBOL. The indirect presentation of a **concept** in **intuition** (in distinction to a schema as a direct presentation); such a presentation is carried out by means of an **analogy** (CJ, Ak 5, p. 352). "The symbol of an idea . . . is the representation of an object in accordance with the analogy, i.e., the same relation to certain consequences" is present as in the object of comparison (Ak 20, p. 280). Thus an absolute monarchy will be symbolized by a hand-mill. Famous and influential was Kant's claim that the **beautiful** is the symbol of the morally **good** (CJ, Ak 5, p. 353), just as in general Kant's critique of aesthetic judgment made it possible for the concept of symbol to gain significance in German aesthetics at the end of the 18th century and in the 19th century. In his *Anthropology from a Pragmatic Point of View*, Kant saw it as an accomplishment of the **enlightenment** to distinguish between the symbolic and the intellectual, that is, between religious observance and religion or between an idol and an ideal (Ak 7, p. 192).

SYNTHESIS (*Synthesis, Verbindung*). A crucial term in Kant's critical philosophy, given that he generally viewed all **thinking** as a mental act of combination that enables us to arrive at the **unity** of a **concept** or of a **judgment**. Synthesis was all the more important to Kant because he regarded the material provided by our **sensibility** to be insufficiently structured for the purposes of the **cognition** of **objects**. This consideration led him to claim that **experience** could be arrived at only by an act of the **understanding**, namely, by a synthesis of the given **manifold**. An indispensable characteristic of such a synthesis was that it had to proceed in accordance with certain clearly determined rules. Kant arrived at this conception of synthesis only during the 1770s, after much struggle with this and related notions. During his **pre-critical** period, he had used the word extensively only in his *Prize Essay* of 1763/1764; here, however, Kant assigned quite a different sense to it, claiming that mathematical definitions are arrived at by means of synthesis, unlike philosophical concepts, for which analysis is the proper means.

At the outset of the "**Transcendental Deduction**" in the *Critique of Pure Reason*, Kant defines synthesis in general as "the action of putting different representations together with each other and comprehending their manifoldness in one cognition." In detail, this means taking up, going through, and combining a multitude of given data (A 77/B 102-3). This threefold process is described in the first edition version of the "Transcendental Deduction," where Kant distinguishes between a "synthesis of **apprehension** in **intuition**," which he also labels a "synopsis of the manifold a priori through sense," a "synthesis of **reproduction** in the **imagination**," and a "synthesis of **recognition** in the concept," also described as the unity through **transcendental apperception** (A 95, 98-104). When the synthesis is effected by the imagination, the synthesized manifold belongs to sensibility, when it is effected by the understanding, the manifold is brought to concepts (A 78/B 103).

In the second edition, in which the role of the imagination is downplayed, synthesis is claimed to be just a function of the understanding (B 130). However, Kant does not completely abandon his earlier conception, though he does replace the previous straightforward, prominently presented trichotomy by the less conspicuously emphasized distinction between a figurative synthesis of the imagination, in which the manifold of sensible intuition is combined, and an intellectual synthesis of the understanding, in which the manifold is thought in accordance with the **category**. Both of these syntheses are claimed to be **transcendental** because they ground the possibility of cognition **a priori**. The synthesis of the imagination evidently serves here (as it already did in the A-version, see, for example, A 124) as an intermediary between sensibility and the understanding, though Kant does not bother in the B-version to explain its exact function at any great length (B 151-54).

Furthermore, Kant distinguishes between the synthesis of an empirical manifold and a **pure** one. The latter is supposed to yield the categories and Kant claims that it must be performed on the a priori forms of intuition of space and time; however, the particulars of this process remain obscure (A 78/B 104). Much clearer is Kant's ascription of synthesis to **transcendental logic** and of **analysis** to general **logic** as well as his accompanying argument that categorical synthesis must precede all analysis, given that dissolution is impossible without previously executed combination (B 130).

In the **"Transcendental Dialectic,"** Kant uses the term 'synthesis' in a somewhat different sense. Instead of speaking of a combination of the manifold of sensibility, he distinguishes here between a progressive synthesis that proceeds from the proximate consequence of a conditioned to the more remote consequences, and a regressive synthesis that proceeds from the condition proximate to a given appearance toward the more remote conditions (A 411/B 438). As the critique of the human cognitive faculties demonstrates, the former pertains to the understanding, the latter to **reason**, whose goal (regress to infinity) can, legitimately, be only problematic and regulative, never **constitutive**.

SYNTHETIC A PRIORI. This is one of the truly revolutionary elements of Kant's **transcendental philosophy**, one with which much of the latter stands or falls. Within Kant's classification of **judgments**, the significance of the undoubtedly important distinction between **analytic a priori** and **synthetic a posteriori** pales in comparison with the magnitude of the conception of the synthetic judgments a priori. While there are historical precedents for the distinction, there is none for the synthetic a priori.

Kant himself declared that the question "how are synthetic propositions a priori possible?" constitutes the "general problem of transcendental philosophy" (B 73). Kant deals with this question by inquiring about the X on which the **understanding** bases itself when it regards the concept of A (for example, something occurs) to be universally and necessarily joined to the concept of B (for example, cause). **Experience** cannot, unlike in the case of the synthetic judgments a posteriori, provide such a foundation (A

9/B 13). It is rather the pure **concepts** of the understanding, the **categories**, on whose employment the synthetic judgments a priori are based. Kant justifies such a usage in his **transcendental deduction** of the pure concepts of the understanding, in which he proves that there would be no experience (empirical **cognition**), if the sensibly given **manifold** were not brought under these concepts. The principles of such a subsumption of the manifold under the categories are the synthetic judgments a priori, which Kant labels "the synthetic principles of the pure understanding." As the necessary conditions of the possibility of both subjective and objective experience, they are objectively valid and thus legitimate (A 154–58/B 193–97).

SYNTHETIC METHOD. *See* ANALYTIC METHOD.

SYSTEM. The notion of system or systematicness was crucial for Kant owing to his conviction that all genuine knowledge had to be systematically ordered. By the latter he understood **cognitions** that were connected according to some principle that precedes the raw data and that orders them, that is, that contains the form and possibly also the purpose of the whole (A 645/B 673). Not surprisingly, Kant's own works are organized in a systematic fashion. This is true especially of the three *Critiques*. Each one has its own **architectonic** structure, but they also form a systematic unity when taken together. Kant thought that human **reason** itself had a tendency toward systematicness, as it considered, for instance, "all cognitions as belonging to a system" (A 474/B 502). Kant regarded the *Critique of Pure Reason* and the *Prolegomena* mainly as efforts to clear the ground, thus titling these works as 'critique' or 'prolegomena' and calling them merely propaedeutic. He did, however, believe that the final aim of **philosophy** was to erect a well-founded **metaphysics** that was to amount to a "system of **pure** reason" (A 841/B 869).

Kant was greatly concerned with showing that the key elements of the first *Critique* formed systems. Hence he laid stress on the fact that the pure **concepts** of the **understanding** (**categories**) were not compiled haphazardly, but were derived according to a principle. Furthermore, he attempted to find some way of systematizing the (empirical) cognitions gained by the understanding on the basis of the categories and the **principles of the understanding**, since these pure concepts could guarantee only a formal unity that did not extend beyond the **form** of cognition. Kant spoke here of reason systematizing the cognitions of the understanding: the unity of reason presupposes the **idea** of the form of the whole of cognition, that is, it postulates a complete **unity** of the cognitions of the understanding, and thanks to this unity such cognitions are not mere **aggregates**, but a system joined in accordance with necessary **laws**. However, such an idea could only be regulative, not **constitutive**. In the "Appendix to the **Transcendental Dialectic**," Kant discussed examples of regulative ideas, and their use in attempting to systematize cognitions, mentioning especially homogeneity, specification, and **continuity** (A 658/B 686). He valued regulative ideas for their methodological utility in guiding our research of nature. In the *Critique of Judgment*, he then suggested that the empirical laws of nature could be systematized by recourse to the notion of a formal **purposiveness** of nature, introducing in this work, moreover, yet another concept for arriving at an ordered whole, namely, the "system of the purposiveness of nature."

In **Neokantianism**, the notion that philosophy had to build a system was as important as it was controversial, especially in regard to its realization. **Hermann Cohen**'s system consisted of four parts (logic, ethics, aesthetics, psychology), and Cohen resorted to aspects of the philosophy of culture and philosophy of consciousness in order to ground it. He wished to explain the unity of culture on the basis of the relation of the three basic modes of production of the cultural consciousness. This unity was to be the subject matter of the fourth part of the system, a part that Cohen never composed; this psychology was to serve as an encyclopedia of the system of philosophy.

Paul Natorp at first followed Cohen's conception, although with a considerably stronger concept of system. After 1912, however, he worked on a "philosophical systematics" that no longer adhered to Kant's or Cohen's notions. For **Heinrich Rickert**, system also remained a part of his program. He pursued the idea of an open system, in which the historical incompleteness of cultural life as well as the supra-historical **validity** of **values** are taken into consideration. His system was to be composed of six areas of value (logic, aesthetics, mysticism, ethics, eroticism, philosophy of religion), to each of which one value, one good, one kind of action of the subject, and one weltanschauung were attributed.

- T -

TABLES OF JUDGMENTS AND CATEGORIES. After much groping, Kant realized that his new epistemology required an indubitable foundation, which, moreover, would have to be complete in some very important sense. He became convinced that he had discovered such an anchor with the theory of **judgment** of the **logic** of his day, claiming that an exhaustive classification of judgments, unencumbered by considerations of the content of the judgments, was the expression of the **form** of the **understanding**. A definitive table of the logical functions in judgment would be complete and would then reflect the structure of all human thought, that is, it would be absolutely valid for any human intellectual endeavor. Modifying the already existing tables somewhat, Kant presented his own version in the *Critique of Pure Reason* (A 70/B 95):

1.
Quantity of Judgments
Universal
Particular
Singular

2.	**3.**
Quality	**Relation**
Affirmative	Categorical
Negative	Hypothetical
Infinite	Disjunctive

4.
Modality
Problematic
Assertoric
Apodictic

Kant thought that every judgment falls under each of the four 'titles' where it exhibits one of the three 'moments.' Thus a judgment's **quantity** expresses the extension of the subject-term, **quality** determines the realities or negations of the predicate, **relation** concerns the relation between the subject and the predicate or the relation between different judgments, and **modality** specifies the relation to thinking in general. Kant put the table of judgments essentially to just one use, namely, to derive from it the table of categories, calling such a process of the derivation of the **categories** a metaphysical **deduction**.

The table of categories is the grid of the pure concepts of the understanding as they relate to objects **a priori**, corresponding to, because allegedly derived from, the table of judgments. The link between the two tables is based on the fact that the understanding performs in both cases the same type of action: in regard to judgments, it "brings the logical form of a judgment into concepts by means of the analytical **unity**"; in regard to the pure concepts of the understanding that pertain to objects a priori, the understanding "brings a transcendental content into its representations by means of the synthetic unity of the **manifold** in **intuition** in general" (A 79/B 105). The difference between the table of judgments and that of the categories corresponds to the difference between general and **transcendental logic**. Kant claimed that the systematic derivation of the categories, namely, the metaphysical **deduction**, ensured that his set of these concepts would be complete. He was then still faced with the further task of proving the objective **validity** of the categories. This he achieved in the so-called **transcendental deduction**. The table of the categories in the *Critique of Pure Reason* (A 80/B 106) is as follows:

1.
Of Quantity
Unity
Plurality
Allness

2.	**3.**
Of Quality	**Of Relation**
Reality	Of Inherence and Subsistence
Negation	(*substantia et accidens*)
Limitation	Of Causality and Dependence
	(cause and effect)
	Of Community (reciprocity between agent and patient)

4.
Modality
Possibility—Impossibility
Existence—Nonexistence
Necessity—Contingence

Among the categories, Kant distinguished mathematical from dynamical ones. The former (quality and quantity) were "concerned with objects of **intuition** (pure and empirical)," the latter (relation and modality) were "directed at the **existence** of these objects (either in relation to one another or to the understanding)" (B 110).

Kant presents two more tables in the first *Critique*, both of which are based on the table of the categories: table of the principles (A 161/B 200) and table of the concepts of the **nothing** (A 292/B 348).

Kant's deduction of the categories from the judgments was not adopted by any major philosopher. Starting with different assumptions, **Johann Gottlieb Fichte** modified Kant's tables as did the other post-Kantian German idealists. **Hermann Cohen** and **Paul Natorp** returned closer to Kant's tables, without, however, taking up his distinction between formal and transcendental logic. Cohen developed a system of 'judgments' of pure cognition, Natorp worked out a system of basic logical functions.

TASTE (*Geschmack*). Originally, this concept was developed in ethics in the 17th century, but in the 18th it became central to **aesthetic** discourse. Taste was considered as both a sensible and a mental **faculty** of the perception, distinction, and **judgment** of objects that were primarily to be found in the fine **arts** or in beautiful **nature**. Nevertheless, taste could still play a role in questions of **morals**.

In his *Anthropology from a Pragmatic Point of View*, Kant defined taste as "the power of the aesthetic faculty of judgment to choose in a universally valid fashion" (Ak 7, p. 241). In this context, he stressed that taste presupposes a social situation in which individuals can communicate their satisfaction with an object to others (CJ, Ak 5, p. 297). The relationship between taste and **genius** is a complex one: on the one hand, taste is not a productive power, but only one of judgment, on the other hand, it serves as a corrective for the products of the unbridled imagination of a genius (pp. 312–13).

The transcendental analytic of the **beautiful** is carried out on the basis of the judgment of taste. Such a judgment, also called aesthetic, is grounded on taste understood as a "*sensus communis*," that is, as "the faculty for judging **a priori** the communicability of the **feelings** that are linked to a given representation" (p. 296).

With the post-Kantian turn of aesthetics toward the philosophy of art, the concept of taste soon lost all its philosophical significance.

TELEOLOGY. Although this expression had already been coined in 1728 by **Christian Wolff**, for whom it signified a part of natural philosophy, it was only with Kant that it gained wide acceptance in philosophy. In general, Kant characterized **philosophy** in accordance with its cosmopolitan concept (*Weltbegriff*) as "the science of the relation of all **cognition** to the essential **ends** of human **reason** (*teleologia rationis humanae*)" (A 839/B 867). He consigned the teleological standpoint, which views the order of the world "**as if** it had sprouted from the intention of a highest reason," to the merely **regulative** use of reason (A 686/B 714). Corresponding to this, he developed in the *Critique of Judgment* a nondoctrinal 'science' of teleology that contains the **a priori principles** of the teleological **judgment** of **nature** (§ 79). These principles concern the only problematically valid "objective **purposiveness**," which may be observed externally between the products of nature and internally in **organisms**. In this context, Kant, following an analogy with human action, interprets nature as a "causality of purpose" (§ 61). He supplements this critical "physical teleology" with a "moral teleology" that declares the human being as a moral being to be the end of creation, thus founding an (ethico-)theology (§§ 86–87).

Kant's adherents and critics took up the concept of 'teleology,' extended it and popularized it. Although critical of the anthropocentrism of the old physico-theology, Friedrich Schiller (1759–1805) pleaded for a conception of world history to which a rational end and a teleological principle ought to be appended. Based on the studies of August Stadler (1850–1910), **Hermann Cohen** newly determined Kant's notion of a regulative teleology of nature as a concept of the transition from the **cognition** of nature to the ideal of **freedom**. In addition, he explicitly credited Kant for securing the legitimacy of teleological thought in ethics. **Wilhelm Windelband**, on the other hand, introduced a teleological element already into his theory of judgment, emphasizing that the grounding of the axioms and norms of philosophy could succeed only by recourse to their teleological meaning, since their specific **validity** was conditioned by the ideal purpose of general validity.

THEODICY.   In the notes that he was compiling for an answer to the prize question raised by the Berlin Academy of Sciences for the year 1755, Kant discussed the relation between the **a priori** grounded optimism of **Gottfried Wilhelm Leibniz** and the empirically justified one of Alexander Pope (Ak 17, pp. 229–39). While in his *An Attempt at Some Reflections on Optimism* of 1759, Kant still argued in favor of the Leibnizian doctrine that **God** had chosen the best of all possible worlds, after his critical turn, namely, in his "On the Miscarriage of all Philosophical Trials in Theodicy" of 1791, Kant completely rejected the notion of a "doctrinal theodicy." He now maintained that human reason was incapable of defending the wisdom of the creator against accusations that arise on the basis of the experience of counter-purposiveness in the world. As the only possible theodicy, Kant at this point regarded a so-called 'authentic' one, consisting of the thought that, within the realm of **practical reason**, God himself is the interpreter of his own creative will.

THEOLOGY.   While the **pre-critical** Kant held the "first principles" of natural theology to be capable of the greatest philosophical evidence (Ak 2,

p. 296), in his *Critique of Pure Reason* he subjected all rational (speculative) theology to devastating criticism. By way of definition, he distinguished between **transcendental** theology, which seeks the **cognition** of **God** by **pure reason** (cosmotheology and ontotheology), and natural theology, which takes the constitution of the **world** as its point of departure and cognizes God either on the basis of the **ends** of **nature** as a **principle** of natural order (physico-theology) or on the basis of the moral end of rational beings as a principle of all moral order (moral theology or ethico-theology) (A 632/B 660; CJ, §§ 85ff.). Because a **transcendent** use of reason is illegitimate, all attempts to derive a speculative theology are invalid. Transcendental theology may, however, be utilized in a negative way, namely, to "ceaselessly censor our reason"; this does leave open the possibility of a moral theology (A 640/B 669). Within the latter, the moral proof of God's **existence** (CJ, § 88) does not entail a theoretical determination of the being of God, but it does carry conviction for the practical use of reason. In his *Conflict of the Faculties*, Kant subjected biblical theology to the supervision of rational theology insofar as the latter was to determine the principles of the interpretation of the Bible, thus conducting the "faith of the churches" back to a pure religious **faith**, based on **practical reason**.

Kant's claim that the genuine purpose of rational religion consisted in the moral improvement of the human being was taken up by Protestant theologians under the heading of 'Rationalism.' Such a position was advocated among others by Kant's student Johann Heinrich Tieftrunk (1759–1837). The basic tenet of this theological movement was the conviction that rational religion arises when the human being accepts the spirit of Jesus in a free, rational manner. Albrecht Ritschl (1822–1889) and Wilhelm Herrmann (1846–1922) took recourse to Kant in the second half of the 19th century in their attempt to found a nonmetaphysical, systematic theology; the latter did so in a lively exchange with the **Marburg School of Neokantianism**.

THING-IN-ITSELF *(Ding an sich)*. A key technical expression in Kant's theoretical and practical **philosophy**. In everyday language, it could be rendered as "things as they are in themselves" or "things as they are outside of our relationship to them." In his **pre-critical** *Inaugural Dissertation* of 1770, Kant still held that the **understanding** could cognize things-in-themselves (Ak 2, p. 392), however, starting with the *Critique of Pure Reason*, he restricted **cognition** to **appearances** as the **objects** of sensible **intuition**. Nevertheless, Kant continued to claim that we cannot avoid supposing the **existence** of the thing-in-itself as a correlate of **sensibility**, given that it would be absurd to maintain that there are appearances without there being anything that appears (B xxvi).

The concept of the thing-in-itself is possibly the most discussed and the most controversial element of Kant's philosophy. The reason for this is that, at least in part, Kant did not focus so much on the concept itself as on the **transcendental** distinction between appearance and thing-in-itself. He determined the thing-in-itself on the one hand as a "**noumenon** in the negative sense" (B 307) and, in the first edition of the first *Critique*, as the "transcendental object" in the sense of an "entirely undetermined thing in general" (A 253). The thing-in-itself thus marks the **boundary** of all cognition of the understanding. Kant was consistent in denying to the thing-in-itself all determination, since it cannot be thought by means of any **category** (A 253, A 288/B 344); he did, unfortunately, also use the expression in plural.

On the other hand, Kant basically admitted the "noumenon in a positive sense" as "an object of sensible intuition," though only as a "problematic concept" (B 344). As such, it justifies the distinction into a sensible **world** and a rational one in Kant's moral philosophy, in which the acting human being may be regarded both as an appearance that is subjected to the laws of nature and as a thing-in-itself (GMM, Ak 4, p. 459). Kant's aim was by no means to introduce an ontological dualism, but only a transcendental distinction, which he hoped would enable him to conceive humans as subject to the laws of **nature** and to the laws of **freedom** without involving himself in a contradiction (p. 459).

The notion of the thing-in-itself, except possibly in the sense of a limiting concept, encountered a generally unfavorable reception, perhaps because it was misunderstood as a determined concept, especially in the sense of an object that affects us (A 19/B 33). Friedrich Heinrich Jacobi (1744–1819) set the tone by claiming in the 'Appendix' to his *David Hume on Belief, or Idealism and Realism* (1787) that without the presupposition that things-in-themselves affect us one cannot enter into Kant's philosophy, but that with this supposition one cannot remain within the system. Other philosophers joined the chorus, evidently because they were reluctant to admit unknowable entities into their field. Criticism was voiced by **Johann Gottlieb Fichte**, **Georg Wilhelm Friedrich Hegel**, and their contemporaries, later by the **Neokantians**, and in the 20th century by the linguistic interpreters of Kant.

Interpretation, critique, and further development of Kant's thought often intermingled. This was true equally of the German Neokantians and of the British reception of Kant in the 19th and 20th centuries. The Scottish philosophers of common sense such as William Hamilton or Henry

Longueville Mansel in Oxford, who sometimes knew Kant only indirectly, measured his teachings on the thing-in-itself against **George Berkeley**'s subjective idealism or Ralph Cudworth's Neoplatonic one; they then tended to accuse Kant of inconsistency, claiming, moreover, that he combined an epistemological skepticism with a metaphysical agnosticism. **Hermann Cohen** interpreted the thing-in-itself exclusively as a boundary concept. The English idealists of the late 19th century (James Hutchison Stirling, Thomas Hill Green, Edward Caird) held the concept of the thing-in-itself to be dogmatic and replaced it with the abstract concept of the **transcendental object**, which they regarded as subsumed, together with the concept of the transcendental subject, in absolute consciousness. The older realists (Shadworth Hollway Hodgson, Andrew Seth) also eliminated the concept of the thing-in-itself by teaching the complete intelligibility of being. Norman Kemp Smith viewed the concept of the transcendental object as a pre-critical remainder. With A. H. Smith, he considered Kant to be a closet rationalist. H. A. Prichard interpreted Kant's thing-in-itself as a critique of the intelligibility of outer objects, taking, however, the further step of rejecting Kant's medium concept of appearance in order to ground his realist epistemology on the two basic concepts of the thing-in-itself and its representation. The linguistic philosophers argued that the distinction between **phenomena** and noumena belonged to the old **metaphysics**, and thus should have been given up by Kant, since Kant had rejected the old metaphysics as well (for example, **Peter F. Strawson**; W. H. Walsh, *Kant's Criticism of Metaphysics*, 1975, pp. 164–66).

THINKING, THOUGHT (*Denken*). In general, 'thinking' for Kant is, as a function of the **understanding** or of **reason**, an act of uniting, combining, or synthesizing isolated data into **concepts**, **judgments**, or conclusions. As such, thinking is distinguished from **intuition**, and is characterized as an act of **spontaneity** rather than of **receptivity**. Laws of thought in general are the subject matter of general (formal) **logic**, laws of thought as it applies to **objects** of **experience** are the concern of **transcendental logic**. Within the realm of the latter, Kant uses the word 'thinking' in two different if related senses. First, thinking is a part of the cognitive process, since pure thought provides the **form** of experience and of **objects**: by producing the form of experience and of its objects, thinking constitutes the necessary conditions of the possibility of experience and of the objects of experience. In this sense, Kant can indeed say that "thinking is cognition through concepts" (A 69/B 94). However, cognition also requires intuition, and where none is given, thinking cannot produce knowledge or **existence**. Second, thinking is distinguished from knowing and cognizing. The latter are re-

stricted to intuitions, while the former is not restricted and may apply to
things-in-themselves. Thinking in this sense plays a central role especially
in practical philosophy; one cannot, for instance, know **freedom**, but one
may think it.

TIME (*Zeit*). In his critical philosophy, Kant presented a radically innovative conception of time. Along with his teachings on the **concepts** and
principles of the **understanding** and on the **ideas** of **reason**, the theory of
space and time constitutes one of the three main pillars of Kant's **transcendental philosophy**. Kant did not greatly occupy himself with reflections on
time during the **pre-critical** period, though there are indications that he
held **Gottfried Wilhelm Leibniz**'s view, according to which time is the
order of external relations between things. Kant's first lengthy exposition
of time occurs in the *Inaugural Dissertation* of 1770, where he defends
essentially the same theory of time as one of the two **forms** of **sensibility**
as he does 11 years later in the *Critique of Pure Reason*. The differences
between the two conceptions are relatively minor; the main one concerns
less time itself and more the altered status of the understanding and its relation to sensibility: while in the earlier work Kant still supposes that sensibility is responsible for ordering the data, in his mature philosophy he assigns this function solely to the understanding. Much of Kant's definitive
theory of time is presented in the "**Transcendental Aesthetic**." Here, the
gist of the matter is summed up by the expression that time and the **objects**
in it are "empirically real but transcendentally ideal." This means that time
is not given empirically, but is an **a priori** form of **intuition**, and therefore
subjective, though not in the sense of differing from one person to the next,
but in the sense of not belonging to objects apart from their relation to human subjects. Thanks to such a conception of subjectivity, Kant is able to
declare that time is fully real and objective, that is, it is necessarily a property of **appearances**, though not of **things-in-themselves**.

Although both in the *Dissertation* and in the "Transcendental Aesthetic" Kant treats space and time jointly, assigning nearly identical properties to them, he subsequently makes different use of each. For one thing,
the properties of time form the basis of the principles of arithmetic, rather
than of geometry as the properties of space do. However, both of these
mathematical disciplines equally owe their a priori status to the a priori status of the two forms of intuition, since both express the manner in which
we necessarily intuit things. Second, time, but not space, makes possible
the application of the pure concepts of the understanding, the **categories**, to
appearances in general, by serving as the basis for the **schematism** of the
pure understanding. As the form of **inner sense**, time is more encompass-

ing than space, and, accordingly, Kant initially assigned to it a more prominent role than he did to space. However, under the dual influence of the charge that his philosophy was a mere regurgitation of **George Berkeley**'s idealism, and of insights that he derived from his development of his philosophy of science, Kant in the second edition of the first *Critique* began to accord a greater role to space. From the point of view of science, the one-dimensionality of time proves to be a disadvantage, making any application of mathematics insufficient. This is reflected in the fact that Kant denies that **psychology**, a science based on time, can ever become truly mathematical and thus truly scientific in the way that **physics**, which is based on space, can be (Ak 4, p. 471). *See also* CONSTRUCTION; CONTINUITY; INFINITY; MATHEMATICS.

TOTALITY. This is the usual English rendition of at least two different German words, namely *'Allheit,'* which Kant qualifies in brackets with the Latin *'universitas'* and which could, and perhaps should, be rendered as 'allness,' and *'Totalität'*; Norman Kemp Smith also translated *'Ganzes'* and *'All'* as 'totality,' though 'whole' and 'all,' respectively, are surely preferable. Unfortunately, Kant himself neither kept these terms completely separate, identifying 'allness' (*Allheit, universitas*) and 'totality' at least twice (B 111, A 322/B 379), nor did he bother to explain how they are related. The term 'allness' appears chiefly as the third of the **categories** of **quantity** and is, as such, defined as "plurality considered as unity" (B 111).

The main use of the term 'totality' (in German almost exclusively as *Totalität*) occurs in the "**Transcendental Dialectic**" of the *Critique of Pure Reason*, where it usually refers to the absolute completeness of conditions to a given conditioned thing. As Kant generally held that it is impossible to attain an unconditioned totality empirically or to determine it **a priori** in accordance with some **principle** (A 759/B 787), the concept of totality ended up signifying some unattainable goal; **reason**'s insistence on reaching it leads to contradictions. Given that such "an unavoidable conflict of reason with itself" is largely the subject matter of the chapter on the **antinomies**, it is not surprising that Kant discusses 'totality' mainly under this heading. Generally speaking, the **ideas** of the antinomies postulate an absolute totality of series of **appearances**, be the series spatial or temporal, although **experience** gives us only some of the elements of such a whole. The only way of avoiding the difficulties arising from such speculative use of ideas beyond the realm of experience is to consider totality as a **problem** for the understanding and not as an axiom (A 508/B 536), that is, to take the cosmological ideas as **regulative** principles and not to posit constitutively an actual totality in such series (A 685/B 713). Kant's remark that disregarding these limitations would make "a category into a transcendental idea" (A 409/B 436) yields a possible clue to a more promising understanding of the relationship between 'allness' and 'totality': the concepts are related as the two sides of a coin, with allness referring to the legitimate application within the bounds of experience, and totality having to do with the illegitimate demand for an unconditioned absolute.

TRANSCENDENT. With the adjective 'transcendent,' Kant characterized **concepts** and especially **ideas, principles** and cognitions, and, even more so, a certain *employment* of such concepts, ideas, or principles. In this use, the **boundaries** of our **cognition** or **experience** are transcended. It is the ideas and principles of **reason** that seduce us to such use, while the concepts and principles of the **pure understanding** function as the conditions of the possibility of experience and are thus only of an *immanent* or empirical employment (A 308/B 365; CJ, § 57). Next to this distinction between transcendent and immanent, a distinction based on the ideas and principles of reason, Kant also opposes a transcendent usage to a **transcendental** one. Unlike in his common usage of 'transcendental' in his critical philosophy, Kant here understands under 'transcendental' the application of "a concept in some principle" to things-in-themselves, distinguishing this use from the empirical application of the concept to **appearances** (A 238–39/B 297–98). Transcendent ideas or principles of reason demand that the boundaries of experience be overstepped; however, the "transcendental use or misuse of the categories" in its application to **things-in-themselves** is a "mere mistake of the **faculty of judgment**," the proper use of such concepts being the empirical one (A 396/B 352–53).

After Kant, transcendence was taken to mean 1) the sphere of the religious that is distinguished from the immanence of all reality in consciousness (Sören Kierkegaard) or the meaning of the idea of God with regard to its content (**Hermann Cohen**); 2) the being of an object thought independently of a consciousness, for example, in **Heinrich Rickert** in the sense of a transcendent **ought**; 3) the constitution of being of the human "there-being" that in its being-in-the-world transcends being (**Martin Heidegger**).

TRANSCENDENTAL. The difference between '**transcendent**' and '**transcendental**,' which prior to Kant was merely a grammatical one, was accorded by him, for the first time, a philosophical significance. Kant discarded the Neoplatonic metaphysical connotations of 'transcendental' and elevated the term to a key position in his thought. Basically (though not always consistently), 'transcendental' refers to the type of **cognition** concerned not with **objects** but with our **a priori concepts** of objects (A

11-12/B 25). Alternatively, one could say that the term points to the need to provide an account of the necessary conditions of possible **experience** or, more generally, to the need to carry out a critique of pure reason. Given that much of Kant's **philosophy** was concerned with these goals, it may, as a whole, be characterized as transcendental.

Kant uses the adjective transcendental in connection with various other terms, yielding, e.g., the titles of parts or divisions of the *Critique of Pure Reason* such as **Transcendental Aesthetic, Transcendental Logic, Transcendental Analytic,** and **Transcendental Dialectic,** or the names of certain components of our cognitive apparatus such as the **Transcendental Unity of Apperception,** or the label of an epistemological dysfunction, the **Transcendental Illusion,** caused by a lack of attention to the need for an examination of the mode of our cognition.

Furthermore, Kant distinguishes transcendental cognition, which itself is a priori, from other a priori cognition, such as **mathematics,** claiming that only the former provides an inspection of the origin and application of the different a priori concepts (A 56/B 80). *See also* EXPOSITION; TRANSCENDENTAL DEDUCTION; TRANSCENDENTAL PHILOSOPHY.

TRANSCENDENTAL AESTHETIC.   The title of the first part of the "Transcendental Doctrine of Elements" in the *Critique of Pure Reason.* In this context, Kant distances his usage of the term 'aesthetic' from its modern meaning as philosophy of beauty, taste, and art. Although loosely connected with *aisthesis,* the ancient Greek word for perception, his employment of the expression is highly technical and restricted. He applies it to **sensibility,** and here more specifically to its **forms** (rather than to its content), which he identifies as **space** and **time.** The main goal of the "Transcendental Aesthetic" is to show that we do not perceive **things-in-themselves,** but, rather, things as they are appear to us through the forms of our sensibility, that is, as they are in space and time. According to a second major thought of the "Transcendental Aesthetic," these forms of sensibility may be represented in **a priori intuitions** and they then serve as the basis for **mathematics** (A 21-22/B 35-36). Kant deals with space and time largely separately, subjecting, in the second edition version, each in its turn to a **metaphysical exposition** and to a **transcendental** one. It is an essential part of Kant's **architectonic** that his treatment of the principles of a priori sensibility is sharply distinguished from his presentation of the concepts of pure thinking; the latter are dealt with in the second part of the "Doctrine of Elements," the "**Transcendental Logic.**" Although the "Transcendental Aesthetic" is relatively short, comprising only some 40 pages in the longer second edition version, it is by no means subservient to the subsequent examination of **pure thought**, but enjoys an equal status. Kant criticizes the **Leibniz-Wolffian** philosophy for failing to recognize that sensibility is an original source of cognition and for treating it instead as an indistinct form of intellectual cognition (A 44/B 61). The significance of the "Transcendental Aesthetic" for all of Kant's theoretical philosophy arises from his basic tenet that all **thought** must be related to sensibility, since **objects** cannot be given to us in any other way than in intuition.

TRANSCENDENTAL ANALYTIC. The First Division of the "**Transcendental Logic**" in the *Critique of Pure Reason*. Unlike the Second Division, the "**Transcendental Dialectic**," which deals with the "**logic of illusion**," this division treats the "**logic of truth**." Kant here concentrates almost exclusively on the **understanding**, first, in Book I ("Analytic of Concepts"), on its **pure concepts**, subsequently, in Book II ("Analytic of Principles"), on its **pure principles**. The former is again subdivided into two parts, namely, into a **metaphysical deduction**, in which Kant attempts to derive the concepts (**table of categories**) from the **table of judgments**, and a **transcendental deduction**, in which he demonstrates that the categories apply to **objects**. The "Analytic of Principles" is concerned with showing how the categories apply to the forms of **intuition**. To this task are devoted especially the first two chapters, dealing, respectively, with the **schematism** of the pure concepts, and with the whole system of the principles, a system that comprises the "**Axioms of Intuition**," the "**Anticipations of Perception**," the "**Analogies of Experience**," and the "**Postulates of Empirical Thought in General**." In the third chapter Kant explains his distinction between **Phenomena** and **Noumena** and stresses that the categories apply to things only as they appear to **sensibility** and not as they are in themselves. Ignoring this fact has misled, for example, the philosophers of the **Leibniz-Wolff** school into taking mere features of concepts for properties of **things-in-themselves**; this type of error is the topic of the Appendix to the "Transcendental Analytic," entitled "**Amphiboly** of Concepts of Reflection."

TRANSCENDENTAL ARGUMENT. Although this expression, which by now has become a standard and integral part of philosophical diction, was not used by Kant himself, it derives from his *Critique of Pure Reason*. In their general structure, transcendental arguments take as their point of departure some undisputed premise, for example, the existence of experience or of the **fact** of science, before proceeding to deduce the necessary conditions of the possibility of the premise. Thus, in his refutation of **idealism**,

Kant begins with the premise that we are directly aware of the temporal order of our consciousness, and he deduces that this is possible only if we also have consciousness of the existence of objects outside of ourselves in **space**. The most famous of Kant's transcendental arguments are the transcendental **exposition** and especially the **transcendental deduction**. *See also* TRANSCENDENTAL METHOD.

TRANSCENDENTAL DEDUCTION. After deriving in the "metaphysical **deduction**" the **categories** from the **table of judgments**, Kant then turns in the following part of the **"Transcendental Analytic"** of the *Critique of Pure Reason* in a series of very elaborate and complicated steps to proving the possibility of the categories "as **a priori cognitions** of **objects** of an **intuition** in general" (B 159). He needed to demonstrate that the categories are not empirical concepts and that they apply to objects not because of any property of the objects themselves, but due to the fact that they provide the necessary conditions of the possibility of the **experience** of objects, or, in Kant's own words, that the laws that govern **appearances** must agree with the a priori **form** of the **understanding**, that is, with the capability of the understanding to synthesize the **manifold** in general (B 164). Kant contrasted such a proof with what he labeled an "empirical deduction," ascribing the latter to **John Locke** and **David Hume**. He claimed that only his own approach could guarantee that the question of *quid juris*, the legitimacy of the categories, would be addressed.

Kant had struggled with the deduction at least since 1772, but when he came to revise the *Critique* in 1787, he almost completely rewrote the corresponding section. The basic goal and the basic ideas, however, remain the same. Thus, both versions are based on the claim that the **transcendental unity of apperception** makes the **synthesis** of the manifold of intuition into objects of experience possible by resort to the categories. However, in the first edition, this process is described in terms of a threefold synthesis, namely, of the **apprehension** of the **representations**, of their reproduction in the **imagination**, and of their **recognition** in the **concept**. In addition, apperception is restricted to uniting the manifold in **time**. In the revised version, the stress on the role of the imagination is dropped, the synthesis of the manifold occurs in both **space** and time, and there is greater interest in proving the objective **validity** of **judgments**. The version of 1781, with its emphasis on the form of **inner sense** and on the faculty of imagination, therefore at least seemingly has a more pronounced psychological dimension than the version of 1787, which is more truly a piece of **transcendental logic**.

Kant offered a transcendental deduction also in his **Opus Postumum**, in which he attempted to prove that **ether** is a necessary condition of the possibility of experience. This deduction occurs at another, less formal and more specific level than the one in the first *Critique*, as the concern now is no longer with a general theory of experience, but rather with a theory of the transition from the **Metaphysical Foundations of Natural Science** to **physics**.

In his *Die logischen Grundlagen der exakten Wissenschaften* (*The Logical Foundations of the Exact Sciences*) of 1910, **Paul Natorp** explicitly reaffirmed the task, set by Kant himself, of a transcendental deduction of the objective validity of the categories. However, he understood the deduction as the problem of developing the basic logical law of the synthetic unity as the basic logical functions of quantity, quality, relation, and modality. Natorp combined in this deduction what Kant had separated into a metaphysical and a transcendental deduction. The first methodical component of this deduction consisted in the explication of the basic relation of the one and the manifold, the second in the operational sequence of the steps beginning, continuation, and conclusion, steps that Natorp regarded as the application of the modal function to quantity, quality, and relation.

TRANSCENDENTAL DIALECTIC. The Second Division of the "**Transcendental Logic**" in the *Critique of Pure Reason*. Here Kant discusses chiefly the misuse of metaphysical concepts. Such misuse is inevitable because it lies in the nature of **reason**; it arises when reason makes inferences without regard to the **limits** of **sensibility**. The "Transcendental Dialectic" is therefore also characterized as the "**logic of illusion**," to be distinguished from the "logic of **truth**" of the "**Transcendental Analytic**." The goal of the 'Dialectic' is to present a "critique of illusion" and thus to effect a cleansing of reason. After an introduction, in which he discusses how **transcendental illusion** arises out of **reason**, Kant then treats in Book I transcendental **ideas** in general, before turning in Book II to the main topic of the "Transcendental Dialectic," namely, the three branches of traditional Special Metaphysics, rational **psychology**, rational **cosmology**, and rational **theology**. Kant considers that only these three types of dialectical (mis)use of reason are possible, as there are only three ways in which reason can deal with the **absolute totality** of the conditions, a totality that is itself unconditioned. However, the 'Dialectic' is not restricted to exercising a merely negative function. Aside from dispelling the transcendental illusion, it also points, as Kant shows in the appendix to this 'Division,' to a legitimate, **regulative** use of the **ideas** of reason. *See also* ANTINOMY; DIALECTIC; IDEAL OF REASON; PARALOGISM.

TRANSCENDENTAL IDEA. Having consigned the term 'idea' to the realm of **reason**, which is not directly concerned with our **cognition of objects**, and having on the other hand defined the expression '**transcendental cognition**' as referring to our a priori cognition of the concepts of objects (A 11-12/B 25), Kant seems to have constructed with the expression "transcendental idea" a self-contradiction. The same problem arises in regard to the "transcendental principles of reason" as they are discussed in the appendix to the **Transcendental Dialectic** of the *Critique of Pure Reason;* being the products of reason, these **principles** cannot be employed to generate any direct cognition of objects. Kant himself was apparently aware of some such difficulty, since at one point he cautions that it would be safer not to speak of cognition in the case of the object that corresponds to a transcendental idea, but that one should restrict oneself to speaking only of a problematic concept (A 339/B 396-97); in a similar vein, he is apparently suggesting that the principles of reason only seem to be transcendental (A 663/B 691). The case against the expressions "transcendental idea" and "transcendental principle of reason" is strengthened by a number of additional considerations. As transcendental they should be provable in an objective **deduction** and they should be necessary. But Kant did not envision an objective deduction of them, only a subjective one (A 336/B 393), nor did he think that they would be susceptible of a transcendental **exposition** in the same manner as **time** and **space** are. And the kind of **necessity** involved here cannot be understood in the same sense as in the case of the **category** of necessity; a subjective necessity is all one may hope for. There have been numerous attempts on the part of the Kant scholarship to explain this issue, but little agreement has been reached beyond the obvious conclusion that Kant used the term 'transcendental' in quite different senses.

TRANSCENDENTAL IDEALISM. This was Kant's preferred expression when he classified his own philosophy within the framework of the traditional realist-idealist dichotomy. He resorted to the alternative, though presumably equivalent expressions "**critical idealism**" and "formal idealism" only infrequently. Kant's philosophical system is idealistic insofar as it claims that we have no **cognition** of **things-in-themselves** and that our **experience** of **objects** is therefore determined by our own cognitive capabilities, that is, by the subjective **concepts** of the **understanding**. The qualifying adjectives are designed to distinguish his own brand of idealism from other philosophies that contain stronger idealistic elements. Kant maintained that his transcendental idealism was compatible with and indeed complementary to empirical **realism**. The idea that pure cognition provides the necessary conditions of the possibility of experience serves as the basis for each of the major parts of the *Critique of Pure Reason:* in the **Transcendental Aesthetic** it manifests itself as the doctrine of the ideal character of **time** and **space**, and helps to explain how **a priori** cognitions in **mathematics** are possible; in the **Transcendental Analytic** it guarantees that the concepts of the understanding are both a priori and applicable to experience, and explains how a priori cognitions in pure **physics** are possible; in the **Transcendental Dialectic** it shows how metaphysical concepts unify in a regulative manner the different cognitions of the understanding.

Kant's philosophy provided the decisive impetus to the main proponents of German idealism **Johann Gottlieb Fichte, Friedrich Wilhelm Joseph Schelling,** and **Georg Wilhelm Friedrich Hegel.** Kant himself witnessed the early part of this development during the last decade or so of his life. He expressed strong disapproval, since he judged the new movement to be a throwback to the older forms of idealism from which he had sought to distance himself. In spite of assigning in his epistemology a crucial role to the subject, Kant always emphasized the need to respect empirical input. The constraints this caveat placed on the role of pure thought were not accepted by his successors.

TRANSCENDENTAL ILLUSION. In his effort to place **philosophy** on a secure foundation, Kant thought that he not only had to point out the errors committed in the metaphysical systems of his predecessors, but that he also had to explain how such errors arose. He claimed that at least some of these fallacies were of a systematic nature, caused by the tendency, inherent in **reason,** to seek greater **cognition** than it was capable of attaining. Kant labeled such an overstepping of the **boundaries** of the legitimate usage of the human cognitive faculties "transcendental illusion." He distinguished it both from empirical (optical) illusion, which occurs when **judgment** is misled by the **imagination,** and from logical illusion, which arises from a failure to attend to a logical **rule.** While the remedy to logical illusion is simple attentiveness, which brings the illusion to an end, the remedy to transcendental illusion is problematic, given that it does not cease even when it is uncovered. Kant compares the persistence of transcendental illusion to the endurance of the illusion that the rising moon appears larger on the horizon in spite of the fact that the astronomer is not deceived. His technical explanation of the stubbornness of the transcendental illusion is based on his claim that certain fundamental rules of reason look like objective **principles,** and that this similarity leads us to confuse the subjective **necessity** of certain connections of our **concepts** with an objective necessity, that is, with a determination of **things-in-themselves** (A 293–98/B 249–55). He thinks there are three ways of committing this error, pertaining in turn to the **soul**, to the **world**, and to **God**. These kinds of **illusion** then occasion the three sections of the **Transcendental Dialectic**.

TRANSCENDENTAL LOGIC. Kant placed the second part of the "Transcendental Doctrine of Elements" of the *Critique of Pure Reason* under the title "Transcendental Logic"; this voluminous part comprises, as its two major subdivisions, the **Transcendental Analytic** and the **Transcendental Dialectic**. Kant defined the concept of "transcendental logic" as the **science** concerned with determining "the **origin**, the domain, and the objective **validity**" of the **cognitions** of **pure understanding** and of **pure reason** (A 57/B 81), claiming, furthermore, that the main task of this discipline is to explain the possibility of **synthetic judgments a priori** (A 154/B 193). He contrasted such a type of logic with general (or formal) **logic**, which abstracts from all content of cognition and deals only with the logical form of thinking.

Within **Neokantianism, Heinrich Rickert** and Emil Lask assigned specific meanings to "transcendental logic." In his famous article "Zwei Wege der Erkenntnistheorie" ("Two Ways of Epistemology," *Kant-Studies* of 1909), Rickert distinguished the objective way of transcendental logic from the subjective way of transcendental psychology. The former takes the meaning of a true proposition as its point of departure, a meaning that consists not in a being, but in a **value** that transcends the being; the latter commences with an act of judgment that is determined as the recognition of a transcendental **ought**. Lask conceived a "logic of philosophy," which has the categories of **validity** as its goal, categories that formed no part of Kant's system. Lask hoped to establish a transcendental logic that was superposed over Kant's transcendental logic.

TRANSCENDENTAL METHOD. This expression was not used by Kant himself, but it did become one of the key concepts of the **critical idealism** of the **Marburg School of Neokantianism**. According to the main representatives of this movement, **Hermann Cohen** and **Paul Natorp, philosophy** was first to refer to the **fact** of science or, analogously, to the factually existing phenomena of culture in order to gain the a priori principles of science and culture, and it was subsequently supposed to justify these principles as the "logical laying of foundations" (Cohen) or as the "differentiations of a unified nomological foundation" (Natorp). This method, inspired in a large measure by **Plato**, implies an abandonment of Kant's distinction between **sensibility** and **thought**, and, in connection with this, leads to a modification of his concepts of **experience** and **reality**. *See also* TRANSCENDENTAL ARGUMENT.

TRANSCENDENTAL OBJECT. The transcendental object resembles the **concept** of a **thing-in-itself** in several respects. It is nothing that is given in **sensibility** nor is it an **object** of **cognition**; Kant calls it nonempirical and employs several times the expression "transcendental object = X." Like the thing-in-itself, it is neither material nor a thinking being in itself, but merely the "ground of **appearances**" (A 379–80, A 288/B 344). However, it differs from the thing-in-itself in also being a concept with a fairly narrow, specific function, namely, to secure the **unity** that is required for turning the given into an object of cognition. Unfortunately, Kant neither offers a well-developed theory of this function nor does he clearly explain how the transcendental object grounds appearances. This expression remains murky not least due to the fact that most of the useful references to it occur only in the first edition of the *Critique of Pure Reason* and are dropped from the revised version of 1787. It is, for example, not clear whether Kant thought of the transcendental object as being the one ground of all appearances or whether he thought that transcendental objects would serve as different grounds of different appearances. As far as the unification of the given is concerned, Kant apparently held that the pure concept of the transcendental object would somehow help to synthesize the **manifold** of **intuition** into an object of cognition, a task that would be effected by the **transcendental unity of apperception** acting in accordance to the **categories** (A 109–10). What is reasonably clear is that separating the transcendental object from sensible data would not yield an object of cognition (A 251–52). The reason for this may be seen in Kant's claim that, when no specific manner of intuition is given, the pure category cannot determine any object, and only the thought of an object in general is expressed (A 247/B 304).

TRANSCENDENTAL PHILOSOPHY. In general any philosophical system, Kant's own or that of any of his followers, which more or less conforms to Kant's definition as a **system** of "all principles of pure reason." Historically, the usage of this expression has varied a great deal, from **Johann Gottlieb Fichte**'s understanding of transcendental philosophy as the systematic development of the human mind to the more widely accepted "investigation of the a priori conditions of the possibility of **experience**." The latter, in its turn, has been variously reinterpreted as an "examination of conditions of **validity**" or, after the linguistic turn in the 20th century, as a "study of the conditions of the possibility of meaning."

Aside from claiming that the general problem of transcendental philosophy is circumscribed by the question "how are synthetic a priori propositions possible?" (B 73), Kant otherwise used the expression in a restricted sense and therefore sparingly. He defined transcendental philosophy as a system of **concepts** "occupied not so much with **objects** but rather with our mode of **cognition** of objects insofar as this is to be possible a priori" (A 11-13/B 25-27). In accordance with the stress this definition places on cognition, Kant used the expression only within the realm of "pure, merely speculative reason," refusing to extend it to the "supreme principles of morality" (A 15/B 29). A further reason for Kant's reticence in using the label may have been related to the fact that he considered much of his effort in epistemology to serve as a mere propaedeutic to transcendental philosophy; this preparation, that is, his project of the **critique of pure reason**, presents only an outline of what the whole system of transcendental philosophy would be.

When he again came to discuss this topic in the chapter on the "**Architectonic** of Pure Reason" at the end of the *Critique of Pure Reason*, Kant correspondingly subsumed transcendental philosophy under the more general heading of **metaphysics**. The propaedeutic, which he put in the place that 'Ontology' (general metaphysics) had occupied in the philosophy of the **Leibniz-Wolff** school, was now defined as the study of "the **understanding** and reason itself in a system of all concepts and principles that are related to objects in general," and was to be distinguished from the "physiology of pure reason" as the study of "the sum total of given objects," that is, from the special metaphysics (**psychology, cosmology, theology**) of the Leibniz-Wolffian tradition (A 845-46/B 873-74).

TRANSCENDENTAL SUBJECT. *See* TRANSCENDENTAL UNITY OF APPERCEPTION.

TRANSCENDENTAL UNITY OF APPERCEPTION. Kant very likely borrowed the term 'apperception' from **Gottfried Wilhelm Leibniz**, in whose mature philosophy it signified consciousness or self-consciousness. Kant himself used the expressions 'apperception,' 'consciousness,' and 'self-consciousness' more or less interchangeably, distinguishing, however, between an empirical apperception (or consciousness, or self-consciousness) and a **transcendental** one. He considered the former, which he usually called **inner sense**, to be 'dispersed' and incapable of providing any abiding self in the stream of inner **appearances**. This task required grounding by the latter, called by Kant variously the 'pure,' 'original,' 'unchanging,' 'necessary,' 'synthetic,' or "transcendental (unity of) apperception."

Transcendental apperception derives its great importance for Kant's theoretical philosophy from the role it plays in his conception of the **understanding** and of **experience**, rather than from what it offers to our consciousness; the last mentioned boils down to "the mere **representation** of the I" (A 117) or, more precisely, to a consciousness "of myself not as I appear to myself, nor as I am in myself, but only that I am" (B 157). The primary function of transcendental apperception is to provide a **transcendental** ground for the unity of consciousness. It guarantees the **a priori** identity of the self and of the self's actions, above all by ensuring that the manifold of representations is united in one consciousness, that is, by ascertaining that the '**I think**,' the form of apperception, can accompany all my representations; if the representations could not be referred to the transcendental unity of apperception, they would be nothing for us, they would certainly not become **cognition**.

Second, transcendental apperception is the highest unity and thus the ground of the necessary **synthesis** or combination of all representations (B 131). Such a combination is an act of the subject's self-activity (B 130). Transcendental apperception is, in this sense, identical with the understanding (B 134). As the transcendental ground of all concepts, it grounds all lawfulness of all appearances and the form of all cognition of objects (B 138–39) and therefore also experience (A 112) and **nature** (A 114). Without the order supplied by the synthesis of the transcendental unity of apperception, we would have neither objects nor experience nor yet nature, and the manifold of perception would be "less than a dream" (A 112).

Kant dealt with the function and status of apperception mainly in the **"Transcendental Deduction"** of his *Critique of Pure Reason*. Although he completely rewrote this chapter for the second edition of 1787, he did not alter his views in regard to the role of apperception in any grand fashion. One significant difference he did introduce reflected the fact that the **imagination**, crucial in the early version, all but disappeared from the later account. Accordingly, apperception in the second edition was no longer supposed to ground the imagination in order to make its synthesis intellectual, as was the case in the earlier version (A 124), but was instead referred to the understanding, whose possibility it was to guarantee (B 131) and of which it formed "the first pure cognition" (B 137).

The second major change concerned the general importance of apperception for the deduction. Although it may be fairly stated that it played a very prominent role already in the first edition, it became even more central in the revamped version. Here, it not only provided Kant's point of departure, it also grounded the transcendental deduction of the **categories** more firmly than it did in the first edition, insofar as Kant stressed the logical significance of apperception for the unity of judgments (B140).

Interestingly enough, Kant completely refrained from employing transcendental apperception in the *Prolegomena*, a work composed in the period that intervened between the two editions of the first *Critique*, basing

instead the **universal** and necessary **validity** of the **judgments** of experience directly on the categories. Whether this omission was caused by Kant's willingness to experiment with an alternative conception or whether it was the consequence of his desire to produce a simplified account is difficult to determine.
Johann Gottlieb Fichte radicalized Kant's conception of the transcendental apperception by attempting to derive the whole of his idealistic system solely out of it. In doing so, he continually ameliorated his concept of the self and of self-consciousness. **Hermann Cohen** suppressed already in his commentary on Kant's theoretical philosophy the importance of transcendental apperception in favor of the supreme principle of the synthetic propositions a priori. In the further development of **Neokantianism**, the transcendental unity of apperception completely lost its philosophical relevance. *See also* PARALOGISMS; PSYCHOLOGY, SOUL.

TRUTH (*Wahrheit*). Playing on his distinction between general (formal) **logic** and **transcendental logic**, Kant claims that the mark of logical truth, namely, the adherence to the principle of contradiction, is a necessary but not sufficient criterion of material truth; failing to grasp this point and attempting to use general logic as the sole criterion of truth is dialectical and leads to **illusion**. Material truth must, in addition, agree with the laws of the **understanding** (**categories** and the **principles** of **pure understanding**), as these serve as the necessary conditions for the possibility of **objects** of **experience**; in that sense, truth is indeed necessarily the agreement of **cognition** with its object (A 58/B 82), since both cognition and object are possible only thanks to the application of the **a priori** laws of the understanding. However, this concerns only "**transcendental** truth" (A 146/B 185), that is, the general **form** of objects. Particular truths about objects must be sought empirically, although such a search stands under the guidance of the a priori laws of the understanding. Aside from this, Kant also drew the distinction between opinion, knowledge, and **belief** in terms of the different types of consciousness of truth; "opinion is taking something to be true with the consciousness that it is subjectively and objectively insufficient," believing with the consciousness that it is subjectively sufficient though objectively insufficient, and knowing with the consciousness that it is both subjectively and objectively sufficient (A 822/B 850).

- U -

UNCONDITIONED (*das Unbedingte*). See ABSOLUTE.

UNDERSTANDING (*Verstand*). One of the major **faculties** of the human **mind**. In the **pre-critical** *Inaugural Dissertation*, Kant held that the understanding could grasp things as they were in themselves (§ 4) and more or less identified it with reason (§ 3), distinguishing it only from **sensibility**. In his **critical philosophy**, he then arrived at the insight that the understanding could cognize things only as they appeared to us, and distinguished it now from both sensibility and **reason**. To this division of the powers of the **mind** corresponds the organization of the main part of the *Critique of Pure Reason*, the "Doctrine of Elements," with its divisions "**Transcendental Aesthetic**," which deals with the faculty of sensibility, "**Transcendental Analytic**," which covers the understanding, and "**Transcendental Dialectic**," which has reason as its main topic.

As the most general definition of the understanding, Kant suggests that it is the faculty of **cognition**, that is, the power of conceptual determination of material in **judgments**, which in turn comes down to the capacity to judge (A 69/B 94). The understanding is the source of pure concepts (**categories**) and **pure principles of the understanding**. Kant offers a number of different characterizations of the understanding: **spontaneity** of cognition in contrast to the **receptivity** of the sensibility; faculty of **thinking**; faculty of **concepts** and also of judgments; faculty of **rules**. All this comes to the same thing, though Kant himself prefers the last mentioned as the most accurate characterization (A 126).

Unlike sensibility, which is the faculty of **intuitions**, the (human) understanding is **discursive**, that is, it provides cognition through concepts. It *thinks* the object of intuition and does not intuit anything (A 67–68/B 92–93). However, as Kant continues to stress, if the understanding is to produce cognition, it must act on data provided by the sensibility. Kant offers a relatively straightforward account of the distinction between the understanding and reason. While the former is "a faculty of **unity** of **appearances** by means of rules," the latter "is the faculty of the unity of the rules of understanding under **principles**," that is, it applies not to **experience** or to any **object**, but to the understanding (A 302/B 359). And while the understanding produces **constitutive** concepts, generates possible experience, and moves within the bounds of experience, reason ventures beyond experience.

UNITY (*Einheit*). Although Kant's philosophy makes use of numerous divisions and distinctions, the concept of unity was very important to him and he employed it in a number of different senses. In the *Critique of Pure Reason*, the highest unity and the source of all other unity was the original, **transcendental unity of apperception**, that is, the purely formal unity of the 'I think' that would guarantee that the **manifold** of **representations** given in an intuition is mine (B 132). He distinguishes it from the empirical unity of apperception, which is properly the subject matter of **psychology** and not of **transcendental philosophy**. Kant held that it not only precedes the understanding, and hence all combination, and hence also the categories (B 131), but that it also serves as a necessary condition even of **perception** (A 123) and of **intuition** (A 98–100). By grounding the synthesis of the manifold in accordance with the **categories** and the **principles of the understanding**, this original unity makes possible the **object of experience**, and, along with it, **cognition** and the unity of experience; the last three mentioned are not given to us, but result from the action of our understanding. Even the unity of **concepts** and of **judgments** would be unthinkable without the highest unity. Kant distinguishes the (qualitative) transcendental unity of apperception from the quantitative unity that is expressed in the category of unity. He also sets it apart from the analytic unity of consciousness that is concerned with common concepts, a topic belonging to general **logic** rather than to **transcendental** one (B 133–34).

Another important sense in which Kant employed the term 'unity' was to refer to the systematic ordering on the part of **reason** of the products of the understanding; reason strives to reduce the manifold of the cognitions produced by the understanding to as small a number of principles as possible. Kant stressed that the unity of appearances produced by the understanding in accordance with rules differed significantly from the unity of reason, in that the former was **constitutive** for experience, while the latter was only regulative. Reason seeks the unconditioned, and may legitimately do so, as long as it does not pretend that it could ever attain this goal. In his **pre-critical** writings, Kant considered **God** to be this highest unity, claiming as late as in the *Inaugural Dissertation* of 1770 that the unity of the connection of substances is a consequence of the dependence of all on God (§ 20). However, in the **critical** period, all collective unity that reaches beyond the distributive synthesis of the understanding can only *aim* at the one final common point, the *focus imaginarius*, but can never achieve this **ideal**.

In addition, Kant includes as mere regulative principles of reason those of a **purposive** unity (A 687/B 715) and of a unity of **nature** (A 693/B 721). The conception of an **architectonic** unity (A 833/B 861) refers to the organization of his own transcendental philosophy.

Among the **Neokantians**, the concept of synthetic unity was taken up especially by **Paul Natorp** who conceived it as a basic relation between the one and the manifold.

UNIVERSALITY (*Allgemeinheit*). A central term for Kant, though one which he did not greatly bother to define or discuss. He held a **concept** or **judgment** to be universal if it was valid for every possible **experience**. He linked strict universality inseparably to **necessity**, and claimed that both were indications of **a priori** cognition (B 4). Ultimately, Kant would admit as universal in a strict sense of the term basically only the concepts or judgments that provide the necessary conditions of possible experience, that is, **synthetic judgments a priori**. What Kant was not greatly interested in was **empirical** or comparative universality, such as is gained by **induction**, since this could make no contribution to his search for certain **cognition**.

- V -

VAIHINGER, HANS (1852–1933). In 1897, Vaihinger established the *Kant-Studien*, in 1905, he founded the Kant Society. His other important contribution to Kantian scholarship was his massive commentary on the Preface, Introduction, and Transcendental Aesthetics of the *Critique of Pure Reason* (2 vols., 1881, 1892). The title of his main philosophical work, *Die Philosophie des Als Ob* (*The Philosophy of the As If*), aptly describes his philosophical teachings. Vaihinger himself called his philosophical standpoint "idealistic positivism." Under the influence of Arthur **Schopenhauer** and **Friedrich Albert Lange**, Vaihinger understood our whole mental world, including scientific cognition, values, and ideals, as a fabric of fictions, that is, as inadequate, subjective, imaginary kinds of representations that are, nevertheless, useful in life.

VALIDITY (*Geltung, Gültigkeit*). In the *Prolegomena*, Kant distinguished between the merely subjective validity of the **judgments** of **perception** and the objective validity of the judgments of **experience** (§§ 18–20); the latter is based on the objective validity of **synthetic** judgments **a priori** (B 197). A judgment in a strict sense of the word as a relation between concepts or propositions is objectively valid (B 142). In his *Groundwork of the Metaphysics of Morals*, Kant discussed the relationship between interest and the universal validity of a moral **law** (Sect. 3).

The concept of validity gained terminological distinction only in the philosophy of Hermann Lotze (1817–1881) and of the **Southwestern German School of Neokantianism**. Here it served to delineate **truth** as the **reality** of a **proposition** (it is true that p = p is valid) from the reality of things or events. Validity was also generally linked to **value**. **Heinrich Rickert**, dissatisfied with Lotze's attempts to interpret the validity of values in terms of Platonic **ideas**, emphasized that validity cannot be attributed on the basis of mere existence. He distinguished three stages of nonreal validity: the individual-subjective validity of the corresponding values, their universal-subjective validity, and their objective validity. Each validity is attached to a **good** and is realized in an act. These classifications and relations apply not only in the theoretical realm but also in the ethical and aesthetic ones. Inspired by German Idealism, **Bruno Bauch** attributed validity also to relations between objects; he distinguished this from the validity of judgments, admitting, however, a reciprocal relationship between the two.

VALUE (*Wert*). Kant touched on the concept of value in the two parts of his *Metaphysics of Morals*. He distinguished between an absolute and a relative value. Things that are useful have a relative value, for which a price is paid. In his *Doctrine of Right* Kant defined price as "a public judgment in regard to the value of a thing" (§ 31). If one were to apply this type of assessment to human beings, it would translate into the notion that the price of a **person** was the external value of his or her utility to others. However, as Kant emphasized in his *Doctrine of Virtue*, a person is an **end** in himself or herself, possesses an **absolute** inner worth, and is therefore exalted above all price (§ 11). Because humans are ends in themselves, Kant attributes an absolute value or worth both to the good **will** and to the being of a person. The moral subject is withdrawn from the realm of relative value, that is, from the market.

Hermann Cohen took up in his *Ethik des reinen Willens* Kant's linkage of value and worth. He considered value as a basic concept of political economics, for which the value of a thing is determined by the value of labor required to produce it. But by connecting the value of labor with the worth of the person of the laborer, he tied Kant's concept of relative value back to his concept of the absolute value of the human being. Hermann Lotze's (1817–1881) extension of the ethical conception of value was motivated by his wish to apply the concept of value, which was closely linked to the concept of the absolute **good**, to other realms of mental life. First, it was applied to **beauty**, which was also understood as a "**relation** valuable in itself." This, however, would tend to transform the moral worth of the rational person into just one value among others. And such a pluralization gave rise to the problem of the mode of being of values. **Wilhelm Windelband** based values on valuations and thus on a valuing **consciousness**. However, he did not conceive this consciousness to be simply free, but considered it to be conducted by the so-called normal laws, that is, by universally valid valuations that serve as the **transcendental** conditions of the

cognition of objects. He thus established the value character of theoretical **propositions**, founding it on the basis of his distinction between **judgment** (*Urteil*) and assessment (*Beurteilung*). In this way, Windelband adhered to Kant's advocacy of the preeminence of **practical reason**. The assessment of the contents of a judgment as to their **truth** value is carried out by means of an inquiry into their validity. Whatever is valid possesses the value of truth. **Heinrich Rickert** explicitly defined epistemology as "the science of theoretical values." By characterizing truth as a value, he ruled out the possibility that the predicate 'true' could be applied to a mere existent, thus undermining any metaphysical doctrine of being. The **a priori** character of cognition that is established by epistemology consists in transcendentally valid theoretical values that build the "transcendental object," that is, the object in accordance to which all thought that is true must proceed.

VIRTUE (*Tugend*). Kant abandons the traditional concept of virtue that was linked to custom, manners, and happiness, describing virtue as the "will's conformity with every **duty**, based on a firm **disposition**" (MM, Ak 6, p. 395). This firmness of the disposition consists in the "strength of the **maxim**" in fulfilling a duty; the strength is recognized by the obstacles, that is, natural **inclinations** that block the path to the fulfillment of duty, that have been surmounted (p. 394). As Kant explains in his *Religion within the Boundaries of Mere Reason*, what is required in order to approach the ideal of virtue (*virtus noumenon*) is, on the one hand, a thorough "revolution in the disposition," and, on the other, a "gradual reformation in the mode of sense" (Ak 6, pp. 47–48). Unfortunately, human nature being what it is, it is necessary to recommence this endeavor time and again (MM, Ak 6, p. 409). Against Friedrich Schiller's criticism of his concept of duty, Kant defends himself in his *Religion* by pointing out that the aesthetic characteristic or temperament of virtue does not consist in a slavish state of mind, but in a joyous heart (Ak 6, pp. 23–24n.). The relation of virtue and **happiness** is described as follows: virtue as "the **dignity** to be happy" builds the supreme condition of all that is worthy of being desired, but virtue constitutes the highest **good** only in conjunction with happiness (CrPR, Ak 5, pp. 110–11).

In accordance with his division of the *Metaphysics of Morals* into a doctrine of right and a doctrine of virtue, Kant, taking a clue from the distinction between perfect and imperfect duties, differentiates between duties of **right** and duties of virtue. The former are external and of "narrow obligation." The latter are of "wide obligation," and this obligation does not concern **actions**, but maxims of actions (Ak 6, p. 390); their end is one's own perfection or the happiness of others (pp. 391ff.).

Hermann Cohen concentrated in his theory of virtue, which constitutes the last part of his ethics, on the subjective, affective aspect of the implementation of morality in the life of individuals. As the affective foundation of virtue, Cohen identified honor or dignity. The first degree virtues based on this are truthfulness, courage, and justice; on the affect of love are based the second degree virtues of modesty, fidelity, and humanity. **Paul Natorp** developed in his *Sozialpädagogik* (1899) a theory of virtue with Platonic overtones; it is oriented on the three levels of human activity of drive, choice, and rational will. Virtue is for Natorp "the right composition of human activity, in accordance with its own law" on each of these levels (purity, courage or moral energy, truth). What is innovative is the linkage between this individualistic ethics of virtue and social education as the "theory of the formation of the will on a communal basis."

VOID (*Leere*) *see* ATOM.

- W -

WAR. Kant had an ambivalent attitude toward war. On the one hand, he condemned it as the "source of all evil and the corruption of morals" (Ak 7, p. 86), or as the "greatest hindrance to the moral," and he expressed the hope that in humankind's progress toward a better future offensive war would completely disappear (Ak 7, p. 93). On the other hand, he found that war had something **sublime** about it, if it was "conducted with order and reverence for civil rights" (Ak 5, p. 263), but, above all, war served, at "the cultural stage, at which mankind is still standing" (Ak 8, p. 121) to develop "all talents . . . to the highest degree" (Ak 5, p. 433). For, on the basis of his philosophy of history, Kant was convinced that **nature** was using war and the readiness for it as a means to attain, "after many devastations, revolutions, and even complete exhaustion," a situation between countries that resembles a civic constitution within a country; he labeled such an association of countries "league of nations" (*Völkerbund*) (Ak 8, pp. 24–28).

WINDELBAND, WILHELM (1848–1915). The founding member of the **Southwestern German School of Neokantianism**. Claiming, like many **Neokantians**, that the best way to understand Kant was to move beyond him, Windelband developed a **transcendental philosophy** of value. He maintained that even theoretical propositions contained values, that, for example, true and false do not enlarge the sphere of cognition, but express approval or disapproval. Logical **laws** were understood as norms that dictate how we ought to think. Although values were for Windelband not objective, since they were the products of a **consciousness**, he did admit "generally valid values" ("normal laws"), grounding them as the transcendental conditions of the cognition of **objects** in a so-called normal consciousness, a consciousness whose existence he postulated. Windelband's emphasis on values or interests enabled him to distinguish between the natural and the historical **sciences** on the basis of their different interests: the former aim to master nature and thus seek to discover general laws, producing 'nomothetic' cognition; the latter are concerned with describing unique events and yield 'idiographic' cognition. This distinction was developed further by Windelband's student **Heinrich Rickert**.

WILL. A key concept in Kant's **ethics**, one which plays a prominent role especially in his *Groundwork of the Metaphysics of Morals*. Under will, Kant understands the faculty of **desire**, insofar as it has its inner ground of determination in the **reason** of the subject. The will is therefore identical with "**practical reason.**" Kant distinguishes, more or less consistently, the will (*Wille*) from the "faculty (or power) of choice" (*Willkür, arbitrium*), mistranslated by Norman Kemp Smith as 'will,' but rendered more suitably in the recent effort by Paul Guyer and Allen W. Wood. "Faculty of choice" refers to the relation of the faculty of desire to **action**, but in such a manner that the faculty of choice may be determined either by sensuous **inclinations** or by pure reason; in the case of the former, Kant speaks of an "animal faculty of choice" (*arbitrium brutum*), in the case of the latter he uses the expression "free faculty of choice" (*liberum arbitrium*). The human power of choice is characterized by the fact that it can determine itself independently of sensuous inclinations to act out of pure will (A 802/B 830; MM, Ak 6, p. 213). *See also* AUTONOMY, HEAUTONOMY, HETERONOMY; GOOD.

WOLFF, CHRISTIAN (1679–1754). The most influential early follower of **Gottfried Wilhelm Leibniz**. The label "Leibniz-Wolffian School" gained prominence already during the first half of the 18th century. Wolffian philosophy came to dominate the German intellectual scene for decades, and it also made more or less significant inroads into Scandinavia, Eastern Europe, Holland, Switzerland, and even France. Wolff's career as a professor of philosophy started at the University of Halle, from where he was expelled in 1723, in good part because he defended **determinism** against Pietist theologians. Subsequently, he taught philosophy at the university of Marburg, before being reinstated in Halle by Frederick the Great in 1740.

An extremely prolific author, Wolff dealt with all areas of knowledge, including philosophy, mathematics, science, jurisprudence, and economics. He wrote his compendia at first in German, subsequently mostly in Latin. Aside from his adherence to Leibniz, Wolff was also greatly influenced by **René Descartes**, and by the neo-scholastic philosophy of Francisco Suárez (1548–1617) and his 17th-century followers. However, Wolff did not defend Leibniz blindly, abandoning, for instance, the central Leibnizian theory of the monads and generally tending to reduce metaphysics to logical analysis. His own thought was highly rationalistic. He took the principles of contradiction and of sufficient reason as his point of departure (attempting to derive the latter from the former). He proceeded systematically, borrowing his demonstrative method in part from mathematics. His writings have often been criticized as pedantic and as ruthlessly boring, though he must be given credit for having developed German philosophical terminology.

The young Kant stood more or less squarely within the Leibniz-Wolff tradition, though, along with other members of this school, he did not accept any of its teachings uncritically. The most heavily Wolffian of Kant's **pre-critical** writings is the *Nova Dilucidatio* of 1755, in which Kant defends Wolff's determinism against Christian August Crusius (1715–1775), one of the major critics of the school (Ak 1, pp. 401–5). However, even at this early stage, Kant already began to distance himself from his famous predecessors, for example, by refusing to unreservedly accept the principles of contradiction and of sufficient reason as the starting points of philosophy. Kant's doubts about the ability of the logical **analysis** of concepts for discovering truth were further expressed in his *Attempt to Introduce Negative Magnitudes into Philosophy* of 1763, in which he argued that there is not only logical contradiction in philosophy but also a real one. This process ultimately culminated in Kant's discovery of the **synthetic judgments a priori**. A further explicit break with the Leibniz-Wolff school occurred in the *Inaugural Dissertation* of 1770, in which Kant rejected the claim that sensible data are merely confused **concepts** of the **understanding** (§ 7), and where he correspondingly elevated **sensibility** to a separate and equal **faculty** of the **mind**.

In his **critical** period, Kant further separated his thought from that of Wolff, though this process of rejection often left its mark on Kant's own philosophical system. Wolff's distinction of philosophy into a general and a special metaphysics, for instance, was transformed: the former was remade into Kant's **Transcendental Aesthetics** and **Transcendental Analytic**, while Wolff's division of special metaphysics into rational cosmology, rational psychology, and natural theology was mirrored in the **Transcenden-**

tal Dialectics of the *Critique of Pure Reason*. On the whole, Kant continued to maintain well into the 1790s the view that the Leibniz-Wolff school exemplified the **dogmatic** method, which had to be overcome by skepticism and eventually by a critical examination of the human cognitive faculties. Wolff is thus always criticized by Kant for his insufficiently critical stance toward the capabilities of reason.

However, though Wolff's thought was in Germany in many ways replaced by Kant's, elements of it were retained by post-Kantian idealistic philosophy. Thus, for example, **Karl Leonhard Reinhold, Johann Gottlieb Fichte**, and **Georg Wilhelm Friedrich Hegel** all returned to Wolff's attempt to ground philosophy in one single principle.

WORLD *(Welt)*. In his **pre-critical** writings, Kant used the word in the sense of a conglomerate of interconnected things, claiming that it is possible that there could be uncounted such worlds; the components of each world would then be unconnected with the components of the other worlds (Ak 1, pp. 22, 414). In a similar vein, throughout the *Universal Natural History and Theory of the Heavens* of 1755, Kant speaks of planetary and stellar systems or of galaxies as worlds that arise on the basis of general mechanical laws, again admitting the possibility of a plurality of such worlds. However, in the *Inaugural Dissertation* of 1770, Kant began to conceive of the notion of a world that is in some way unattainable. He discussed the fact that the **sensibility** can join parts without ever reaching a whole (world) that is itself not a part, though at this point Kant still thought that our **understanding** could grasp the concept of an unchangeable, essential form of the world (§§ 1-2).

In the *Critique of Pure Reason*, 'world' was still viewed as the subject of **cosmology**, but Kant now classified it only as an **idea**, that is, not as an **object** of possible **experience**, and therefore not as a legitimate object of **cognition**. If one made the mistake of treating the world as an object of cognition, for example, if one attempted to define its spatial or temporal boundaries or the limits of its composition or division, one would become enmeshed in contradictions, that is, in **antinomies**. In this context, Kant admits that 'world' is often taken to mean the same as '**nature**,' but he insists on clearly distinguishing the two concepts. World, in Kant's own terms, "signifies the mathematical whole of all appearances and the totality of their synthesis in the great as well as in the small, that is, in their progress through composition as well as through division" (A 418/B 446), or, similarly, "in the transcendental sense the word 'world' signifies the absolute totality of the sum total of existing things" (A 419/B 447). Nature, on the other hand, is not just an idea, it is an object of cognition. In the section on the antinomies, Kant generally ascribes to 'world' or to 'world-con-cepts' attributes such as an "absolute totality in the synthesis of appearances" or an unconditioned totality (A 408/B 434).

Not directly linked to but consistent with this antinomial sense of the term, Kant criticizes the distinction, employed especially in the Leibniz-Wolff school and to some extent also by himself in his **pre-critical** inaugural dissertation *De Mundi Sensibilis atque Intelligibilis Forma et Principiis*, between a sensible and an intelligible world. He claimed that such a dichotomy misleadingly suggests that the world of sense comprises the sum total of **appearances** so far as it is intuited, while the world of understanding is the connection of the appearances according to the general **laws** of the understanding. Instead, Kant's own, critical period distinction between the human powers of sensibility and understanding cuts across the older distinction: he now stresses that the understanding can only be used in regard to appearances (that is, the world of sense), but not beyond (A 256–57/B 312–13).

However, although no cognition of intelligible objects or of an intelligible world is possible, Kant does admit the idea of an intelligible world in the sense of a **moral** world. Such a world would be in conformity with moral laws and it would be free from all elements of sensibility, that is, from all impurities of human nature (A 808/B 836). In such a world, **humans** would be considered as **noumena** and would be governed by the **causality** of **freedom**. Accordingly, in the *Groundwork of the Metaphysics of Morals*, Kant describes such an intelligible world as a world of rational beings, as a **kingdom of ends**, in which all **persons** as members give their own **laws** (Ak 4, p. 438). However, as Kant continually stresses, such a world is only an *idea* of practical reason, since humans always are, as a matter of fact, also parts of the sensible world.

In the *Critique of Judgment*, Kant elaborates on the legitimate **regulative** use of the term 'world' that is suggested in the antinomies; we are now allowed to *think* of a world as a purposive whole. As Kant argues, if we recognize that the human being as a moral being is the **purpose** of creation, then we have a ground "for regarding the world as a whole connected in accordance with purposes and as a system of final causes" (§ 86).

BIBLIOGRAPHY

Under the heading "Primary Sources," we first list the four most common German language editions, namely the so-called *Akademie*-Edition, the *Cassirer*-Edition, the *Weischedel*-Edition, and the *Meiner*-Edition. The first of these is generally considered to be the standard edition, though some of its volumes are outdated and user unfriendly; this latter fact explains the frequent recourse on the part of German readers to the other editions; it also accounts for the plans for a revision of at least some of the older volumes. In spite of these shortcoming, the *Akademie*-Edition serves as the standard for most of the English-language renderings. The section "English Translations" includes first the volumes that have already appeared of the Cambridge Edition, which will likely become standard for English language Kant scholarship, then a fairly large number of the other important translations.

Under the heading "Secondary Sources," we offer only a small selection from the very large mass of scholarly literature dealing with Kant. Preference is given to recent titles (except in the section "Kantianism") and to book publications; articles are included only sparingly. Furthermore, the list is weighted in favor of English-language works; for works that have been translated into English only the translation is included (again with the exception of the section "Kantianism"). The "Secondary Sources" are subdivided in a straightforward, standard manner. The following comments should nevertheless help to explain the structure of the list and to correlate the titles to Kant's own works. Our recommendations for further reading along with our comments are necessarily even more contingent than our overall selection; it is simply not possible to list all the works that have proven helpful to us and/or from which the reader could benefit in some respect or other.

Among the "Reference Works," the two Kant dictionaries by Rudolf Eisler (*Kant-Lexikon*) and Howard Caygill (*A Kant Dictionary*) are both useful, though the former, mainly a collection of quotes, is somewhat outdated while the latter includes a great deal of historical material with emphasis on scope rather than on precision. From the section "Historical Background and Context," we would highly recommend Lewis White Beck's *Early German Philosophy*, which not only provides a wealth of detailed, reliable background information on German philosophy in the 17th

292 Bibliography

and 18th centuries but also contains a very good introductory chapter on Kant's life and thought.

Under "Biographies," we have included books that deal primarily with Kant's life, even if they often contain valuable commentaries on Kant's writings; conversely, some of the titles presented under "General Surveys" include important biographical data. Among the biographies, Manfred Kuehn's recent *Kant: A Biography* largely supersedes all previous efforts in this area. Among the "General Surveys," the collections of essays edited by Lewis White Beck (*Kant Studies Today*), Paul Guyer (*The Cambridge Companion to Kant*) and Robert Paul Wolff (*Kant: A Collection of Critical Essays*) include articles by leading Kant scholars and cover a large part of Kant's work. Especially useful for beginners are John Kemp's *The Philosophy of Kant* and Otfried Höffe's *Immanuel Kant*.

The section "Pre-critical Writings" contains works that concentrate on Kant's early thought, that is, on the period before the publication of the *Critique of Pure Reason* in 1781. The recently published collection of essays edited by Tom Rockmore (*New Essays on the Precritical Kant*) provides a good overview of the scholarly endeavor that is presently being devoted to this period of Kant's life, while Martin Schönfeld's *The Philosophy of the Young Kant* offers an interesting reading of the interrelation between Kant's early pieces. Even if one ultimately does not accept all of Schönfeld's interpretation, the book is invaluable for its detailed and accurate description of the intellectual setting, in which the pre-critical Kant wrote and in which he finally came to work out his critical philosophy. Additional material on the young Kant can be found in the biographies as well as in numerous works on the mature philosophy, in which the continuities and discontinuities in Kant's lifelong intellectual development are noted.

The titles listed under "Epistemology and Metaphysics" deal almost exclusively with the *Critique of Pure Reason* and the *Prolegomena to Any Future Metaphysics*. The vast majority of these titles concentrate on particular aspects of Kant's theoretical philosophy; our recommendations are restricted only to those works that treat the whole or at least large parts of this subject matter. Of the commentaries on the first *Critique*, Norman Kemp Smith's *Commentary to Kant's "Critique of Pure Reason"* is still useful, in spite of its many peculiarities. Far more solid is H. J. Paton's *Kant's Metaphysic of Experience;* unfortunately, it does not cover the "Transcendental Dialectic." The much more recent commentary edited by Georg Mohr and Marcus Willaschek (*Immanuel Kant: Kritik der reinen Vernunft*) does cover the whole of the first *Critique*, and is useful, even if the articles in English or German by the different contributors explain the different parts of the *Critique* from different perspectives and are of an uneven quality. Henry E. Allison's *Kant's Transcendental Idealism* and Paul Guyer's *Kant and the Claims of Knowledge* provide very helpful detailed overviews of Kant's epistemology. Gottfried Martin's *Kant's Metaphysics and Theory of Science* can be recommended to intermediate students of Kant. Martin discusses a number of problems that an attentive first-time reader of the *Critique of Pure Reason* is likely to encounter.

Under "Philosophy of Science" are included mostly titles having to do with the *Metaphysical Foundations of Natural Science*, the *Opus Postumum*, and those aspects of the first *Critique* that are closely connected to Kant's reflections on science. As a commentary on the *Metaphysical Foundations*, Jules Vuillemin's *Physique et métaphysique kantiennes* is still very helpful, if only for its examination of the relationship of the principles of Kant's philosophy of physics to the "Principles of Pure Understanding" from the first *Critique*. Also useful are the collection of essays edited by Robert E. Butts (*Kant's Philosophy of Physical Science*) and the exhaustive commentary by Konstantin Pollok, *Kants "Metaphysische Anfangsgründe der Naturwissenschaft."* On the *Opus postumum*, one may consult the collection of articles edited by the "Forum für Philosophie Bad Homburg" (*Übergang*) and Michael Friedman's *Kant and the Exact Sciences*, which discusses the significance of the developments in physics and especially chemistry for Kant's late philosophy of science.

The section "Moral Philosophy" contains works focused mainly on the *Critique of Practical Reason, The Groundwork of the Metaphysics of Morals*, and the *Metaphysical First Principles of the Doctrine of Virtue*, that is, the second part of *The Metaphysics of Morals*. Lewis White Beck's *Commentary on Kant's Critique of Practical Reason* is the standard overview of Kant's moral philosophy, especially of those parts that are presented in the second *Critique* and in the *Groundwork*. Guyer's *Kant on Freedom, Law, and Happiness* contains a more recent as well as a more comprehensive assessment of Kant's ethics. One aspect that Beck did not much consider is the teleological aspect of morality and, related to this, the problem of bridging the gap between Kant's epistemology and ethics. These questions have since been addressed by Thomas Auxter (*Kant's Moral Teleology*), John E. Atwell (*Ends and Principles in Kant's Moral Thought*) and Richard L. Velkley (*Freedom and the End of Reason*). A staunch defense of the transcendental character of Kant's ethics is offered by Henry E. Allison (*Kant's Theory of Freedom*), while Sandra Jane Fairbanks (*Kantian Moral Theory*) presents an appraisal that is at least equally critical. Worthy of mention are Christine M. Korsgaard's *Creating the Kingdom of Ends*, in which the realization of morals in a community is explored, and Onora O'Neill's *Con-*

structions of Reason, in which the attempt is made to apply Kant's ethics to questions of international relations. The titles included under "Political Philosophy" deal with Kant's smaller works, such as his essay on *Perpetual Peace* as well as with the *Metaphysical First Principles of the Doctrine of Right*, the first part of *The Metaphysics of Morals*. A number of these titles discuss the implications of Kant's ethics for his political thought. Patrick Riley's *Kant's Political Philosophy* offers a useful overview for beginners as well as for more advanced students of Kant. A historically oriented presentation of Kant's philosophy of peace may be found in Georg Cavallar's *Kant and the Theory and Practice of International Right*. The relationship of Kant's political thought to his other work is explored in Hanna Arendt's *Lectures on Kant's Political Philosophy*, in which the dependence on the *Critique of Judgment* is especially emphasized, and in Hans Saner's *Kant's Political Thought*, where it is argued that peace is the fundamental idea on which Kant's theoretical and practical philosophy converge. The question of the present-day relevance of Kant's political philosophy is examined in the collections of essays edited by Ronald Beiner and William James Booth (*Kant and Political Philosophy*) and James Bohman and Matthias Lutz-Bachmann (*Perpetual Peace*). The social aspects of Kant's political thought are dealt with by Alexander Kaufman (*Welfare in the Kantian State*), who explores the implications of Kant's political theory for questions of social justice, and by Harry Van der Linden (*Kantian Ethics and Socialism*), who examines Kant from the perspective of the tradition of the Neokantian concept of ethical socialism.

The works concentrating on the *Critique of Judgment* are subdivided, in accordance with Kant's own organization, into two sections, the first of which concentrates on works on aesthetics, the second on teleology. Among the former, Henry E. Allison's *Kant's Theory of Taste* offers a comprehensive, systematic study that closely follows Kant's own text on aesthetics. The same may be said of Paul Guyer's *Kant and the Claims of Taste*, except that here, the author chooses a more topical approach. In her *Ästhetik der Sitten*, Birgit Recki deals with the relationship between Kant's aesthetics and his moral philosophy; Wolfgang Wieland's *Urteil und Gefühl* is a precise investigation of the role of the faculty of judgment in Kant's philosophy. On teleology, Peter McLaughlin in his *Kant's Critique of Teleology in Biological Explanation* presents a concise overview of Kant's reception of contemporary biology.

Under "Philosophy of History, Anthropology, and Empirical Psychology" are listed works dealing essentially with Kant's essays on history or with his late publication *Anthropology from a Pragmatic Point of View*.

Helpful here is Reinhard Brandt's commentary on the *Anthropology*, while John H. Zammito (*Kant, Herder, and the Birth of Anthropology*) elucidates the historical background.

Under "Philosophy of Religion" are included titles concerned especially with Kant's *Religion within the Limits of Reason Alone*. Especially useful is Stephen Palmquist's *Kant's Critical Religion*, in which both the historical situation and the philosophical issues relevant to Kant's conception of religion and theology are discussed; for the latter, one may also consult Allen W. Wood's *Kant's Rational Theology*.

The section "Kantianism" includes works that were heavily influenced by Kant and that the reader would consult less for learning about Kant himself than for learning about the particular author of that book. Of course, these works are often highly instructive for providing a broader perspective on Kant's own thought as well. The selection here is even more parsimonious than in the rest of the bibliography, in part because we have had to take into consideration works spanning all of the 19th and early 20th centuries and not just recent titles, in part because the number of works that pertain to Kantianism in one way or another is immense. We have therefore restricted our selection only to works in which the influence of Kant is both profound and conspicuous. This section is divided into five subsections in order to better reflect the historical development of Kantianism. The early reactions to Kant mainly in Germany, but to some extent also in Great Britain, are documented in the first subsection; they came from writers representing a variety of philosophical directions. The next two subsections document the rise and spread of the movement known as Neokantianism. The development of Kantianism in the English-speaking world did not proceed in parallel with that in Germany, and it is documented in the fourth subsection. Finally, the last subsection presents a small selection of 20th-century titles that were heavily influenced by Kant. Secondary sources dealing with Kantianism are listed under the last heading "Kant's Influence." In this section, we have largely avoided listing the numerous studies on post-Kantian German Idealism (especially on Georg Wilhelm Friedrich Hegel) as well as those on Martin Heidegger, in spite of the fact that many include background material on Kant. (For ample bibliographical as well as philosophical material on Hegel's and Heidegger's relationship to Kant see *The Historical Dictionary of Hegel's Philosophy* and *The Historical Dictionary of Heidegger*, respectively.)

For books with two or more places of publication we have listed only the first one. With the exception of the *Kant-Studies*, we have omitted mentioning the series within which the books have appeared.

There are numerous bibliographies available to the reader, in addition to those included in titles dealing with Kant's philosophy. Worth mentioning are the lists that have been published in the *Kant-Studies* since 1969 as well as the running "Bibliography of Kant Literature" that is released periodically by the North American Kant Society. Highly useful is also Margit Ruffing's *Kant-Bibliographie 1945–1990* (see infra under "Reference Works"). If the continuation proceeds as planned, the volumes should eventually provide a very exhaustive list of both primary and secondary sources pertaining to Kant.

Articles on Kant are published in many different journals and collections of essays. However, two journals are devoted nearly exclusively to Kant, namely, the *Kant-Studies*, founded in 1896 (for information on the history of the journal see *Kant-Studies* 87, 1996: 385–89), and the *Kantian Review*, published since 1997 and more specifically focused on Kantian themes in today's philosophy. In addition, the *Proceedings of the International Kant Congresses (Akten der Internationalen Kant Kongresse)* include a wealth of articles; especially noteworthy are the proceedings of the congresses held in Rochester (1970), Mainz (1974, 1981, 1990), Pennsylvania State University (1985), Memphis (1995), and Berlin (2000).

There are a number of websites devoted specifically to Kant. The following are especially helpful and may be expected to significantly exceed the customarily low life expectancy of material posted on the Internet: www.uni-marburg.de/kant (website of the *Kant Forschungsstelle* of the University of Marburg; includes a number of links to other relevant sites); www.uni-mainz.de/~kant/kfs (website of the *Kant Forschungsstelle* of the University of Mainz; it also includes the home page of the *Kant-Studies*); naks.ucsd.edu (website of the North American Kant Society).

OUTLINE OF BIBLIOGRAPHY

I. Primary Sources
   A. Kant's Works: German Editions
   B. English Translations

II. Secondary Sources
   A. Reference Works
   B. Historical Background and Context
   C. Biographies
   D. General Surveys
   E. Pre-critical Writings

F. Epistemology and Metaphysics
G. Philosophy of Science
H. Moral Philosophy
I. Political Philosophy and Philosophy of Law
J. The Third Critique: Comprehensive Studies and Aesthetics
K. The Third Critique: Teleology and Philosophy of Biology
L. Philosophy of History, Anthropology, and Empirical Psychology
M. Philosophy of Religion
N. Kantianism
O. Studies on Kant's Influence and on Kantianism

I. PRIMARY SOURCES

A. KANT'S WORKS: GERMAN EDITIONS

The Akademie-*Edition*

Kants gesammelte Schriften, ed. (Königlich) Preussische Akademie der Wissenschaften, subsequently Deutsche Akademie der Wissenschaften. Thirty-four parts in 29 volumes. Berlin: Georg Reimer, subsequently Walter de Gruyter, 1900– . The edition is divided into four parts: *Werke* (volumes 1–9), *Briefe* (volumes 10–13), *Handschriftlicher Nachlass* (volumes 14–23), *Vorlesungen* (volumes 24–29).

Other 20th-Century Editions

Ernst Cassirer, ed. *Werke,* 2 vols. Berlin: Bruno Cassirer, 1912–1922.

Wilhelm Weischedel, ed. *Werke in sechs Bänden.* Wiesbaden: Insel Verlag, 1956–1962. Reprinted in 12 vols. with the original pagination by Suhrkamp Verlag, Frankfurt am Main, 1968. Unlike the *Akademie* edition, this contains German translations of Kant's several Latin works.

Individual works are also published in the *Philosophische Bibliothek* of Felix Meiner Verlag, Hamburg. These include:
Anthropologie in pragmatischer Hinsicht. Ed. Reinhard Brandt. 2000.
Briefwechsel. Ed. Rudolf Malter. 3rd ed. 1986 (includes letters that are not in the *Akademie* edition).
Der Streit der Fakultäten. Ed. Piero Giordanetti. 2004.

Die Religion innerhalb der Grenzen der bloßen Vernunft. Ed. Bettina Stangneth. 2003.

Grundlegung zur Metaphysik der Sitten. Ed. Bernd Kraft, Dieter Schönecker. 1999.

Kritik der reinen Vernunft. Ed. Jens Timmermann. 1998.

Kritik der praktischen Vernunft. Eds. Horst D. Brandt, Heiner F. Klemme. 2003.

Kritik der Urteilskraft. Ed. Heiner F. Klemme. 2001.

Metaphysische Anfangsgründe der Naturwissenschaft. Ed. Konstantin Pollok. 1997.

Metaphysische Anfangsgründe der Rechtslehre: Metaphysik der Sitten, Erster Teil. Ed. Bernd Ludwig. 1986.

Metaphysische Anfangsgründe der Tugendlehre: Metaphysik der Sitten, Zweiter Teil. Ed. Mary Gregor, Bernd Ludwig. 1990.

Prolegomena zu einer jeden künftigen Metaphysik. Ed. Konstantin Pollok. 2001.

Edition on CD-ROM

Kant im Kontext II. Komplettausgabe. Berlin: Karsten Worm, 2003 (includes all of Kant's own published and unpublished work).

B. ENGLISH TRANSLATIONS

The Cambridge Edition of the Works of Immanuel Kant, Cambridge: Cambridge University Press, 1992– , is in the process of becoming the English-language standard edition, likely to supersede most earlier translations. It will provide new or revised translations of all of Kant's published works and selections from his correspondence, notes, and lectures. The following volumes have already appeared:

Correspondence. Trans. Arnulf Zweig, 1999.

Critique of the Power of Judgment. Ed. Paul Guyer, trans. Paul Guyer, Eric Matthews, 2000.

Critique of Pure Reason. Trans. Paul Guyer, Allen W. Wood, 1997.

Lectures on Ethics. Ed. Peter Heath, J. B. Schneewind, trans. Peter Heath, 1996.

Lectures on Logic. Trans. J. Michael Young, 1992.

Lectures on Metaphysics. Trans. Karl Ameriks, Steve Naragon, 1997.

Opus postumum. Ed. Eckart Förster, trans. Eckart Förster, Michael Rosen, 1993.
Practical Philosophy. Trans. Mary J. Gregor, 1996.
Religion and Rational Theology. Trans. Allen W. Wood, George di Giovani, 1996.
Theoretical Philosophy, 1755–1770. Trans. David Walford, Ralf Meerbote, 1992.
Theoretical Philosophy after 1781. Trans. Henry Allison, Peter Heath, 2002.

Selection of Other Important Translations

Anthropology from a Pragmatic Point of View. Trans. Mary J. Gregor. The Hague: Martinus Nijhoff, 1974.
Anthropology from a Pragmatic Point of View. Trans. Victor Lyle Dowdell, ed. Hans H. Rudnick. Carbondale: Southern Illinois University Press, 1978.
The Conflict of the Faculties. Trans. Mary J. Gregor. New York: Abaris, 1979 (new ed., Lincoln: University of Nebraska Press, 1992).
Critick of Pure Reason. Trans. Francis Haywood. London: William Pickering, 1838.
Critique of Judgment. Trans. J. H. Bernard. New York: Hafner, 1951.
Critique of Judgment: Including the First Introduction. Trans. Werner S. Pluhar. Indianapolis: Hackett, 1987.
Critique of Practical Reason. Trans. Lewis White Beck. Indianapolis: Bobbs-Merrill, 1956.
Critique of Practical Reason. Trans. Mary J. Gregor. Cambridge: Cambridge University Press, 1997.
Critique of Practical Reason, and Other Writings in Moral Philosophy. Trans. Lewis White Beck. Chicago: University of Chicago Press, 1949 (reprinted, New York: Garland, 1976).
Critique of Pure Reason. Trans. J. M. D. Meiklejohn. London: Bohn, 1855 (reprinted, New York: Prometheus, 1990).
Critique of Pure Reason. Trans. Max Müller. London: Macmillan, 1881 (new ed., New York: Doubleday, 1966).
Critique of Pure Reason. Trans. Norman Kemp Smith. London: Macmillan, 1929.
Critique of Pure Reason: A Revised and Expanded Translation Based on Meiklejohn. Ed. Vasilis Politis. London: Everyman, 1993.

Critique of Pure Reason. Trans. Werner Pluhar. Indianapolis: Hackett, 1996.

The Doctrine of Virtue. Trans. Mary J. Gregor. New York: Harper & Row, 1964.

Dreams of a Spirit-Seer. Trans. E. F. Goerwitz. London: Swan Sonnenschein, 1900 (reprinted, with an introduction by Frank Sewall, Bristol: Thoemmes, 1992).

The Educational Theory of Immanuel Kant. Trans. Edward Franklin Buchner. Philadelphia: J. B. Lippincott, 1904.

First Introduction to the Critique of Judgment. Trans. James Haden. Indianapolis: Bobbs-Merrill, 1965.

Foundations of the Metaphysics of Morals and What Is Enlightenment? Trans. Lewis White Beck. Indianapolis: Bobbs-Merrill, 1959. (*Foundations* reissued with Critical Essays, ed. Robert Paul Wolff. Indianapolis: Bobbs-Merrill, 1969.)

Groundwork of the Metaphysics of Morals. Trans. Mary J. Gregor. Cambridge: Cambridge University Press, 1998.

The Kant-Eberhard Controversy: An English Translation together with Supplementary Materials and a Historical-Analytic Introduction of Immanuel Kant's On a Discovery According to Which Any New Critique of Pure Reason Has Been Made Superfluous by an Earlier One. Trans. Henry E. Allison. Baltimore: Johns Hopkins University Press, 1973.

Kant: On History. Ed. Lewis White Beck, trans. Lewis White Beck, Robert E. Anchor, Emil Fackenheim. Indianapolis: Bobbs-Merrill, 1963.

Kant's Critique of Judgement. Trans. James Creed Meredith. Oxford: Clarendon Press, 1952.

Kant's Critique of Practical Reason and Other Works on the Theory of Ethics. Trans. Thomas Kingsmill Abbott. 2nd ed. London: Longmans Green, 1879.

Kant's Introduction to Logic and His Essay on the Mistaken Subtilty (sic) of the Four Figures. Trans. Thomas Kingsmill Abbott. London: Longmans Green, 1885 (new ed., Westport: Greenwood, 1972).

Kant's Latin Writings: Translations, Commentaries, and Notes. Trans. Lewis White Beck, Mary J. Gregor, Ralf Meerbote, John A. Reuscher. New York: Peter Lang, 1986.

Kant's Political Writings. Ed. Hans Reiss, trans. H. B. Nisbet. Cambridge: Cambridge University Press, 1970 (2nd ed., 1990).

Kant: Philosophical Correspondence 1759-1799. Trans. Arnulf Zweig. Chicago: University of Chicago Press, 1967.

Lectures on Ethics. Trans. Louis Infield. London: Methuen, 1930 (reprinted, with an introduction by Lewis White Beck, New York: Harper & Row, 1963).

Lectures on Philosophical Theology. Trans. Allen W. Wood, Gertrude M. Clark. Ithaca, N.Y.: Cornell University Press, 1978.

Logic. Trans. Robert S. Hartmann, Wolfgang Schwarz. Indianapolis: Bobbs-Merrill, 1974 (new ed., New York: Dover, 1988).

The Metaphysical Elements of Justice: Part I of The Metaphysics of Morals. Trans. John Ladd. Indianapolis: Bobbs-Merrill, 1965 (new ed., Indianapolis: Hackett, 1999).

Metaphysical Foundations of Natural Science. Trans. James Ellington. Indianapolis: Bobbs-Merrill, 1970 (reprinted, with *Prolegomena,* in *Philosophy of Material Nature,* Indianapolis: Hackett, 1985).

The Metaphysical Principles of Virtue: Part II of The Metaphysics of Morals. Trans. James Ellington. Indianapolis: Bobbs-Merrill, 1964 (reprinted, with *Foundations of the Metaphysics of Morals,* in *Ethical Philosophy,* Indianapolis: Hackett, 1983).

The Metaphysics of Morals. Trans. Mary J. Gregor. Cambridge: Cambridge University Press, 1991 (new ed., 1996).

The Moral Law: Or Kant's Groundwork of the Metaphysics of Morals. Trans. H. J. Paton. London: Hutchinson, 1949 (new ed., *Groundwork of the Metaphysics of Morals.* New York: Harper, 1964).

Observations on the Feeling of the Beautiful and Sublime. Trans. John T. Goldthwait. Berkeley: University of California Press, 1960.

On the Old Saw: That May Be Right in Theory but It Won't Work in Practice. Trans. E. B. Ashton. Philadelphia: University of Pennsylvania Press, 1974.

The One Possible Basis for a Demonstration of the Existence of God. Trans. Gordon Treash. New York: Abaris, 1979 (new ed., Lincoln: University of Nebraska Press, 1994).

Perpetual Peace. Trans. Lewis White Beck. Indianapolis: Bobbs-Merrill, 1957.

Perpetual Peace and Other Essays on Politics, History, and Morals. Trans. Ted Humphrey. Indianapolis: Hackett, 1983.

Perpetual Peace: A Philosophical Essay. Trans. M. Campbell Smith. London: Sonnenschein, 1903 (reprinted, Bristol: Thoemmes, 1992).

Prolegomena to Any Future Metaphysics. Trans. Lewis White Beck. Indianapolis: Bobbs-Merrill, 1950.

Prolegomena to Any Future Metaphysics That Will Be Able to Come Forward as Science: With Selections from the Critique of Pure Reason. Trans. Gary Hatfield, Cambridge: Cambridge University Press, 1997.

Religion within the Boundaries of Mere Reason and Other Writings. Trans. Allen W. Wood, George Di Giovanni. Cambridge: Cambridge University Press, 1998.

Religion within the Limits of Reason Alone. Trans. by Theodore M. Greene, Hoyt H. Hudson, with a new essay "The Ethical Significance of Kant's *Religion"* by John R. Silber. New York: Harper & Row, 1960.

Selected Pre-Critical Writings and Correspondence with Beck. Trans. G. B. Kerferd and D. E. Walford, with a contribution by P. G. Lucas. Manchester: Manchester University Press, 1968.

Universal Natural History and Theory of the Heavens. Trans. W. Hastie. Ann Arbor: University of Michigan Press, 1969.

Universal Natural History and Theory of the Heavens. Trans. Stanley L. Jaki. Edinburgh: Scottish Academic Press, 1981.

What Real Progress Has Metaphysics Made in Germany since the Time of Leibniz and Wolff? Trans. Ted Humphrey. New York: Abaris, 1983.

II. SECONDARY SOURCES

A. REFERENCE WORKS

Adickes, Erich. *German Kantian Bibliography.* 2 vols. Boston: B. Franklin, 1895–96 (reprinted, Würzburg, Liebing, 1970. Annotated bibliography of 2,832 titles on Kant up to 1887.)

Caygill, Howard. *A Kant Dictionary.* Oxford: Blackwell, 1995.

Eisler, Rudolf. *Kant-Lexikon. Nachschlagewerk zu Kants sämtlichen Schriften, Briefen und handschriftlichem Nachlaß.* Berlin: E. S. Mittler, 1930 (reprinted, Hildesheim: Georg Olms, 1961).

Kantian Ethical Thought: A Curricular Report and Annotated Bibliography. Tallahassee, Fla.: Council for Philosophical Studies, 1984.

Martin, Gottfried. *Personenindex zu Kants gesammelten Schriften.* Berlin: Walter de Gruyter, 1969.

———. *Sachindex zu Kants Kritik der reinen Vernunft.* Berlin: Walter de Gruyter, 1967.

Mellin, G. S. A. *Encyklopädisches Wörterbuch der kritischen Philosophie.* 6 vols. 1797–1804 (reprinted, Aalen: Scientia, 1970–1971).

Ratke, Heinrich. *Systematisches Handlexikon zu Kants Kritik der reinen Vernunft.* Leipzig: Felix Meiner, 1929 (reprinted, Hamburg: Meiner, 1972).

Reuscher, Jay. *A Concordance to the* Critique of Pure Reason. New York: Peter Lang, 1996.

Ruffing, Margit, ed. *Kant-Bibliographie 1945–1990*. Frankfurt a.M.: Vittorio Klostermann, 1998. (Includes 12,000 titles. Further volumes should eventually cover all editions of Kant's works as well as all secondary literature dealing with Kant starting with 1750.)

Schmid, Carl C. E. *Wörterbuch zum leichtern Gebrauch der Kantischen Schriften*. 4th ed. Jena: Cröker, 1798 (reprinted, Brussels: Culture et civilisation, 1974; Darmstadt: Wissenschaftliche Buchgesellschaft, 1976).

B. HISTORICAL BACKGROUND AND CONTEXT

Beck, Lewis White. *Early German Philosophy: Kant and His Predecessors*. Cambridge, Mass.: Harvard University Press, 1969 (reprinted, Bristol: Thoemmes Press, 1996).

Beiser, Frederick C. *The Fate of Reason: German Philosophy from Kant to Fichte*. Cambridge, Mass.: Harvard University Press, 1987.

Buchdahl, Gerd. *Metaphysics and the Philosophy of Science: The Classical Origins Descartes to Kant*. Oxford: Basil Blackwell, 1969.

Cassirer, Ernst. *Freiheit und Form: Studien zur deutschen Geistesgeschichte*. 3rd ed. Darmstadt: Wissenschaftliche Buchgesellschaft, 1961.

———. *The Philosophy of the Enlightenment*. Trans. Fritz C. A. Koelln and James P. Pettegrove. Princeton, N.J.: Princeton University Press, 1951.

Emundts, Dina, ed. *Immanuel Kant und die Berliner Aufklärung*. Wiesbaden: Reichert, 2000.

Heimsoeth, Heinz. *Studien zur Philosophiegeschichte: Gesammelte Abhandlungen, Band II*. Kant-Studien Ergänzungsheft 82. Bonn: Bouvier, 1961.

Oberhausen, Michael, ed. *Vernunftkritik und Aufklärung: Studien zur Philosophie Kants und seines Jahrhunderts*. Stuttgart-Bad Cannstatt: Frommann-Holzboog, 2001.

Rosenkranz, Karl. *Geschichte der Kant'schen Philosophie*. Leipzig: Leopold Voss, 1840 (reprinted, Berlin: Akademie Verlag, 1987).

Schneewind, Jerome B. *The Invention of Autonomy. A History of Modern Moral Philosophy*. Cambridge: Cambridge University Press, 1998.

———, ed. *Moral Philosophy from Montaigne to Kant: An Anthology*. 2 vols. Cambridge: Cambridge University Press, 1990.

Tonelli, Giorgio. *Kant's Critique of Pure Reason within the Tradition of Modern Logic. A Commentary on Its History.* Ed. David H. Chandler. Hildesheim: Georg Olms, 1994.

Wundt, Max. *Die deutsche Schulphilosophie im Zeitalter der Aufklärung.* Tübingen: J. C. B. Mohr, 1945 (reprinted, Hildesheim: Georg Olms, 1964).

C. BIOGRAPHIES

Cassirer, Ernst. *Kant's Life and Thought.* Trans. James Haden. New Haven, Conn.: Yale University Press, 1981.

Dietzsch, Steffen. *Immanuel Kant. Eine Biographie.* Leipzig: Reclam, 2003.

Geier, Manfred. *Kants Welt. Eine Biographie.* Reinbek: Rowohlt, 2003.

Gerhardt, Volker. *Immanuel Kant. Vernunft und Leben.* Stuttgart: Reclam, 2002.

Gross, Felix, ed. *Immanuel Kant: Sein Leben in Darstellungen von Zeitgenossen. Die Biographien von L. E. Borowski, R. B. Jachmann, und E. A. Ch. Wasianski.* Berlin: Deutsche Bibliothek, 1912 (new ed., with an introduction by Rudolf Malter, Darmstadt: Wissenschaftliche Buchgesellschaft, 1993).

Gulyga, Arsenij. *Immanuel Kant: His Life and Thought.* Trans. Marijan Despalatovi . Boston: Birkhäuser, 1987.

Kuehn, Manfred. *Kant. A Biography.* Cambridge: Cambridge University Press, 2001.

———, ed. *Kant Biographien.* 8 vols. Bristol: Thoemmes, 2002.

Ritzel, Wolfgang. *Immanuel Kant: Eine Biographie.* Berlin: Walter de Gruyter, 1985.

Vorländer, Karl. *Immanuel Kant: Der Mann und das Werk.* 2 vols. 2nd ed., ed. Rudolf Malter. Hamburg: Felix Meiner, 1977.

———. *Immanuel Kants Leben.* 4th ed., ed. Rudolf Malter. Hamburg: Felix Meiner, 1986.

D. GENERAL SURVEYS

Allison, Henry E. *Idealism and Freedom: Essays on Kant's Theoretical and Practical Philosophy.* Cambridge: Cambridge University Press, 1996.

Ameriks, Karl. *Interpreting Kant's "Critiques."* Oxford: Clarendon Press, 2003.

Beck, Lewis White. *Studies in the Philosophy of Kant.* Indianapolis: Bobbs-Merrill, 1965.

————. *Essays on Kant and Hume.* New Haven, Conn.: Yale University Press, 1978.

————, ed. *Kant Studies Today.* La Salle, Ill.: Open Court, 1969.

Burnham, Douglas. *Kant's Philosophies of Judgement.* Edinburgh: Edinburgh University Press, 2004.

Cassirer, Ernst. *Rousseau, Kant, Goethe.* Trans. James Gutmann, Paul Oskar Kristeller, and John Herman Randall, Jr. Princeton, N.J.: Princeton University Press, 1945 (new ed., with an introduction by Peter Gay, New York: Harper & Row, 1963).

Chadwick, Ruth, ed. *Immanuel Kant: Critical Assessments.* 4 vols. London: Routledge, 1992.

Dancy, R. M. *Kant and Critique: New Essays in Honor of W. H. Werkmeister.* Dordrecht: Kluwer, 1993.

Delekat, Friedrich. *Immanuel Kant. Historisch-kritische Interpretation der Hauptschriften.* 3rd ed. Heidelberg: Quelle & Meyer, 1969.

De Vleeschauwer, Herman–Jean. *La déduction transcendentale dans l'oeuvre de Kant.* 3 vols. Antwerp: De Sikkel; Paris: Champion; and The Hague: Martinus Nijhoff, 1934–37.

————. *The Development of Kantian Thought: The History of a Doctrine.* Trans. A. R. C. Duncan. London: Thomas Nelson & Sons, 1962.

Den Ouden, Bernard, and Marcia Moen, eds. *New Essays on Kant.* New York: Peter Lang, 1987.

Dörflinger, Bernd. *Das Leben theoretischer Vernunft: Teleologische und praktische Aspekte der Erfahrungstheorie Kants.* Berlin: Walter de Gruyter, 2000.

Döring, Eberhard. *Immanuel Kant. Eine Einführung.* Wiesbaden: Marix Verlag, 2004.

Findlay, J. N. *Kant and the Transcendental Object: A Hermeneutic Study.* Oxford: Clarendon Press, 1981.

Förster, Eckart, ed. *Kant's Transcendental Deductions: The Three 'Critiques' and the 'Opus postumum.'* Stanford, Calif.: Stanford University Press, 1989.

Fulda, Hans Friedrich, and Jürgen Stolzenberg, eds. *Architektonik und System in der Philosophie Kants.* Hamburg: Felix Meiner, 2001.

Gerhardt, Volker, and Friedrich Kaulbach. *Kant.* Erträge der Forschung, Band 105. Darmstadt: Wissenschaftliche Buchgesellschaft, 1979.

Gram, Moltke S., ed. *Interpreting Kant*. Iowa City: University of Iowa Press, 1982.

Guyer, Paul, ed. *The Cambridge Companion to Kant*. Cambridge: Cambridge University Press, 1992.

Heimsoeth, Heinz. *Studien zur Philosophie Immanuel Kants. Metaphysische Ursprünge und Ontologische Grundlagen*. Cologne: Kölner Universitäts-Verlag, 1956.

———. *Studien zur Philosophie Immanuel Kants II*. Kant-Studien Ergänzungsheft 100. Bonn: Bouvier, 1970.

Heimsoeth, Heinz, and Dieter Henrich, Giorgio Tonelli, eds. *Studien zu Kants philosophischer Entwicklung*. Hildesheim: Georg Olms, 1967.

Heintel, Peter, and Ludwig Nagl, eds. *Zur Kantforschung der Gegenwart*. Darmstadt: Wissenschaftliche Buchgesellschaft, 1981.

Henrich, Dieter. *The Unity of Reason: Essays on Kant's Philosophy*. Trans. Jeffrey Edwards, Louis Hunt, Manfred Kuehn, Guenter Zoeller. Cambridge, Mass.: Harvard University Press, 1994.

Höffe, Otfried. *Immanuel Kant*. Trans. Marshall Farrier. Albany: State University of New York Press, 1994.

Hutter, Axel. *Das Interesse der Vernunft. Kants ursprüngliche Einsicht und ihre Entfaltung in den transzendentalphilosophischen Hauptwerken*. Hamburg: Felix Meiner, 2003.

Irrlitz, Gerd. *Kant-Handbuch: Leben und Werk*. Stuttgart: J. B. Metzler, 2002.

Kemp, John. *The Philosophy of Kant*. London: Oxford University Press, 1968.

Kennington, Richard, ed. *The Philosophy of Immanuel Kant*. Washington, D.C.: Catholic University of America Press, 1985.

Klemme, Heiner F., and others, eds. *Aufklärung und Interpretation. Studien zu Kants Philosophie und ihrem Umkreis*. Würzburg: Königshausen & Neumann, 1999.

Körner, Stephan. *Kant*. Harmondsworth: Penguin Books, 1955.

Laberge, Pierre and others, eds. *Proceedings of the Ottawa Congress on Kant in the Anglo-American and Continental Traditions Held October 10–14, 1974*. Ottawa: University of Ottawa Press, 1976.

Lauener, Henri. *Hume und Kant. Eine systematische Gegenüberstellung einiger Hauptpunkte ihrer Lehren*. Bern: Francke, 1969.

Loock, Reinhard. *Idee und Reflexion bei Kant*. Hamburg: Felix Meiner, 1998.

Neiman, Susan. *The Unity of Reason. Rereading Kant*. Oxford: Oxford University Press, 1994.

Oberer, Hariolf, and Gerhard Seel, eds. *Kant: Analysen – Probleme – Kritik.* 3 vols. Würzburg: Königshausen & Neumann, 1988, 1996, 1997.
Piché, Claude. *Das Ideal. Ein Problem der Kantischen Ideenlehre.* Bonn: Bouvier, 1984.
Prauss, Gerold, ed. *Kant: Zur Deutung seiner Theorie von Erkennen und Handeln.* Cologne: Kiepenheuer & Witsch, 1973.
Puech, Michel. *Kant et la causalité. Étude sur la formation du système critique.* Paris: J. Vrin, 1990.
Rescher, Nicholas. *Kant and the Reach of Reason. Studies in Kant's Theory of Rational Systematization.* Cambridge: Cambridge University Press, 2000.
Rotenstreich, Nathan. *Experience and Its Systematization: Studies in Kant.* 2nd ed. The Hague: Martinus Nijhoff, 1972.
Schaper, Eva, and Wilhelm Vossenkuhl, eds. *Bedingungen der Möglichkeit: 'Transcendental Arguments' und transzendentales Denken.* Stuttgart: Klett-Cotta, 1984.
Schönecker, Dieter, and Thomas Zwenger, eds. *Kant verstehen. Understanding Kant.* Darmstadt: Wissenschaftliche Buchgesellschaft, 2001.
Schönrich, Gerhard and Yasushi Kato, eds. *Kant in der Diskussion der Moderne.* Frankfurt am Main: Suhrkamp, 1996.
Shell, Susan Meld. *The Embodiment of Reason. Kant on Spirit, Generation, and Community.* Chicago: University of Chicago Press, 1996.
Simon, Josef. *Kant. Die fremde Vernunft und die Sprache der Philosophie.* Berlin: Walter de Gruyter, 2003.
Thomson, Garrett. *On Kant.* Belmont, Calif.: Wadsworth, 2000.
Van Cleve, James. *Problems from Kant.* Oxford: Oxford University Press, 1999.
Walker, Ralph C. S. *Kant.* London: Routledge & Kegan Paul, 1978.
Werkmeister, W. H. *Kant's Silent Decade: A Decade of Philosophical Development.* Tallahassee: University Presses of Florida, 1979.
———. *Kant: The Architectonic and Development of His Philosophy.* LaSalle, Ill.: Open Court, 1980.
———, ed. *Reflections on Kant's Philosophy.* Gainesville: University Presses of Florida, 1975.
Whitney, George Tapley, and David F. Bowers, eds. *The Heritage of Kant.* Princeton, N.J.: Princeton University Press, 1939.
Wolff, Robert Paul, ed. *Kant: A Collection of Critical Essays.* Garden City, N.Y.: Doubleday Anchor, 1967.
Wood, Allen W., ed. *Self and Nature in Kant's Philosophy.* Ithaca, N.Y.: Cornell University Press, 1984.

E. PRE-CRITICAL WRITINGS

Hinske, Norbert. *Kants Weg zur Transzendentalphilosophie: Der dreißig-jährige Kant.* Stuttgart: Kohlhammer, 1970.

Kreimendahl, Lothar. *Kant—Der Durchbruch von 1769.* Cologne: Jürgen Dinter, 1990.

Laberge, Pierre. *La théologie kantienne précritique.* Ottawa: Éditions de l'Université d'Ottawa, 1973.

Laywine, Alison. *Kant's Early Metaphysics and the Origins of the Critical Philosophy.* Atascadero, Calif.: Ridgeview, 1993.

Polonoff, Irving I. *Force, Cosmos, Monads and Other Themes of Kant's Early Thought.* Kant-Studien Ergänzungsheft 107. Bonn: Bouvier, 1973.

Reuscher, John A. "A Clarification and Critique of Kant's Principiorum Primorum Cognitionis Metaphysicae Nova Dilucidatio." *Kant-Studien* 68 (1977): 18–32.

Rockmore, Tom, ed. *New Essays on the Precritical Kant.* Amherst, N.Y.: Humanity Press, 2001.

Schilpp, Paul Arthur. *Kant's Pre-Critical Ethics.* 2nd ed. Evanston, Ill.: Northwestern University Press, 1960 (reprint of 1938 ed., Bristol: Thoemmes, 1998).

Schmucker, Josef. *Die Ursprünge der Ethik Kants in seinen vorkritischen Schriften und Reflektionen.* Meisenheim: Anton Hain, 1961.

———. *Die Ontotheologie des vorkritischen Kants.* Kant-Studien Ergänzungsheft 112. Berlin: Walter de Gruyter, 1980.

———. *Kants vorkritische Kritik der Gottesbeweise. Ein Schlüssel zur Interpretation des theologischen Hauptstücks der transzendentalen Dialektik der Kritik der reinen Vernunft.* Wiesbaden: Franz Steiner, 1983.

Schönfeld, Martin. *The Philosophy of the Young Kant. The Precritical Project.* Oxford: Oxford University Press, 2000.

Theis, Robert. *Gott. Untersuchung zur Entwicklung des theologischen Diskurses in Kants Schriften zur theoretischen Philosophie bis hin zum Erscheinen der Kritik der reinen Vernunft.* Stuttgart: Frommann-Holzboog, 1994.

Waschkies, Hans-Joachim. *Physik und Physikotheologie des jungen Kant. Die Vorgeschichte seiner Allgemeinen Naturgeschichte und Theorie des Himmels.* Amsterdam: Grüner 1987.

F. EPISTEMOLOGY AND METAPHYSICS

Abela, Paul. *Kant's Empirical Realism.* Oxford: Clarendon Press, 2002.

Adickes, Erich. *Kant und das Ding an sich.* Berlin: Pan-Verlag, 1924.

————. *Kants Lehre von der doppelten Affektion unseres Ich als Schlüssel zu seiner Erkenntnistheorie.* Tübingen: J. C. B. Mohr, 1929.

Al-Azm, Sadik J. *The Origins of Kant's Arguments in the Antinomies.* Oxford: Clarendon Press, 1972.

Allison, Henry E. *Kant's Transcendental Idealism: An Interpretation and Defense.* New Haven, Conn.: Yale University Press, 1983.

Allison, Henry E., ed. *Kant's Critical Philosophy. The Monist* 72/2 (1989) (special issue multiple-author anthology).

Ameriks, Karl. *Kant's Theory of Mind: An Analysis of the Paralogisms of Pure Reason.* Oxford: Clarendon Press, 1982.

————. "Recent Work on Kant's Theoretical Philosophy." *American Philosophical Quarterly* 19 (1982): 1–24.

Aquila, Richard E. *Representational Mind: A Study of Kant's Theory of Knowledge.* Bloomington: Indiana University Press, 1983.

————. *Matter in Mind: A Study of Kant's Transcendental Deduction.* Bloomington: Indiana University Press, 1989.

Aschenbrenner, Karl. *A Companion to Kant's Critique of Pure Reason: Transcendental Aesthetic and Analytic.* Lanham, Md.: University Press of America, 1983.

Baum, Manfred. *Deduktion und Beweis in Kants Transzendentalphilosophie: Untersuchungen zur Kritik der reinen Vernunft.* Königstein: Athenäum, 1986.

Baumanns, Peter. *Kant Philosophie der Erkenntnis. Durchgehender Kommentar zu den Hauptkapiteln der Kritik der reinen Vernunft.* Würzburg: Königshausen & Neumann, 1996.

Beck, Lewis White, ed. *Kant's Theory of Knowledge: Selected Papers from the Third International Kant Congress.* Dordrecht: D. Reidel, 1974.

Becker, Wolfgang. *Selbstbewußtsein und Erfahrung: Zu Kants transzendentaler Deduktion und ihrer argumentativen Rekonstruktion.* Freiburg: Karl Alber, 1984.

Bencivenga, Ermanno. *Kant's Copernican Revolution.* Oxford: Oxford University Press, 1987.

Bennett, Jonathan. *Kant's Analytic.* Cambridge: Cambridge University Press, 1966.

————. *Kant's Dialectic.* Cambridge: Cambridge University Press, 1974.

Bieri, Peter, Rolf-Peter Horstmann, and Lorenz Kruger, eds. *Transcendental Arguments and Science: Essays in Epistemology.* Dordrecht: D. Reidel, 1979.

Bird, Graham. *Kant's Theory of Knowledge: An Outline of One Central Argument in the* Critique of Pure Reason. London: Routledge & Kegan Paul, 1962.

Böhme, Gernot. *Philosophieren mit Kant. Zur Rekonstruktion der Kantischen Erkenntnis- und Wissenschaftstheorie.* Frankfurt am Main: Suhrkamp, 1986.

Bossart, W. H. *Apperception, Knowledge, and Experience.* Ottawa: University of Ottawa Press, 1994.

Brandt, Reinhard. *The Table of Judgments: Critique of Pure Reason A 67–76, B 92–101.* Trans. Eric Watkins. Atascadero, Calif.: Ridgeview, 1995.

Broad. C. D. *Kant: An Introduction.* Ed. C. Levy. Cambridge: Cambridge University Press, 1978.

Brook, Andrew. *Kant and the Mind.* Cambridge: Cambridge University Press, 1994.

Bubner, Rüdiger, Konrad Cramer, and Reiner Wiehl. *Zur Zukunft der Transzendentalphilosophie. Neue Hefte für Philosophie* 14 (1978) (special issue multiple-author anthology).

Buchdahl, Gerd. *Kant and the Dynamics of Reason. Essays on the Structure of Kant's Philosophy.* Oxford: Blackwell, 1992.

Buroker, Jill Vance. *Space and Incongruence: The Origin of Kant's Idealism.* Dordrecht: D. Reidel, 1981.

Butts, Robert E. *Kant and the Double Government Methodology: Supersensibility and Method in Kant's Philosophy of Science.* Dordrecht: D. Reidel, 1984.

————, ed. *Kant's* Critique of Pure Reason, *1781–1981. Synthese* 47 (Nos. 2 and 3) (1981) (special issues multiple-author anthology).

Carl, Wolfgang. *Der schweigende Kant: Die Entwürfe zu einer Deduktion der Kategorien vor 1781.* Göttingen: Vandenhoeck & Ruprecht, 1989.

————. *Die Transzendentale Deduktion der Kategorien in der ersten Auflage der Kritik der reinen Vernunft. Ein Kommentar.* Frankfurt am Main: Vittorio Klostermann, 1992.

Collins, Arthur W. *Possible Experience. Understanding Kant's* Critique of Pure Reason. Berkeley: University of California Press, 1999.

Cramer, Konrad. *Nicht-reine synthetische Urteile a priori: Ein Problem der Transzendentalphilosophie Immanuel Kants.* Heidelberg: Carl Winter Universitätsverlag, 1985.

Dickerson, A. B. *Kant on Representation and Objectivity.* Cambridge: Cambridge University Press, 2004.

Dryer, D. P. *Kant's Solution for Verification in Metaphysics.* London: George Allen & Unwin, 1966.

Edwards, Jeffrey. *Substance, Force, and the Possibility of Knowledge: On Kant's Philosophy of Material Nature.* Berkeley: University of California Press, 2000.

Erdmann, Benno. *Kants Kriticismus in der ersten und in der zweiten Auflage der Kritik der reinen Vernunft. Eine historische Untersuchung.* Leipzig: Leopold Voss, 1878.

Ertl, Wolfgang. *Kants Auflösung der "dritten Antinomie". Zur Bedeutung des Schöpfungskonzepts für die Freiheitslehre.* Freiburg: Karl Alber, 1996.

Ewing, A. C. *Kant's Treatment of Causality.* London: Kegan Paul, 1924.

———. *A Short Commentary on Kant's* Critique of Pure Reason. Chicago: University of Chicago Press, 1938.

Falkenstein, Lorne. *Kant's Intuitionism: A Commentary on the Transcendental Aesthetic.* Toronto: University of Toronto Press, 1995.

Flach, Werner. *Die Idee der Transzendentalphilosophie. Immanuel Kant.* Würzburg: Königshausen & Neumann, 2002.

Frischbier, Reinhard. *Kant und die Mathematik.* Halle: Hallescher Verlag, 2001.

Gardner, Sebastian. *Kant and the* Critique of Pure Reason. London: Routledge, 1999.

Garnett, Christopher B., Jr. *The Kantian Philosophy of Space.* New York: Columbia University Press, 1939.

Gibbons, Sarah L. *Kant's Theory of Imagination: Bridging Gaps in Judgement and Experience.* Oxford: Clarendon Press, 1994.

Gram, Moltke S. *Kant, Ontology, and the* A Priori. Evanston, Ill.: Northwestern University Press, 1968.

———. *The Transcendental Turn: The Foundations of Kant's Idealism.* Gainesville: University of Florida Press, 1984.

———, ed. *Kant: Disputed Questions.* Chicago: Quadrangle Books, 1967.

Greenberg, Robert. *Kant's Theory of "a priori" Knowledge.* University Park: Pennsylvania State University Press, 2001.

Grier, Michelle. *Kant's Doctrine of Transcendental Illusion.* Cambridge: Cambridge University Press, 2001.

Gurwitsch, Aron. *Kants Theorie des Verstandes.* Ed. Thomas M. Seebohm. Dordrecht: Kluwer, 1990.

Guyer, Paul. *Kant and the Claims of Knowledge.* Cambridge: Cambridge University Press, 1987.

Hanna, Robert. *Kant and the Foundations of Analytic Philosophy.* Oxford: Oxford University Press, 2001.

Harper, William L., and Ralf Meerbote, eds. *Kant on Causality, Freedom, and Objectivity.* Minneapolis: University of Minnesota Press, 1984.

Heckmann, Reinhard. *Kants Kategoriendeduktion. Ein Beitrag zu einer Philosophie des Geistes.* Freiburg: Karl Alber, 1997.

Heidemann, Ingeborg, and Wolfgang Ritzel, eds. *Beiträge zur Kritik der reinen Vernunft 1781–1981.* Berlin: Walter de Gruyter, 1981.

Heimsoeth, Heinz. *Atom, Seele, Monade: Historische Ursprünge und Hintergründe von Kants Antinomie der Teilung.* Wiesbaden: Franz Steiner, 1960.

———. *Transzendentale Dialektik: Ein Kommentar zu Kants Kritik der reinen Vernunft.* 4 vols. Berlin: Walter de Gruyter, 1966–1971.

Heinrich, Richard. *Kants Erfahrungsraum: Metaphysischer Ursprung und kritische Entwicklung.* Freiburg: Karl Alber, 1986.

Henrich, Dieter. "The Proof-Structure of Kant's Transcendental Deduction." *Review of Metaphysics* 22 (1969): 640–59.

———. *Identität und Objektivität: Eine Untersuchung über Kants transzendentale Deduktion.* Heidelberg: Carl Winter Universitätsverlag, 1976.

Hinsch, Wilfried. *Erfahrung und Selbstbewusstsein: Zur Kategoriendeduktion bei Kant.* Hamburg: Felix Meiner, 1986.

Hintikka, Jaakko. *Knowledge and the Known: Historical Perspectives in Epistemology.* Dordrecht: D. Reidel, 1974.

Höffe, Otfried. *Kants Kritik der reinen Vernunft. Die Grundlegung der modernen Philosophie.* Munich: Beck, 2003.

Holzhey, Helmut. *Kants Erfahrungsbegriff. Quellengeschichtliche und Bedeutungsanalytische Untersuchungen.* Basel: Schwabe, 1970.

Hossenfelder, Malte. *Kants Konstitutionstheorie und die Transzendentale Deduktion.* Berlin: Walter de Gruyter, 1978.

Howell, Robert. *Kant's Transcendental Deduction.* Dordrecht: Kluwer, 1992.

Kaulbach, Friedrich. *Die Metaphysik des Raumes bei Leibniz und Kant.* Cologne: Kölner Universitäts-Verlag, 1960.

———. Philosophie als Wissenschaft. *Eine Anleitung zum Studium von Kants Kritik der reinen Vernunft in Vorlesungen.* Hildesheim: Gerstenberg, 1981.

Keller, Pierre. *Kant and the Demands of Consciousness.* Cambridge: Cambridge University Press, 1998.

Kemp Smith, Norman. *A Commentary to Kant's 'Critique of Pure Reason.'* 2nd ed. London: Macmillan, 1923 (new ed., with an introduction by Sebastian Gardner, New York: Palgrave Macmillan, 2003).

Kitcher, Patricia. *Kant's Transcendental Psychology.* Oxford: Oxford University Press, 1990.

Klemme, Heiner F. *Kants Philosophie des Subjekts. Systematische und entwicklungsgeschichtliche Untersuchungen zum Verhältnis von Selbstbewußtsein und Selbsterkenntnis.* Hamburg: Felix Meiner, 1996.

Kopper, Joachim, and Rudolf Malter, eds. *Materialien zu Kants "Kritik der reinen Vernunft."* Frankfurt am Main: Suhrkamp, 1975.

Kopper, Joachim, and Wolfgang Marx, eds. *200 Jahre Kritik der reinen Vernunft.* Hildesheim: Gerstenberg, 1981.

Koriako, Darius. *Kants Philosophie der Mathematik. Grundlagen—Voraussetzungen—Probleme.* Hamburg: Felix Meiner, 1999.

Kugelstadt, Manfred. *Synthetische Reflexion. Zur Stellung einer nach Kategorien reflektierenden Urteilskraft in Kants theoretischer Philosophie.* Berlin: Walter de Gruyter, 1998.

Langton, Rae. *Kantian Humility: Our Ignorance of Things in Themselves.* Oxford: Oxford University Press, 2001.

Lauener, Henri, ed. *Proceedings of the IVth International Colloquium in Biel. Dialectica* 35, 1-2 (1981). (Essays on the *Critique of Pure Reason.*)

Longueness, Béatrice. *Kant and the Capacity to Judge: Sensibility and Discursivity in the Transcendental Analytic of the* Critique of Pure Reason. Trans. Charles T. Wolfe. Princeton, N.J.: Princeton University Press, 1998.

Maier, Anneliese. *Kants Qualitätskategorien.* Kantstudien Ergänzungsheft 65. Berlin: Pan-Verlag, 1930.

Malzkorn, Wolfgang. *Kants Kosmologie-Kritik. Eine formale Analyse der Antinomienlehre.* Kantstudien Ergänzungsheft 134. Berlin: Walter de Gruyter, 1999.

Martin, Gottfried. *Kant's Metaphysics and Theory of Science.* Trans. P. G. Lucas. Westport, Conn.: Greenwood Press, 1974.

———. *Arithmetic und Combinatorics: Kant and His Contemporaries.* Trans. Judy Wubnig. Carbondale: Southern Illinois University Press, 1985.

Melnick, Arthur. *Kant's Analogies of Experience.* Chicago: University of Chicago Press, 1973.

———. *Space, Time, and Thought in Kant.* Dordrecht: Kluwer, 1989.

Meyer, Michel. *Science et métaphysique chez Kant.* Paris: Presses Universitaires de France, 1988.

Michel, Karin. *Untersuchungen zur Zeitkonzeption in Kants Kritik der reinen Vernunft.* Kant-Studien Ergänzungsheft 145. Berlin: Walter de Gruyter, 2003.

Mohanty, J. N., and Robert W. Shahan, eds. *Essays on Kant's Critique of Pure Reason.* Norman: University of Oklahoma Press, 1982.

314   *Bibliography*

Mohr, Georg. *Kommentar. Kants Grundlegung der kritischen Philosophie.* Frankfurt am Main: Suhrkamp, 2004.

Mohr, Georg, and Marcus Willaschek, eds. *Immanuel Kant: Kritik der reinen Vernunft.* Berlin: Akademie Verlag, 1998.

Nagel, Gordon. *The Structure of Experience: Kant's System of Principles.* Chicago: University of Chicago Press, 1983.

Natterer, Paul. *Systematischer Kommentar zur* Kritik der reinen Vernunft: *Interdisziplinäre Bilanz der Kantforschung seit 1945.* Kant-Studien Ergänzungsheft 141. Berlin: Walter de Gruyter, 2002.

Neujahr, Philip J. *Kant's Idealism.* Macon, Ga.: Mercer, 1995.

Oberhausen, Michael. *Das neue Apriori. Kants Lehre von einer 'ursprünglichen Erwerbung' apriorischer Vorstellungen.* Stuttgart: Frommann-Holzboog, 1997.

Parsons, Charles. *Mathematics in Philosophy: Selected Essays.* Ithaca, N.Y.: Cornell University Press, 1983.

Paton, H. J. *Kant's Metaphysic of Experience: A Commentary on the First Half of the* Kritik der reinen Vernunft. 2 vols. London: George Allen & Unwin, 1936.

Pippin, Robert B. *Kant's Theory of Form: An Essay on the* Critique of Pure Reason. New Haven, Conn.: Yale University Press, 1982.

Posy, Carl J. ed. *Kant's Philosophy of Mathematics: Modern Essays.* Dordrecht: Kluwer, 1992.

Powell, C. Thomas. *Kant's Theory of Self Consciousness.* Oxford: Clarendon Press, 1990.

Prauss, Gerold. *Erscheinung bei Kant: Ein Problem der "Kritik der reinen Vernunft."* Berlin: Walter de Gruyter, 1971.

———. *Kant und das Problem der Dinge an sich.* 2nd ed. Bonn: Bouvier, 1977.

Prichard, H. A. *Kant's Theory of Knowledge.* Oxford: Clarendon Press, 1909.

Reich, Klaus. *The Completeness of Kant's Table of Judgments.* Trans. Jane Kneller, Michael Losonsky. Stanford, Calif.: Stanford University Press, 1992.

Rescher, Nicholas. *Kant's Theory of Knowledge and Reality. A Group of Essays.* Washington, D.C.: University Press of America, 1983.

Reuter, Peter. *Kants Theorie der Reflexionsbegriffe. Eine Untersuchung zum Amphiboliekapitel der Kritik der reinen Vernunft.* Würzburg: Königshausen & Neumann, 1989.

Robinson, Hoke, ed. *The Spindel Conference 1986: The B-Deduction.* The *Southern Journal of Philosophy* 25 Supplement (1987) (special issue multiple-author anthology).

Rosales, Alberto. *Sein und Subjektivität bei Kant: zum subjektiven Ursprung der Kategorien.* Berlin: Walter de Gruyter, 2000.

Roussett, Bernard. *La doctrine kantienne de l'objectivité.* Paris: J. Vrin, 1967.

Sans, Georg. *Ist Kants Ontologie naturalistisch? Die "Analogien der Erfahrung" in der* Kritik der reinen Vernunft. Stuttgart: Kohlhammer, 2000.

Schaper, Eva, and Wilhelm Vossenkuhl, eds. *Reading Kant: New Perspectives on Transcendental Arguments and Critical Philosophy* Oxford: Basil Blackwell, 1989.

Schmauke, Stephan. *"Wohlthätigste Verirrung." Kants kosmologische Antinomien.* Würzburg: Königshausen & Neumann, 2002.

Schmucker, Josef. *Das Weltproblem in Kants Kritik der reinen Vernunft. Kommentar und Strukturanalyse des ersten Buches und des zweiten Hauptstücks des zweiten Buches der transzendentalen Dialektik.* Bonn: Bouvier, 1990.

Schönrich, Gerhard. *Kategorien und transzendentale Argumentation. Kant und die Idee einer transzendentalen Semiotik.* Frankfurt am Main: Suhrkamp, 1981.

Schneeberger, Guido. *Kants Konzeption der Modalbegriffe.* Basel: Verlag für Recht und Gesellschaft, 1952.

Schulthess, Peter. *Relation und Funktion.Eine systematische und entwicklungsgeschichtliche Untersuchung zur theoretischen Philosophie Kants.* Kant-Studien Ergänzungsheft 113. Berlin: Walter de Gruyter, 1981.

Schwyzer, Hubert. *The Unity of Understanding: A Study in Kantian Problems.* Oxford: Clarendon Press, 1990.

Sellars, Wilfrid. *Science and Metaphysics: Variations on Kantian Themes.* London: Routledge & Kegan Paul, 1968.

Smith, A. H. *Kantian Studies.* Oxford: Clarendon Press, 1947.

Smyth, Richard A. *Forms of Intuition: An Historical Introduction to the Transcendental Aesthetic.* The Hague: Martinus Nijhoff, 1978.

Srzednicki, Jan T. *The Place of Space and Other Themes.* The Hague: Martinus Nijhoff, 1983.

Strawson, P. F. *The Bounds of Sense: An Essay on Kant's* Critique of Pure Reason. London: Methuen, 1966.

Stuhlmann-Laeisz, Rainer. *Kants Logik: Eine Interpretation auf der Grundlage von Vorlesungen, veröffentlichten Werken und Nachlass.* Berlin: Walter de Gruyter, 1976.

Swing, Thomas K. *Kant's Transcendental Logic.* New Haven, Conn.: Yale University Press, 1969.

Thöle, Bernhard. *Kant und das Problem der Gesetzmäßigkeit der Natur.* Berlin: Walter de Gruyter, 1991.

Tonelli, Giorgio. *Kant's Critique of Pure Reason within the Tradition of Modern Logic. A Commentary on Its History,* ed. David H. Chandler. Hildesheim: Georg Olms, 1994.

Tuschling, Burkhard, ed. *Probleme der "Kritik der reinen Vernunft": Kant-Tagung Marburg 1981.* Berlin: Walter de Gruyter, 1984.

Vaihinger, Hans. *Commentar zu Kants Kritik der reinen Vernunft.* 2 vols. Stuttgart: W. Spemann 1881, and Union Deutsche Verlagsgesellschaft, 1892.

Van Cleve, James, and Robert E. Frederick, eds. *The Philosophy of Right and Left. Incongruent Counterparts and the Nature of Space.* Dordrecht: Kluwer, 1991.

Walker, Ralph C. S., ed. *Kant on Pure Reason.* Oxford: Oxford University Press, 1982.

Walsh, W. H. *Kant's Criticism of Metaphysics.* Edinburgh: Edinburgh University Press, 1975.

Waxman, Wayne. *Kant's Model of the Mind: A New Interpretation of Transcendental Idealism.* Oxford: Oxford University Press, 1991.

Weldon, Thomas D. *Kant's Critique of Pure Reason.* 2nd ed. Oxford: Clarendon Press, 1958.

Westphal, Kenneth R. *Kant's Transcendental Proof of Realism.* Cambridge: Cambridge University Press, 2004.

White, F. C. *Kant's First Critique and the Transcendental Deduction.* Aldershot: Avebury, 1996.

Wike, Victoria S. *Kant's Antinomies of Reason: Their Origin and Their Resolution.* Washington, D.C.: University Press of America, 1982.

Wilkerson, T. E. *Kant's Critique of Pure Reason: A Commentary for Students.* Oxford: Clarendon Press, 1976.

Williams, Terrence C. *The Unity of Kant's Critique of Pure Reason: Experience, Language, and Knowledge.* Lewiston, N.Y.: Edwin Mellen Press, 1987.

Winterbourne, Anthony. *The Ideal and the Real: An Outline of Kant's Theory of Space, Time, and Mathematical Construction.* Dordrecht: Kluwer, 1988.

Wolff, Michael. *Die Vollständigkeit der kantischen Urteilstafel.* Frankfurt am Main: Klostermann, 1995.

Wolff, Robert Paul. *Kant's Theory of Mental Activity: A Commentary on the Transcendental Analytic of the Critique of Pure Reason.* Cambridge, Mass.: Harvard University Press, 1963.

Wolff-Meternich, Brigitta-Sophie. *Die Überwindung des mathematischen Erkenntnisideals. Kants Grenzbestimmung von Mathematik und Philosophie.* Berlin: Walter de Gruyter, 1995.

Zöller, Günter. *Theoretische Gegenstandsbeziehung bei Kant.* Kant-Studien Ergänzungsheft 117. Berlin: Walter de Gruyter, 1984.

G. PHILOSOPHY OF SCIENCE

Adickes, Erich. *Kants Opus postumum dargestellt und beurteilt.* Kant-Studien Ergänzungsheft 50. Berlin: Reuther und Reichard, 1920 (reprinted, Vaduz: Topos, 1978).

———. *Kant als Naturforscher.* 2 vols. Berlin: Walter de Gruyter, 1924–1925.

Brittan, Gordon G., Jr. *Kant's Theory of Science.* Princeton, N.J.: Princeton University Press, 1978.

Butts, Robert E., ed. *Kant's Philosophy of Physical Science: Metaphysische Anfangsgründe der Naturwissenschaft 1786–1986.* Dordrecht: D. Reidel, 1986.

Emundts, Dina. *Kants Übergangskonzeption im Opus Postumum. Zur Rolle des Nachlasswerkes für die Grundlegung der empirischen Physik.* Berlin: Walter de Gruyter, 2004.

Falkenburg, Brigitte. *Kants Kosmologie. Die wissenschaftliche Revolution der Naturphilosophie im 18. Jahrhundert.* Frankfurt am Main: Vittorio Klostermann, 2000.

Förster, Eckart. *Kant's Final Synthesis. An Essay on the* Opus postumum. Cambridge, Mass.: Harvard University Press, 2000.

Forum für Philosophie Bad Homburg, ed. *Übergang: Untersuchungen zum Spätwerk Immanuel Kants.* Frankfurt am Main: Vittorio Klostermann, 1991.

Friedman, Michael. *Kant and the Exact Sciences.* Cambridge, Mass.: Harvard University Press, 1992.

Gloy, Karen. *Die Kantische Theorie der Naturwissenschaft: Eine Strukturanalyse ihrer Möglichkeit, ihres Umfanges und ihrer Grenzen.* Berlin: Walter de Gruyter, 1976.

Hahn, Robert. *Kant's Newtonian Revolution in Philosophy.* Carbondale: Southern Illinois University Press, 1988.

Hoppe, Hansgeorg. *Kants Theorie der Physik: Eine Untersuchung über das Opus postumum von Kant.* Frankfurt am Main: Vittorio Klostermann, 1969.

Mathieu, Vittorio. *Kants Opus postumum.* Ed. Gerd Held. Frankfurt am Main: Vittorio Klostermann, 1989.

Mudroch, Vilem. *Kants Theorie der physikalischen Gesetze.* Kant-Studien Ergänzungsheft 119. Berlin: Walter de Gruyter, 1987.

Plaass, Peter. *Kants Theorie der Naturwissenschaft: Eine Untersuchung zur Vorrede von Kants "Metaphysischen Anfangsgründen der Naturwissenschaft."* Göttingen: Vandenhoeck & Ruprecht, 1965.

Pollok, Konstantin. *Kants "Metaphysische Anfangsgründe der Naturwissenschaft": Ein kritischer Kommentar.* Hamburg: Felix Meiner, 2001.

Schäfer, Lothar. *Kants Metaphysik der Natur.* Berlin: Walter de Gruyter, 1966.

Tuschling, Burkhard. *Metaphysische und transzendentale Dynamik in Kants Opus postumum.* Berlin: Walter de Gruyter, 1971.

Vuillemin, Jules. *Physique et métaphysique kantiennes.* Paris: Presses Universitaires de France, 1955.

Watkins, Eric, ed. *Kant and the Sciences.* New York: Oxford University Press, 2000.

H. MORAL PHILOSOPHY

Acton, H. B. *Kant's Moral Philosophy.* London: Macmillan, 1970.

Allison, Henry E. *Kant's Theory of Freedom.* Cambridge: Cambridge University Press, 1990.

———, ed. *Kant's Practical Philosophy. The Monist* 72/3 (1989) (special issue multiple-author anthology).

Ameriks, Karl, and Dieter Sturma, eds. *Kants Ethik. Beiträge aus der angloamerikanischen und kontinentaleuropäischen Philosophie.* Paderborn: Mentis, 2004.

Atwell, John E. *Ends and Principles in Kant's Moral Thought.* Dordrecht: Martinus Nijhoff, 1986.

Aune, Bruce. *Kant's Theory of Morals.* Princeton, N.J.: Princeton University Press, 1979.

Auxter, Thomas. *Kant's Moral Teleology.* Macon, Ga.: Mercer University Press, 1982.

Banham, Gary. *Kant's Practical Philosophy: From Critique to Doctrine.* Basingstoke: Palgrave Macmillan, 2003.

Baron, Marcia W. *Kantian Ethics Almost without Apology.* Ithaca, N.Y.: Cornell University Press, 1995.

Baumgarten, Hans-Ulrich, and Carsten Held, eds. *Systematische Ethik mit Kant.* Freiburg: Karl Alber, 2001.

Beck, Lewis White. *A Commentary on Kant's Critique of Practical Reason.* Chicago: University of Chicago Press, 1960.

Bielefeldt, Heiner. *Kants Symbolik. Ein Schlüssel zur kritischen Freiheitsphilosophie.* Freiburg: Karl Alber, 2001.

Bittner, Rüdiger, and Konrad Cramer, eds. *Materialien zu Kants 'Kritik der praktischen Vernunft.'* Frankfurt am Main: Suhrkamp, 1975.

Böckerstette, Heinrich. *Aporien der Freiheit und ihre Aufklärung durch Kant.* Stuttgart: Frommann-Holzboog, 1982.

Brinkmann, Walter. *Praktische Notwendigkeit: eine Formalisierung von Kants Kategorischem Imperativ.* Paderborn: Mentis, 2003.

Carnois, Bernard. *The Coherence of Kant's Doctrine of Freedom.* Trans. David Booth. Chicago: Chicago University Press, 1987.

Chalier, Catherine. *What Ought I to Do? Morality in Kant and Levinas.* Ithaca, N.Y.: Cornell University Press, 2002.

Cox, J. Gray. *The Will at the Crossroads: A Reconstruction of Kant's Moral Philosophy* Lanham, Md.: University Press of America, 1984.

Delbos, Victor. *La philosophie pratique de Kant.* Paris: Presses Universitaires de France, 1969.

Düsing, Klaus. "Das Problem des höchsten Gutes in Kants praktischer Philosophie." *Kant-Studien* 62 (1971): 5–42.

Esser, Andrea Marlen. *Eine Ethik für Endliche. Kants Tugendlehre in der Gegenwart.* Stuttgart: Frommann-Holzboog, 2003.

Fairbanks, Sandra Jane. *Kantian Moral Theory and the Destruction of the Self.* Boulder, Colo.: Westview Press, 2000.

Forkl, Markus. *Kants System der Tugendpflichten. Eine Begleitschrift zu den* Metaphysischen Anfangsgründen der Tugendlehre. Frankfurt am Main: Peter Lang, 2001.

Frierson, Patrick R. *Freedom and Anthropology in Kant's Moral Philosophy.* Cambridge: Cambridge University Press, 2003.

Gregor, Mary J. *Laws of Freedom: A Study of Kant's Method of Applying the Categorical Imperative in the* Metaphysik der Sitten. Oxford: Basil Blackwell, 1963.

Grossmann, Michael. *Wertrationalität und notwendige Bildung. Immanuel Kants praktische Philosophie in ihrer Bedeutung für eine heutige pädagogische Ethik.* Frankfurt am Main: Peter Lang, 2003.

Guevara, Daniel. *Kant's Theory of Moral Motivation.* Boulder, Colo.: Westview Press, 2000.

Guyer, Paul. *Kant and the Experience of Freedom. Essays on Aesthetics and Morality.* Cambridge: Cambridge University Press, 1993.

———. *Kant on Freedom, Law, and Happiness.* Cambridge: Cambridge University Press, 2000.

———, ed. *Kant's* Groundwork of the Metaphysics of Morals: *Critical Essays.* Lanham, Md.: Rowman & Littlefield, 1998.

Henrich, Dieter. "Über Kants früheste Ethik." *Kant-Studien* 54 (1963): 404–31.

Herman, Barbara. *Morality as Rationality: A Study of Kant's Ethics.* New York: Garland, 1990.

Hill, Thomas E., Jr. *Dignity and Practical Reason in Kant's Moral Theory.* Ithaca, N.Y.: Cornell University Press, 1992.

Himmelmann, Beatrix. *Kants Begriff des Glücks.* Kant-Studien Ergänzungsheft 143. Berlin: Walter de Gruyter, 2003.

Hochberg, Gary M. *Kant: Moral Legislation and Two Senses of 'Will.'* Washington, D.C.: University Press of America, 1982.

Höffe, Otfried. *Ethik und Politik. Grundmodelle und -probleme der praktischen Philosophie.* Frankfurt am Main: Suhrkamp, 1979.

———. *Kategorische Rechtsprinzipien. Ein Kontrapunkt der Moderne.* Frankfurt am Main: Suhrkamp, 1990.

———, ed. *Grundlegung der Metaphysik der Sitten: Ein kooperativer Kommentar.* Frankfurt am Main: Vittorio Klostermann, 1989.

Hudson, Hud. *Kant's Compatibilism.* Ithaca, N.Y.: Cornell University Press, 1994.

Hutchings, Patrick Æ. *Kant on Absolute Value: A Critical Examination of Certain Key Notions in Kant's* Groundwork of the Metaphysic of Morals *and of His Ontology of Personal Value.* London: George Allen & Unwin, 1972.

Jones, Hardy E. *Kant's Principle of Personality.* Madison: University of Wisconsin Press, 1971.

Jones, W. T. *Morality and Freedom in the Philosophy of Kant.* London: Oxford University Press. 1940.

Kaulbach, Friedrich. *Das Prinzip Handlung in der Philosophie Kants.* Berlin: Walter de Gruyter, 1978.

Köhl, Harald. *Kants Gesinnungsethik.* Berlin: Walter de Gruyter, 1990.

König, Peter. *Autonomie und Autokratie. Über Kants Metaphysik der Sitten.* Berlin: Walter de Gruyter, 1994.

Korsgaard, Christine M. *Creating the Kingdom of Ends.* Cambridge: Cambridge University Press, 1996.

Krüger, Gerhard. *Philosophie und Moral in der Kantischen Kritik.* Tübingen: J. C. B. Mohr, 1931 (2nd ed., 1967).

Lo, P. C. *Treating Persons as Ends: An Essay on Kant's Moral Philosophy.* Lanham, Md.: University Press of America, 1987.

Löhrer, Guido. *Menschliche Würde. Wissenschaftliche Geltung und metaphorische Grenze der praktischen Philosophie Kants.* Freiburg: Karl Alber, 1985.

Louden, Robert: *Kant's Impure Ethics: From Rational Beings to Human Beings.* Oxford: Oxford University Press, 2000.

Malibabo, Balimbanga. *Kants Konzept einer kritischen Metaphysik der Sitten.* Würzburg: Königshausen & Neumann, 2000.

Milz, Bernhard. *Der gesuchte Widerstreit. Die Antinomie in Kants Kritik der praktischen Vernunft.* Kant-Studien Ergänzungsheft 139. Berlin: Walter de Gruyter, 2002.

Mulholland, Leslie A. *Kant's System of Rights.* New York: Columbia University Press. 1990.

Munzel, G. Felicitas. *Kant's Conception of Moral Character. The 'Critical' Link of Morality, Anthropology, and Reflective Judgement.* Chicago: University of Chicago Press, 1999.

Nell, Onora (O'Neill). *Acting on Principle: An Essay on Kantian Ethics.* New York: Columbia University Press, 1975.

Nisters, Thomas. *Kants Kategorischer Imperativ als Leitfaden humaner Praxis.* Freiburg: Karl Alber, 1989.

O'Neill, Onora. *Constructions of Reason: Explorations of Kant's Practical Philosophy.* Cambridge: Cambridge University Press, 1989.

Paton, H. J. *The Categorical Imperative: A Study in Kant's Moral Philosophy.* London: Hutchinson, 1947.

Potter, Nelson T., and Mark Timmons. *Morality and Universality: Essays on Ethical Universalizability.* Dordrecht: D. Reidel, 1985.

Prauss, Gerold. *Kant über Freiheit als Autonomie.* Frankfurt am Main: Vittorio Klostermann, 1983.

————, ed. *Handlungstheorie und Transzendentale Philosophie.* Frankfurt am Main: Vittorio Klostermann, 1986.

Rawls, John. "Kantian Constructivism in Moral Theory." *Journal of Philosophy* 77 (1980): 515–72.

Reiner, Hans. *Duty and Inclination: The Fundamentals of Morality Discussed and Redefined with Special Regard to Kant and Schiller.* Trans. Mark Santos. The Hague: Martinus Nijhoff, 1983.

Ross, Sir David. *Kant's Ethical Theory: A Commentary on the* Grundlegung zur Metaphysik der Sitten. Oxford: Clarendon Press, 1954.

Rossvær, Viggo. *Kant's Moral Philosophy: An Interpretation of the Categorical Imperative.* Oslo: Universitetsforlaget, 1979.

Rothenstreich, Nathan. *Practice and Realization. Studies in Kant's Moral Philosophy.* The Hague: Martinus Nijhoff, 1979.

Sala, Giovanni B. *Kants Kritik der praktischen Vernunft. Ein Kommentar.* Darmstadt: Wissenschaftliche Buchgesellschaft, 2004.

Schönecker, Dieter. *Kant: Grundlegung III. Die Deduktion des kategorischen Imperativs.* Freiburg: Karl Alber, 1999.

Schönecker, Dieter, and Allen W. Wood. *Kants Grundlegung zur Metaphysik der Sitten. Ein einführender Kommentar.* Paderborn: Schöningh, 2002.

Schnoor, Christian. *Kants Kategorischer Imperativ als Kriterium der Richtigkeit des Handelns.* Tübingen: J. C. B. Mohr (Paul Siebeck), 1989.

Schwaiger, Clemens. *Kategorische und andere Imperative. Zur Entwicklung von Kants praktischer Philosophie bis 1785.* Stuttgart: Frommann-Holzboog, 1999.

Seidler, Victor J. *Kant, Respect and Injustice: The Limits of Liberal Moral Theory.* London: Routledge & Kegan Paul, 1986.

Seung, T. K. *Kant's Platonic Revolution in Moral and Political Philosophy.* Baltimore, Md.: John Hopkins University Press, 1994.

Silber, John R. "Kant's Conception of the Highest Good as Immanent and Transcendent." *The Philosophical Review* 68 (1959): 469–93.

———. "The Importance of the Highest Good in Kant's Ethics." *Ethics* 73 (1962–3): 179–97.

Singer, Marcus G. *Generalization in Ethics: An Essay in the Logic of Ethics, with the Rudiments of a System of Moral Philosophy.* New York: Alfred A. Knopf, 1961.

Sommerfeld-Lethen, Caroline. *Wie moralisch werden? Kants moralistische Ethik.* Freiburg: Karl Alber, 2004.

Steigleder, Klaus. *Kants Moralphilosophie. Die Selbstbezüglichkeit reiner praktischer Vernunft.* Stuttgart: J. B. Metzler, 2002.

Stevens, Rex P. *Kant on Moral Practice.* Macon, Ga.: Mercer University Press, 1981.

Stratton-Lake, Philip. *Kant, Duty and Moral Worth.* London: Routledge, 2000.

Sullivan, Roger J. *Immanuel Kant's Moral Theory.* Cambridge: Cambridge University Press, 1989.

———. *An Introduction to Kant's Ethics.* Cambridge: Cambridge University Press, 1994.

Timmermann, Jens. *Sittengesetz und Freiheit. Untersuchungen zu Immanuel Kants Theorie des freien Willens.* Berlin: Walter de Gruyter, 2003.

Timmons, Mark, ed. *Kant's Metaphysics of Morals: Interpretative Essays.* Oxford: Oxford University Press, 2002.

Velkley, Richard L. *Freedom and the End of Reason: On the Moral Foundations of Kant's Critical Philosophy* Chicago: University of Chicago Press, 1989.

Ward, Keith. *The Development of Kant's View of Ethics.* Oxford: Blackwell, 1972.

Wike, Victoria S. *Kant on Happiness in Ethics.* Albany: State University of New York Press, 1994.

Williams, T. C. *The Concept of the Categorical Imperative: A Study of the Place of the Categorical Imperative in Kant's Ethical Theory.* Oxford: Clarendon Press, 1968.

Wolff, Robert Paul. *The Autonomy of Reason: A Commentary on Kant's Groundwork of the Metaphysics of Morals.* New York: Harper & Row, 1973.

Wood, Allen W. *Kant's Ethical Thought.* Cambridge: Cambridge University Press, 1999.

Yovel, Yirmiyahu, ed. *Kant's Practical Philosophy Reconsidered: Papers Presented at the Seventh Jerusalem Philosophical Encounter, December 1986.* Dordrecht: Kluwer, 1989.

I. POLITICAL PHILOSOPHY AND PHILOSOPHY OF LAW

Arendt, Hannah. *Lectures on Kant's Political Philosophy.* Ed. Ronald Beiner. Chicago: University of Chicago Press, 1982.

Batscha, Zwi, ed. *Materialen zu Kants Rechtsphilosophie.* Frankfurt am Main: Suhrkamp, 1976.

Beiner, Ronald, and William James Booth, eds. *Kant and Political Philosophy: The Contemporary Legacy.* New Haven, Conn.: Yale University Press, 1993.

Bohman, James, and Matthias Lutz-Bachmann, eds. *Perpetual Peace: Essays on Kant's Cosmopolitan Ideal.* Cambridge, Mass.: MIT Press, 1997.

Brandt, Reinhard. *Eigentumstheorien von Grotius bis Kant.* Stuttgart: Frommann-Holzboog, 1974.

———, ed. *Rechtsphilosophie der Aufklärung.* Berlin: Walter de Gruyter, 1982.

Budelacci, Orlando. *Kants Friedensprogramm. Das politische Denken im Kontext der praktischen Philosophie.* Oberhausen: Athena, 2003.

Burg, Peter. *Kant und die Französische Revolution.* Berlin: Duncker & Humblot, 1974.

Busch, Werner. *Die Entstehung der kritischen Rechtsphilosophie Kants, 1762-1780.* Kant-Studien Ergänzungsheft 110. Berlin: Walter de Gruyter, 1979.

Cavallar, Georg. *Kant and the Theory and Practice of International Right.* Cardiff: University of Wales Press, 1999.

Deggau, Hans-Georg. *Die Aporien der Rechtslehre Kants.* Stuttgart: Frommann-Holzboog, 1983.

Flickschuh, Katrin. *Kant and Modern Political Philosophy.* Cambridge: Cambridge University Press, 2000.

Friedrich, Rainer. *Eigentum und Staatsbegründung.* Kant-Studien Ergänzungsheft 146. Berlin: Walter de Gruyter, 2004.

Gerhardt, Volker. *Immanuel Kants Entwurf 'Zum ewigen Frieden.' Eine Theorie der Politik.* Darmstadt: Wissenschaftliche Buchgesellschaft, 1995.

Haensel, Werner. *Kants Lehre vom Widerstandsrecht: Ein Beitrag zur Systematik der Kantischen Rechtsphilosophie.* Kant-Studien Ergänzungsheft 60. Berlin: Pan-Verlag, 1926.

Höffe, Otfried. *"Königliche Völker." Zu Kants kosmopolitischer Rechts- und Friedensethik.* Frankfurt am Main: Suhrkamp, 2001.

————. *Metaphysische Anfangsgründe der Rechtslehre.* Berlin: Akademie Verlag, 1999.

————, ed. *Immanuel Kant: Zum ewigen Frieden.* Berlin: Akademie Verlag, 1995.

Hüning, Dieter, and Burkhard Tuschling, eds. *Recht, Staat und Völkerrecht bei Immanuel Kant.* Berlin: Duncker & Humblot, 1998.

Hutchings, Kimberly. *Kant, Critique and Politics.* London: Routledge, 1996.

Kaufman, Alexander. *Welfare in the Kantian State.* Oxford: Oxford University Press, 1999.

Kersting, Wolfgang. *Wohlgeordnete Freiheit: Immanuel Kants Rechts- und Staatsphilosophie.* Berlin: Walter de Gruyter, 1984.

————. *Kant über Recht.* Paderborn: Mentis, 2004.

Kühl, Kristian. *Eigentumsordnung als Freiheitsordnung: Zur Aktualität der Kantischen Rechts- und Eigentumslehre.* Freiburg: Karl Alber, 1984.

Küsters, Gerd-Walter. *Kants Rechtsphilosophie.* Darmstadt: Wissenschaftliche Buchgesellschaft, 1988.

Laberge, Pierre, Guy Lafrance, and Denis Dumas, eds. *L'Année 1795. Kant. Essai sur la paix.* Paris: J. Vrin, 1997.

Langer, Claudia. *Reform nach Prinzipien: Untersuchungen zur politischen Theorie Immanuel Kants.* Stuttgart: Klett-Cotta, 1986.

Ludwig, Bernd. *Kants Rechtslehre.* Hamburg: Felix Meiner, 1988.

Lutz-Bachmann, Matthias, and James Bohman, eds. *Frieden durch Recht. Kants Friedensidee und das Problem einer neuen Weltordnung.* Frankfurt am Main: Suhrkamp, 1996.

Merkel, Reinhard, and Roland Wittmann, eds. *Zum ewigen Frieden. Grundlagen, Aktualität und Aussichten einer Idee von Immanuel Kant.* Frankfurt a.m.: Suhrkamp, 1996.

Murphy, Jeffrie G. *Kant: The Philosophy of Right.* London: Macmillan, 1970 (reprinted, Macon, Ga.: Mercer University Press, 1994).

Oberer, Hariolf. "Zur Frühgeschichte der Kantischen Rechtslehre." *Kant-Studien* 64 (1973): 88–102.

Riley, Patrick. *Kant's Political Philosophy.* Totowa, N.J.: Rowman & Littlefield, 1983.

Ritter, Christian. *Der Rechtsgedanke Kants nach den frühen Quellen.* Frankfurt am Main: Vittorio Klostermann, 1971.

Saage, Richard. *Eigentum, Staat und Gesellschaft bei Immanuel Kant.* Stuttgart: Kohlhammer, 1973.

Saner, Hans. *Kant's Political Thought: Its Origins and Development.* Trans. E. B. Ashton. Chicago: University of Chicago Press, 1973.

Shell, Susan Meld. *The Rights of Reason: A Study of Kant's Philosophy and Politics.* Toronto: University of Toronto Press, 1980.

Tuck, Richard. *The Rights of War and Peace. Political Thought and the International Order from Grotius to Kant.* Oxford: Oxford University Press, 1999.

Van der Linden, Harry. *Kantian Ethics and Socialism.* Indianapolis: Hackett, 1988.

Vlachos, Georges. *La pensée politique de Kant. Métaphysique de l'ordre et dialectique du progrès.* Paris: Presses Universitaires de France, 1962.

Williams, Howard L. *Kant's Political Philosophy.* New York: St. Martin's Press, 1983.

———, ed. *Essays on Kant's Political Philosophy.* Cardiff: University of Wales Press, 1992.

Zotta, Franco. *Immanuel Kant. Legitimität und Recht. Eine Kritik seiner Eigentumslehre, Staatslehre und seiner Geschichtsphilosophie.* Freiburg: Karl Alber, 2000.

J. THE THIRD CRITIQUE: COMPREHENSIVE STUDIES AND AESTHETICS

Allison, Henry E. *Kant's Theory of Taste: A Reading of the Critique of Aesthetic Judgment.* Cambridge: Cambridge University Press, 2001.

Banham, Gary. *Kant and the End of Aesthetics.* Basingstoke: Macmillan, 1999.

Bartuschat, Wolfgang. *Zum systematischen Ort von Kants Kritik der Urteilskraft.* Frankfurt am Main: Vittorio Klostermann, 1972.

Burnham, Douglas. *An Introduction to Kant's Critique of Judgment.* Edinburgh: Edinburgh University Press, 2001.

Cassirer, Heinrich Walter. *A Commentary on Kant's Critique of Judgment.* London: Methuen, 1938.

Caygill, Howard. *Art of Judgement.* Oxford: Basil Blackwell, 1989.

Cheetham, Mark A. *Kant, Art, and Art History: Moments of Discipline.* Cambridge: Cambridge University Press, 2001.

Cohen, Ted, and Paul Guyer, eds. *Essays in Kant's Aesthetics.* Chicago: University of Chicago Press, 1982.

Coleman, Francis X. J. *The Harmony of Reason: A Study in Kant's Aesthetics.* Pittsburgh, Pa.: University of Pittsburgh Press, 1974.

Crawford, Donald W. *Kant's Aesthetic Theory.* Madison: University of Wisconsin Press, 1974.

Crowther, Paul. *The Kantian Sublime: From Morality to Art.* Oxford: Clarendon Press, 1989.

Dumouchel, Daniel. *Kant et la genèse de la subjectivité esthétique. Esthétique et philosophie avant la Critique de la faculté de juger.* Paris: J. Vrin, 1999.

Dunham, Barrows. *A Study in Kant's Aesthetics: The Universal Validity of Aesthetic Judgments.* Lancaster, Pa.: no publisher, 1934.

Esser, Andrea Marlen. *Kunst und Symbol. Die Struktur ästhetischer Reflexion in Kants Theorie des Schönen.* Munich: Wilhelm Fink, 1997.

Felten, Gundula. *Die Funktion des "sensus communis" in Kants Theorie des ästhetischen Urteils.* Paderborn: Wilhelm Fink, 2003.

Fistioc, Mihaela C. *The Beautiful Shape of the Good: Platonic and Pythagorean Themes in Kant's Critique of the Power of Judgment.* New York: Routledge, 2002.

Frank, Manfred, and Véronique Zanetti, eds. *Einführender Kommentar zu Kants Ästhetischen Schriften.* 3 vols. Frankfurt am Main: Suhrkamp, 2001.

Fricke, Christel. *Kants Theorie des reinen Geschmacksurteils.* Berlin: Walter de Gruyter, 1990.

Gasche, Rodolphe. *The Idea of Form: Rethinking Kant's Aesthetics.* Stanford, Calif.: Stanford University Press, 2003.

Guyer, Paul. *Kant and the Claims of Taste.* Cambridge, Mass.: Harvard University Press, 1979 (2nd ed., Cambridge: Cambridge University Press, 1997).

Henrich, Dieter. *Aesthetic Judgment and the Moral Image of the World.* Stanford, Calif.: Stanford University Press, 1992.

Kemal, Salim. *Kant and Fine Art: An Essay on Kant and the Philosophy of Fine Art and Culture.* Oxford: Clarendon Press, 1986.

———. *Kant's Aesthetic Theory. An Introduction.* New York: St. Martin's Press, 1992.

Kirwan, James. *The Aesthetic in Kant: A Critique.* London: Continuum, 2004.

Kohler, Georg. *Geschmacksurteil und ästhetische Erfahrung. Beiträge zur Auslegung von Kants "Kritik der ästhetischen Urteilskraft."* Kant-Studien Ergänzungsheft 111. Berlin: Walter de Gruyter, 1980.

Krämling, Gerhard. *Die systembildende Rolle von Ästhetik und Kulturphilosophie bei Kant.* Freiburg: Karl Alber, 1985.

Kulenkampff, Jens. *Kants Logik des ästhetischen Urteils.* Frankfurt am Main: Vittorio Klostermann, 1978.

Lebrun, Gérard. *Kant et la mort de la métaphysique: Essai sur la "Critique de la faculté de juger."* Paris: Colin, 1970.

McCloskey, Mary A. *Kant's Aesthetic.* London: Macmillan, 1987.

Macmillan, R. A. C. *The Crowning Phase of the Critical Philosophy: A Study in Kant's Critique of Judgment.* London: Macmillan, 1912 (reprinted, New York: Garland, 1976).

Makkreel, Rudolf A. *Imagination and Interpretation in Kant. The Hermeneutical Import of the* Critique of Judgment. Chicago: Chicago University Press, 1990.

Meerbote, Ralph, ed. *Kant's Aesthetics.* Atascadero, Calif.: Ridgeview, 1991.

Menzer, Paul. *Kants Ästhetik in ihrer Entwicklung.* Abhandlungen der Deutschen Akademie der Wissenschaften zu Berlin, Klasse für Gesellschaftswissenschaften, Jahrgang 1950, No. 2. Berlin: Akademie-Verlag, 1952.

Mertens, Helga. *Kommentar zur ersten Einleitung in Kants Kritik der Urteilskraft: Zur systematischen Funktion der Kritik der Urteilskraft für das System der Vernunftkritik.* Munich: Johannes Berchman, 1975.

Mothersill, Mary. *Beauty Restored.* Oxford: Clarendon Press, 1984.

Nerheim, Hjördis. *Zur kritischen Funktion ästhetischer Rationalität in Kants* Kritik der Urteilskraft. Frankfurt am Main: Peter Lang, 2001.

Parret, Herman, ed. *Kants Ästhetik = Kant's Aesthetics = L'Esthétique de Kant.* Berlin: Walter de Gruyter, 1998.

Pillow, Kirk. *Sublime Understanding: Aesthetic Reflection in Kant and Hegel.* Cambridge, Mass.: MIT Press, 2000.

Podro, Michael. *The Manifold in Perception: Theories of Art from Kant to Hildebrand.* Oxford: Clarendon Press, 1972.

Pieper, Hans-Joachim. *Geschmacksurteil und ästhetische Einstellung. Eine Untersuchung zur Grundlegung transzendentalphilosophischer Ästhetik bei Kant und ein Entwurf zur Phänomenologie der ästhetischen Erfahrung.* Würzburg: Königshausen & Neumann, 2001.

Pries, Christine. *Übergänge ohne Brücken. Kants Erhabenes zwischen Kritik und Metaphysik.* Berlin: Akademie Verlag, 1995.

Recki, Birgit. *Ästhetik der Sitten. Die Affinität von ästhetischem Gefühl und praktischer Vernunft bei Kant.* Frankfurt am Main: Vittorio Klostermann, 2001.

Rogerson, Kenneth F. *Kant's Aesthetics: The Roles of Form and Expression.* Lanham, Md.: University Press of America, 1986.

Savile, Anthony. *Aesthetic Reconstructions: The Seminal Writings of Lessing. Kant, and Schiller.* Oxford: Blackwell, 1987.

―――. *Kantian Aesthetics Pursued.* Edinburgh: Edinburgh University Press, 1993.

Schaper, Eva. *Studies in Kant's Aesthetics.* Edinburgh: Edinburgh University Press, 1979.

Uehhing, Theodore E., Jr. *The Notion of Form in Kant's Critique of Aesthetic Judgment.* The Hague: Mouton, 1971.

Wieland, Wolfgang. *Urteil und Gefühl. Kants Theorie der Urteilskraft.* Göttingen: Vandenhoeck & Ruprecht, 2001.

Zammito, John H. *The Genesis of Kant's Critique of Judgment.* Chicago: University of Chicago Press, 1992.

Zeldin, Mary-Barbara. *Freedom and the Critical Undertaking: Essays on Kant's Later Critiques.* Ann Arbor, Mich.: UMI Monographs, 1980.

K. THE THIRD CRITIQUE: TELEOLOGY AND PHILOSOPHY OF BIOLOGY

Düsing, Klaus. *Die Teleologie in Kants Weltbegriff.* Kant-Studien Ergänzungsheft 96. Bonn: Bouvier, 1968 (2nd ed., 1986).

Hermann, István. *Kants Teleologie.* Budapest: Akadémiai Kiadó, 1972.

Löw, Reinhard. *Philosophie des Lebendigen: Der Begriff des Organischen bei Kant, sein Grund und seine Aktualität.* Frankfurt am Main: Suhrkamp, 1980.

McFarland, J. D. *Kant's Concept of Teleology.* Edinburgh: Edinburgh University Press, 1970.

McLaughlin, Peter. *Kant's Critique of Teleology in Biological Explanation: Antinomy and Teleology.* Lewiston, N.Y.: Mehlen, 1990.

Menzer, Paul. *Kants Lehre von der Entwicklung in Natur und Geschichte.* Berlin: Georg Reimer, 1911.

Zumbach, Clark. *The Transcendent Science: Kant's Conception of Biological Methodology.* The Hague: Martinus Nijhoff, 1984.

L. PHILOSOPHY OF HISTORY, ANTHROPOLOGY, AND EMPIRICAL PSYCHOLOGY

Booth, William James. *Interpreting the World: Kant's Philosophy of History and Politics.* Toronto: University of Toronto Press, 1986.

Brandt, Reinhard. *Kritischer Kommentar zu Kants Anthropologie in pragmatischer Hinsicht (1798).* Hamburg: Felix Meiner, 1999.

————. *Universität zwischen Selbst- und Fremdbestimmung. Kants* Streit der Fakultäten. *Mit einem Anhang zu Heideggers "Rektoratsrede."* Berlin: Akademie Verlag, 2003.

Ferrari, Jean, ed. *L'Année 1798. Kant et la naissance de l'anthropologie au siècle des lumières.* Paris: J. Vrin, 1997.

Galston, William A. *Kant and the Problem of History.* Chicago: University of Chicago Press, 1975.

Jacobs, Brian, and Patrick Kain, eds. *Essays on Kant's Anthropology.* Cambridge: Cambridge University Press, 2003.

Kaiser-El-Safti, Margret. *Die Idee der wissenschaftlichen Psychologie. Immanuel Kants kritische Einwände und ihre konstruktive Widerlegung.* Würzburg: Königshausen & Neumann, 2001.

Kant: philosophie de l'histoire. Revue Germanique Internationale 6 (1996) (special issue multiple-author anthology).

Kleingeld, Pauline. *Fortschritt und Vernunft. Zur Geschichtsphilosophie Kants.* Würzburg: Königshausen & Neumann, 1995.

Philonenko, Alexis. *La théorie kantienne de l'histoire.* Paris: J. Vrin, 1986.

Van de Pitte, Frederick P. *Kant as Philosophical Anthropologist.* The Hague: Martinus Nijhoff, 1971.

Weyand, Klaus. *Kants Geschichtsphilosophie: Ihre Entwicklung und ihr Verhältnis zur Aufklärung.* Kant-Studien Ergänzungsheft 85. Cologne: Kölner Universitäts-Verlag, 1963.

Yovel, Yirmiyahu. *Kant and the Philosophy of History.* Princeton, N.J.: Princeton University Press, 1980.

Zammito, John H. *Kant, Herder, and the Birth of Anthropology.* Chicago: University of Chicago Press, 2001.

M. PHILOSOPHY OF RELIGION

Axinn, Sidney. *The Logic of Hope: Extensions of Kant's View of Religion.* Amsterdam: Rodopi, 1994.

Bohatec, Josef. *Die Religionsphilosophie Kants in der "Religion innerhalb der Grenzen der bloßen Vernunft." Mit besonderer Berücksichtigung ihrer theologisch-dogmatischen Quellen.* Hildesheim: Georg Olms, 1966.

Bruch, Jean-Louis. *La philosophie religieuse de Kant.* Paris: Aubier-Montaigne, 1968.

Caropreso, Paolo. *Von der Dingfrage zur Frage nach Gott: zum eigentlichen Ursprung von Religiosität in Kants Transzendentalphilosophie.* Berlin: Walter de Gruyter, 2003.

Dell'Oro, Regina O. M. *From Existence to the Ideal: Continuity and Development in Kant's Theology.* New York: Peter Lang, 1994.

Despland, Michel. *Kant on History and Religion.* Montreal: McGill-Queen's University Press, 1973.

Fischer, Norbert, ed. *Kants Metaphysik und Religionsphilosophie.* Hamburg: Meiner, 2004.

Fukumitsu, Mizue. *Kants Gottesbegriff und seine kopernikanische Wende.* Hamburg: Kovac, 2001.

Loades, Ann J. *Kant and Job's Comforters.* Newcastle upon Tyne: Avero, 1985.

Michalson, Gordon E., Jr. *Fallen Freedom. Kant on Radical Evil and Moral Regeneration.* Cambridge: Cambridge University Press, 1990.

———. *Kant and the Problem of God.* Oxford: Blackwell, 1999.

Moore, A. W. *Noble in Reason, Infinite in Faculty: Themes and Variations in Kant's Moral and Religious Philosophy.* New York: Routledge, 2003.

Palmquist, Stephen. *Kant's Critical Religion.* Aldershot: Ashgate, 2000.

Ricken, Friede, and François Marty, eds. *Kant über Religion.* Stuttgart: Kohlhammer, 1992.

Rossi, Philip J., and Michael Wreen, eds. *Kant's Philosophy of Religion Reconsidered.* Bloomington: Indiana University Press, 1991.

Reardon, Bernard M. G. *Kant as Philosophical Theologian.* Totowa, N.J.: Barnes and Noble, 1988.

Reboul, Olivier. *Kant et le problème du mal.* Montreal: Presses de l'Université de Montréal, 1971.

Sala, Giovanni. *Kant und die Frage nach Gott. Gottesbeweise und Gottesbeweiskritik in den Schriften Kants.* Kant-Studien Ergänzungsheft 122. Berlin: Walter de Gruyter, 1990.

Schmucker, Josef. *Das Problem der Kontingenz der Welt: Versuch einer positiven Aufarbeitung der Kritik Kants am kosmologischen Argument.* Freiburg: Herder, 1969.

Schulte, Christoph. *Radikal Böse. Die Karriere des Bösen von Kant bis Nietzsche.* Munich: Wilhelm Fink, 1988.

———. *Die jüdische Aufklärung. Philosophie, Religion, Geschichte.* Munich: Beck, 2002.

Stangneth, Bettina. *Kultur der Aufrichtigkeit. Zum systematischen Ort von Kants Religion innerhalb der Grenzen der bloßen Vernunft.* Würzburg: Königshausen & Neumann, 2000.

Thiede, Werner. *Glauben aus eigener Vernunft? Kants Religionsphilosophie und die Theologie.* Göttingen: Vandenhoeck & Ruprecht, 2004.

Webb, Clement C. J. *Kant's Philosophy of Religion.* Oxford: Clarendon Press, 1926.

Wimmer, Reiner. *Kants kritische Religionsphilosophie.* Kant-Studien Ergänzungsheft 124. Berlin: Walter de Gruyter, 1990.

Winter, Alois. *Der andere Kant. Zur philosophischen Theologie Immanuel Kants.* Hildesheim: Georg Olms, 2000.

Wood, Allen W. *Kant's Moral Religion.* Ithaca, N.Y.: Cornell University Press, 1970.

———. *Kant's Rational Theology.* Ithaca, N.Y.: Cornell University Press, 1978.

N. KANTIANISM

1. Early Responses to Kant

Beck, Jakob Sigismund. *Erläuternder Auszug aus den critischen Schriften des Herrn Prof. Kant.* 3 vols. Riga: Hartknoch, 1793–1796 (reprinted, Brussels: Culture et civilisation, 1968; Frankfurt am Main: Minerva, 1975).

———. *Grundriss der critischen Philosophie.* Halle: Renger, 1796 (reprinted, Brussels: Culture et civilisation, 1970).

———. *The Principle of Critical Philosophy, selected from the Works of Emmanuel Kant . . . and Expounded by James Sigismund Beck Translated from German by an Auditor of the Latter.* London: J. Johnson, 1797.

———. *Commentar über Kants Metaphysik der Sitten, 1. Theil welcher die metaphysischen Principien des Naturrechts enthält.* Halle: Renger, 1798 (reprinted, Brussels: Culture et civilisation, 1970).

Beddoes, Thomas. *Observations on the Nature of Demonstrative Evidence; with an Explanation of Certain Difficulties Occurring in the Elements of Geometry: and Reflections on Language.* London: J. Johnson, 1793 (reprinted, Bristol: Thoemmes, 1990).

Eberhard, Johann August. *Der Streit mit Johann August Eberhard*, ed. Marion Lauschke, Manfred Zahn. Hamburg: Meiner, 1998.

Fichte, Johann Gottlieb. *Versuch einer Critik aller Offenbarung.* Königsberg: Hartung, 1792.

————. *Attempt at a Critique of all Revelation*, trans. Garrett Green. Cambridge: Cambridge University Press, 1978.

————. *Grundlage der gesammten Wissenschaftslehre: Als Handschrift für seine Zuhörer.* Leipzig: Christian Ernst Gabler, 1794.

————. *Science of Knowledge (Wissenschaftslehre) with the First and Second Introductions*, trans. Peter Heath, John Lachs. New York: Appleton-Century-Crofts, 1970.

Fries, Jakob Friedrich. *Wissen, Glauben und Ahndung.* Jena, 1805.

————. *Neue oder anthropologische Kritik der Vernunft*, 2nd ed. 3 vols. Heidelberg: Winter, 1828-31.

Hegel, Georg Wilhelm Friedrich. *Differenz des Fichte'schen und Schelling'schen Systems der Philosophie in Beziehung auf Reinhold's Beyträge zur leichtern Übersicht des Zustands der Philosophie zu Anfang des neunzehnten Jahrhunderts, etc.* Jena, 1801.

————. *Difference between Fichte's and Schelling's System of Philosophy in Connection with the First Fascicle of Reinhold's Contributions to a more Convenient Survey of the State of Philosophy at the Beginning of the Nineteenth Century*, trans. Walter Cerf, H.S. Harris. Albany: State University of New York Press, 1976.

————. *Jenaer kritische Schriften. 3, Glauben und Wissen, oder die Reflexionsphilosophie der Subjektivität, in der Vollständigkeit ihrer Formen, als Kantische, Jacobische und Fichtesche*, eds. Hans Brockard, Hartmut Buchner. Hamburg: Meiner, 1986.

————. *Faith and Knowledge: or, The Reflective Philosophy of Subjectivity in the Complete Range of its Forms as Kantian, Jacobian, and Fichtean Philosophy*, trans. Walter Cerf, H. S. Harris. Albany: State University of New York Press, 1976.

Herder, Johann Gottfried. *Verstand und Erfahrung. Eine Metakritik zur Kritik der reinen Vernunft.* 2 vols. Leipzig: Hartknoch, 1799 (reprinted, Brussels: Culture et civilisation, 1969).

Landau, Albert, ed. *Rezensionen zur Kantischen Philosophie. Band I: 1781-1787.* Bebra: Landau, 1991.

Maimon, Salomon. *Versuch über die Transcendentalphilosophie.* Berlin: Voss und Sohn, 1790 (reprinted, Darmstadt: Wissenschaftliche Buchgesellschaft, 1972; Hildesheim: Georg Olms, 2000).

————. *Versuch einer neuen Logik oder Theorie des Denkens.* Berlin: Felisch, 1794 (reprinted, Hildesheim: Georg Olms, 1970).

Nitsch, Friedrich August. *A General and Introductory View of Professor Kant's Principles concerning Man, the World, and the Deity.* London: J. Downes, 1796.

O'Keeffe, J. A. *An Essay on the Progress of the Human Understanding.* London: V. Griffiths, 1795.

Reinhold, Karl Leonhard. *Beyträge zur Berichtigung bisheriger Missverständnisse der Philosophen.* 2 vols. Jena: Johann M. Mauke, 1790–1792.

————. *Briefe über die Kantische Philosophie.* 2 vols. Leipzig: Göschen, 1790/1792 (early versions of some of the Letters appeared in 1786/87).

————. *Versuch einer neuen Theorie des menschlichen Vorstellungsvermögens.* Prague and Jena: C. Widtmann and I. M. Mauke, 1789.

Richardson, John. *The Principles of Critical Philosophy, selected from the Works of Emmanuel Kant . . . and Expounded by James Sigismund Beck . . . Translated from the German by an Auditor of the Latter.* London: Escher, 1797.

Rink, Friedrich T. *Mancherley zur Geschichte der metacritischen Invasion. Nebst einem Fragment einer ältern Metacritik von Johann Georg Hamann.* Königsberg: Nicolovius, 1800 (reprinted, Brussels: Culture et civilisation, 1969).

Sassen, Brigitte, ed. and trans. *Kant's Early Critics. The Empiricist Critique of the Critical Philosophy.* Cambridge: Cambridge University Press, 2000. (Translation of criticism raised against Kant between 1781 and 1789.)

Schelling, Friedrich Wilhelm Joseph. *Philosophische Briefe über Dogmatismus und Kriticismus (1795); Neue Deduction des Naturrechts (1796/97); Antikritik (1796),* ed. Hartmut Buchner. Stuttgart: Frommann-Holzboog, 1982.

Schopenhauer, Arthur. *Ueber die vierfache Wurzel des Satzes vom zureichenden Grunde: eine philosophische Abhandlung.* Rudolstadt: Hof-Buch- und Kunsthandlung, 1813.

————. *On the Fourfold Root of the Principle of Sufficient Reason,* trans. E. F. J. Payne. La Salle, Ill.: Open Court, 1974.

————. *Die Welt als Wille und Vorstellung. Vier Bücher nebst einem An-hang, der die Kritik der Kantischen Philosophie enthält, etc.* Leipzig: Brockhaus, 1819.

————. *The World as Will and Representation*, trans. E. F. J. Payne, 2 vols. Indian Hills, Colo.: Falcon's Wing Press, 1958.

Schultz, Johann. *Exposition of Kant's* Critique of Pure Reason, trans. James C. Morrison. Ottawa: University of Ottawa Press, 1995.

Stewart, Dugald. "Dissertation Exhibiting a General View of the Progress of Metaphysical, Ethical, and Political Philosophy, since the Revival of Letters in Europe." In *Supplement to the Fourth, Fifth, and Sixth Editions of the Encyclopedia Britannica.* Vol. 1, pp. 1–66, Vol. 5, pp. 1–257. Edinburgh, 1824.

Willich, A. F. M. *Elements of the Critical Philosophy.* London: T. N. Longman, 1798 (reprinted, New York: Garland, 1977).

2. Precursors of Neokantianism

Beneke, Friedrich Eduard. *Kant und die philosophische Aufgabe unserer Zeit.* Berlin: Mittler, 1832 (reprinted, Brussels: Culture et civilisation, 1969).

Fischer, Kuno. *Immanuel Kant.* 2 vols. Mannheim: Bassermann, 1860.

————. *A Commentary on Kant's Critick of the Pure Reason.* London: Longmans, Green, 1866 (reprinted, New York: Garland, 1976).

Helmholtz, Hermann von. "Über das Sehen des Menschen. Vortrag gehalten zu Königsberg am 27. Februar 1855." In *Vorträge und Reden.* 5th ed., vol. 1, pp. 85–117. Braunschweig: Vieweg, 1903.

Lange, Friedrich Albert. *Geschichte des Materialismus und Kritik seiner Bedeutung in der Gegenwart.* 2 vols., ed. Alfred Schmidt. Frankfurt am Main: Suhrkamp, 1974 (first ed. 1866).

————. *Die Arbeiterfrage in ihrer Bedeutung für Gegenwart und Zukunft beleuchtet.* Duisburg: W. Falk & Volmer, 1865 (reprinted, Hildesheim: Georg Olms, 1979).

Liebmann, Otto. *Kant und die Epigonen. Eine kritische Abhandlung.* Stuttgart: Carl Schober, 1865 (new ed. by Bruno Bauch, Berlin: Reuther & Reichard, 1912; reprinted, Erlangen, 1991).

————. *Über den objectiven Anblick. Eine kritische Abhandlung.* Stuttgart: Schober, 1869.

Lotze, Hermann. *Metaphysic: In Three Books, Ontology, Cosmology, and Psychology.* Trans. Bernard Bosanquet. Oxford: Clarendon Press, 1884 (first German ed., Leipzig: Weidmann, 1841).

————. *Logic: In Three Books, of Thought, of Investigation, and of Knowledge.* Trans. Bernard Bosanquet. Oxford: Clarendon Press, 1884 (reprinted, New York: Garland, 1980; 2nd German ed., Leipzig: S. Hirzel, 1880).

Stadler, August. *Die Grundsätze der reinen Erkenntnisstheorie in der kantischen Philosophie.* Leipzig: S. Hirzel, 1876.

————. *Kants Teleologie und ihre erkenntnisstheoretische Bedeutung.* Berlin: F. Dümmler, 1874.

————. *Kants Theorie der Materie.* Leipzig: S. Hirzel, 1883.

Weisse, Christian Hermann. *In welchem Sinn die deutsche Philosophie jetzt wieder an Kant sich zu orientiren hat. Eine akademische Antrittsrede.* Leipzig: Dyk, 1847.

3. Neokantianism

Bauch, Bruno. *Immanuel Kant.* 3rd ed. Berlin: Göschen, 1923 (first ed. 1917). Review by Paul Natorp, "Bruno Bauchs *Immanuel Kant* und die Fortbildung des Systems des kritischen Idealismus." *Kant-Studien* 22 (1918): 426–59.

Cassirer, Ernst. "Kant und die moderne Mathematik. (Mit Bezug auf Bertrand Russells und Louis Couturats Werke über die Prinzipien der Mathematik.)" *Kant-Studien* 12 (1907): 1–49.

————. *Substance and Function and Einstein's Theory of Relativity,* trans. William Curtis Swabey. Chicago: Open Court, 1923.

Cohen, Hermann. *Ästhetik des reinen Gefühls.* 2 vols. 2nd ed. Berlin: Bruno Cassirer, 1912 (reprinted, Hildesheim: Georg Olms, 1982).

————. *Der Begriff der Religion im System der Philosophie.* Giessen: Töpelmann, 1915 (reprinted, Hildesheim: Georg Olms, 1996).

————. *Ethik des reinen Willens.* 2nd ed. Berlin: Bruno Cassirer, 1907 (reprinted, Introduction in English by Steven S. Schwarzschild, Hildesheim: Georg Olms, 1981).

————. *Kants Begründung der Ästhetik.* Berlin: Ferdinand Dümmler, 1889.

————. *Kants Begründung der Ethik.* 2nd ed. Berlin: Bruno Cassirer, 1910 (reprinted, Hildesheim: Georg Olms, 2001).

————. *Kants Theorie der Erfahrung.* 3rd ed. Berlin: Bruno Cassirer, 1918 (reprinted, Hildesheim: Georg Olms, 1987).

————. *Logik der reinen Erkenntnis.* 2nd ed. Berlin: Bruno Cassirer, 1914 (reprinted, Hildesheim: Georg Olms, 1977).

————. *Religion of Reason out of the Sources of Judaism*. Trans. Simon Kaplan. New York: Frederick Ungar Publishing Co., 1972.

Cohn, Jonas. *Geschichte des Unendlichkeitsproblems im abendländischen Denken bis Kant*. Leipzig: W. Engelmann, 1896 (reprinted, Hildesheim: Georg Olms, 1960, 1983).

————. *Theorie der Dialektik. Formenlehre der Philosophie*. Leipzig: F. Meiner, 1923 (reprinted, Darmstadt: Wissenschaftliche Buchgesellschaft, 1965).

Kellermann, Benzion. *Das Ideal im System der Kantischen Philosophie*. Berlin: C. A. Schwetschke & Sohn, 1920.

Kuntze, Friedrich. *Die kritische Lehre von der Objektivität. Versuch einer weiterführenden Darstellung des Zentralproblems der kantischen Erkenntniskritik*. Heidelberg: Winter, 1906.

Lask, Emil. *Die Logik der Philosophie und die Kategorienlehre. Eine Studie über den Herrschaftsbereich der logischen Form*. Tübingen: J.C.B. Mohr (Paul Siebeck), 1911 (2nd ed. 1923, reprinted, 1993).

Natorp, Paul. *Die logischen Grundlagen der exakten Wissenschaften*. 2nd ed. Leipzig: Teubner, 1921 (first ed. 1910).

————. "Kant und die Marburger Schule." *Kant-Studien* 17 (1912): 193–221.

Nelson, Leonard. *Die kritische Ethik bei Kant, Schiller, und Fries: Eine Revision ihrer Prinzipien*. Göttingen: Vandenhoeck & Ruprecht, 1914.

————. *Progress and Regress in Philosophy: From Hume and Kant to Hegel and Fries*. Ed. Julius Kraft, trans. Humphrey Palmer. 2 vols. Oxford: Basil Blackwell, 1970–1.

Rickert, Heinrich. "Zwei Wege der Erkenntnistheorie. Transcendentalpsychologie und Transcendentallogik." *Kant-Studien* 14 (1909): 169–228 (Separate edition, Würzburg: Königshausen & Neumann, 2002).

————. *Der Gegenstand der Erkenntnis. Einführung in die Transzendentalphilosophie*. 3rd ed. Tübingen: J. C. B. Mohr (Paul Siebeck), 1915.

————. *Kant als Philosoph der modernen Kultur. Ein geschichtsphilosophischer Versuch*. Tübingen: J. C. B. Mohr (Paul Siebeck), 1924.

Riehl, Alois. *Der philosophische Kriticismus und seine Bedeutung für die positive Wissenschaft*. 3 vols. Leipzig: W. Engelmann, 1876–87.

Vorländer, Karl. "Kant und der Sozialismus." *Kant-Studien* 4 (1900): 361–412.

Windelband, Wilhelm. *Präludien. Aufsätze und Reden zur Philosophie und ihrer Geschichte*. 2 vols. 9th ed. Tübingen: J. C. B. Mohr (Paul Siebeck), 1924 (first ed. 1883).

4. Kant in 19th-Century Great Britain and America

Adamson, Robert. *On the Philosophy of Kant.* Edinburgh: Douglas, 1879 (reprinted, London: Routledge, 1993).

———. *The Development of Modern Philosophy.* 2 vols. Ed. W. R. Sorley. Edinburgh: Blackwood, 1903.

Caird, Edward. *A Critical Account of the Philosophy of Kant, with an Historical Introduction.* Glasgow: MacLehose, 1877 (reprinted, Bristol: Thoemmes, 1999).

———. *The Critical Philosophy of Immanuel Kant.* 2 vols. Glasgow: James Maclehose & Sons, 1889 (reprinted, New York: Kraus, 1968).

DeArmey, Michael, and James A. Good, eds. *St. Louis Hegelians.* 3 vols. Bristol: Thoemmes, 2001 (reprint of articles by the St. Louis group).

Good, James A., ed. *The Journal of Speculative Philosophy, 1867–1893.* 22 vols. Bristol: Thoemmes, 2002 (reprint of all volumes of *The Journal*).

———. *The Early American Reception of German Idealism.* 5 vols. Bristol: Thoemmes, 2002 (reprints of works first published between 1841 and 1882).

Green, Thomas Hill. *Prolegomena to Ethics.* Ed. A. C. Bradley. Oxford: Clarendon, 1883 (reprinted, New York: Kraus, 1969; Bristol: Thoemmes, 1997; Oxford: Clarendon, 2003).

Hamilton, William. *Discussions on Philosophy and Literature.* Ed. Robert Turnbull. New York: Harper & Brothers, 1853 (first ed. London: Longman, 1852).

———. *Lectures on Metaphysics and Logic.* 4 vols. Eds. H. L. Mansel and J. Veitch. Edinburgh: W. Blackwood, 1859–1860.

Hamilton, William, and Henry L. Mansel, Andrew Seth, Thomas Hill Green. *Philosophy of the Unconditioned, On the Philosophy of Kant, The Development from Kant to Hegel, and Lectures on the Philosophy of Kant.* London: Routledge/Thoemmes, 1993 (reprints of works that appeared in 1829, 1856, 1882, and 1890, respectively).

Haywood, Francis. *An Analysis of Kant's Critick of Pure Reason.* London: William Pickering, 1844 (reprinted, Bristol: Thoemmes, 1990).

McCosh, James. *A Criticism of the Critical Philosophy.* New York: C. Scribner, 1884.

Mansel, Henry Longueville. *A Lecture on the Philosophy of Kant, delivered at Magdalen College, May 20, 1856.* Oxford: John Henry and James Parker, 1856.

Peirce, Charles Sanders. "On a New List of Categories." *Proceedings of the American Academy of Arts and Sciences* 7 (1868): 287–98.

————. *Collected Papers.* 8 vols. Eds. Charles Hartshorne, Paul Weiss, A. W. Burks. Cambridge, Mass.: Harvard University Press, 1931–1958 (reprinted, Bristol: Thoemmes, 1997).

————. *Writings of Charles S. Peirce. A Chronological Edition.* Ed. M. H. Fish et al. Bloomington: Indiana University Press, 1982–.

Seth, Andrew. *The Development from Kant to Hegel.* London: Williams and Norgate, 1882 (reprinted, New York: Garland, 1976).

————. *Scottish Philosophy: A Comparison of the Scottish and German Answers to Hume.* Edinburgh: Blackwood & Sons, 1885 (reprinted, New York: Franklin, 1971; New York: Garland, 1983).

Stirling, James Hutchison. *Text-Book to Kant. The* Critique of Pure Reason: *Aesthetic, Categories, Schematism. Translation, Reproduction, Commentary, Index. With a Biographical Sketch.* Edinburgh: Oliver & Boyd, 1881 (reprinted, London: Routledge, 1993).

Watson, John. *Kant and his English Critics. A Comparison of Critical and Empirical Philosophy.* New York: MacMillan, 1881 (reprinted, New York: Garland, 1976).

Whewell, William. *History of the Inductive Sciences, from the Earliest to the Present Times.* 3 vols. London: J. W. Parker, 1837 (reprinted, London: Cass, 1967; Hildesheim: Olms, 1976; Bristol: Thoemmes, 2001).

————. *The Philosophy of the Inductive Sciences Founded upon their History.* 2 vols. London: J. W. Parker, 1840 (reprinted, London: Cass, 1967; New York: Johnson, 1967; London: Routledge, 1996; Bristol: Thoemmes, 2001).

5. Twentieth-Century Kantianism

Blaha, Ottokar. *Die Ontologie Kants. Ihr Grundriss in der Transzendentalphilosophie.* Salzburg, Munich: Anton Pustet, 1967.

Davidson, Donald. "Mental Events." In *Essays on Actions and Events*, pp. 207–25. Oxford: Clarendon Press, 1980.

Heidegger, Martin. *Kant und das Problem der Metaphysik.* Bonn: Cohen, 1929 (English: *Kant and the Problem of Metaphysics.* Trans. James S. Churchill. Bloomington: Indiana University Press, 1962).

————. *Die Frage nach dem Ding: Zu Kants Lehre von den transzendentalen Grundsätzen.* Tübingen: Max Niemeyer, 1962.

————. *Kants These über das Sein.* Frankfurt am Main: Klostermann, 1963.

Heimsoeth, Heinz. "Metaphysische Motive in der Ausbildung des kritischen Idealismus." *Kant-Studien* 29 (1924): 121–59.

―――――. "Persönlichkeitsbewusstsein und Ding an sich in der Kantischen Philosophie." In *Kant-Festschrift der Albertus-Universität Königsberg in Preussen*, pp. 41-80. Leipzig: Dietrich, 1924.

Lewis, C. I. *Mind and the World Order*. New York: Charles Scribner's Sons, 1929.

―――――. *An Analysis of Knowledge and Valuation*. La Salle, Ill.: Open Court, 1946.

Przywara, Erich. *Kant heute. Eine Sichtung*. Munich: Oldenbourg, 1930.

Strawson, Peter. *Individuals: An Essay in Descriptive Metaphysics*. London: Methuen, 1959.

Vaihinger, Hans. *Die Philosophie des Als Ob. System der theoretischen, praktischen und religiösen Fiktionen der Menschheit auf Grund eines idealistischen Positivismus. Mit einem Anhang über Kant und Nietzsche.* Berlin: Reuther & Reichard, 1911 (10th ed. Leipzig, 1927, reprinted, Aalen: Scientia, 1986; English: *The Philosophy of "As If": A System of the Theoretical, Practical and Religious Fictions of Mankind*. Trans. C. K. Ogden, London: Kegan Pau etc., 1924, reprinted, London: Routledge, 2000).

Wundt, Max. *Kant als Metaphysiker: Ein Beitrag zur Geschichte der deutschen Philosophie im 18. Jahrhundert.* Stuttgart: Ferdinand Enke, 1924.

O. STUDIES ON KANT'S INFLUENCE AND ON KANTIANISM

Ameriks, Karl. *Kant and the Fate of Autonomy: Problems in the Appropriation of the Critical Philosophy.* Cambridge: Cambridge University Press, 2000.

Creighton, J. E. "The Philosophy of Kant in America." *Kant-Studien* 2 (1899): 237-52 (further reports on literature on Kant in America in subsequent issues of the *Kant-Studien*).

Dufour, Eric. *Les Néokantiens: Valeur et vérité*. Paris: Vrin, 2003.

Duncan, George M. "English Translation of Kant's Writings." *Kant-Studien* 2 (1899): 253-8.

Edel, Geert. *Von der Vernunftkritik zur Erkenntnislogik. Die Entwicklung der theoretischen Philosophie Hermann Cohens.* Freiburg: Karl Alber, 1988.

Ferrari, Massimo. *Retours à Kant. Introduction au néo-kantisme*. Paris: Les Éditions du Cerf, 2001.

Funke, Gerhard. *Von der Aktualität Kants*. Bonn: Bouvier, 1979.

Hanewald, Christian. *Apperzeption und Einbildungskraft. Die Auseinandersetzung mit der theoretischen Philosophie Kants in Fichtes früher Wissenschaftslehre.* Berlin: Walter de Gruyter, 2001.

Heidemann, Dietmar H., and Kristina Engelhard, eds. *Warum Kant heute? Systematische Bedeutung und Rezeption seiner Philosophie in der Gegenwart.* Berlin: Walter de Gruyter, 2004.

Henrich, Dieter. *Grundlegung aus dem Ich. Untersuchungen zur Vorgeschichte des Idealismus. Tübingen—Jena 1790-1794.* 2 vols. Frankfurt am Main: Suhrkamp, 2004.

Hoaglund, John. "The Thing in Itself in English Interpretations of Kant." *American Philosophical Quarterly* 10 (1973): 1-14.

Holzhey, Helmut. *Cohen und Natorp.* 2 vols. Basel: Schwabe, 1986.

———, ed. *Ethischer Sozialismus. Zur politischen Philosophie des Neukantianismus.* Frankfurt am Main: Suhrkamp, 1994.

Hubbert, Joachim. *Transzendentale und empirische Subjektivität in der Erfahrung bei Kant, Cohen, Natorp und Cassirer.* Frankfurt am Main: Peter Lang, 1993.

Köhnke, Klaus Christian. *The Rise of Neo-Kantianism: German Academic Philosophy between Idealism and Positivism.* Trans. R. J. Hollingdale. Cambridge: Cambridge University Press, 1991.

Krijnen, Christian. *Nachmetaphysischer Sinn. Eine problemgeschichtliche und systematische Studie zu den Prinzipien der Wertphilosophie Heinrich Rickerts.* Würzburg: Königshausen & Neumann, 2001.

Krijnen, Christian, and Ernst Wolfgang Orth, eds. *Sinn, Geltung, Wert. Neukantianische Motive in der modernen Kulturphilosophie.* Würzburg: Königshausen & Neumann, 1998.

Kuklick, Bruce. "Seven Thinkers and how they Grew: Descartes, Spinoza, Leibniz; Locke, Berkeley, Hume; Kant." In *Philosophy in History*, eds. Richard Rorty, J. B. Schneewind, Quentin Skinner, pp. 125-39. Cambridge: Cambridge University Press, 1984.

Lehmann, Gerhard. *Geschichte der nachkantischen Philosophie. Kritizismus und kritisches Motiv in den philosophischen Systemen des 19. und 20. Jahrhunderts.* Berlin: Junker & Dünnhaupt, 1931.

MacDonald Ross, George, and Tony McWalter, eds. *Kant and his Influence.* Bristol: Thommes, 1990.

Marshall, N. H. "Kant und der Neukantianismus in England." *Kant-Studien* 7 (1902): 385-408.

Ollig, Hans-Ludwig. *Der Neukantianismus.* Stuttgart: J. B. Metzler, 1979.

———, ed. *Materialien zur Neukantianismus-Diskussion.* Darmstadt: Wissenschaftliche Buchgesellschaft, 1987.

Orth, Ernst Wolfgang, and Helmut Holzhey, eds. *Neukantianismus. Perspektiven und Probleme.* Würzburg: Königshausen & Neumann, 1994.

Pätzold, Detlev, and Christian Krijnen, eds. *Der Neukantianismus und das Erbe des deutschen Idealismus. Die philosophische Methode.* Würzburg: Königshausen & Neumann, 2002.

Piché, Claude, ed. *Années 1781–1801. Kant, Critique de la raison pure: vingt ans de réception.* Paris: Vrin, 2002.

Ritzel, Wolfgang. *Studien zum Wandel der Kantauffassung. Die Kritik der reinen Vernunft nach Alois Riehl, Hermann Cohen, Max Wundt und Bruno Bauch.* Meisenheim a.G.: Hain, 1952.

Rotenstreich, Nathan. *Reason and Its Manifestations: A Study on Kant and Hegel.* Stuttgart: Frommann-Holzboog, 1996.

Schmid, Peter A., and Simone Zurbuchen, eds. *Grenzen der kritischen Vernunft.* Basel: Schwabe, 1997.

Sedgwick, Sally, ed. *The Reception of Kant's Critical Philosophy: Fichte, Schelling, and Hegel.* Cambridge: Cambridge University Press, 2000.

Shaw, Gisela. *Das Problem des Dinges an sich in der englischen Kantinterpretation.* Kant-Studien Ergänzungsheft 97. Bonn: Bouvier, 1969.

Sieg, Ulrich. *Aufstieg und Niedergang des Marburger Neukantianismus. Die Geschichte einer philosophischen Schulgemeinschaft.* Würzburg: Königshausen & Neumann, 1994.

Stolzenberg, Jürgen. *Ursprung und System. Probleme der Begründung systematischer Philosophie im Werk Hermann Cohens, Paul Natorps und beim frühen Martin Heidegger.* Göttingen: Vandenhoeck & Ruprecht, 1995.

Vorländer, Karl. *Kant und Marx. Ein Beitrag zur Philosophie des Sozialismus.* 2nd ed. Tübingen: J. C. B. Mohr (Paul Siebeck), 1926.

Wellek, René. *Immanuel Kant in England 1793–1838.* Princeton, N.J.: Princeton University Press, 1931.

Wildfeuer, Armin. *Praktische Vernunft und System. Entwicklungsgeschichtliche Untersuchungen zur ursprünglichen Kant-Rezeption Johann Gottlieb Fichtes.* Stuttgart-Bad Cannstatt: Frommann-Holzboog, 1999.

Willey, Thomas. *Back to Kant: The Revival of Kantianism in German Social and Historical Thought.* Detroit, Mich.: Wayne State University Press, 1978.

APPENDIX A: KANT'S PUBLISHED WRITINGS

The following list of the first publications of Kant's writings is chronologically arranged. The few short pieces that were not published immediately after being written are listed according to the date of their composition. However, the notes on Kant's lectures are ordered by the date of their publication. The list presents the original German or Latin title, followed by the place of publication as well as an English rendering of the title. It also includes information on the location of the German text in the *Akademie*-Edition of Kant's writings (cited as 'Ak' followed by the volume and the page numbers) and, wherever possible, on the location of the English translation in the *Cambridge Edition of the Works of Immanuel Kant* (cited as 'CE' together with the name of the volume and the page numbers). A facsimile reprint of a number of the 18th-century German publications is available from Harald Fischer Verlag (Erlangen).

1749   *Gedanken von der wahren Schätzung der lebendigen Kräfte und Beurtheilung der Beweise, derer sich Herr von Leibnitz und andere Mechaniker in dieser Streitsache bedienet haben, nebst einigen vorhergehenden Betrachtungen, welche die Kraft der Körper überhaupt betreffen*, Königsberg, 1749 (Ak 1, 1–181).
        Thoughts on the True Estimation of Living Forces, and criticism of the proofs propounded by Herr von Leibniz and other mechanists in their treatment of this controversy, along with some preliminary observations concerning the force of bodies in general (CE, *Natural Science*).

1754   "Untersuchung der Frage, ob die Erde in ihrer Umdrehung um die Achse, wodurch sie die Abwechslung des Tages und der Nacht hervorbringt, einige Veränderungen seit den ersten Zeiten ihres Ursprungs erlitten habe und woraus man sich ihrer versichern könne, welche von der Königl. Akademie der Wissenschaften zu Berlin zum Preise für das jetzt laufende Jahr aufgegeben worden," *Wöchentliche Königsbergische Frag- und Anzeigungs-Nachrichten*, Nos. 23 and 24 of 8 and 15 June (Ak 1, 183–91).

"Inquiry into the Question Whether the Earth in its Rotation Around its Axis, by which it Produces the Change of Day and Night, Has Undergone any Alterations since the Time of its Origin" (CE, *Natural Science*).

1754   "Die Frage: ob die Erde veralte, physikalisch erwogen," *Wöchentliche Königsbergische Frag- und Anzeigungs-Nachrichten,* Nos. 32–37 of 10 August to 14 September (Ak 1, 193–213).
"The Question Whether the Earth is Aging, Considered from a Physicalist Point of View" (CE, *Natural Science*).

1755   *Allgemeine Naturgeschichte und Theorie des Himmels, oder Versuch von der Verfassung und dem mechanischen Ursprunge des ganzen Weltgebäudes nach Newtonischen Grundsätzen abgehandelt,* Königsberg und Leipzig (Ak 1, 215–368).
Universal Natural History and Theory of the Heavens, or An Essay on the Constitution and Mechanical Origin of the Entire World Edifice Treated According to Newtonian Principles (CE, *Natural Science*).

1755   *Meditationum quarundam de igne succincta delineatio,* first published in *Kant, Sämtliche Werke,* eds. Karl Friedrich Rosenkranz and Friedrich Wilhelm Schubert, Vol. 5, pp. 233–54, Leipzig, 1839 (Ak 1, 369–84).
On Fire (CE, *Natural Science*).

1755   *Principiorum primorum cognitionis metaphysicae nova dilucidatio,* Königsberg (Ak 1, 385–416).
A New Elucidation of the First Principles of Metaphysical Cognition (CE, *Theoretical Philosophy, 1755–1770,* pp. 1–45).

1756   "Von den Ursachen der Erderschütterungen bei Gelegenheit des Unglücks, welches die westliche Länder von Europa gegen das Ende des vorigen Jahres betroffen hat," *Wöchentliche Königsbergische Frag- und Anzeigungs-Nachrichten,* Nos. 4 and 5 of 24 and 31 January (Ak 1, 417–27).
"Concerning the Causes of the Terrestrial Convulsions on the Occasion of the Disaster which Afflicted the Western Countries of Europe towards the End of Last Year" (CE, *Natural Science*).

1756   *Geschichte und Naturbeschreibung der merkwürdigsten Vorfälle des Erdbebens, welches an dem Ende des 1755sten Jahres einen grossen Theil der Erde erschüttert hat,* Königsberg (Ak 1, 429–61).

History and Natural Description of the Most Remarkable Occurrences Associated with the Earthquake which at the end of 1755 Shook a Large Part of the World (CE, *Natural Science*).

1756   "Fortgesetzte Betrachtungen der seit einiger Zeit wahrgenommenen Erderschütterungen," *Wöchentliche Königsbergische Frag- und Anzeigungs-Nachrichten*, Nos. 15 and 16 of 10 and 17 April (Ak 1, 463–72).

"Further Observation on the Terrestrial Convulsions which have been for Some Time Observed" (CE, *Natural Science*).

1756   *Metaphysicae cum geometria iunctae usus in philosophia naturali, cuius specimen I. continet monadologiam physicam*, Königsberg (Ak 1, 473–87).

The Employment in Natural Philosophy of Metaphysics combined with Geometry, of which Sample I contains the Physical Monadology (CE, *Theoretical Philosophy, 1755–1770*, pp. 47–66).

1756   *Neue Anmerkungen zur Erläuterung der Theorie der Winde, wodurch er zugleich zu seinen Vorlesungen einladet*, Königsberg (Ak 1, 489–503).

New Notes towards a Discussion of the Theory of Winds (CE, *Natural Science*).

1757   *Entwurf und Ankündigung eines Collegii der physischen Geographie, nebst dem Anhange einer kurzen Betrachtung über die Frage: Ob die Westwinde in unsern Gegenden darum feucht seien, weil sie über ein großes Meer streichen*, Königsberg (Ak 2, 1–12).

Outline and Announcement of a Course of Lectures on Physical Geography, together with an Appendix of an Inquiry into the Question of Whether the West Winds in our Regions are Humid because they have Traversed a Great Sea (CE, *Natural Science*).

1758   *Neuer Lehrbegriff der Bewegung und Ruhe, und der damit verknüpften Folgerungen in den ersten Gründen der Naturwissenschaft, wodurch zugleich seine Vorlesungen in diesem halben Jahre angekündigt werden*, Königsberg (Ak 2, 13–25).

New Conception of Motion and Rest and its Consequences for the Primary Grounds of Natural Science, through which at the same time his Lectures for this Semester are Announced (CE, *Natural Science*).

1759   *Versuch einiger Betrachtungen über den Optimismus von M. Immanuel Kant, wodurch er zugleich seine Vorlesungen auf das* bevorstehende halbe Jahr ankündigt, Königsberg (Ak 2, 27–35).

An Attempt at some Reflections on Optimism by M. Immanuel Kant, also Containing an Announcement of his Lectures for the Coming Semester (CE, *Theoretical Philosophy, 1755–1770*, pp. 67–76).

1760   *Gedanken bei dem frühzeitigen Ableben des Hochwohlgebornen Herrn, Herrn Johann Friedrich von Funk, in einem Sendschreiben an seine Mutter,* Königsberg (Ak 2, 37–44).

Thoughts on the Premature Expiration of Herr Johann Friedrich von Funk, in an Epistle to his Mother.

1762   *Die falsche Spitzfindigkeit der vier syllogistischen Figuren erwiesen von M. Immanuel Kant,* Königsberg (Ak 2, 45–61).

The False Subtlety of the Four Syllogistic Figures Demonstrated by M. Immanuel Kant (CE, *Theoretical Philosophy, 1755–1770,* pp. 85–105).

1763   *Der einzig mögliche Beweisgrund zu einer Demonstration des Daseins Gottes von M. Immanuel Kant,* Königsberg (Ak 2, 63–163).

The Only Possible Argument in Support of a Demonstration of the Existence of God by M. Immanuel Kant (CE, *Theoretical Philosophy, 1755–1770,* pp. 107–201).

1763   *Versuch den Begriff der negativen Größen in die Weltweisheit einzuführen von M. Immanuel Kant,* Königsberg (Ak 2, 165–204).

Attempt to Introduce the Concept of Negative Magnitudes into Philosophy by M. Immanuel Kant (CE, *Theoretical Philosophy, 1755–1770,* pp. 203–41).

1764   *Beobachtungen über das Gefühl des Schönen und Erhabenen,* Königsberg (Ak 2, 205–56).

Observations on the Feeling of the Beautiful and the Sublime.

1764   "Versuch über die Krankheiten des Kopfes," *Königsbergsche Gelehrte und Politische Zeitungen,* Nos. 4–8 of 13–27 February (Ak 2, 257–71).

"An Essay on the Maladies of the Mind" (CE, *Anthropology, History, and Education*).

1764   "Recension von Silberschlags Schrift: Theorie der am 23. Juli 1762 erschienenen Feuerkugel," *Königsbergsche Gelehrte und Politische Zeitungen,* No. 15 of 23 March (Ak 2, 272a–272d).

"Review of Silberschlag's Essay on the Fireball of 1762" (CE, *Natural Science*).

1764   *Untersuchung über die Deutlichkeit der Grundsätze der na-*
türlichen Theologie und der Moral. Zur Beantwortung der
Frage, welche die Königl. Akademie der Wissenschaften zu
Berlin auf das Jahr 1763 aufgegeben hat, Berlin (Ak 2,
273–301).
Inquiry Concerning the Distinctness of the Principles of
Natural Theology and Morality, Being an Answer to the
Question Proposed for Consideration by the Berlin Royal
Academy of Sciences for the Year 1763 (CE, *Theoretical*
Philosophy, 1755–1770, pp. 243–75).

1765   *M. Immanuel Kants Nachricht von der Einrichtung seiner*
Vorlesungen in dem Winterhalbenjahre von 1765–1766, Kö-
nigsberg (Ak 2, 303–13).
M. Immanuel Kant's Announcement of the Programme of his
Lectures for the Winter Semester 1765–1766 (CE, *Theoretical*
Philosophy, 1755–1770, pp. 287–300).

1766   *Träume eines Geistersehers, erläutert durch Träume der*
Metaphysik, Königsberg (Ak 2, 315–73).
Dreams of a Spirit-Seer Elucidated by Dreams of Metaphysics
(CE, *Theoretical Philosophy, 1755–1770*, pp. 301–59).

1768   "Von dem ersten Grunde des Unterschiedes der Gegenden im
Raume," *Wöchentliche Königsbergische Frag- und Anzei-*
gungs-Nachrichten, Nos. 6–8 (Ak 2, 375–83).
"Concerning the Ultimate Ground of the Differentiation of
Directions in Space" (CE, *Theoretical Philosophy, 1755–1770*,
pp. 361–72).

1770   *De mundi sensibilis atque intelligibilis forma et principiis,*
Königsberg (Ak 2, 385–419).
On the Form and Principles of the Sensible and the Intelligible
World (CE, *Theoretical Philosophy, 1755–1770*, pp. 373–416).

1771   "Recension von Moscatis Schrift: Von dem körperlichen
wesentlichen Unterschiede zwischen der Structur der Thiere
und Menschen," published anonymously in *Königsbergsche*
Gelehrte und Politische Zeitungen, No. 67 of 23 August, pp.
265–6 (Ak 2, 421–5).
"Review of Moscati's Book: On the Essential Physical Differences between the Structures of Animals and Humans" (CE,
Anthropology, History, and Education).

1775   *Von den verschiedenen Racen der Menschen zur Ankündigung*
der Vorlesungen der physischen Geographie im Sommer-
halbenjahre 1775, Königsberg (Ak 2, 427–43).

On the Different Human Races (CE, *Anthropology, History, and Education*).

1776–1777   "Aufsätze, das Philanthropin betreffend," *Königsbergsche Gelehrte und Politische Zeitungen,* 28 March 1776 and 27 March 1777 (Ak 2, 445–52).

"On the Dessau Philanthropin Academy" (CE, *Anthropology, History, and Education*).

1777   Untitled Latin address in response to Johann Gottlieb Kreutzfeld's *Dissertatio philologico-poetica de principiis fictionum generalioribus,* first published in *Altpreussische Monatsschrift,* Vol. 47, No. 4 (1910), pp. 663–70 (Ak 15, 903–35).

Concerning Sensory Illusion and Poetic Fiction.

1781   *Kritik der reinen Vernunft,* Riga (Ak 4, 1–252).

Critique of Pure Reason (CE, *Critique of Pure Reason*).

1782   "Nachricht an Ärzte," *Königsbergsche Gelehrte und Politische Zeitungen,* No. 31 of 18 April (Ak 8, 5–8).

"Report to Physicians" (CE, *Anthropology, History, and Education*).

1783   *Prolegomena zu einer jeden künftigen Metaphysik, die als Wissenschaft wird auftreten können,* Riga (Ak 4, 253–383).

Prolegomena to Any Future Metaphysics that will be Able to Come Forward as Science (CE, *Theoretical Philosophy after 1781*).

1783   "Recension von Schulz's Versuch einer Anleitung zur Sittenlehre für alle Menschen ohne Unterschied der Religion," *Räsonnierendes Bücherverzeichnis,* No. 7 of April, pp. 93–104 (Ak 8, 9–14).

"Review of Schulz's Attempt at an Introduction to a Doctrine of Morals for all Human Beings Regardless of Different Religions" (CE, *Practical Philosophy*, pp. 1–10).

1784   "Idee zu einer allgemeinen Geschichte in weltbürgerlicher Absicht," *Berlinische Monatsschrift,* Vol. 4 of 11 November, pp. 385–411 (Ak 8,15–31).

"Idea for a Universal History with a Cosmopolitan Purpose".

1784   "Beantwortung der Frage: Was ist Aufklärung?" *Berlinische Monatsschrift,* Vol. 4 of 12 December, pp. 481–94 (Ak 8, 33–42).

"An Answer to the Question: What is Enlightenment?" (CE, *Practical Philosophy*, pp. 11–22).

1785   "Recensionen von Johann Gottfried Herders Ideen zur Philosophie der Geschichte der Menschheit," *Allgemeine Litteratur-*

zeitung, No. 4 of 6 January 1785, pp. 17–20, Supplement *(Beilage)* to No. 4, pp. 21–2, and issue No. 271 of 15 November, pp. 153–6 (Ak 8, 43–66).
"Reviews of Johann Gottfried Herder's Ideas on the Philosophy of the History of Humankind."

1785   "Über die Vulkane im Monde," *Berlinische Monatsschrift,* Vol. 5, pp. 199–213 (Ak 8, 67–76).
"The Volcanoes on the Moon" (CE, *Natural Science*).

1785   "Von der Unrechtmäßigkeit des Büchernachdrucks," *Berlinische Monatsschrift,* Vol. 5, pp. 403–17 (Ak 8, 77–87).
"On the Wrongfulness of Unauthorized Publishing of Books" (CE, *Practical Philosophy,* pp. 23–35).

1785   "Bestimmung des Begriffs einer Menschenrace," *Berlinische Monatsschrift,* Vol. 6 of November, pp. 390–417 (Ak 8, 89–106).
"On the Different Human Races" (CE, *Anthropology, History, and Education*).

1785   *Grundlegung zur Metaphysik der Sitten,* Riga (Ak 4, 385–463).
Groundwork of the Metaphysics of Morals (CE, *Practical Philosophy,* pp. 37–108).

1786   *Metaphysische Anfangsgründe der Naturwissenschaft,* Riga (Ak 4, 465–565).
Metaphysical Foundations of Natural Science (CE, *Theoretical Philosophy after 1781*).

1786   "Muthmaßlicher Anfang der Menschengeschichte," *Berlinische Monatsschrift,* Vol. 7 of January, pp. 1–27 (Ak 8, 107–23).
"Conjectures on the Beginning of Human History."

1786   "Recension von Gottlieb Hufeland's Versuch über den Grundsatz des Naturrechts," *Allgemeine Litteraturzeitung,* Vol. 2 of 18 April, pp. 113–6 (Ak 8, 125–30).
"Review of Hufeland's Essay on the Principle of Natural Right" (CE, *Practical Philosophy,* pp. 109–17).

1786   "Was heißt: Sich im Denken orientieren?" *Berlinische Monatsschrift,* Vol. 8 of October, pp. 304–30 (Ak 8, 131–47).
"What does it Mean to Orient Oneself in Thinking?" (CE, *Religion and Rational Theology,* pp. 1–18).

1786   *De medicina corporis, quae philosophorum est* (Ak 15, 939–53).
On the Philosophers' Medicine of the Body.

1787   *Kritik des reinen Vernunft. Zweite, hin und wieder verbesserte Auflage,* Riga (Ak 3).

Critique of Pure Reason (CE, *Critique of Pure Reason*).

1788   "Über den Gebrauch teleologischer Principien in der Philosophie," *Teutscher Merkur*, 1st Quarter, No. 1, pp. 36–52, No. 2, pp. 107–36 (Ak 8, 157–84).
"On the Use of Teleological Principles in Philosophy" (CE, *Aesthetics and Teleology*).

1788   *Kritik der praktischen Vernunft*, Riga (Ak 5, 1–163).
Critique of Practical Reason (CE, *Practical Philosophy*, pp. 133–271).

1790   *Kritik der Urtheilskraft*, Berlin und Libau (2nd ed., Berlin, 1793) (Ak 5, 165–485).
Critique of (the Power of) Judgment (CE, *Critique of the Power of Judgment*).

1790   "Erste Einleitung in die Kritik der Urteilskraft," ed. Otto Buek in *Kant's Werke*, vol. V, ed. Ernst Cassirer, 1914 (Ak 20, 193–251).
"First Introduction to the Critique of the Power of Judgement" (CE, *Critique of the Power of Judgment*, pp. 1–51).

1790   *Über eine Entdeckung, nach der alle neue Critik der reinen Vernunft durch eine ältere entbehrlich gemacht werden soll*, Königsberg (Ak 8, 185–251).
On a Discovery whereby any New Critique of Pure Reason is to be Made Superfluous by an Older One (CE, *Theoretical Philosophy after 1781*).

1791   "Über das Mißlingen aller philosophischen Versuche in der Theodicee," *Berlinische Monatsschrift*, Vol. 18 of September, pp. 194–225 (Ak 8, 253–71).
"On the Miscarriage of all Philosophical Trials in Theodicy" (CE, *Religion and Rational Theology*, pp. 19–37).

1791   *Über die von der Königl. Akademie der Wissenschaften zu Berlin für das Jahr 1791 ausgesetzte Preisfrage: Welches sind die wirklichen Fortschritte, die die Metaphysik seit Leibnitzens und Wolf's Zeiten in Deutschland gemacht hat?*, ed. Friedrich Theodor Rink, Königsberg, 1804 (Ak 20, 253–351).
Concerning the Prize Question Posed by the Royal Academy of Sciences in Berlin for the Year 1791: What Real Progress has Metaphysics Made in Germany since the Time of Leibniz and Wolff? (CE, *Theoretical Philosophy after 1781*).

1793   *Die Religion innerhalb der Grenzen der bloßen Vernunft*, Königsberg (2nd ed., Frankfurt and Leipzig, 1794) (Ak 6, 1–202).

Religion within the Boundaries of Mere Reason (CE, *Religion and Rational Theology*, pp. 39–215).

1793   "Über den Gemeinspruch: Das Mag in der Theorie richtig sein, taugt aber nicht für die Praxis," *Berlinische Monatsschrift*, Vol. 22, pp. 201–84 (Ak 8, 273–313).

"On the Common Saying: That May be Correct in Theory, but it is of no Use in Practice" (CE, *Practical Philosophy*, pp. 273–309).

1794   "Etwas über den Einfluß des Mondes auf die Witterung," *Berlinische Monatsschrift*, Vol. 23, pp. 392–407 (Ak 8, 315–24).

"Something on the Moon's Influence over the Weather" (CE, *Natural Science*).

1794   "Das Ende aller Dinge," *Berlinische Monatsschrift*, Vol. 23, pp. 495–522 (Ak 8, 325–39).

"The End of all Things" (CE, *Religion and Rational Theology*, pp. 217–31).

1795   *Zum ewigen Frieden. Ein philosophischer Entwurf,* Königsberg (2nd ed., 1796) (Ak 8, 341–86).

Toward Perpetual Peace: A Philosophical Project (CE, *Practical Philosophy*, pp. 311–51).

1796   "Von einem neuerdings erhobenen vornehmen Ton in der Philosophie," *Berlinische Monatsschrift*, vol. 27, pp. 387–426 (Ak 8, 387–406).

"On a Recently Arisen Tone of Superiority in Philosophy" (CE, *Theoretical Philosophy after 1781*).

1796   "Verkündigung des nahen Abschlusses eines Tractats zum ewigen Frieden in der Philosophie," *Berlinische Monatsschrift*, Vol. 28, pp. 485–504 (Ak 8, 411–22).

"Proclamation of the Imminent Conclusion of a Treaty of Perpetual Peace in Philosophy" (CE, *Theoretical Philosophy after 1781*).

1796   *Zu Sömmering über das Organ der Seele,* Königsberg.

To Sommering Concerning the Organ of the Soul (CE, *Anthropology, History, and Education*).

1797   *Die Metaphysik der Sitten: 1. Metaphysische Anfangsgründe der Rechtslehre, 2. Metaphysische Anfangsgründe der Tugendlehre,* Königsberg (Ak 6, 203–493).

The Metaphysics of Morals: Part I. Metaphysical First Principles of the Doctrine of Right, Part II. Metaphysical First

Principles of the Doctrine of Virtue (CE, *Practical Philosophy*, pp. 353–603).

1797   "Über ein vermeintes Recht aus Menschenliebe zu lügen," *Berlinische Blätter*, No. 10 of 6 September, pp. 301–14 (Ak 8, 423–30).
"On a Supposed Right to Lie from Philanthropy" (CE, *Practical Philosophy*, pp. 605–15).

1798   *Der Streit der Fakultäten*, Königsberg (Ak 7, 1–116).
The Conflict of the Faculties (CE, *Religion and Rational Theology*, pp. 233–309)

1798   *Anthropologie in pragmatischer Hinsicht*, Königsberg (Ak 7, 117–333).
Anthropology from a Pragmatic Point of View.

1800   *Logik. Ein Handbuch zu Vorlesungen*, ed. Gottlob Benjamin Jäsche, Königsberg (Ak 9, 1–150).
The Jäsche Logic (CE, *Lectures on Logic*, pp. 517–640).

1800   *Nachschrift zu Christian Gottlieb Mielckes Littauisch-deutschem und deutsch-littauischem Wörterbuch* (Ak 8, 443–45).
Postscript to Mielkes' Lithuanian-German and German-Lithuanian Dictionary (CE, *Anthropology, History, and Education*).

1802   *Physische Geographie*, ed. Friedrich Theodor Rink, Königsberg (Ak 9, 151–436).
Physical Geography (CE, *Natural Science*).

1803   *Immanuel Kant über Pädagogik*, ed. Friedrich Theodor Rink, Königsberg (Ak 9, 437–99).
Education.

1817   *Kants Vorlesungen über die philosophische Religionslehre*, ed. Karl Heinrich Ludwig Pölitz (Ak 28, 989–1126).
Lectures on the Philosophical Doctrine of Religion (CE, *Religion and Rational Theology*, pp. 335–446).

1821   *Kants Vorlesungen über die Metaphysik*, ed. Karl Heinrich Ludwig Pölitz, Erfurt (Ak 28, 193–350, 525–609).
Lectures on Metaphysics (CE, *Lectures on Metaphysics*, pp. 19–106, 299–354).

1922   *Briefwechsel* (Ak 10–13).
Correspondence (CE, *Correspondence*).

1924   *Eine Vorlesung Kants über Ethik*, ed. Paul Menzer (Ak 27, 237–473).
Moral Philosophy: Collins's Lecture Notes (CE, *Lectures on Ethics*, pp. 37–222).

1925–1934   *Reflexionen* (Ak 14–19).
1936–1938   *Opus postumum,* ed. Artur Buchenau and Gerhard Lehmann
            (Ak 21 and 22).
            Opus Postumum (CE, *Opus Postumum*).

APPENDIX B: NINETEENTH-CENTURY ENGLISH TRANSLATIONS OF KANT

The following list contains the most important 19th-century English translations of Kant's works in chronological order.

Kant's Metaphysic of Ethics. Trans. John W. Semple. Edinburgh: T. Clark, 1836 (includes *The Doctrine of Virtue*, part of the *Critique of Practical Reason*).

The Metaphysical Works of the Celebrated Kant. Trans. John Richardson. London: W. Simpkin and R. Marshall, 1836 (includes the *Prolegomena*).

Religion within the Boundary of Pure Reason. Trans. John W. Semple. Edinburgh: T. Clark, 1838.

Critick of Pure Reason. Trans. Francis Haywood. London: William Pickering, 1838.

Critique of Pure Reason. Trans. J. M. D. Meiklejohn. London: Bohn, 1855.

Kant's Critical Philosophy for English Readers. Trans. John P. Mahaffy. 2 vols. London: Longmans & Co, 1872–1874 (vol. 1: *Kritik of Pure Reason Explained and Defended;* vol 2: *Prolegomena*).

Kant's Critique of Practical Reason and Other Works on the Theory of Ethics. Trans. Thomas Kingsmill Abbott. London: Longmans, Green and Co., 1873 (5th ed. 1898).

Critique of Pure Reason. Trans. Max Müller. London: Macmillan, 1881.

Kant's Prolegomena and Metaphysical Foundations of Natural Science. Trans. E. B. Bax. London: G. Bell and Sons, 1883 (2nd ed. 1891).

The Philosophy of Law: An Exposition of the Fundamental Principles of Jurisprudence as the Science of Right. Trans. William Hastie. Edinburgh: T. & T. Clark, 1887 (translation of the "Metaphysical First Principles of the Doctrine of Right").

Kant's Principles of Politics, Including his Essay on Perpetual Peace. Trans. William Hastie. Edinburgh: T. Clark, 1891.

Kant's Kritik of Judgement. Trans. J. H. Bernard. London: Macmillan, 1892.

Fundamental Principles of the Metaphysic of Ethics. Trans. T. K. Abbott. London: Longmans & Co., 1895.

APPENDIX C: GLOSSARY

The following list contains Kant's basic philosophical vocabulary as well as some of the key terms of later German-language Kantianism. In regard to the meaning of the terms, we have followed Kant's own usage rather than the modern German one, which occasionally differs significantly. However, in keeping with present day practice, we have modernized the orthography of the 18th-century German words. Obvious cognates (e.g., Abstrakt = abstract) are generally not included.

GERMAN-ENGLISH

Abfolge	succession
Absicht	aim, intention, respect
absondern	separate
Achtung	respect, reverence
allgemein	general, universal
Allgemeingültigkeit	universal validity
Allheit	allness
an sich	in itself
angeboren	innate
angenehm	agreeable
Anlage	predisposition
Anmut	gracefulness
anschauen	intuit
anschaulich	intuitive
Anschauung	intuition
Antrieb	impulse
Anziehung	attraction
Äther	ether
Aufgabe	problem
aufgegeben	given as a problem
aufheben	abolish, cancel, remove
Auflösung	dissolution, resolution, solution
Aufklärung	enlightenment
Ausdehnung	extension

Äußere	external(thing)
äußerlich	external
Bedeutung	meaning, significance
Bedingung	condition
Bedürfnis	need
Begehrungsvermögen	faculty of desire
Begierde	desire
begreifen	comprehend
Begriff	concept, notion
beharren	persist
beharrlich	persistent
Beharrlichkeit	persistence
bejahen	affirm
besondere	particular, special
bestimmen	determine
Bestimmung	determination
Betrachtung	consideration
beurteilen	assess, judge
Beurteilung	estimation, judgment
Bewegung	motion
Beweggrund	motive
Beweis	proof
Beweisgrund	ground of proof
Bewusstsein	consciousness
Beziehung	relation
Böse	evil
Bösartigkeit	depravity
Bosheit	malice
bürgerlich	civil
Bürgerrecht	citizenship
darstellen	exhibit, present
Dasein	existence
Dauer	duration
denken	conceive, think
Denken	thought
Denkart	way of thinking
Ding	thing
Einbildungskraft	(faculty of) imagination

Eindruck	impression
Einerleiheit	identity
Einfluß	influence
Einheit	unity
einsehen	have insight into, see (into), understand
einschränken	limit
Einstimmung	agreement
Einteilung	division
Einwilligung	consent
Empfänglichkeit	receptivity
Empfindung	sensation
Endabsicht	final aim
endlich	finite
Endzweck	final end
entäussern	divest
Entgegensetzung	opposition
Entschließung	decision
Erfahrung	experience
erhaben	sublime
Erhaltung	conservation
erkennen	cognize, recognize
Erkenntnis	cognition, knowledge
Erkenntnislehre	epistemology
Erkenntnistheorie	epistemology
Erklärung	declaration, definition, explanation
Erlaubnis	permission
Erläuterung	clarification, elucidation, illustration
Erörterung	exposition
Erscheinung	appearance
erweiternd	ampliative
Erweiterung	amplification, expansion, extension
erzeugen	generate, produce
Fortschritt	progress
Freiheit	freedom
Friede	peace
Fürwahrhalten	taking to be true
Ganze	entirety, whole
Gattung	genus
Gebot	command

Gedankending	thought-entity
Gefühl	feeling
Gegenstand	object
Gegenstück	counterpart
Gegenwirkung	counter-effect
Geist	mind, spirit
Geltung	validity
gemein	common
Gemeinschaft	community
Gemüt	mind
Gerechtigkeit	justice
Geschichte	history
Geschicklichkeit	skill
Geselligkeit	sociability
Gesellschaft	society
Gesetz	law
Gesetzgeber	legislator
Gesetzmäßigkeit	conformity to law, lawfulness
Gesinnung	disposition
Gewissen	conscience
Gewohnheit	custom, habit
Glaube	belief, faith
gleichartig	homogeneous
Glückseligkeit	happiness
Gnade	grace
Grad	degree
Grenze	bound(ary)
Größe	magnitude
Grund	basis, ground
Grundkraft	fundamental faculty or power
Grundlage	foundation
Grundlegung	laying of foundations
Grundsatz	principle
gültig	valid
Gültigkeit	validity
Gut	good
Handlung	action
Hang	propensity
Herrschaft	dominion, mastery
hineinlegen	insert, put in

Ich	ego, self
Inbegriff	sum total
Inhalt	content
Kenntnis	acquaintance, information, knowledge
Klugheit	prudence
Körper	body
körperlich	corporeal
Kraft	force, faculty, power
Krieg	war
Kunst	art
Lage	position
Laster	vice
Läuterung	purification
Leben	life
Lebenswandel	life conduct
Leere	void
Lehre	doctrine
Lehrsatz	theorem
Leiden	suffering, passivity
Leidenschaft	passion
Leitfaden	guiding thread
Letztbegründung	ultimate foundation
Liebe	love
Lüge	lie (n.)
Lust	pleasure
Macht	power
mannigfaltig	manifold (adj.)
Mannigfaltigkeit	manifold (n.)
Materie	matter
Meinung	opinion
Menge	amount, multiplicity, multitude
Mensch	human being
Möglichkeit	possibility
Nacheinander	succession
Naturanlage	natural predisposition
Naturell	natural temper
Neigung	inclination

Nichts	nothing
notwendig	necessary, necessarily
Notwendigkeit	necessity
Nutzen	usefulness, utility
Obersatz	major premise
Öffentlichkeit	public
Pflicht	duty
Probierstein	touchstone
Quelle	source
Raum	space
recht	right
Recht	juridical law
Regel	rule
Reich	kingdom
Reihe	series
Reihenfolge	succession, successive series
rein	pure
Ruhe	rest
Sache	thing
Satz	principle, proposition, sentence
Schätzung	appraisal
Schein	illusion
schlechthin	absolutely
schließen	infer
Schluß	conclusion, inference
Schmerz	pain
Schönheit	beauty
Schöpfer	creator
Schranke	limitation
Schuld	guilt
Schwärmerei	enthusiasm
schwer	heavy
Schwere	gravity
Schwerkraft	gravitational force
Seele	soul
Selbstbewusstsein	self-consciousness

Selbsterkenntnis	self-knowledge
Selbstsetzung	self-positing
Selbsttätigkeit	self-activity
setzen	place, posit, put
Sinn	sense (n.)
sinnlich	sensible
Sinnlichkeit	sensibility
Sitten	manners
Sittlichkeit	morals
sollen	ought
Stoff	material, matter
Tätigkeit	activity
Tatsache	fact
Trägheit	inertia
Trieb	drive, impulse
Triebfeder	incentive
Tugend	virtue
Übel	ill
Übergang	transition
Überlegung	reflection
Undurchdringlichkeit	impenetrability
Unendlichkeit	infinity
Unlust	displeasure, pain
unmittelbar	immediate, immediately
Unsterblichkeit	immortality
Untersatz	minor premise
Unterscheidung	distinction
Unterschied	difference
Untersuchung	investigation
Urbild	archetype
Urgrund	original ground
Ursache	cause
Ursprung	origin
Urteil	judgment
urteilen	judge
Urteilskraft	(faculty or power of) judgment
Urwesen	original being
Veränderung	alteration

Verbindlichkeit	obligation
Verbindung	combination, synthesis
Verdienst	merit
Vereinigung	union
Verfassung	constitution
Verhältnis	relation
Vergleichung	comparison
Verknüpfung	connection
Vermögen	capacity, faculty
verneinen	deny, negate
Vernunft	reason
vernünfteln	rationalize, ratiocinate
vernünftelnd	sophistical
Vernunftschluß	inference of reason, syllogism
Verschiedenheit	difference
Verstand	understanding
verstehen	understand
Vertrag	contract
Verwandtschaft	affinity
Vielheit	plurality
Volk	peoples
Voraussetzung	presupposition
vorherbestimmt	preestablished
Vorsatz	intention, resolution
vorstellen, sich	imagine, represent
Vorstellung	representation
Wahrheit	truth
Wahrnehmung	perception
Wahrscheinlichkeit	probability
Wärmestoff	ether, caloric
wechselseitig	reciprocal
Wechselwirkung	community, interaction
Welt	world
Weltall	world-whole
Weltbegriff	cosmological concept, cosmopolitan concept
Weltganzes	world-whole
Weltkörper	heavenly body
Weltweisheit	philosophy
Wert	value

Wesen	being, essence
Widerlegung	refutation
Widerspruch	contradiction
Widerstand	resistance
Widerstreit	conflict, opposition
Willkür	(faculty of) choice, will
willkürlich	arbitrary, voluntary
Wirklichkeit	actuality
Wirkung	effect
Wissen	knowledge
Wissenschaft	science
Wohlwollen	benevolence
wollen	will
Wollen	volition
Würde	dignity
Zahl	number
Zeit	time
Zeitfolge	temporal sequence
Zergliederung	analysis
zufällig	contingent
zugleich	simultaneous
Zurechnung	imputation
Zusammenhang	connection, interconnection, nexus
Zusammensetzung	composition
Zustand	state, condition
Zwang	coercion, compulsion
Zweck	end, purpose
zweckmäßig	purposive, suitable
Zweckmäßigkeit	finality, purposiveness

ENGLISH-GERMAN

abolish	aufheben
absolute(ly)	schlechthin, absolut
action	Handlung
activity	Tätigkeit
actuality	Wirklichkeit
affinity	Verwandtschaft, Affinität
affirm	bejahen

agreeable	angenehm
agreement	Einstimmung
aim	Absicht
allness	Allheit
alteration	Veränderung
ampliative	erweiternd
amplification	Erweiterung
analysis	Zergliederung, Analyse
appearance	Erscheinung
appraisal	Schätzung
arbitrary	willkürlich
archetype	Urbild
art	Kunst
assess	beurteilen
attraction	Anziehung
beauty	Schönheit
being (n.)	Sein, Wesen
belief	Glaube
benevolence	Wohlwollen
body	Körper
bound(ary)	Grenze, Schranke
caloric	Wärmematerial, Wärmestoff
cancel	aufheben
capacity	Fähigkeit (capacitas), Vermögen
cause	Ursache
change (n.)	Wechsel
choice, faculty of	Willkür
citizenship	Bürgerrecht
civil	bürgerlich
clarification	Erläuterung
clue	Leitfaden
coercion	Zwang
cognition	Erkenntnis (cognitio)
cognize	erkennen (cognoscere)
combination	Verbindung (combinatio)
command	Gebot
common	gemein
community	Gemeinschaft, Wechselwirkung
comparison	Vergleichung

composition	Zusammensetzung
comprehend	begreifen (comprehendere)
compulsion	Zwang
conceive	denken
concept	Begriff (conceptus)
conclusion	Schluß
condition	Bedingung, Zustand
conflict	Streit, Widerstreit
connection	Verknüpfung (connexio), Zusammen-hang (nexus, conjunctio)
conscience	Gewissen
consciousness	Bewusstsein
consent	Einwilligung
conservation	Erhaltung
consideration	Betrachtung
constitution	Verfassung
content	Gehalt, Inhalt
contingent	zufällig
contract	Vertrag
contradiction	Widerspruch
corporeal	körperlich
counter-effect	Gegenwirkung
counterpart	Gegenstück
creator	Schöpfer
custom	Gewohnheit
decision	Entschließung
definition	Erklärung, Definition
degree	Grad
deny	verneinen
depravity	Bösartigkeit
desire	Begierde
determination	Bestimmung
determine	bestimmen
difference	Unterschied, Verschiedenheit, Differenz
dignity	Würde
displeasure	Unlust, Schmerz
disposition	Gesinnung
distinction	Unterscheidung
divest	entäussern
doctrine	Lehre, Doktrin

dominion	Herrschaft
drive	Trieb
duration	Dauer
duty	Pflicht
effect	Wirkung
ego	Ich
elucidation	Erläuterung
end	Zweck
enduring	bleibend
enlightenment	Aufklärung
enthusiasm	Schwärmerei
epistemology	Erkenntnislehre, Erkenntnistheorie
essence	Wesen
estimation	Beurteilung
ether	Äther, Wärmestoff
evil	Böse
exhibit	darstellen
existence	Dasein, Existenz
expansion	Erweiterung
experience	Erfahrung
explanation	Erklärung
exposition	Erörterung, Exposition
extension	Ausdehnung, Erweiterung
external (thing)	äußerlich, Äußeres
fact	Tatsache, Faktum
faculty	Vermögen (facultas)
faculty of desire	Begehrungsvermögen
faith	Glaube
feeling	Gefühl
final aim	Endabsicht
final end	Endzweck
finality	Zweckmäßigkeit
finite	endlich
force	Kraft
foundation	Grundlage
foundation, ultimate	Letztbegründung
freedom	Freiheit
fundamental power	Grundkraft

general	allgemein
genus	Gattung
given	gegeben
given as a problem	aufgegeben
good	Gut
grace	Gnade
gracefulness	Anmut
gravitational force	Schwerkraft
gravity	Schwere
ground	Grund
guide	leiten
guiding thread	Leitfaden
guilt	Schuld
habit	Gewohnheit
happiness	Glückseligkeit
heavenly body	Weltkörper
heavy	schwer
homogeneous	gleichartig, homogen
hope	Hoffnung
human being	Mensch
identity	Einerleiheit, Identität
illusion	Schein, Illusion
imagination	Einbildung, Einbildungskraft
imagine	einbilden, sich vorstellen
immediate(ly)	unmittelbar
immortality	Unsterblichkeit
impenetrability	Undurchdringlichkeit
impression	Eindruck
impulse	Antrieb
imputation	Zurechnung
in itself	an sich (selbst)
incentive	Triebfeder
inclination	Neigung
inertia	Trägheit
infer	schließen
inference	Schluß
infinity	Unendlichkeit
influence	Einfluß (influxus)
innate	angeboren

insert	hineinlegen
insight	Einsehen (perspicere)
intention	Absicht, Vorsatz
interaction	Wechselwirkung
interconnection	Zusammenhang
intuit	anschauen
intuition	Anschauung (intuitus)
intuitive	anschaubar, anschaulich
investigation	Untersuchung
judge (v.)	urteilen
judgment	Urteil, Urteilskraft
justice	Gerechtigkeit
kingdom	Reich
know	kennen (noscere), wissen (scire)
knowledge	Erkenntnis, Kenntnis, Wissen (scientia)
law	Gesetz
law, conformity to	Gesetzmäßigkeit
law, juridical	Recht
laying of foundations	Grundlegung
legislator	Gesetzgeber
lie	Lüge
life	Leben
life conduct	Lebenswandel
limit (v.)	einschränken
limit(ation)	Einschränkung, Grenze, Schranke
love	Liebe (eros, amor)
magnitude	Größe
major premise	Obersatz
malice	Bosheit
manifold (adj.)	mannigfaltig
manifold (n.)	Mannigfaltigkeit
manners	Sitten
material	Stoff
matter	Materie
merit	Verdienst
mind	Gemüt, Geist
minor premise	Untersatz

morals	Sittlichkeit
motion	Bewegung
motive	Beweggrund
multiplicity	Menge
multitude	Menge
necessary	notwendig
necessity	Notwendigkeit
need (n.)	Bedürfnis
negate	verneinen
nexus	Zusammenhang
nothing	Nichts
notion	Begriff
number	Zahl
object	Gegenstand, Objekt
obligation	Verbindlichkeit
opposition	Entgegensetzung, Widerstreit, Opposition
origin	Ursprung
original being	Urwesen (ens originarium)
original ground	Urgrund
ought	sollen
outer	äußerlich
outside	außer
pain	Schmerz, Unlust
particular	besondere
passion	Leidenschaft
peace	Friede
peoples	Volk
perception	Wahrnehmung
perfection	Vollkommenheit
permission	Erlaubnis
persist	beharren
persistence	Beharrlichkeit
philosophy	Weltweisheit, Philosophie
pleasure	Lust
plurality	Vielheit
posit	setzen
position	Lage, Setzung, Position

possibility	Möglichkeit
power	Gewalt, Kraft, Macht
predisposition	Anlage
preestablished	vorherbestimmt
present (v.)	darstellen
presupposition	Voraussetzung
principle	Grundsatz, Satz, Prinzip, Prinzipium
probability	Wahrscheinlichkeit
problem	Aufgabe, Problem
progress	Fortschritt, Fortgang
proof	Beweis
propensity	Hang
proposition	Satz
prudence	Klugheit
public (n.)	Öffentlichkeit
pure	lauter, rein
purification	Läuterung
purpose	Zweck
purposive	zweckmäßig
ratiocinate	vernünfteln
rationalize	vernünfteln
real	real, wirklich
reason	Vernunft
receptivity	Empfänglichkeit
refutation	Widerlegung
relation	Beziehung, Verhältnis, Relation
remove	aufheben
represent	vorstellen
representation	Vorstellung (repraesentatio)
resolution	Vorsatz
respect	Achtung
rest	Ruhe
right	Recht
rule	Regel
science	Wissenschaft (scientia)
self	Ich
self-activity	Selbsttätigkeit
self-consciousness	Selbstbewusstsein
self-knowledge	Selbsterkenntnis

self-positing	Selbstsetzung
self-sufficient	selbständig
sensation	Empfindung (sensatio)
sense (n.)	Sinn
sensibility	Sinnlichkeit
sensible	sinnlich
sentence	Satz
separate	absondern
sequence	Folge
series	Reihe
simultaneous	zugleich
sociability	Geselligkeit
society	Gesellschaft
solution	Auflösung
sophistical	vernünftelnd
soul	Seele
source	Quelle
space	Raum
state	Zustand, Staat
sublime	erhaben
succeed	nachfolgen
succession	Abfolge, Nacheinandersein, Sukzession
suffering (n.)	Leiden
sum	Summe
sum total	Inbegriff
syllogism	Vernunftschluss, Syllogismus
synthesis	Verbindung, Synthese
take (to be true)	Fürwahrhalten
temporal sequence	Zeitfolge
theorem	Lehrsatz
thing	Ding, Sache
think	denken
thought	Denken
thought-entity	Gedankending (ens rationis)
time	Zeit
touchstone	Probierstein
transition	Übergang
truth	Wahrheit
understand	verstehen (intelligere)

understanding	Verstand (intellectus)
union	Vereinigung
unity	Einheit
universal	allgemein
universal validity	Allgemeingültigkeit
utility	Nutzen
valid	gültig
validity	Geltung, Gültigkeit
value	Wert
vice	Laster
virtue	Tugend
void	Leere
volition	Wollen
voluntary	willkürlich
war	Krieg
whole	Ganze
will (n.)	Wille, Willkür
will (v.)	wollen
world	Welt
world-whole	Weltganzes, Weltall

ABOUT THE AUTHORS

HELMUT HOLZHEY (M.A., Ph.D., University of Zurich) is professor emeritus at the University of Zurich. His books on Kantianism include *Kants Theorie der Erfahrung* (*Kant's Theory of Experience*) and *Cohen und Natorp*. Many of his published articles deal with Kant and especially with Neokantianism. In 1969, he founded the Hermann Cohen Archive at the University of Zurich, which serves to coordinate international research on Neokantianism and under whose direction an edition of the collected works of Hermann Cohen is being published. In 2004, in recognition of his work on the Marburg School of Neokantianism, he was awarded an honorary doctorate from the University of Marburg.

VILEM MUDROCH (B.A., M.A., McMaster University; Ph.D., University of Zurich) is a research associate at the University of Zurich. His publications on Kant include *Kants Theorie der physikalischen Gesetze* (*Kant's Theory of the Laws of Physics*) as well as several articles and book reviews. His main area of research is centered on themes of general intellectual history of the 17th and 18th centuries. With Helmut Holzhey and others he has edited a book on the Scottish Enlightenment as well as volumes of the German-language encyclopedia of the history of philosophy *Grundriss der Geschichte der Philosophie* dealing with philosophy in Germany, Scandinavia, and Eastern Europe in the 17th century and in Great Britain, North America, and Holland in the 18th century. Currently, both authors are working on the volumes that will cover 18th-century philosophy in France and in Germany. The latter volume will include chapters on Kant and on his early opponents and adherents.